THE WORLD OF CONSUMPTION

Consumption has become one of the leading topics across the social sciences and vocational disciplines such as marketing and business studies. As a result of this, a number of overlapping analytical problems have arisen: how to integrate contributions from the different disciplines; how to address the relationship between society and the individual in a postmodernist world; and how to bring material and cultural factors together. This book provides an answer.

In this comprehensively updated and revised new edition, traditional approaches as well as the most recent literature are fully addressed and incorporated, with wide reference to theoretical and empirical work. Fine's refreshing and authoritative text includes a critical examination of such themes as:

- economics imperialism and globalisation;
- the world of commodities;
- systems of provision and culture;
- the consumer society;
- public consumption.

This book presents an updated analysis of the cluttered landscape of studies of consumption that will make it required reading for students from a wide range of backgrounds including political economy, history and social science courses generally.

Ben Fine is Professor of Economics and Director of the Centre for Economic Policy for Southern Africa, School of Oriental and African Studies, University of London. He is the author of several books for Routledge, including *Social Capital versus Social Theory* (2000).

ECONOMICS AS SOCIAL THEORY
Series edited by Tony Lawson
University of Cambridge

Social theory is experiencing something of a revival within economics. Critical analyses of the particular nature of the subject matter of social studies and of the types of method, categories and modes of explanation that can legitimately be endorsed for the scientific study of social objects are re-emerging. Economists are again addressing such issues as the relationship between agency and structure, between economy and the rest of society, and between the enquirer and the object of enquiry. There is a renewed interest in elaborating basic categories such as causation, competition, culture, discrimination, evolution, money, need, order, organisation, power probability, process, rationality, technology, time, truth, uncertainty, value, etc.

The objective for this series is to facilitate this revival further. In contemporary economics the label 'theory' has been appropriated by a group that confines itself to largely asocial, ahistorical, mathematical 'modelling'. Economics as Social Theory thus reclaims the 'theory' label, offering a platform for alternative rigorous, but broader and more critical, conceptions of theorising.

Other titles in this series include:

ECONOMICS AND LANGUAGE
Edited by Willie Henderson

RATIONALITY, INSTITUTIONS AND ECONOMIC METHODOLOGY
Edited by Uskali Mäki, Bo Gustafsson and Christian Knudsen

NEW DIRECTIONS IN ECONOMIC METHODOLOGY
Edited by Roger Backhouse

WHO PAYS FOR THE KIDS?
Nancy Folbre

RULES AND CHOICE IN ECONOMICS
Viktor Vanberg

BEYOND RHETORIC AND REALISM IN ECONOMICS
Thomas A. Boylan and Paschal F. O'Gorman

THE WORLD OF CONSUMPTION

The material and cultural revisited

Second edition

Ben Fine

London and New York

First published 2002
by Routledge
11 New Fetter Lane, London EC4P 4EE

Simultaneously published in the USA and Canada
by Routledge
29 West 35th Street, New York, NY 10001

Routledge is an imprint of the Taylor & Francis Group

Typeset in Baskerville by Taylor & Francis Books Ltd
Printed and bound in Great Britain by Biddles Ltd, Guildford and King's Lynn

British Library Cataloguing in Publication Data
A catalogue record for this book is available from the British Library

Library of Congress Cataloging-in-Publication Data
Fine, Ben.
The world of consumption : the material and cultural revisited / Ben Fine – 2nd ed.
(Economics as social theory)
Includes bibliographical references (p.) and index.
1. Consumption (Economics) I. Title II Series.
HB801 .F52 2002
339.4'7–dc21
2001048675

ISBN 0–415–27944–5 (hbk)
ISBN 0–415–27945–3 (pbk)

CONTENTS

PREFACE

A decade has passed since the first edition of *World of Consumption* was drafted. In the interim, the contours and context of the study of consumption have changed enormously, if not out of all recognition. This new edition offers the opportunity to take stock. In doing so, the volume has been so much revised that it is essentially a new publication altogether. The structure, the sequencing and the vast majority of the content of the original have been set aside. Newly written material has replaced the old, and the scattered chunks of the old that remain have been heavily rewritten, amended or reorganised. The vast majority of references in this new edition did not appear in the old one!

Yet, despite these drastic measures, the core approach and arguments of the original stand as before. Indeed, they have been strengthened not only through the new text but also through the impression that the system of provision approach that the original pioneered is growing in popularity and influence, although evidence occasionally takes the form of criticism, some extremely harsh, as well as praise. So why and how is the content of the new edition being changed, far above major updating? It is necessary to explain the nature of, and reasons for, the revisions.

At the time of the first edition, the burgeoning literature on consumption had begun to depart from its infancy but it still remains short of adulthood and maturity. As explained then, and again in Chapters 5 and 6 of this edition, much of the understanding of consumption has been organised 'horizontally', addressing theories and factors *within* social science disciplines and across a range, possibly not delimited, of consumption goods or aspects of consumer behaviour. The original edition established this in Chapters 3 to 5 (and elsewhere in the text), covering consumer studies, economics and psychology, respectively. With the exception of economics, now sited in Chapter 7, these chapters have now simply been omitted.

The opening chapter of these three on different disciplines was unusual since it addressed consumer studies, a discipline that has primarily been developed and practised in the United States. Nonetheless, it had a wider relevance. Analytically, it has been based on an amalgam of marketing, psychology, business, marketing and any other disciplinary fragments that proved convenient in such an academic mongrel. The fate of consumer studies, in degenerating into what its own circumspect practitioners confess is a chronic state of fragmented disarray, serves as a salutary lesson to the more scholarly pretensions of those newly engaging in the study of consumption. For the problems of consumer studies as a discipline did not derive from any lack of intellectual integrity or quality of research and methods (deficient though they may have been when viewed loftily from the standards of more established disciplines). Rather, the goal of consumer studies has been at fault in seeking to stack together a collection of horizontal theories to provide for analytical generality and comprehensiveness in case studies.

The inadequacy of horizontal and intra-disciplinary approaches remains, as does the relevance of the warning against simplistic and forced interdisciplinary articulations. These propositions are less controversial and more familiar than before, as the study of consumption has become more analytically street-wise. In particular, and in addition, the hazards associated with intra-disciplinary and naïve interdisciplinary research have been recognised. Instead, a different issue now challenges, possibly haunts, the study of consumption. It is, or should be, at a higher intellectual level than before and locates itself across disciplines. Latterly, in the vanguard of social theory and not just the study of consumption, is the issue of how to relate material and cultural factors to one another. Material culture as an object and subject of study was by no means new or negligible at the time of the first edition. Indeed, our volume was itself an attempt to place the culture of consumption on a sounder footing by emphasising its material determinants. But material culture has grown in prominence in the study of consumption over the past decade. Nor is this simply a matter of the weight of its popularity and a count of publications. The relationship between material and cultural factors has correctly become seen as decisive for the study of consumption as for other aspects of social theory. This is a healthy reaction against the economicless 'subjectivity' of postmodernism and the cultureless 'objectivity' of economic reductionism.

As a result, the opening chapters have totally shifted in content and orientation. Instead of exposing the shortcomings of the horizontal and the intra-disciplinary, they have engaged with the leading social theory concerned with material culture. Key concepts in this regard are use value, exchange value, commodity, money, gift and capital. Whilst not always immediately and directly relevant to consumption, such categories have been increasingly incorporated in studying it over the past decade. The mode of doing so has often been casual, inconsistent, arbitrary and ill-conceived, not least because postmodernism, or its influence, has usually been the poor starting point of departure from which something more substantive has been attempted. There has, however, also been extremely rewarding insight and scholarship. This study of consumption, then, begins not with how the various disciplines have addressed consumption but with the social forms in which contemporary consumption primarily presents itself.

This has also involved moving forward some of the material from the old edition that was concerned with the contribution of, and debates over, Marx and the study of consumption. Marx, after all, even by his numerous detractors, is widely recognised as the theorist *par excellence* of many of the concepts listed towards the beginning of the previous paragraph. Misunderstandings and misapplications of his theory have been rife. Together with dissatisfaction with the limited, if far from negligible, insights that Marx himself provided on consumption, it has often been presumed that his approach precluded further progress. As is shown, the opposite is the case, and Marx's concepts are rich in potential for addressing the material culture of consumption.

The rise of interest in material culture is not the only significant shift in the cultural climate that is recognised and highlighted. Over the last ten years, economics imperialism, or the colonisation of other social sciences by economics, has accelerated in scope and depth. Whilst previously gaining a presence where rational choice had already been accepted, certain theoretical developments *within* economics have strengthened its appeal and potential across a much wider range of social theory. Thus, there has been an epidemic of new economic fields, dealing in politics, institutions, geography and welfare as well as customs, norms, culture, and so on. With limited exceptions, consumption has not fallen victim to the dubious charms of the dismal science.

This provides two reasons for retaining and revising the chapter on the economics of consumption. First, like the dog that did not bark, the limitation of economics in colonising the study of consumption reveals some of the strengths of existing approaches from other disciplines that might otherwise go unrecognised by them for being taken for granted. These concern the nature of culture and its irreducible contextual content properly understood. Second, by the same token, economics is pitifully inadequate with respect to the more traditional factors commonly treated within its own discipline in comprehending the economics of consumption itself (the nature and sources of technology etc.). But this situation has been far from conducive to a challenge to mainstream economics. For social theory has tended to retreat from the economic in addressing consumption (and more generally), not least because of the lingering legacy of an economicless postmodernism, the alien and absurd postures of mainstream economics, and the formidable intimidation posed by its technical virtuosity and pompous and invalid claims to science and rigour. Despite the limitations and failings of mainstream economics (and the now longstanding wish for consumption not to be reduced to production), it remains imperative that the economic be treated as central to the study of consumption. But mainstream economics must not be taken as its starting point even for departure.

One highly telling indication of the weakness of mainstream economics in addressing consumption or otherwise, and despite economics imperialism, is its inability to participate in debate over globalisation. Its methodological individualism and corresponding discomfort with, or denial of, systemic or holistic analysis pre-empts its contributing except in a piecemeal fashion along the lines of recognising, and generally welcoming, more international openness in trade and finance etc. Yet globalisation has been the most prominent concept across the social sciences from the 1990s onwards and has inescapable economic connotations. Consequently, Chapter 7, on economics and consumption, has been complemented by one, Chapter 2, on economics imperialism and globalisation. This precedes the chapters on commodities, gifts, etc., in order to set the latter against what are shown to be appealing, at times insightful, but ultimately flawed starting points.

The inclusion of a chapter on economics imperialism and globalisation (and the retention of one on economics) is paradoxical in light of a further thematic shift from the old to the new edition. Much of the previous volume, written by dissenting economists, took persuasion of economists as an important goal, partly through the critique of economics itself and partly through the introduction to them of material from other social sciences. The response from this intended audience has been underwhelming if not non-existent. For the intervening period has unambiguously demonstrated that this effort is a futile waste of time and effort. Despite considerable interest in the system of provision approach across the social sciences, there has been none from mainstream economics, not even in the form of dissent. As a result, the inclusion of more economics material, despite the absence of an audience of economists, needs to be justified. The intention in the new edition has been twofold. As already indicated, one is to advise on the dangers of economics imperialism and globalisation as sources of economic analysis for the study of consumption. The other is to reiterate the importance of the economy whatever the deficiencies of economics.

In short, the major change in, and influence upon, thematic priorities in the new edition have been derived from consideration of culture, and how to relate it to the economic. But this is not all. Neglect of culture has long been the charge made against those who emphasise the economic. There is, however, a counter charge that can be made with some venom, and is equally serious to the extent that such things can be quantified. This, as noted but not redressed in the first edition, is lack of interest in public consumption – rarely, if not proscribed from being, the subject of semiotic analysis. The new edition begins to make up this deficiency with two new chapters. The first seeks to explain why public consumption should fail to enter popular and academic discourse over and above the obvious reason that it might be construed as too mundane (and there has, in any case, been a cultural turn to the everyday). The answer is simply that once consumption becomes public it begins no longer to be construed as consumption as such unless ideologically as a pale imitation of, and alternative to, private provision.

The second chapter addresses the leading illustration of this point, the welfare state from which both 'public' and 'consumption' have overtly been terminologically dropped. Recent developments in how the welfare state has been understood are critically assessed, revealing how the aforementioned economics imperialism is becoming increasingly influential. Alternative approaches are urgently needed, those drawing from the insights of material culture and its application to consumption. In a sense, two steps need to be taken at once – to make up for the failure of postmodernism to deconstruct the welfare state, and to locate welfare as a form of material provision. Suggestions are made along these lines, drawing upon the systems of provision approach.

The new opening chapter, as introduction and overview, necessarily reflects the changing content of the volume already reported. The closing chapter has also been replaced. The old looked forward to public consumption, the new takes advantage of the passage of time to review briefly some contributions to food studies. This is less as a means to present case studies and more by way of exploring themes developed earlier in the book.

Finally, though, reference must be made to other departures in content from the original. They had not outlived their useful life but room had to be found for the new and more contemporary material already described. Chapter 17 of the previous edition critically assessed the theory of consumption classes, closely associated with Peter Saunders, and very much a response to different forms of housing tenure and the privatisation of public (council) housing. A decade ago, the idea gained both appeal and notoriety, both of which have mercifully subsided. Chapter 20 contained a close, technical and critical review of the idea of retail capital as a generic form of capital. The purpose, apart from dealing in retail itself, was to provide an illustration of the pitfalls of proceeding with hori-zontal categories of analysis (as well as with horizontal theories). Retail capital is distinguished more by the different commodities to which it is attached than by its common attributes as a form of capital without connection to specific systems of provision – the same applies to advertising or a putative design capital for example. Whilst the chapter remains a pertinent contribution, the length, detail and narrow specialisation of the content led these to be put aside, not least because the general point about horizontal approaches will already have been covered and more readily be accepted. Third, what again might be considered too esoteric a contribution is the discussion of the relationship between Baudrillard and Sraffa, previously found in the old Chapter 19. This showed that they are, in a sense, mirror images of one another. One departs from exchange value by exclusive preoccupation with its constructed use value; the other targets exchange value by exclusive preoccupation with unreconstructed use value. Whatever the merits in omitting these contributions, they remain available to the dedicated reader in the old edition.

The same applies to the case studies and illustrations from the original volume. It is with great reluctance that these have not been included, as initially planned, in the revised edition. For the proof of the theoretical pudding, as well as its illumination, lies in its more concrete digestion. But space simply did not allow, with the application of the systems of provision approach previously taking up a third or more of the first edition. The discussion of the history of clothing, food adulteration, advertising, and the critique of trickle-down approaches and of the putative consumer revolution of the eighteenth century, could have remained much as before with minor editing and updating. The case studies of food have, to some extent, been supplemented and also complemented by subsequent work (Fine *et al.* 1996, Fine 1998c). However, the initial contributions belonged more to the present-day than the other case studies, and food has been subject to significant change and attention over the past decade. So the new edition closes with food around, as previously mentioned, material and cultural themes.

The new, like the old, edition covers a vast subject matter. The depth of scholarship and attention to detail are uneven from topic to topic. Occasionally, a footnote has flown off on a tangent with days of investigation to make an esoteric point and reference or three. At other times, major issues have only been treated cursorily. By the same token, some parts are more up to date than others, although the volume as a whole is skewed towards addressing and incorporating the most recent literature. Success in doing so has depended in part on the vagaries of what has been available once identified as of interest. Where Internet access has been used, page references have been omitted even though published versions might also exist. For the reader seeking to dabble, and not necessarily interested in consumption or foundations for studying it, each chapter has been made relatively self-contained, a few basic ideas apart, without unduly incurring the cost of overlap. Study of globalisation is to be found in Chapter 2, the welfare state in Chapter 10, food in Chapter 11, the gift in Chapter 3, cultural systems in Chapter 6, and so on.

I take this opportunity to thank all who have commented on and contributed to the research. Most of it was undertaken as part of a broader initiative between March 1999 and March 2001. I was then in receipt of a Research Fellowship from the UK Economic and Social Research Council (ESRC) under award number R000271046 to study The New Revolution in Economics and Its Impact upon Social Sciences, although the final writing up took another six months. The book is dedicated to Jack whose special needs delayed completion and more careful scholarship but also allowed significant pause for contemplation over content and structure. Last, but by no means least, the new edition has lost an author. Ellen Leopold did not participate directly in the redrafting of the new, and generously and selflessly allowed the old to be drastically shorn to make way for it. Nonetheless, her contribution to the systems of provision approach remains immense as does her influence across each page of what follows. The pity for the content and the reader is that other obligations precluded her from being more fully involved in the new edition.

References

Fine, B. (1998c) *The Political Economy of Diet, Health and Food Policy*, London: Routledge.
Fine, B. et al. (1996) *Consumption in the Age of Affluence: The World of Food*, London: Routledge.

1

INTRODUCTION AND OVERVIEW

Introduction

The study of consumption has expanded prodigiously over the last twenty years. The first edition of *World of Consumption* was written as the field was reaching its adolescence with all that this entails in terms of growing pains and experimental pleasures. The following decade has witnessed an accelerating interest in the subject. Now, far from occupying a subordinate academic niche, consumption is increasingly served by a bewildering range of contributions (Glennie 1995: 164–5). These draw upon the different objects of consumption themselves, their social significance, the sequence of activities that lead to consumption, and the different sites of consumption across country and household, quite apart from the wealth of illustrations across time and space. Equally varied have been the methods and theories for investigation of consumption both within and across the social sciences, as is evidenced by a number of surveys, which are often necessarily partial, specialised and rapidly dated in their coverage (e.g. Fine and Leopold 1993, Miller 1995b, Gabriel and Lang 1995, de Grazia and Furlough 1996, Holbrook 1995, Miller (ed) 2002).[1] To the extent that such surveys have dropped off in numbers, the reason is that the subject matter has become too vast to cover. In short, consumption is a moving, expanding and an evasive target, especially in view of the array of analytical weapons with which it has been assaulted.

In the previous edition, a warning was signalled that unless it was careful, the study of consumption would be liable to degenerate into a more scholarly version of US consumer studies, a hodgepodge of eclectic theoretical and empirical elements, leading to a self-confessed chronic state of disarray.[2] Is the same true of the more academic study of consumption that only lags the emergence of consumer studies by a decade or so?[3]

Although not addressing this issue directly, and not necessarily departing from the assessment to follow, Miller *et al*, (1998: 1) would seem to suggest otherwise. They see consumption as shifting from 'academic outcast' through three stages of research over the past two decades.[4] The earlier works are perceived to have emphasised lack of theory and empirical studies and the diversity of social relations attached to consumption, rendering it a confusing catch-all in taking account of gender, kinship, ethnicity, age, locality, etc. Apart from concern with interdisciplinarity and with knowledge and meaning, the literature was marked by being unfocused and by endless debate over central terms. This first stage was prompted by four motives: to make consumption more visible through study of the new landscapes of consumption (supermarkets, retail parks, shopping malls); to counterpose consumption to production; to place culture in opposition to political economy; and, primarily through advertising, to inspire interpretative studies especially around subcultures. The second stage is characterised by five aspects: the creation of a presence for consumption as its own subfield within disciplines; consumption is set adrift from production; emphasis is placed upon subjectivity, self and identity; the scope of study is expanded to include festivals, collecting and the like; and consumption is seen as a key aspect of the history of modernity through display and gaze, tied to time, place and construction. Finally, the third stage reflects five main issues: the restoration of production and the inclusion of distribution, thereby incorporating the active role of consumers and workers; emphasis upon material culture and the interaction between the subjects and objects of consumption; corresponding interest in contextual specificity; more work on the history of consumption; and also on space and place as instrumental in the making of consuming identities.

As a broad brush, the account of Miller *et al.* has much to commend it. But, not surprisingly, it is far too neat and tidy, leaving as many questions unposed as answered. In particular what is the timing of this periodisation (and can three stages be squeezed into two decades), and does it fit equally across disciplines and topics? Although the study of consumption across the social sciences may have exhibited some changing emphases and postures, it can also be interpreted as having become increasingly chaotic, not least because the progress identified by Miller *et al.* is far from uniform or complete across the literature, with successive stages supplementing rather than displacing one another. Not everyone can be in, let alone recognise, the analytical vanguard. Even those that have been in the lead in some respects are capable of straddling the divides posited by Miller *et al.*, as in Ritzer's (1993, 1998) successive contributions, ultimately leading to a brutally frank stages-defying amalgam within a single contribution let alone across the literature as a whole (Ritzer 1999a: 76):[5]

> In the end, this is not a work in postmodern theory, or any other theory for that matter. The goal is to gain a greater understanding of the new means of consumption and to that end theoretical tools that work will be employed, whatever their origins. In order to create the theoretical framework for this book, I have borrowed the ideas of exploitation, control, rationalization, and disenchantment from modern social theory and the notion of reenchantment from postmodern theory. This book offers what the postmodernists call a 'pastiche' (a mixture of sometimes seemingly contradictory ideas) of modern and postmodern ideas in order to analyze the cathedrals of consumption. The latter, of course,

2

are themselves combinations of modern, postmodern, and even premodern elements. Both the subject matter and the theoretical perspective of this book stand with one foot in some of social theory's oldest ideas and the other in some of its most contemporary thinking.

If periodisation *within* the study of consumption is questionable, a notable neglect in Miller *et al.* is consideration of the broader intellectual context as if the study of consumption has experienced a self-contained inner momentum of its own. But its evolution, as is at least implicit in their account, has depended upon a much broader renegotiation across the social sciences of the relationship between what might be conveniently termed economy and culture, although other oppositions are represented and representative, not least production and consumption. Thus, Ashkenazi and Clammer (2000) acknowledge how consumption has been at the forefront of the study of material culture in view of its bringing together a number of core and classical themes – gender, class, critical theory, mass society – and new themes such as media studies, popular culture and the ethnography of conformity and resistance in everyday life. The study of consumption emerged during, out of, and as a major part of the rise of postmodernism. The social sciences are now, unevenly and variously, on retreat from its excesses. What exactly has this all entailed?

One consequence has been a number of notable achievements in the study of consumption. Six readily spring to mind, and these will be elaborated and justified at greater length during the course of the chapters that follow. First, as already mentioned, contributions have been both wide ranging and diverse. In addition, in contrast to a decade ago, it is no longer so common to find studies of consumption that are motivated or rationalised by the wish to balance its neglect relative to production. But the pendulum between the two has now swung towards or past its midpoint, if not so far as presumed by Quataert (2000: 1), 'the consumption of goods, not their production, drives history. ... Modernity is also marked by the rise of mass consumerism, and by its ascendancy of the consumer over the producer'.[6] Indeed, the pendulum has in some respects begun its return, albeit perturbed, journey. Many have become interested in bringing production back into the study of consumption.

Second, rational choice methodologies, or those more generally based on methodological individualism, have made remarkably little headway in the literature on consumption. The two obvious candidates for rendering this otherwise are economics and psychology. In their mainstream versions both have generally been studiously, even contemptuously, ignored. From psychology, the idea of consumption as the means by which to fulfil natural, instinctive or biologically determined needs has proved an anathema both to postmodernist preoccupations with the meaning of identity and the objects of consumption themselves and to social theory more traditionally based on structures, relations and agencies.

If such psychology is dead for consumption, economics might be considered undead. For everyone recognises that prices and incomes, and the economy more generally, are vital to the study of consumption. But much of that vitality has been lost in the cultural turn. As a result, more by accident than design, the study of consumption has not fallen prey to 'economics imperialism', the process by which the traditional subject matter of the other social sciences has been appropriated by economics, as discussed in Chapters 2 and 7. This is despite the success with which economics imperialism is currently sweeping, albeit unevenly, across the other social sciences. Whilst it now purports to incorporate history, institutions, custom and culture, mainstream economics remains empty when it comes to the meaning of the consumed to the consumer (and, indeed, treats the consumer much like a mini-enterprise with utility as its sole product). Given the meaning of consumption as starting point, and production as point of departure, it is apposite that mainstream economics should be studiously ignored in the recent rise of the study of consumption.

Third, not surprisingly, the study of consumption took the popular notions of consumer society or consumerism as an initial analytical prompt in two different, if closely related, ways. On the one hand, following the pioneering work of McKendrick *et al.* (1982), the birth of a consumer society is seen as part of the historical landscape. On the other hand, whether through the questionable notion of consumer sovereignty or through the less sanguine perspective organised around the diseases of affluence, consumerism has encouraged an unduly ethical reading of consumption. Is it good or bad? Humphery (1998: 209) observes an intellectual legacy of 'participation in consumption cultures as socially destructive, culturally bereft and politically dangerous'. But there has been some shift towards less negative approaches over the last two decades as well as celebration of consumption as resistance. Further, Humphery

> emphasises the importance of the *mundane* and the *everyday*, rather than the spectacular. ... Consumption is undoubtedly connected to these fantastic worlds. But it may be that pleasure and excitement are overly 'written in' when it comes to the cultural analysis of consumer society.
>
> (p. 26)

However, whether for ethics or for history, on which see Chapter 8, the notion of consumer society has been so widely and indiscriminately used that it has become recognisably empty of precision and explanatory content.

Fourth, with the major exception of economics, the study of consumption has been highly conducive to interdisciplinarity. An initial phase in the literature like so many newly emerging topics, was marked by the simple intra-disciplinary application of ready-made, off-the-shelf theory to consumer and consumed. But this has given way to genuine fertilisation across disciplines in appropriate recognition that the subject of consumption knows no analytical boundaries. The exceptional exclusion of economics is paradoxical. For it reflects both the authority and impenetrability of the discipline – to other social sciences and as it presents itself, it is technically formidable – and the narrowness of the analytical terrain upon which it exercises its command. The result is both an absence of mainstream economics and a neglect of the economic, a point to be taken up later and throughout.

Fifth, whilst consumption may have taken production as its point of departure, it has increasingly rejected a simple dichotomy between production and consumption. The literature has liberally incorporated other, intermediate activities between production and consumption, and recognised them to be of significance. This is true of design, retail, advertising, shopping and so on.

Finally, primarily as a reaction against the interpretative excesses of postmodernism, the study of consumption has increasingly sought to integrate material and cultural factors. What objects are and how they are perceived are inextricably linked to one another, and to the processes by which they are brought to the consumer and used (and discarded).

The approach to consumption as material culture, however, confronts a major stumbling block – its relationship to the economy and to economics. How can the economy be brought back in following the postmodernist cultural turn, and the much longer standing divide between social and cultural and economic analysis? In many ways, this is how the first edition of *World of Consumption* can be interpreted and justified. It represented an attempt to convince cultural theorists of consumption to take the economy seriously (and economists to do likewise for culture). There is a world out there that must be acknowledged as a source not only of the objects of consumption but also of how they are and can be interpreted. Hopefully, this message is now increasingly pushing against a door that is ajar if not fully open. As a result, it is possible to move on to a new message, one that avoids the horns of the dualism between the material and the cultural.

The new message is disarmingly simple. Consumption in the modern world is primarily served by capital and capitalism, and these must analytically figure prominently both as material and cultural categories in the study of consumption. Whilst mainstream economics is appropriately set aside as being incapable of providing that material, let alone the cultural, element, a political economy of capitalism is essential. It must address the nature of commodities and money, for example, as the unavoidable conduits in the provision of consumption as well as those of its aspects, cultural or otherwise, that appear to evade or negotiate commercialism. But this is to anticipate the content of what is to follow for which an overview is now provided.

Overview

The next chapter establishes certain features of the present intellectual environment. Currently, there is a dual retreat, uneven and faltering, from the excesses both of neo-liberalism and of postmodernism. On the one hand, the idea no longer prevails that the market does or could work perfectly. Consequently, greater interest has been stimulated in examining how economic and non-economic factors, the market and the non-market, interact with one another. At or below the national level, for example, this has allowed the notion of social capital to flourish. On the other hand, emphasis on the interpretation or deconstruction of the meaning of the material world is conceding ground to attention over how that world is materially created. In this respect, to an even greater extent than the fashionable social capital, the idea of globalisation has exploded across the social sciences during the last decade. It too has sought to confront the articulation of the economic and the non-economic. It has tended to do so by positing them as being in opposition to one another – as the heterogeneity of the national, social, etc., is washed over by the homogeneous tidal wave of the global economic. The culture of consumption, in particular, is perceived to be resistant to globalisation despite McDonaldisation.

Globalisation has, then, provided a ready-made framework for examining a wide range of economic and social phenomena. But it is flawed not so much in terms of being exaggerated or not, the dominant issue in a literature marked by pros and antis, but in its understanding of the economic and the corresponding opposition drawn with the non-economic. This is demonstrated in Chapter 2 by discussion of finance, the markets for which have been understood to be the epitome of, and metaphor for, globalisation.

It follows that globalisation has limited purchase in explaining rather than describing the articulation of the material and the cultural. Another candidate has, however, presented itself for the task, economics imperialism. Again, over the past decade or so, mainstream economics has sought to colonise the other social sciences and has succeeded as never before. This is because it has moved from an approach based on the non-economic, as if reducible to being equivalent to a perfect market, to one in which the non-economic is to be understood as the rational response to market imperfections. The new phase of economics imperialism has, however, made limited impact on the study of consumption because it is incapable of genuinely addressing the social construction of the meaning of objects, taking these (as well as the identity of consumers) as self-evident.

What, then, are the alternatives to economics imperialism and globalisation? This is the subject of Chapters 3 and 4 in which a critical but constructive review is undertaken of a number of traditional concepts deployed across the social sciences. Two broad conclusions are drawn. First, in Chapter 3, the dichotomy between commodity and gift is discussed and shown to be an invalid dualism. What is crucial is to uncover the social relations underpinning the forms that these represent. For the two broad categories conceal a diverse range of material and cultural relations. Little is to be gained, and much to be lost, in treating all commodities and commodity forms as mutually equivalent in some other sense and also as the 'other' world of an equally heterogeneous category of non-commodities or gifts. As the literature has come to recognise, commodities can express gift relations and vice versa. Nonetheless, the chapter concludes, a full understanding of capital commodity production is an appropriate starting point for examining the differentiated nature of more general forms of exchange – putatively commodity, gift or otherwise.

Chapter 4 is concerned to establish, contrary to much received wisdom, that capitalist commodity production as analytical starting point does not preclude an appropriate study of use values as opposed to exchange value. It takes Haug's (1986) aesthetic illusion as point of departure. Haug argues that commodities tend to be degraded in their material properties in pursuit of profitability through cheaper production. To guarantee sale, this is veiled by endowing them with a sexual content through advertising. Significantly, Haug establishes the connection between how commodities are produced and how they are construed. But his analysis is too narrow in presuming that commodities are always worsened and that compensation only comes in the form of sexuality and advertising. Commodities pick up their highly diverse meanings from a variety of sources. Nor is it a matter of adding more means and content to the making of their use values. For this leaves open to a large extent the systemic source of initial meanings and whether and how these are reproduced, transformed or set aside rather than simply supplemented.

In posing the system of provision approach in Chapter 5, Haug's approach can be interpreted as being extended, possibly beyond recognition. The argument is that commodities designed for consumption belong to distinct 'vertically' integrated chains of activities – incorporating production, distribution, retailing, etc. The food is distinct from the clothing system in the way in which the different moments along their provision are linked together. The system of provision approach is defended against criticisms that have been made against it, particularly that consumption is so 'leaky' across commodity chains that they are not distinguishable from one another. Further, Chapter 6 moves beyond the idea of a circuit of culture by arguing that each system of provision is attached to a cultural system that conditions the meanings taken by consumption.

Chapter 7 returns to economic issues more centrally, examining in detail why mainstream economics is incapable of contributing to a material culture of consumption. This is done both through close consideration of the work of Gary Becker and through debate over how consumer durables should be understood. For Becker, all economic and social phenomena can be reduced to the aggregated behaviour of individuals single-mindedly maximising utility. Both individuals and objects of consumption are unproblematically taken as given – an unpromising starting point for a material culture of consumption. But the emptiness of the approach can be seductive. Rather than simply being questioned and rejected in light of its emptiness, the latter allows omitted factors to be appended as qualification or critique. This needs to be recognised so that a more appropriate economic (and cultural) analysis can be broached as is illustrated by the discussion of consumer durables.

More generally, the insidious persistence of Becker's economic approach is marked by informal appeal to supply and demand as explanatory tools, where these can range over any material or cultural factor. Such is the impetus behind the idea of consumer society, where the demand blade comes to the fore out of the market scissors. Chapter 8 is concerned with the notion of consumer society, consumerism or the consumer revolution. These concepts are popularly used to explain, and often to condemn, the mores and practices of present-day society, with its presumed opposition between the creation and satisfaction of 'false' and 'real' needs. But as a concept with analytical content, consumer society is found to be both vague and insubstantial. First, a glance at some of the history of consumption reveals that consumer society can be traced back hundreds of years. Applied to the distant past, it has too readily been associated with bursts of consumption, often of particular, newly available items, even though this is almost inevitably a concomitant of any period of economic growth. It is more noticeable in retrospect because of association with the luxury or conspicuous consumption of the wealthy, and hence more likely to have survived and to have acquired antique value in the present.

For the nineteenth and twentieth centuries, however, the analysis of the consumer revolution is inevitably richer. It has been linked to particular transmission mechanisms, such as the retail or distribution revolutions (via transport and communications). It has been seen as the counterpart to the mass production of uniform consumption goods. Advertising has been considered crucial in creating a domestic revolution around the working-class consumer, primarily represented through the purchases of the housewife – with the major exception of the male prerogative over the motor car. Paradoxically, the consumer revolution has served simultaneously to suggest increasing uniformity, even democratisation, of consumption *and* increasing differentiation as particular market segments, whether men or women, rich or poor, young or old, are cast as vanguards of demand, leading the economy forward. Critical assessment of such notions confirms the usefulness of the alternative systems of provision approach based on the presumed co-existence of heterogeneous systems of provision.

Chapters 9 and 10 turn from private to public consumption. The first of these chapters puzzles over why public consumption should so readily disappear off the agenda of consumption studies. An answer is offered in terms of the discursive and practical transformation of consumption into something else once it becomes recognisably public. This is illustrated in Chapter 10 by consideration of the welfare state as an alternative both to private and public consumption. In addition, in reviewing recent literature, the book returns to its beginnings in showing how mythologies around globalisation and the economics (imperialism) of welfare have been increasingly influential.

The final chapter offers a whistle-stop tour of some recent developments in food provision and food studies, suggesting that the system of provision approach is capable of addressing them. In this way, earlier themes are illustrated, not least that the cluttered landscape of consumption (studies) can be placed in some order, especially if drawing upon a critical appreciation of capital and capitalism as both material and cultural categories.

2

FROM ECONOMICS
IMPERIALISM TO
GLOBALISATION?

Introduction

Those wedded to traditional Marxist political economy must view the contemporary prominence and popularity of the idea of globalisation across a wide range of discourses as a mixed blessing. For, on the one hand, it recognises the systemic nature of capitalism on a world scale in contemporary conditions. It opens up questions both of power (and powerlessness) and of underlying economic and social forces. On the other hand, globalisation is the correspondingly anodyne equivalent of the Third Way, open to multiple and shifting interpretations and definitively forestalling certain perspectives, not least those associated with the idea of imperialism.

This chapter is concerned with ideas, specifically the relationship between *economics* imperialism and globalisation. Because the notion of globalisation has shot to prominence in academia and popular discourse on the nature of contemporary capitalism, it has inevitably drawn attention to economic issues, even where the economic is not the immediate focus of attention. Yet, remarkably, globalisation essentially remains unexamined within the discipline of economics itself. In a sense, this is not so surprising, after reflection, for two separate reasons. First, mainstream economics has strengthened its attachment to an analytical framework based on the optimising behaviour of individual agents. This is hardly conducive to use of historically specific, even contemporary, concepts of a systemic type, especially when pitched at a global level. Second, economic theory itself has shifted towards examining the incidence and consequences of market (and non-market) imperfections, precisely those factors that are supposed to impede globalisation. Consequently, within mainstream economics, globalisation tends to be understood implicitly as the piecemeal and incomplete removal of barriers to the free flow of resources and knowledge. At best, mainstream economics understands globalisation as international expansion and integration of trade, finance and investment, as convergence of fluctuations, and the emergence of, and need for, international as opposed to national regulation.

It follows that the attention to globalisation across the social sciences other than economics offers an opportunity for the re-emergence of radical political economy. It has sorely declined over the past two decades both within economics itself, which has been particularly intolerant of any alternative to the increasingly esoteric mainstream, and across the other social sciences as well as a result of the rise of postmodernism and its own intolerance of determinism, economism, reductionism, and many other -isms. With the extremes of postmodernism also under retreat, political economy is well placed to gain in influence not least because, in principle, it is dedicated to systemic analysis of the sort needed to address significant shifts in the nature of contemporary capitalism.

Yet it would be a mistake to presume that political economy will rise phoenix-like from the analytical ashes of mainstream economics and postmodernism. For, I have argued elsewhere that economics is currently undergoing a significant shift in its orientation.[1] On the basis of the new micro-foundations or information-theoretic approach, it is seeking to colonise the other social sciences as never before. Accordingly, there is considerable tension between the two processes that I have identified. Mainstream economics is particularly unsuited to contribute to systemic analysis of the sort required to handle concepts such as globalisation. Yet it is exerting influence, to a greater or lesser extent and in varied ways, over the other social sciences that are more at home in examining contemporary capitalism as a system.

In this light, the next section briefly lays out the features of the aforementioned revolution in or, more exactly, around economics. It is followed in the third section by a short and selective overview of literature on globalisation that seeks to bring out its complexity and range. The fourth section examines finance arguing that, despite its often being presumed to serve as an exemplary illustration of globalisation, it is far from doing so. Indeed, precisely because of differentiation of financial systems, a role is created for mainstream economics to contribute to the understanding of the globalisation of finance in terms of its information-theoretic approach. This is to be contrasted to an approach based on the political economy of finance that is briefly outlined.

What is the relevance of all of this for consumption? First, the issues addressed by the overlapping notions of the economy and of globalisation are of vital significance for consumption. Sometimes this is recognised explicitly as, for example, in theses organised around (post-)Fordism or McDonaldisation. It hardly seems to be necessary to make the case that the economy and globalisation are of direct relevance to consumption. But each needs to be carefully addressed rather than casually incorporated. Second, at other times, the economy and globalisation are taken almost as the antithesis of consumption, as its point of departure for privileging and examining the 'cultural' and the 'local' (down to the individual) in any number of ways ranging over the subjectivity and identity of the consumer. Such oppositions are, however, limited in part because of their stylised understanding of the economy and globalisation. Accordingly, it is appropriate to examine economics imperialism and globalisation (of finance) in general terms. For, in doing so, false understanding of the economy and of the global may be avoided in more direct study of consumption whether the economic and the global are explicitly incorporated or not.

Revolution across the social sciences

In a collection in one of the leading mainstream economics journals, anticipating prospects for the discipline over the next fifty years, Lazear (2000) contributes an article on economic imperialism. In doing so, he certainly was not inspired by the spirit of Hobson or Lenin. Indeed, Lazear is a specialist in personnel economics. What he had in mind might be better termed economics imperialism, signifying the colonisation of the other social sciences by economics. Lest Lazear be considered an eccentric and his article idiosyncratic, it is worth emphasising that the term economic(s) imperialism is far from new and is increasingly being explicitly peddled both by colonists and colonised. Swedberg (1990a: 14) reports the term as having been introduced in the 1930s by Ralph William Souter, who suggested that:

> The salvation of Economic Science in the twentieth century lies in an enlightened and democratic 'economic imperialism', which invades the territories of its neighbors, not to enslave them or swallow them up but to aid and enrich them and promote their autonomous growth in the very process of aiding and enriching itself.

Lindbeck (2000), Chair of the Nobel Prize Committee for Economics, literally cites it as one of the criteria for making the award.

Unfortunately if not surprisingly as an enthusiastic participant, Lazear's account of economics imperialism is weak on four major counts.[2] First, it is entirely celebratory, selectively and uncritically highlighting examples with little or no sense of their relationship to the continuing traditions and concerns of the disciplines or topics being appropriated. Second, this is a consequence of an equally uncritical attachment to mainstream economics itself. It is understood to be 'scientific' and 'rigorous', terms punishingly familiar to heterodox economists, in contrast to the other social sciences.[3] This is because of its attachment to mathematical models (axiomatic deductivism), to rational choice (everything can be reduced to optimising behaviour of individuals), and to falsifiability (theories can be tested against the facts). To other social theorists, and to the increasingly rare, more methodologically cultured economists, these propositions border on the laughable for their naïveté and ignorance.

Yet, third, putting these huge reservations about methodology aside, Lazear's account is profoundly ahistorical. If economics is the only true social science, why is it only recently that such virtues have come to light and illuminated the subject matter variously distributed across the other social sciences? Indeed, the sort of economics peddled by Lazear emerged through the marginalist revolution of the 1870s. Has it taken a century for its superiority to be recognised by its own and other practitioners? Further, the marginalist revolution depended upon confining its method to the economy or, more narrowly, to the market in order to set economics apart as a separate discipline.

Finally, and most important for the purposes here, Lazear primarily misreads the current dynamic of economics imperialism itself. Unduly emphasising the contributions of Gary Becker, his main concern is with how optimising behaviour of individuals leads to efficient and stable outcomes across economy and society more generally. But, as will be explained, the current virulence of economics imperialism derives from an entirely different world vision on the part of economists – the idea that optimising individuals interact through market and non-market in ways that are conducive to inefficiency and instability.

In a nutshell, Lazear is primarily referring to economics imperialism in what might be termed its old or non-revolutionary version. In this, for which Becker has been by far the leading exponent, all economic and social phenomena are reduced to a world as if a perfect market, inhabited by 'rational', optimising individuals who balance costs against benefits. This is so for decisions over education, fertility, crime, addiction and so on, see Chapter 7. Such economics imperialism has achieved some success, most notably with the idea of human capital. But its scale and scope have been limited, not least because *social* theorists, of whatever persuasion, are wedded to the idea that the non-market is not reducible to the market, and society is not reducible to a sack of otherwise unconnected individuals. Significantly, human capital has become widely used across the social sciences because it has been able to conceal and, to some extent, to shed its origins in the methodological extremities of mainstream economics – education is simply an asset over which individuals make optimising decisions![4]

Indeed, the division between the other social sciences and mainstream economics has traditionally been one of methodology and not of content. As Becker's work obsessively indicates, the sphere of application of what he terms the 'economic approach' is unlimited since rationality as utility maximisation is not confined to the economy. Only by convention and in establishing itself as a separate discipline did economics become so restricted in scope. No doubt a certain deference to realities also limited the claims of economists to fall short of what has previously been the traditional terrain of the other social sciences – perceived by mainstream economists to be the irrational and the social as opposed to the rational and economic (Zafirovski 2000).

Thus, mainstream neo-classical economics has proceeded on the basis of a science of the economy in which the latter fills out a definite terrain that, negatively, defines the non-economic. Initially, the economic is synonymous with market relations. When Lionel Robbins (in)famously defined economics as the allocation of scarce resources between competing ends, for most economists the implicit assumption was that the market would be doing the allocating. On this basis, more or less complex models of equilibrium are constructed, ranging from supply and demand in a single market to general equilibrium which incorporates all markets including those spreading out into the indefinite future. Such models have two important analytical properties. First, they provide a standard against which the 'real world' can be judged. As Carrier (1997a: 16) argues, the models are surrounded by a *cordon sanitaire*, since any empirical and theoretical anomalies can be rationalised in terms of market imperfections, or the non-correspondence of the economy to the economic model. Second, predominantly in practice if not in principle, the analytical content of mainstream economics is specific to market relations. Yet the well-worn technical devices – organised around optimisation, production and utility functions, and inputs and outputs – are ahistorical and asocial. Consequently, it is only by convention and caution that the domain of economics is restricted to the market, where prices prevail.

No such customary limits are to be respected amongst the economic imperialists in the Becker-mould. For them, the economic approach is universal, applicable across all activity. Consequently, as Carrier (1997b: 152–3) reveals by referencing the critical commentary of others, Becker essentially obliterates the distinction between the economic and the non-economic except as the consequence of (economic) choices made by optimising agents. Indeed, as much of non-economic life as possible is explained by the economic approach. Whatever falls outside is deemed to be non-economic by virtue of being irrational.

Why has this simple if shifting division between the economic and the non-economic (and economics and the other social sciences) begun to change (in ways overlooked by Lazear), especially as the recent neo-liberal period has been associated with an intellectual climate conducive both to individualism (rational choice) and to the market? To some extent, academia itself has experienced a reaction against neo-liberalism, not least because it has to make at least a pretence at originality – and there are only so many ways of saying leave things to the market. Most important, though, in enabling a new 'revolutionary' phase of economics imperialism has been developments within mainstream economics itself, what one of its leading practitioners, Joe Stiglitz (1994), has termed the information-theoretic approach. Unlike the old Becker-style approach, this is based on the old idea of market imperfections but with a novel twist. This is the emphasis placed upon informational imperfections – all knowledge is not available to all and some have more than others, dubbed informational asymmetry. On this basis, despite continuing and unquestioning reliance upon methodological individualism in the form of utility maximisation, the new approach purports to be able to explain the presence and impact of economic and social structures, institutions, customs and culture, and even apparent violation of 'rational' behaviour as their consequence.

To see why and how, consider one of the classic texts of the new approach, Akerlof's (1970) 'Market for Lemons', where the title is drawn from US slang and refers to second-hand cars not to fruit. Unscrupulous (i.e. utility-maximising) second-hand car dealers know more about the quality of their cars than potential buyers. At any given price for a standard model, the average quality of those on sale within the market will be brought down by the withdrawal of those of considerably higher than average quality and the offer of those of considerably lower (neither distinguishable as such by the buyer). As a result, while the market may appear to be efficient in terms of equating supply with demand, it will not be so. For there will be those who wish to sell higher quality cars at a higher price and those who would be prepared to buy them as such.

Of course, it would be possible to regulate the market, offering or requiring tests, standards and warranties. This is, however, to begin to recognise how the new phase of economics imperialism proceeds. For such regulation would be perceived as the rational, non-market response to a market (informational) imperfection. Once in place, appropriate collective solutions could command conformity from optimising individuals.

Now consider a labour market in which all workers appear identical to employers but they differ by virtue of their skills, alternative job opportunities and motivation. In order to attract more skilled, less mobile and more committed workers, a wage might be offered that is higher than the going rate. Such an 'efficiency wage', as it is termed, more than pays back the extra cost incurred through higher productivity and reduced turnover. The result, though, is potential excess supply in the labour market. Workers drawn by the higher wages would work for less but the employer holds both to the higher wages and the level of employment warranted by production conditions.

This example demonstrates how economic (labour market) structures can be deemed to be explained, rather than taken for granted, on the basis of opti-mising individuals. For, whilst there are differences between workers, these are unknown to employers who structure the labour market into employed and unemployed by holding to the efficiency wage. Further, if there is some informa-tion about workers that gives the slightest indication of their productivity or whatever, this will be used as a proxy for deciding who to hire. Thus, so the story goes, gender and race might be used to structure the labour market because, for whatever reason, productivity is higher for white males on average. There are also knock-on effects, with the distribution of wage and employment opportuni-ties inducing workers to adopt corresponding strategies over education, allocation of domestic responsibilities, etc. Once again, informational asymme-tries purport to explain economic *and* social outcomes.

A final example is provided by health insurance for the old or infirm. At any premium price, only those at sufficiently bad risk of claiming will apply. The average health of applicants worsens as premiums rise. It is possible that there is no premium at which revenue exceeds expected costs of claims for treatment. There will be no market at all for health insurance for those most at risk. Such exclusion from the market is seen as a way of explaining both its scope and the rationale for non-market intervention, most notably by the state.

In short, as these three examples illustrate, informational imperfections are used to explain why markets might be inefficient, might not clear (supply and demand remain out of equilibrium), or might not emerge at all. As a result, whilst still drawing upon a methodology of optimising individuals, it is able to suggest why economic *structures* might arise – as, for example, in the division between the employed and unemployed when the labour market does not clear. Whilst this is a significant result *within* mainstream economics, just as important are the implications for other social sciences. For non-economic or non-market behaviour is now understood as the rational, i.e. individual optimising behaviour, response to market imperfections. It is appropriate in face of informational, and hence market, imperfections to form social structures, as reflected in collectives, institutions and the state, and to engage in what would otherwise appear to be non-rational behaviour, as in customs, trust and norms. Relative to the old, the new approach adds market imperfections in the form of informational asymmetries but, on this basis alone, it also extends the scope of the analysis more or less indefinitely across the social sciences. Both the economic and the non-economic are reduced to the historically evolved but rational response to (informational) market imperfections.

Such simple analytical advances considerably expand the capacity of economics to colonise the other social sciences, not least because of the formal and abstract nature of the models employed within economics. There has been a proliferation of applications in and around economics – the new institutional economics, the new household economics, the new economic sociology, the new welfare economics, the new political economy, the new growth theory, the new labour economics, the new economic geography, the new financial economics, the new development economics, the new economic history, and so on.[5] The analytical principles can be called forth in any context open to interpretation as an imperfect (non-)market situation. As the principles involved have no historical or social roots, they leave the historical, the social and the specific open to be imposed, as if painting on an empty canvas. For, in content, the theory relies entirely upon categories such as utility, production, inputs and informational uncertainties, quite apart from the timeless and rootless optimising of individuals, themselves located in history and society only by virtue of the preceding optimising of their ancestors. Thus, to reiterate, the new, like the old, approach is characterised in its starting point by excising social and historical content in anything other than name. Consequently, the historical can be (re)introduced formally as path dependence (or dynamics and multiple equilibrium) in some form. This allows the claim to be made that history matters, as do institutions, customs, culture and the like. But these are history etc. in a form that is shallow and would be scarcely recognised by the vast majority of social theory. Notably absent is any notion of the historically and socially rooted meaning of the categories of analysis themselves.

This explains why consumption has been relatively untouched by the new phase of economics imperialism. Nonetheless, the experience from other colonised areas is instructive. The alien methodology of economics does not present an impenetrable barrier to incursions elsewhere. This is because they proceed by concealing their origins or, more exactly, their underlying content, by informally adopting and adapting the concepts and language of the occupied analytical terrain.

A crucial conclusion is that the current relationship between economics and the other social sciences is highly fluid and by no means predetermined in its ebb and flow. The present success in the study of consumption in resisting economics imperialism is by no means a guarantee for the future. Nor does it, in and of itself, compensate for the weakness in the economic analysis of consumption that is the inheritance of the cultural turn. Whilst mainstream economics has strengthened its colonising designs both by refusing to tolerate other perspectives within its own discipline and by shifting from an as if perfect to an as if imperfect world, its underlying methodology remains alien to the vast majority of social science other than that based on rational choice. In addition, as social science reverses its cultural turn and returns to the material, including the economy, it is as yet ill placed to offer alternative political economy of its own. Indeed, as the following discussion of globalisation illustrates, social theorists often display a limited and dated understanding of the economy and of (mainstream) economics.

Globalising concepts[6]

In less than a decade, the notion of globalisation has become extremely common across the other social sciences.[7] In this respect, it shares in common some of the features of other concepts that have gained similar levels of prominence in the past – those such as consumer society, modernisation, Keynesian/welfarism and, its most recent predecessors, postmodernism and flexibility.[8] Each of these notions has been notable for representing the analytical response to what are presumed to be generalised empirical developments. Each has initially been relatively simple in its conceptual content but, on reflection and further study, has evolved prodigiously in scope and detail. Each has drawn upon the particular intellectual and ideological milieu in which it is situated and, because of vagueness and flexibility, allowed wide participation across disciplines and methods. As Gollan (1995a: 1) observes of globalisation:

> Critics often point to its theoretical weakness, vagueness or at least malleability as a serious and irreconcilable concern, while others see its vagueness as an asset for its popularity because of its capacity to elucidate virtually anything, ensuring its continued use and application.

Yet, the corresponding promise of opening interdisciplinary study has yielded a sequence of false dawns. Further, each of these notions has ultimately given way to new fashions and concerns, leaving a greater or lesser impression on how the world is understood and theoretically (re)constructed.

In the case of globalisation, there is already sufficient literature for these and other features to be apparent. Initially, the idea has been most simply associated with the hypothesis that developments at an international level have gained predominance over those at and between national levels. However, this has induced a number of reactions. In an apocalyptic vision, Beck (2000: 161–2) imagines that:

> The neo-liberals have won, even against themselves. The national state has been cleared away ... the 'Deutsche Bank' ... is now called the 'World Bank'. ... Similarly, in place of the United Nations, an organization has appeared which calls itself United Coca-Cola.

Others are more measured. For Hirst and Thompson (1996), it is argued that such internationalisation is not unique, its having been at least as strong at the end of the nineteenth century, although Bairoch and Kozul-Wright (1996) rightly warn against the dangers of seeing the two periods as in some sense similar.[9] Others, such as Sassen (1995), Gertler (1997), Boyer and Drache (1996), Boyer (1996), Levi-Faur (1997), Wade (1996), Weiss (1998), Fulcher (2000), Petras and Veltmeyer (2000) and Sutcliffe and Glyn (2000) have powerfully argued for the continuing salience of the nation-state.[10] Indeed, Helleiner (1997a, b) has suggested that, far from simply being the victims of globalisation, some nation-states promote and benefit from it.[11] Such positive support could equally be withdrawn in the future, for capital and trade controls for example, as occurred with the protectionist stances adopted in the interwar period.

This is all primarily to draw attention to globalisation as the economic and its effects – economic or otherwise – on nations, states and nation-states. It paints too narrow and distorted a picture relative to the vast weight of literature. For Therborn (2000b) there are at least five discourses around globalisation – competitive economics, social criticism, state (im)potence, culture and ecology. Bartelson (2000) perceptively observes that the vast majority of the literature accepts the fact of globalisation[12] and deploys this common starting point to restructure discourse in one of three ways, what he terms transference, transformation and transcendence. These are, respectively, more interaction between units, especially nation-states (more trade and investment, for example), systemic change leaving units as before (from competition between firms of nations to competition between firms and nations), and effective dissolution of units (end of the nation-state). Equally, such insights can be applied to globalisation as understood outside the immediate economic arena.

But one of the most common responses to the globalisation hypothesis is to associate it, if not always to contradict it, with heterogeneity and differentiation as, for example, in Eade (1997a), Jones (1995), Amin and Thrift (1994a), Appadurai (1996), Garrett (1998) and Berger and Dore (1996).[13] To a large extent, this follows from the particular response of the nation-state or whatever to the presumed universalising pressure associated with globalisation. As the impact of the latter is contested, outcomes are open ended (Amin and Thrift 1994b, Waterman 1996, Thomas 1995). The sharpest expression of the coupling of globalisation with differentiation is, however, through the notion of 'glocalisation'. The global universal is only realised through the local particular. These interact with one another and can even lead to the local being raised to the level of the global. In rather different terms, Therborn (2000a: 149) suggests that:

> In comparison with the pre-occupations of the social sciences 100 years earlier, the current overriding interest in globalization means two things. First of all, a substitution of *the global* for *the universal*; second, a substitution of *space* for *time*.

Glocalisation is itself indicative of three separate features of the literature. First, the confrontation between local and global is just a special case of a more general juxtaposition of a variety of underlying factors whose interaction is understood as mediating the global. Anthony Giddens is, for example, often taken as a point of reference with his understanding of the modern condition being based on the compression of time and space. For Appadurai (1996), globalisation is associated with the drawing of five different landscapes – those of ethnos, media, techno, finance and ideo.[14] Second, then, as there can be as many such landscapes as we care to choose, globalisation becomes open to increasingly diverse understandings. For Dunning (1993), for example, more or less confining his understanding of globalisation to extensive internationalisation (of production), there are as many as a hundred or more factors which affect the operation of multinational corporations. Significantly, this is the consequence of the extension of his highly popular *eclectic* theory of international production.[15] Third, then, there is an uneasy relationship between the abstract and the concrete, between the theoretical and the empirical. As for glocalisation, for example, the mix of local and global in outcomes can be readily understood in terms of corresponding theoretical constructs – even more so as the glocal is unpacked into an ever-expanding variety of Appadurai-type 'X-scapes'.[16]

Multiplicity of perspectives, and corresponding definitional conundrums, inevitably raises issues of methodology and theory that, not surprisingly, are extremely diverse across analyses of globalisation. The considerations of the previous paragraph can, at one extreme, be wrapped up in dialectical terms or, at the other, as a simple interpretative narrative. Implicitly or otherwise, a number of interconnected themes are pervasive. One is the relationship of theory to structures, not least how globalisation, in the form of financial markets or transnational production for example, relates to the nation-state. For Lewis *et al.* (1996), globalisation raises the issue of what are the units of competition – nation-states or corporations? And, what are the mechanisms of competition – resources, culture or organisation? A second theme is the role of (underlying) processes, not least as the parent of them all, globalisation, is unpacked into its constituent and interacting elements. A third is that of agency – who is the bearer and creator of structures and processes? Fourth is whether an approach is adopted at a holistic or atomistic level (Jones 1995). Is the global the reflection of a world system or the interaction of its constituent parts? Finally, there is the connection to be forged between causes and consequences. Is globalisation responsible for increasing inequality and poverty at a world level, for under-mining the power and independence of the nation-state, for subjecting democracy, let alone social democracy and welfarism, to the dictates of the global (financial) market?[17]

Of course, these concerns are not specific to the issue of globalisation. They are the nuts and bolts of all social science and the differences between and within various schools of thought. Consequently, the literature is marked by the extent that it draws upon existing conceptual frameworks, if now applied to the global rather than at some other level or object. Consequently, Watson *et al.* (1997: 276) can observe, 'Debates in sociology on globalisation have superseded the preoccupation with the transition from modernity to post-modernity.' Yet Baylis and Smith (1997a) consider that there is a close connection between the theories of modernisation and globalisation, with the latter raising the former to the international level, albeit in a different ideological context and with different theoretical emphases.[18] In particular, globalisation has been associated with a different assessment of the world situation, one marked by the end of the Cold War, the new World Order, the triumph of neo-liberalism and 'the market' and the decline of the nation-state. In addition, it should be recognised that literature on globalisation has often been deployed with a careless, shallow and implicit understanding of the nation-state. Not surprisingly, this makes it relatively easy to allow globalisation either to set it aside or to be impeded by it.

Paradoxically, however, globalisation has come to the fore just as the intellec-tual climate across the social sciences has sought to address the significance of institutions and regulation which, especially when operative at a national level, bring into question simple propositions concerning the nature and consequences of globalisation. Post-Fordism, for example, with its emphasis on flec-spec (or flexible specialisation in production and product), suggests the importance of subnational social and political organisation, most notably through industrial districts. Even mainstream economics which has been the source of the most virulent analytical support in practice to the neo-liberal project has sought to understand the importance of institutions and how they make a difference in performance between economic units, most notably in the new growth theory which seeks to investigate whether economies converge and, if not, why not.[19] This is mirrored in the World Bank's shift in ideological stance to a post-Washington consensus, in which the market is heavily associated with imperfections, which may be corrected by an interventionist state.[20] More gener-ally, emphasis upon institutional thickness,[21] forms of embeddedness,[22] the cultural as an economic factor,[23] state capabilities,[24] etc., have served both to finesse the differential impact of globalisation as well as to draw upon contempo-rary theoretical concerns, usually applied previously to the nation-state. It is the height of irony that those progressives who have fought long and hard against the non-interventionism attached to the neo-liberal Washington consensus should view the post-Washington consensus as too little too late, with globalisa-tion having undermined the potential for replicating the East Asian miracles.

Polanyi can rest in peace: the great transformation is over – unless it can be promoted at an international level.

So much for the new conceptual order around globalisation. Not surprisingly, one of its key features is the prominence of economic factors, even if indirectly in the emphasis, for example, on speed and cost of communication. The importance of the economic might be thought to be natural in view of the object of enquiry but it cannot be taken for granted since globalisation is probably first historically linked to the cultural, not least in (the reaction against) Americanisation and US hegemony in non-economic, especially cultural and military, arenas. Added impetus to the economic has been provided by the reaction against the extremes of postmodernism. Globalisation directs attention to the constraints within which we run our lives as opposed to the subjectivities with which we can interpret them. By the same token, it follows that the economic skills which social science in general can bring to bear upon the global are limited not only for having been neglected over the recent period but also for having been concentrated upon market versus state debates. Nor, as already observed, does economics as a discipline itself provide a useful counterweight since it is methodologically ill-suited to deal with globalisation other than as the atomistic outcome of individual decision making. As a consequence, it is unable to address economic globalisation, other than as a particular outcome of market imperfections, nor its broader social and cultural implications other than as economics by other means.

Globalisation as finance

Simplifying drastically, the result has been the use in other social sciences of the economic and economics as a metaphor for globalisation itself in its pure form. Further, an element in the metaphor is the power of economic globalisation itself over the non-economic arena. It is the rule of the market or companies at an international level without regard to, and overriding, the non-economic. The global is the footloose multinational corporation and, more generally, the discipline of mobile capital on wages, competitiveness and government policy. Everything else, especially the non-economic, is a reaction against such factors, impeding or promoting, conforming to its dictates or exploiting the autonomy it endows. Further, if the global is the economic as metaphor, the financial system and finance are themselves the metaphor of the economic. Appadurai (2000: 3) provides a sharp illustration:[25]

> Globalization is inextricably linked to the current workings of capital on a global scale; in this regard it extends the earlier logics of empire, trade, and political dominion in many parts of the world. Its most striking feature is the runaway quality of global finance, which appears remarkably independent of traditional constraints of information transfer, national regulation, industrial productivity, or 'real' wealth in any particular society, country, or region.

In short, international finance is the symbol of globalisation. It has grown enormously over the past twenty years: it is internationally mobile and respects no national boundaries; it compresses time and space through computer dealing and communications faster and with greater scope than for any other market; it is homogeneous in seeking out the highest rates of return: and last, but by no means least, it is no respecter of national sovereignty, visiting speculative crises on those who do not respect its requirements for fiscal and other forms of commercial discipline.

The literature on the globalisation of finance is, however, far less secure in providing the pure model for globalisation either as metaphor for emulation or as the point of departure for non-economic heterogeneity and differentiation. First of all, the notion of the globalisation of finance as an undifferentiated entity is itself extremely misleading, as if finance were simply an extremely fluid set of interchangeable monies. As Coleman (1996) observes, there have been three aspects of globalisation of financial services. There is the growth of international markets in such services; the growing integration between financial services within domestic markets; and the deepening of domestic markets by which is meant the creation of ever more financial products and derivatives. Further, the last is indicative of a continuing heterogeneity within the financial sector, which covers a wide range of assets and services from consumer credit through to stock exchanges and government bonds. In other words, finance can only be globalised on the basis of an increasingly complex set and structure of financial instruments, uneven in distribution, character and fungibility.

Second, such differentiation is itself the product of distinctive national financial systems. A voluminous literature has arisen on the nature and significance of the differences between market-based and bank-based financial systems, corresponding to Anglo-American and German–Japanese banking, respectively, with one relying on short-term and the other on long-term financing and monitoring of industry.[26] This also points to the need to consider the relationship between finance and the rest of the economy rather than allowing finance to float freely in a global ether.

Third, the globalisation of finance has raised the issue of national sovereignty. For Cohen (1998), for example, money has been effectively deterritorialised to the extent that business can be carried out in any currency. This has consequences for national independence, in the conduct of macroeconomic policy and access to seignorage, for example. Nonetheless, Cohen interprets the current situation as one in which national monopolies over money supply have been displaced by a competitive oligopoly, with different currencies vying for market demand. In a different way, the same conclusion is drawn by Helleiner (1997b) although, for him, the United States and the UK encouraged liberalisation, and hence globalisation, of financial markets in order to promote their own position.

Fourth, there is concern about the stability of financial markets as they putatively break free from national control (Porter 1996, McKenzie and Khalidi 1996). This gives rise to consideration of (re)regulation at national and international levels, leading to reliance upon recent theoretical developments, such as the new institutional economics. This is a result of the supposed rapidity of globalisation of finance having resulted from the particularly large impact of reductions in transactions costs and speed of communications. For Cerny (1994), for example, the reduction of transactions costs in international finance has undermined the economies of scale of national financial regulation since the latter would simply disadvantage national finance in international competition, with some other government prepared to lessen regulatory requirements. Yet Lütz (1998) argues that Germany has witnessed a strengthening of the nation-state in its regulation of the stock exchange in response to globalised financial markets. Agnes (2000) demonstrates that there is no 'end of geography' in the functioning of financial markets, with the continuing salience of locally embedded knowledge and social relations.

From this extremely selective dip into the literature on the globalisation of finance, it follows that it cannot serve as an ideal type against which to assess other forms of, and reactions against, globalisation. For global finance is itself equally differentiated and heterogeneous. And finance is not culture nor sovereignty as such. This is not to deny finance its global importance. Indeed, I would argue that the period since the collapse of the postwar boom has been marked by the prominence of international finance, and the ways in which it has intervened in the restructuring of the international and domestic economies. The goal here, though, is less to establish the importance of global finance, and its corresponding implications, as to dismiss its, usually unquestioned, role as metaphor and exemplar for the essence of globalisation (like perfect competition as pure model of the economy).

For completeness, although tangential to primary purpose, this section closes by examining how are we to understand the heterogeneity of global finance. Surely *not* as in the new financial economics with its emphasis upon asymmetric information as the primary explanatory device? This has five weaknesses.[27] First, it tends to take the nature and availability of information as given or, at the very least, derived from exogenously given parameters.[28] This reflects lack of systemic analysis as a consequence of underlying dependence upon methodological individualism. In contrast, the uncertainties attached to capitalism are of its own making, the consequence of its specific economic and social relations.[29] Second, information-theoretic economics focuses on the *intrinsic* content of the exchange between agents, at most taking the extrinsic content as given or as a matter of policy or regulation. This is to set aside economic, political and ideological leverage that derives from the class positions occupied by agents. Third, by the same token, there is sore neglect of the structure, tendencies and processes attached to capitalism, quite apart from issues of power and conflict. Fourth, in effect, there is no specific understanding of money (and of its role within capitalism) as the theory of market imperfections is equally applicable to any market. Finally, the mainstream literature has undermined itself in its own empirical work which has shown that clear-cut differences between stereotyped financial systems simply do not prevail – in light of composition of different types of assets, for example.[30]

Marxist political economy offers an alternative approach, with some of its features shared by post-Keynesian monetary theory.[31] First, apart from understanding capitalism in terms of class relations, it structures the economy into spheres of production and exchange, the one responsible for creating (surplus) value, and the other for circulating and realising it. Second, the sphere of exchange is itself structured. On the one hand, there is a broad distinction between interest-bearing capital and commercial capital – one funding accumulation of capital, and the other facilitating its results in the buying and selling of commodities. On the other hand, each of these forms of capital in exchange has become extremely fragmented by sector and function and mutually embroiled. In principle, and in practice, a divorce is created between the 'real' accumulation of capital in production and its representation and movement in exchange, as paper (increasingly electronic) claims on (surplus) value are created and bought and sold in volumes and type that bear no necessary relationship to underlying 'fundamentals'. Third, such capital in exchange can facilitate the accumulation of capital, indeed it is necessary for it, by speeding up sale and purchase and making money capital available for investment.

Fourth, though, as in speculative bubbles, but more generally and less dramatically, capital in exchange can be built up in nominal terms alone, even over long periods of time. This is reflected in the rise of finance over the last thirty years. The effects are not to be recognised exclusively in the accumulation of financial assets and the spread of financial activities. Equally they are to be found in almost every aspect of economic and social life, from the distributional gains and leverage of those attached to finance, to the bloated resources devoted to turning the wheels of finance, quite apart from the transformation of those cities dedicated to financial services.[32] In addition, the life-styles associated with the captains of finance, well captured in the notion of yuppie, have a profound impact on elite consumption – quite apart from the easily forgotten, often casualised and poorly paid service workers to finance, who survive on entirely different standards of consumption.

How is it possible for financial assets and activity to be persistently excessive relative to real activity? If financial markets were perfect, it would be impossible since prices for their services would fall. But financial markets cannot be perfect. If they were in the classical sense of price taking, with indefinite borrowing and lending at all times at given rates of interest, no one would ever pay back on loans since all obligations could be met on the basis of further borrowing. Further, models of imperfect competition in financial services can be used not only to establish constraints on markets where information is asymmetric. For 'local' monopolies for finance can lead to excessive product differentiation and financial activity.[33] The position of Marxist political economy is different since it does not treat finance as if it were simply some other sector of the economy. Taking the structural separation of production and exchange as its starting

23

point, the competitive process within the sphere of exchange in access to finance is different from that within production (and trading capital within exchange). This is because competition across industry depends upon access to finance as larger capitals tend to beat out the smaller in productivity and survival. The financial sector is not liable to provide finance for competition with itself. This is not to deny the presence of competition within the financial sector, only to acknowledge that it is distinctive, as recognised in the need for regulation to constrain excessive systemic creation of finance as individual financial enter-prises pursue their own profitability, possibly collectively at the expense of overall financial stability.[34]

Fifth, as sharply evidenced by recent financial crises, quite apart from building up slowly, financial assets can be destroyed rapidly with severe conse-quences for the 'industrial' capital to which they are attached. The relationship between real and fictitious capital is, however, not simply one arising out of informational and market imperfections. It reflects fundamental conflicts of interest between finance and industry, in which the former has prevailed despite its ultimate dependence on the latter. It remains to be seen whether recent finan-cial turbulence leads to a reining in of the powers of finance. It has been so at ideological and academic levels, with calls for cancellation of Third World debt, for a Tobin tax, or for other forms of international regulation with much being made of the parallels with the movement in the nineteenth century to national regulation of local banking. Less emphasis has been placed on the scope for domestic regulation of finance (apart from opposition to Neanderthal neo-liberal goals of rapid and full deregulation), although there has been some resurgence of interest in capital controls.[35] Whether at a national or international level, the issue is less whether controls can be effective and more who will exercise them and in whose interests. In this light, financial policy cannot be considered in isolation from underlying (national) economic and political interests and the mix of other policies with which they inevitably interact.

Concluding remarks

In the dual intellectual retreat from the excesses of neo-liberalism (leave every-thing to the market) and postmodernism (leave everything to the imagination), economics and the economy hold peculiar and ambiguous positions, especially as far as the study of the economy is concerned. On the one hand, the new phase of economics imperialism, based on informational imperfections, offers a complete solution to the (re)integration of the economic with the non-economic, of the market with the non-market, the private with the public, and to the incor-poration of the social, historical, institutional, customary and even the cultural. It is not a satisfactory solution for those antagonistic to methodological individu-alism in the form adopted by mainstream economists nor to those concerned with the meaning of consumption to the consumer. Yet economics imperialism holds certain attractions to social theorists, reflected in its considerable albeit uneven successes, not least where it conceals its analytical weaknesses in slipping across interdisciplinary boundaries and apparently adopting, whilst transforming, the traditional concepts and concerns of its newly adopted homes.

Globalisation, on the other hand, is at least as wide ranging as economics imperialism in pretending both to incorporate anything and to resolve everything. It tends to proceed, however, by drawing upon an idealised model of the economy, one presumed to be especially attuned to the financial world, in which the economic sweeps all before it, conquering and homogenising local differences. Inevitably, the local (from national down to community and even the individual consumer) strikes back, furnishing an alternative, complementary model. Whether it be derived from the economic itself, or the cultural or whatever, globalisation is set against the refinements associated with resistance and specificity.

Taken together, economics imperialism and globalisation form a dream team, if uncomfortably so. One hails from mainstream economics, the other from social theory. Both are all-embracing in terms of topics to be addressed and explanatory factors to be incorporated, but they complement rather than compete with one another (although social theorists often believe they are criticising mainstream economics, simply by rejecting the virtual world of perfect competition).[36] Yet, each is profoundly flawed, in targeted scope of generalisation and the content with which it is endowed. In the chapters that follow, an alternative approach is followed. It begins with the basic categories of capitalism (the commodity, the gift and capital itself), addresses consumption in terms of systems of provision and, ultimately, illustrates its merits (and the deficiencies of its rivals) by application to the welfare state as the most important example of (public) consumption.

3

THE WORLD OF COMMODITIES

Introduction

Initially, the literature on consumption grew on the basis of applying existing theories and concepts to a previously neglected topic. For sociologists, it was a matter of distinction and emulation and, for postmodernists, meaning and identity. Each discipline within the social sciences could interpret consumption from its own traditional, 'horizontal' perspective by theme and theory. More recently, the literature has become more circumspect, seeking greater analytical depth in rooting out the sources and meanings of consumption. It has necessarily involved more abstract and distant considerations, those that in the first instance seem far removed from consumption itself. In particular, questions are raised over the relationship between the material and the cultural, the social and the economic, the private and the public, the micro and the macro, and so on. Consumption is used to interrogate such issues as well as to shed light upon them. Further, if consumption is differentiated by class, gender, glocalisation or whatever, these too become of significance in their own right, and a matter for reassessment, as part of the study of consumption. By the same token, there has also been renewed interest in the nature of the commodity and of money as these are essential for contemporary access to consumption. This chapter seeks to clarify some of the analytical confusion that surrounds much of this latter literature. It does so by drawing the conclusion in the fourth section that capitalist commodity production is an appropriate starting point for examining modern consumption, even where such consumption does not itself necessarily depend directly upon (capitalist) commodity production.

The route to this conclusion is taken by a number of steps. The first, in the next section, is to explore the relationship between use value and exchange value, but with emphasis on exchange value. It is shown, following Marx's theory of commodity fetishism that, whilst money provides a common measure across commodities, it only does so by seemingly setting aside the underlying social relations, structures and processes by which use values are made available for consumption. The fashionable trainer does not display the child labour upon which its provision depends.[1] More generally, for Marx, both how production is organised and how labour is expended under the control of capital are of crucial

26

importance in underpinning the exchange value of commodities. His labour theory of value is not simply a theory of the quantitative determination of price but a qualitative theory with the potential for tracing the passage from production through to consumption.

The implications for use value of Marx's understanding of the commodity are taken up in the next chapter. The third section of this chapter undertakes a preliminary ground-clearing exercise. In anthropology, an opposition has been drawn between the commodity and the gift, with the first representing the quantitative, impersonal, private and homogenised world of commerce, and the second, the qualitative, personal, public and heterogeneous world of ritual, custom and culture. Each of these worlds tends to be associated with different forms and meanings of consumption. The gift is ethnographically rich, authentic, the product of a nostalgically viewed era that only survives in the interstices of contemporary private lives (or marginalised and threatened primitive societies). The commodity is debased by commercial imperatives, homogenised and impersonal, lacking depth and quality. Postmodernism has, however, blasted this dichotomy to pieces, not least through emphasising the complex semiotic narratives that can be woven around the sign values of commodities.

Initially, the gift and commodity were associated, respectively, with primitive and commercial societies. But capitalism has been shown to exhibit gift-like features, not least because it is not and cannot be reduced to commercial relations alone, even within commerce itself with each market sustained and marked by its own non-economic characteristics, such as institutions and customs. Ultimately, the distinction between gift and commodity has only been retained by ranging societies or aspects of them along a continuum between the two extreme poles of pure gift and pure commodity. This too has proven unsatisfactory since the social character of commodities is no less rich than that of gifts. Consequently, the opposition between gift and commodity is rejected. At most gifts can stand as a marker for absence of the commodity, for a generalised notion of exchange other than through the market. As such, it is highly diverse in the social relations it represents and incorporates, and highly misleading as a general category, suggesting commonalities across what is not common. The gift has also served the negative function of monopolising attention on use value, thereby impoverishing understanding of the use value aspect of the commodity even though this is one of its essential components.

With the rejection of the gift/commodity duality (and the gift itself other than as heuristic device), the fourth section further investigates the commodity as itself representing a range of diverse social relations, from simple exchange of commodities, independently produced, through to the mass production of advanced capitalism. Objects can even adopt the form of the commodity, exchange with money, without being commodities, as in payments made for bribery (the price of principle) or articles that are sold but cannot be reproduced such as antiques.[2] These can be classified by, but not reduced to, their points of departure from capitalist production. They are not commodity production by other means but they are heavily conditioned by the world of commodities they inhabit. Like articles that are never exchanged, such as family heirlooms, it is crucial to recognise that their distinctiveness as items of consumption necessarily derives in part from their not being commodities. They are in a sense a counter-culture, irreducibly if invisibly attached to the culture (and the shop counter) from which they are notable by their absence. Accordingly, a general theory of consumption across all such items, whether they be directly attached to the market or not (casual monetary exchange or heirlooms), is liable to be limited by failing to differentiate their origins both outside commodity production and their connections to it.

Use value and exchange value

In modern times, consumption predominantly presents itself as attached to a world of commodities. But the commodity is both simple and mysterious. For it has a double life in the world of thought. On the one hand, like consumption itself, it is so commonplace that it can be taken for granted. 'You pays your money, you makes your choice.' But even this simple adage opens up a wealth of conundrums. How much do you pay, and why this choice rather than that one? On the other hand, then, the commodity has been subject to close scholarly scrutiny, not least in the attempt to discover what makes it distinctive – from the 'gift', for example, as discussed in the next section.

Starting back at least as far as classical political economy of the eighteenth century, it has long been recognised that the commodity is both a use value and an exchange value. Adam Smith, for example, puzzled over the diamond/water paradox. How could one have so little use value and yet be so valuable, and the other so invaluable to life and be so cheap? In modern parlance, especially main-stream economics, use value and exchange value have fallen into disuse and have been replaced by the notions of utility and price (with the idea of the commodity giving way to the idea of goods). The diamond/water paradox is resolved by reference to insatiable needs competing for attention in the face of scarce productive resources – although diamonds would be very much cheaper but for the century-old cartel organised by de Beers.[3] In most respects, the reduction to utility and price strips the commodity of most of the interesting questions that can be asked of it, as shown in Chapter 7. In particular, what is it that makes objects useful: is this a matter of physical or cultural properties; is it a result of individual preferences or social determinants?

Significantly, this last batch of questions has nothing as such to do with the commodity precisely because they are confined to use value. The latter neces-sarily prevails across all societies irrespective of whether commodities are present or not. This is not to say that use value is unimportant to the commodity, nor that how the commodity gains its use value is irrelevant or trivial. Use value is an essential ingredient of the commodity. But, look as long as we like at the commodity purely as a use value and we will learn nothing about the commodity as characteristic of particular societies or particular activities within societies. The same is true, of course, of the gift as use value. Objects may reveal very little about the societies from which they are drawn.

The exchange value of the commodity seems more promising as an analytical can opener for society. But it is deceptively troublesome. For the incidence of exchange within and across societies is highly variable so that a generalised notion of commodity or market exchange is inappropriate. Although in economics, exchange and monetary exchange tend to be used synonymously, with former more common usage for brevity, in other social sciences exchange is used to denote most if not all personal and social interactions. An exchange of views, vows, blows and so on readily springs to mind. What distinguishes commodity exchange is the use of money as an intermediary by the parties involved. So, to understand commodity exchange, we have to understand money. To clarify the point, as will be discussed in the fourth section, barter is *not* commodity exchange in the absence of money. Barter is a direct exchange of use values. Simple commodity exchange can have this effect – sell for money in order to buy something else. But commodity exchange is always an exchange of a use value against money. Although money is itself a use value with many aspects, it is a *specific* use value. Barter allows, in principle, for exchange between *any* two use values. Commodity exchange does not. Money must always be present in some form on one or other sides of the exchange. As a result, there is a major difference between barter and commodity exchange. For the latter, the seller goes away with a use value, money, that can in principle *and* practice be exchanged against any other available use value at any time or place.

This last point has led commentators, especially economists, to see barter as an elementary and inefficient form of monetised market exchange. Money simply does what barter does, only more effectively and efficiently. Accordingly, money can be set aside as simply catalytic. This is true of Gary Becker, for example, whose work is considered in some detail in Chapter 7. As shown in Fine (2001a: Chapter 3), despite purporting to be able to explain all rational behaviour as economic, in whatever sphere of human endeavour, his economic approach never draws upon, even mentions, the presence of money as a feature of the economy – and much the same is true of unemployment! This is despite the emergence in his work of a plethora of capitals, physical, human, personal, social and so on. But economists are not unique in seeing barter in terms of what Godbout (1998: 114) calls a simple 'economic evolutionism' from some form of barter to money, with gift exchange, to be examined in the next section, having preceded barter. Appadurai (1986a: 9) defines barter as 'the exchange of objects for one another *without* reference to money and *with* maximum feasible reduction of social, cultural, political, or personal transaction costs', the two qualifications placing barter, respectively, between the gift and the commodity. As Strathern (1992: 169) observes:

> It is a curiosity that anthropological attempts to describe non-monetary transactions may well end up concentrating on their monetary aspects. … It (barter) was regarded as a strategy through which people obtained things that they needed, that is, doing in the absence of money what people with money also do. In short, it was understood in 'monetary' terms.

In similar vein, Gregory (1987: 525) tartly observes of 'the habit of beginning an argument with an analysis of barter in an "early and rude state of society"', that, 'the barter economies of these theories are figments of a Eurocentric imagination that bears no resemblance at all to actual tribal economies'.

The effect of such imagination is to underrate and misunderstand the importance of money itself. For, from this perspective, it simply becomes the oil that eases the movement of the market that is itself construed as a perfected system of bartering. But, once money mediates exchange, it not only takes on a life of its own but so do the motives of the parties in exchange. For money has the effect of homogenising exchange in the sense that all goods are measurable against one another in the single dimension of money. Whilst commodities necessarily have different use values, they almost appear to lose them in being set against money. In the market everything has its price. As Simmel (1900: 394) puts it, cited and critically discussed in Fine and Lapavitsas (2000: 371), money 'forces an extraneous standard upon things, a standard that is quite alien to distinction'.

Some caution is appropriate at this stage. First, of course, not everything is or can be in the market. So not all relations between agents are attached to such homogenisation. As Dodd (1994) is at pains to point out, Simmel is not arguing that money homogenises everything. Rather, the idea that money can do so is extremely powerful and very much enters our understanding of capitalist society. In more eloquent terms, Oscar Wilde referred to those who knew the price of everything and the value of nothing. This distinction between the idea of money and the practices in reality to which it is attached is extremely important. As Gronow (1997) is crystal clear on the matter, he is worth quoting at length. He begins by noting how Simmel emphasises the variety of social influences (on consumption) of which money, in particular, is especially important but not unique (p. 159):

> Simmel's society consists of innumerable, different and simultaneous forms of sociation, of which no single one is self-evidently more important than another: every form can be taken as an object of social analysis, but it is not possible, even in principle, to make a total evaluation of the degree of complexity or purity of social forms. … There is,

however, one social phenomena, money which to Simmel's mind is the symbol of modern society, and the cultural influence which reaches most social phenomena (as analysed by Simmel in his *Philosophy of Money*). One could almost say that it permeates the whole of modern society. Money is a symbol – an empirical and narrow one – of the unity of all being. It is fixed to or grows from every style of life almost like a part of the body, and overcomes all 'one-sidedness'.

But, in interpreting Simmel, Gronow is careful to distinguish between this symbolic role of money and the formation of culture in practice (p. 191):

> In *The Philosophy of Money* one cannot find any general view about general aestheticization of modern culture followed by the increasing influence of money. If such a connection exists, it is much more indirect and complex and one should look for it in the general differentiation of modern culture, in the plurality and complexity of all those social forms in which an individual takes part, rather than in the one-dimensionality of money.

Although Simmel did posit general theories of aestheticisation, what would now be called trickle-down and also be concerned with the adornment of women for men's pleasure and status, this is not the point at issue here. Rather it is to recognise both that money sets a standard of homogenisation but that it does not command a monopoly by doing so. In short, the idea of money as homogenising is not all-conquering. As a result, Radin (1996), for example, argues that to treat everything as if it were a commodity, the reduction of everything to monetary value, is to encourage the process of commodification itself. Her general concern is how the idea of 'universal commodification' leads to a failure to appreciate the non-market aspects of market relations as well as non-market values. She cites Hobbes' dictum, 'the Value or WORTH of a man ... is as of all other things, his Price; that is to say, so much as would be given for the use of his Power' (p. 6). This is paramount to condoning slavery, child labour and other ethically unacceptable practices that would be encouraged, even allowed, by the philosophy of universal commodification, for 'we cannot both know the price of something and know that it is unmonetizable, or priceless' (p. 101). Universal commodification requires a narrow view of both nature and humanity (p. 5); not least, in the method of mainstream economics, it imagines 'a thin self that does *not* change' (p. 77), one without context and meaning. One particular concern is how the new economics of law would understand sexual violence as a crime against personal property with a corresponding monetary damage to be paid at the expense or exclusion of broader ethical considerations. Her stance, outside the most committed and crudest of 'economics imperialism', discussed in Chapter 2, would surely command agreement. Everything should not and cannot be reduced to its price. Not surprisingly, the relationship between the ideology of leaving everything to the market, the neo-liberalism of Thatcher and Reagan, and its outcomes in practice has had mixed results as far as withdrawal of the state from the market is concerned.

In short, Radin is arguing that the idea of universal commodification leads to objectification and subordination to the market in principle and, as a result, in practice. By the same token, this is to accept that homogenisation by the market, commodities and money is not absolute. Indeed, in the work of Zelizer (1987, 1988, 1994, 1996, 1998), the approach to money, markets and commodities is turned the other way around. Emphasis is placed upon the capacity of agents to retain heterogeneity, their own contexts and meanings, and to express the social relations to which they are attached. Thus, Zelizer (1988: 618) deploys a notion of the market as 'one among many different possible arrangements, such as barter or gift exchange, that involve economic processes' and sees 'its essence (as) the rational calculation of costs and benefits and the regulation of exchange by the price mechanism'. Similarly, for her, money is heterogeneous, so that 'different cultural and social settings introduce special forms of controls, restrictions, and distinctions in the uses, users, allocation, regulation, sources, and meanings of money' (p. 631). In Russell Banks' novel, *Continental Drift*, for example, the 'hero' is determined to return the roll of banknotes, which he has received for smuggling illegal immigrants, to the community of Haitians that paid for his services. This follows after those in his boatload are thrown overboard and drowned in an attempt to elude capture. The money itself cannot reveal his crime and guilt but it carries those marks for him.

Such emphasis on heterogeneity of markets, commodities and money appears to deny the latter's homogenising power (see Fine and Lapavitsas (2000) in debate with Zelizer (2000)). The point of the former's critique is not to assert universal commodification, as Radin would term it, in practice. Rather, it is necessary to isolate what is special about all commodities that allows them to be homogenised in one, if not all, respects – their equivalence with money. This, as Simmel is aware, requires a quantitative theory of value, on which Zelizer is completely silent. Unfortunately, Simmel himself has nothing much to offer beyond vague notions of the socialised subjectivity of worth that derives from the process of exchange. The same is true of Carruthers and Babb. For them:

> Our argument is informed by two general observations. The first is that markets have certain preconditions without which they cannot function. The second is that markets function very differently at different times, in different places, and in different spheres of economic life.
>
> (p. 4)

Further, 'Four key elements constitute that foundation: property, buyers and sellers, money and information' (p. 5). Markets are seen as embedded, by which is meant 'that markets coexist with, are shaped by, and depend on, other social relations' (p. 7). Thus, 'together, institutions and cultural meanings constitute two different sorts of nonmarket social relationships in which markets are embedded' (p. 9). Consequently, 'the fact that capitalism possesses some core features does not, however, mean that markets are always and everywhere the same' (p. 11). But they offer little by way of identifying and explaining these core features, without which the diversity floats freely across non-market factors rather than subjective worth as for Simmel.

The second caution in dealing with the homogenisation attached to commodities and money has already been covered under the first. The distinction between the idea and practice of homogenisation means that the latter is not the only relation between the agents. Whatever is bought and sold, and how, can affect the agents concerned. In any case, markets require all sorts of institutional supports for them to survive, not least in defining and safeguarding property. Again, this has led some to emphasise the heterogeneity of markets, to distinguish them according to the networks, cultures and so on in which they are embedded, following the work of Granovetter (1985) and ultimately leading to the idea that the functioning of markets depends upon their associated social capital (see Fine (2001a) for a critique). Callon (1998a, b) even goes so far as to suggest that heterogeneity in the formation of markets is driven by the extent to which they are understood to incorporate externalities by economists or others (see Fine (2001f) for a critique). In either case, the market is more or less impersonal despite its use of money to homogenise and quantify. It can be impersonal, especially in money or other financial markets themselves as exchanges take place at the press of a keyboard. But, even here, when loans are under consideration, the characteristics of the agents and the connections between them can be paramount, as reviewed by Uzzi (1999) and critically discussed by Lapavitsas (2000). In short, money does homogenise, and not only in the mind, but its homogenising power is not and, it should be added, cannot be absolute. A key issue is how commodities and money, and ultimately consumption, accommodate the homogeneity of exchange value and the heterogeneity of use value. The answer cannot be found in the forms themselves.

These cautions aside, for the moment, it suffices to establish that a distinguishing feature of the commodity (in order eventually to be able to purchase other commodities with the money realised) is that it is sold for money.[4] And, if it is sold for money, that must inform the motives and activities that have brought it to the market. Such observations are almost certainly uncontroversial although opinions differ sharply over whether this is a good thing or not. Proponents of the market argue that it allows resources to be allocated efficiently, for innovation to thrive and for consumer needs to be met. In contrast, critics of commercialism in general, and consumerism in particular, perceive the market as overpowering and eliminating anything other than the monetary motive and, a different point, leading to the manipulation of consumers in pursuit of sales.

In both of these perspectives, it is correctly perceived that commodities are produced *for* the market and not, as for barter, merely being the more or less accidental exchange of one use value for another or, more likely, for money in particular. An immediate corollary is that the market is itself more extensive than the exchange of commodities. It does not include barter but, once the market for commodities and money is extensive, they can be used for other purposes, possibly replicating more easily what would otherwise have to be achieved through other means. This is true of casual sale of second-hand items or the payment of bribes. Both adopt the market form of commanding a price but neither constitutes a commodity.

A crucial question is why do some things become, in the clumsy term, commodified or commoditised, and others not so. Some consideration to this issue will be given later. By the same token, why do other things become decommodified? This is one way of interpreting the impact of the welfare state as labour is no longer required to enter the labour market to obtain income, an interpretation offered by Esping-Andersen's theory of welfare regimes that is critically assessed in Chapter 10. The issue is, however, more complex than this for it has just been shown that there is a tripartheid division between those things that command a price and those that do not – money cannot buy me love, for example, although there is a market for sex. Further, amongst those things that can be bought and sold, some are not commodities – more or less casual sale of articles that thereby assume the trappings of commodities as opposed to representing systematic production for the market.

Much confusion has prevailed across the literature for failing to draw these simple distinctions. For, without them, very different sorts of over-generalised categories of goods and activities (labour, for example) are treated analytically as if they were all of a feather. The limit is reached where all of the distinctions involved are erased, and everything is reduced to 'goods' as in mainstream economics. It inappropriately leads to the search for a theory of goods that prevails across all times and places. From the perspective adopted here, it is essential to deal first with commodities proper. This is because they are of overwhelming importance in contemporary society and set the conditions for the presence and nature of those goods that are not within their immediate orbit and ambit. Both the market for casual sale and for bribery are heavily influenced, if indirectly and in different ways, by what is going on around them in the world of commodities.

A long analytical journey has been traced in order to gain a simple vantage point. The commodity as exchange value is governed by, but not reducible to, production for the market as the quantitative means of access to money. Our journey, however, does not end here but has only just begun. For what makes it possible in social organisation for products to take the form of commodities? Marx, who possibly examined the anatomy of the commodity in this respect more than any other, provides a particular, controversial answer. First, he excludes use value as the determining factor. There are good reasons for doing so. Use values, both in their material and cultural properties, are infinitely diverse and, as has already been argued above, none can be singled out as always being present in exchange. For economists, though, utility is used to represent the presence of use value of whatever content, and reduce it to a single dimension, in order to motivate exchange. Higher marginal utility commands higher price. But there are many sources of utility that do not lead to commodity production, not least because it is a universal and ahistorical category of analysis, present across all societies. In other words, the secret of the commodity cannot be found in its property as use value as bearer of (marginal) utility (Fine 1982: 97–8).

Second, Marx seeks out the social property that renders the commodity possible. He positively selects labour as the quantitative source of value. His reasons for doing so are complex and sophisticated. Most important is the idea that, when commodities are exchanged against one another, they are not simply measured against money but, equally if indirectly, the different labours that have gone into producing the commodities are also measured against one another. Further, this is a social property uniquely characteristic of commodity-producing societies. Different labours are not measured against one another in other societies, or at least not in the same way through the unconscious medium of money. A centrally planned economy might measure labour contributions, and even weight some more or less than others (and, a slightly different point, remunerate them differently). But, in doing so, the equivalence between the labours is established in an entirely different way, by conscious calculation.

It has been traditional to understand Marx's value theory as incorporating two aspects. The qualitative aspect has just been discussed and will be taken up again below. The quantitative aspect concerns the relationship between Marx's notion of value (the labour time of production) and price. Does value equal price or, both different and slightly less demanding in some respects, does value determine or cause price? The latter would mean that strict equality between value and price is not necessary but that labour time is the sole source of value and makes price what it is (Elson 1979, Fine (ed) 1986, Saad-Filho 1997). This 'dual' approach to Marx's value theory is inappropriate. For Marx, commodity production necessarily establishes a relationship for labourers as producers – from factories and fields, say; throughout the world, different labourers are brought into equivalence with one another, or measured against one another through the mechanism of market exchange. The issue is less one of whether value and price equal one another or what is the more complex mathematical relationship between the two as prices come to reflect the difference in capital–labour relations, wages, technology, trade, monopoly and so on. Rather, in interpreting commodities as the products of labour which are brought into equivalence with one another, the political economy of commodities is opened up for further analysis. It is not closed as an esoteric solution to price theory. In particular, Marx's value theory raises the question of *how*, in the widest sense of the term, values become prices. What are the processes, structures, relations and mechanisms by which the fragmented and diverse distribution and allocation of work are brought together and balanced off against one another through the market?

The pertinence of this approach is highlighted by Marx's theory of commodity fetishism. He argues that the world of commodities presents itself as a relationship between things – x of commodity X is worth y of commodity Y and so on although, in reality, the representation of value is much more abstract as it takes the form of price and not of comparison between use values. Purchase merely requires the handing over of money, the presentation of a piece of plastic, or an electronic transfer of funds. It is not wrong to see commodities in these terms. Indeed, it is essential for everyday existence. But, however much you examine the payment mechanism, the relative price of diamonds and water, or the properties of the commodity as a material object, it will be impossible to discover the social relations under which they have been created. Commodity relations positively conceal their social origins. There is little or no trace, other than in their use values, of how they have come to the market. Whatever knowledge we have of this derives from sources other than the market form itself.

In putting forward his theory of commodity fetishism, Marx's concern is to highlight how relations between producers are both represented through, and concealed by, commodity equivalence in the market. In further positing that labour itself is the source of value, he is able to develop both a theory of exploitation and laws of development of capitalism. The veracity of these analyses is not of concern for the moment. But it is worth observing that they undoubtedly involve a privileging of production and labour in Marx's analytical framework. Why is production, for example, more important than distribution, finance, invention, entrepreneurship or whatever? And, with production privileged, why should labour take precedence over capital equipment, raw materials or even location? One way of highlighting this privileging of labour is by reference to the modern environmental movement. For, in the case of many commodities, the impact of their sourcing upon the environment cannot be identified in the goods themselves or their pricing. Thus, environmental and many other social relations are also concealed by commodity fetishism, an issue taken up in Chapters 4 and 6 in the context of the social construction of use value and Chapter 9 for the meaning of public consumption. Similarly, the difficulties of imposing trade sanctions for political purposes reveal that the 'nationality' of goods is rarely transparent in the nature of commodities themselves.

So why privilege production and labour? Answers can be given to these questions and debated. They involve Marx's general conclusions concerning the importance of modes of production in periodising history, distinguishing feudalism from capitalism, for example. Societies are different according to how they organise relations between producers for the purposes of generating and appropriating a surplus: not only who works and who gains but how. Where commodities are present, the answer is very different than for slavery and for feudalism where labour or its surplus product can be appropriated directly (although commodities and money and elementary types of capital can also be present in non-capitalist societies).

A second rationale for privileging production and labour rests more along the lines of the proof of the pudding being in the eating. The task of unravelling the structures, relations and processes by which commodities come to the market has already been exposed. Can value theory à la Marx deliver the goods? Once again the answer remains subject to debate in terms of the meaning, validity and relevance of Marx's theory of exploitation, accumulation of capital, development of production, productivity and the labour process, the financial system, monopolisation, social reproduction, ideology, the role of the state, globalisation, uneven development and the nature and incidence of crises.

These themes will surface from time to time throughout the book, although it is of note how they are all part and parcel of Marx's analytical ingredients. The academic and popular turn to consumption, though, has been heavily associated with a swing away from Marx's pudding. Three related but distinct charges have been brought against him. These are that his preoccupation with exchange value has been at the expense of use value; that his privileging of production is at the expense of consumption; and, as a special case of the latter, Marx's analysis precludes appropriate consideration of consumption other than as a passive response to the determining role played by production or the economy more generally as opposed to the cultural. These propositions also carry under- often overtones of the denial of subjectivity and identity in Marx, not least through the parallel analytical privileging of class alongside labour and production.

Gift versus commodities?

At best, these criticisms reflect relative emphasis in Marx's work. They will be disputed in detail in the next chapter, not to restore Marx to position of head chef, but to shift discussion to the issue of use value and how it is to be understood in relationship to the commodity and exchange value. The remainder of this chapter is devoted to sharpening the understanding of the commodity by contrasting it with the gift. In popular parlance, a gift is associated with Christmas, birthdays or gratuitous generosity. In pure form, it seems to be detached from commercial motives. Yet the gift is heavily bound to custom and culture, even anxiety and fear of stigma – for the giver, what is an appropriate gift in type or value? It also sets up reciprocal obligations – what must I, as recipient, give in return? The term present might be best used for such gifts, for the latter has a more general and analytical meaning within anthropology. It has come to stand for a whole range of exchanges that only have in common the absence of the market. Over the past decade or more, there has been an increasing interest across the social sciences in the theory of the gift and its relationship to the commodity. As Schrift (1997a: 1) observes:

> Since Marcel Mauss … in 1924, gifts and gift exchange have been frequent topics of inquiry within the field of anthropology. But for other disciplines in the social sciences and humanities, gifts and gift giving were not a theme able to sustain much attention. Until quite recently, that is. In fact, over the past two decades, the theme of gifts

and gift giving has emerged as a central issue within a range of divergent fields.

This spread of attention to the gift from its home in anthropology has also involved a shift in its application. For, from analysis of primitive societies for which it was first developed, use of gift analysis has been motivated by the wish to study contemporary capitalism. In this respect, it represents a specific example of a more general, but previously still limited phenomenon, of the anthropological method being projected back upon the societies from which it had originated. Whilst the fieldworker has hardly become the fieldwork, the western household has become a site of anthropological as well as sociological exploration. The study of consumption by Douglas and Isherwood (1980) is an early classic. Appadurai (1986a: 24), for example, sees Mary Douglas as bringing out the 'primitive' in 'modern industrial societies', imagery that provokes ridicule as the intrepid anthropologist penetrates the heart of the darkest Surbiton household. Subsequently, suburbia has become a well-trodden field for ethnographic study.

Cheal (1988) suggests two reasons for the erstwhile neglect of the gift in analysing modern society. First, it has been perceived to be appropriate only to an elemental anthropology. Gifts belong primarily if not exclusively to a past world, of the primitive even if honourable. For Miller (1997: 21–2):

> There exists a model of modern life ... which views the present time as a kind of fall from grace when compared with the past. ... One of the main disciplines that contributed to this image of lost community was anthropology. It has often been held that contemporary non-industrial societies are in some ways equivalents of the historical if not social evolutionary origins of present industrial societies. Within anthropology, this distinction between modern and traditional communities is probably most fully developed in the opposition between the gift and the commodity.

Second, the heavy hand of political economy is seen to have marginalised the relevance of the gift through three theses. The thesis of capitalist transformation has displaced social morals or mores by those of the market. The thesis of emotional sequestration argues there has been a privatisation of emotions and their shift out of the public arena. Finally, the thesis of economic rationalisation is associated with the pursuit of self-interest.

Whatever the validity of this rationale, what is left unexplained is why the gift should have emerged from its anthropological wrappings. One reason has been 'the emergence of the current interest in consumption among anthropologists and cultural sociologists' (Clammer 1997: 15), especially under the umbrella of postmodernism for which notions of the elemental need to be critically deconstructed. Moreover, in this context, private mores, emotions and interests are positively pursued in constructing individual identity. The three theses are

rendered not so much redundant in banishing the gift from contemporary capitalism as instrumental in raising its profile, prompting and heralding its
triumphant return. In short, postmodernism in general and consumption in
particular have been good news for widening the scope of the gift beyond the
primitive, as taken up later.

Nor have the anthropological bearers of the gift been unwelcome intruders
upon the subject matter previously reserved as the territory of other disciplines.
They have been warmly embraced for adding an otherwise absent yet invaluable
explanatory element, those social relations that lie outside the immediate logic of
commercial society. In this vein, an opposition is posed between the commodity
and the gift, with this duality itself symbolising a range of others – the private
and the public, the personal and the impersonal, the social and the economic,
the rational and the customary, the commercial and the cultural, the market and
the non-market, and so on, respectively. Carrier (1995a) tellingly observes that
the gift–commodity diode can be required to carry the burden of distinguishing
between *Gemeinschaft* and *Gesellschaft*, affective and instrumental rationality,
mechanical and organic solidarity, even feudalism and capitalism. As Strathern
(1988: 143) puts it in referencing Gregory's (1982) classic opposition between gift
and commodity:

> The category goods [often used in mainstream economics] implies a
> subjective relation between an individual and an object of desire –
> goods are pre-defined as things that people want. Categories such as
> commodity and gift refer instead to the organization of relations.
> Commodity exchange … establishes a relationship between the objects
> exchanged, whereas gift exchange establishes a relation between the
> exchanging subjects. In a commodity oriented economy, people thus
> experience their interest in commodities as a desire to appropriate
> goods; in a gift oriented economy, the desire is to expand social relations.

Here, Strathern points to another rationale for adding or counterposing gift to
commodity – the capacity to address differences in social relations. Such considerations lead Gregory (1982: 210) to reject mainstream economics for its failure
to distinguish gift from commodity – since each simply comprises 'goods' in the
'economics approach', thereby leaving it inferior to the 'Political Economy
approach'. As a result, discussion of the gift is relevant to consumption for three
reasons. First, if not extensively, it has itself been applied directly to the study of
consumption. Second, the way in which the gift is understood is indicative of
how other factors have been applied to consumption, as in those raised in the
previous paragraph. Third, as a special case of the second point, the gift sheds
light on the commodity as its putative *alter ego*.

Mauss (1925) is the classic starting point for the gift. A key concept within his
approach is the idea of reciprocity – that the act of giving creates an obligation
to return something, even the same thing, at a later date. This contrasts with

commodity exchange where both parties can in principle walk away from the sale/purchase with no further requirement to conduct business. As Gregory (1987: 25) puts it, citing Mauss:[5]

> The wage-labourer in a capitalist society gives a 'gift' which is not returned. Capitalism for Mauss then was a system of non-reciprocal gift exchange: a system where the recipients were under no obligation to make a return gift.

As is apparent, the primitive/gift society is constructed in opposition to, as other than, capitalism. Miller (1997: 22) recognises that the absence of the gift is perceived to be symbolic of an absence of social relations, 'commodities do not involve the construction of social relations'. Similarly, for Narotzky (1997: 43):

> The gift appeared as a form of transaction very different to the acts of exchange taking place in our society. Indeed, in Western contemporary societies, people appeared separated from their social context and confronted as individuals during transactions: things were severed from people in an autonomous realm of exchange.

There is a stunning parallel between this view of the commodity, in its contrast to the gift, and the idea that money homogenises and devalues. Significantly, though, for Gregory, wage labour is puzzlingly and essentially characterised in terms that might be described as a giftless gift. This is because the gift and the commodity are perceived to have something in common – they are both special forms of generalised exchange where, of necessity, this refers to much more than market exchange. This has meant that understanding of both gift and commodity has occasionally been tied by analogy to language or communication more generally, not least where a focus is placed upon meaning incorporated into such exchanges.[6] In addition, like value for the commodity, Mauss was searching for something in the gift itself that guaranteed its return or reciprocity, leading him in mystical directions as observed by Gregory (1987: 525):[7]

> Gifts therefore become embodied with the 'spirit' of the giver and this 'force' in the thing given compels the recipient to make a return.

But, without suggesting anything other than a crude overview, the gift/commodity literature initially took Mauss as point of departure in two ways. First, it expanded the realm of factors that constitute the gift, adding to or refining Mauss's dual emphasis upon reciprocity and inalienable labour. This was an inevitable consequence of more intensive and extensive application of the gift to case studies, across time and place, giver and recipient, and the objects of exchange themselves. This element in the analytical evolution of the gift understands it as the polar opposite of the commodity, with societies driven to one extreme or the other. As Lapavitsas (2000) puts it:

> Gifts, moreover, penetrate into areas of social life that are not immedi-
> ately and obviously touched by the market: to give in order to establish
> a relationship and in expectation of a reciprocal gesture is fundamental
> to interpersonal relations, to family relations, to friendship, to relations
> at work, to political and social intercourse. By the same token, gift-
> giving appears to possess a transhistorical aspect that captures
> something of the deeper reality of human beings. Given that
> commodity exchangeability (especially as exchange value and money
> price) is the province *par excellence* of economics, the appeal of the gift as
> vehicle for analysis of the non-market aspects of social life is evident.
> The gift can act as terrain and metaphor for analysis of social relations
> that differ in kind from the cash-nexus at the heart of markets. It
> appears conducive to analysis of social obligation, trust, hierarchy, pres-
> tige, solidarity, and so on, in ways not available when analytical focus is
> on commodities and markets.

Accordingly, the distinction between gift and commodity takes on a historical as
well as an analytical role, with the spread of capitalism (and commodity relations) displacing pre-capitalist societies (based on varieties of gift relations),
except where commoditisation is obstructed by culture. For Kopytoff (1986: 73):

> The counterdrive to this potential onrush of commoditization is
> culture. In the sense that commoditization homogenizes value, while the
> essence of culture is discrimination, excessive commoditization is anti-
> cultural. ... Culture ensures that some things remain unambiguously
> singular, it resists the commoditization of others; and it sometimes
> resingularizes what has been commoditized. In every society, there are
> things that are publicly precluded from being commoditized.

This approach to the gift/commodity relationship is based on an abstraction or
construction of ideal types. All commodities are treated as synonymous with one
another and are stripped of all social connections and properties other than their
sharing in common their attachment to monetary exchange. On the other hand,
the gift ranges over all activities that do not involve monetary exchange and
defines its realm negatively relative to the commodity. The gift covers everything
from ceremonial exchange of shells and religious artefacts (kula) to feasting as
wasteful display of wealth to the point of its destruction (potlatch). In turn,
major social theorists have sought to crack the enigma of the gift. For Levi-
Strauss's functionalism, Gregory (1987: 525–6) sees that his

> innovation is to argue that women are the 'supreme gift' and that the
> incest taboo is the key to understanding gift exchange. ... Whatever its

shortcomings his theory nevertheless manages to establish the important link between gift giving and the social organization of kinship and marriage.

Karl Polanyi delves into the gift as embodying reciprocity, (re)distribution, household production and autarky, 'with custom, law, magic and religion cooperating to induce the individual to comply with the rules of behaviour' (Gregory 1987: 526). For Bourdieu (1977: 5), 'in every society it may be observed that, if it is not to constitute an insult, the counter-gift must be *deferred* and *different*'. Godbout (1998: 5) argues that 'the magic of the gift can only operate as long as the underlying rules are not formulated. As soon as they become explicit ... the gift is reduced to reciprocity.' Further, 'even more than Marx's capital, the gift is not a thing but a social connection' (p. 7). Hence, 'the gift is nothing less than the embodiment of the system of interpersonal social relations' (p. 18). Within the domestic sphere the gift incorporates emotional exchange, the rendering of services, passing of heirlooms and ritual (p. 50). More generally, it should involve giving, receiving, reciprocity and disinterestedness or ambiguity in outcome otherwise it is liable to become equivalent to a commercial exchange. In contrast to Titmuss's (1969) classic study of blood donors, the welfare state is not perceived as offering gifts to its beneficiaries as it is understood as reflecting rights rather than socially organised gifts.

Ultimately, as a second point of departure from Mauss, as is already apparent, the unavoidable result of the expanding domain of the gift has been to discover that it is not confined to its own self-contained primitive worlds but that it is also alive and well in contemporary capitalism. This is most obvious in those activities that are not commercialised. Accordingly, the existence of gift and commodity as polar extremes is accepted only by way of exception. Further, exchange of commodities is only entirely stripped of the personal and the social in the rarefied trading rooms of the financial institutions (and even these can be perceived to have a social content, most notably and recently in yuppie culture, for example). Commodity trade can even depend upon and construct the personal, as in the use of networks of trust for quality or payment. Moreover, even in capitalist societies dominated by commodity production, gift exchange remains pervasive outside the world of (direct) commerce, most notably in the home, work and continuing personal and social relations in general. For Cheal (1988: 19), for example, the modern gift is rendered redundant on grounds of its attachment to moral economy, but it remains essential for guaranteeing non-economic reproduction:[8]

> We can therefore define the gift economy as *a system of redundant transactions within a moral economy, which makes possible the extended reproduction of social relations*.

There is a sharp contradiction between the two ways of building upon Mauss. For one accepts the division between gift and commodity and focuses on expanding knowledge of the gift in a commodity-less world. The other takes the increasing scope of the gift to indicate that the commodity and its world are *not* giftless. A simple, if unsatisfactory, resolution of the contradiction is provided by understanding the gift and commodity as no longer mutually exclusive but merely as polar ideal types, with a continuum of outcomes, both for individual exchanges and for societies as a whole, forged between the extremes attached to gift and commodity in their pure forms. As Lapavitsas (2000) argues:

> Others have rejected the notion of sharp dichotomy between commodity and gift, preferring to see the two as poles in a 'spectrum of give-and-take' that extends from transactions 'dictated by a sense of obligation and commitment' (the gift pole) to transactions 'merely or principally dictated by a desire to obtain certain objects by means of exchange' (the commodity pole) (Valeri 1994: 18).

At a mundane level, for example, Davis (1992) can ask whether we should regret the commercialisation of Xmas or welcome the Xmasisation of commerce (as DIY tools are sold with holly attached). A more general and striking example is provided by Offer (1997). He explicitly addresses the terrain lying 'between the gift and the market', and occupies it with an abstract category of his own, 'the economy of regard'. He then proceeds to address the historical balance between market and non-market in terms of shifting comparative advantage, even deploying the simplistic framework of supply and demand curves. In short (p. 471):

> The economy of regard operates wherever incentives are affected by personal relations. Its core is in the household, but it extends whenever people work in small groups or negotiate face to face. Gift exchange is sensitive to the cost of information and the cost of time. As market incomes rise, so does the cost of time. On the other hand, the cost of information is declining. These trends work in opposite directions.

On this basis, a whole range of activities, from donations through charity to the household, a whole range of societies, from the kula system to modern capitalism, and a whole range of writers from Adam Smith to Mauss, are accommodated. As Strathern (1997: 297–8) aptly if implicitly comments:

> It is because society is likened to an environment that it is possible for Euro-Americans to think of individual persons as relating not to other persons but to society as such, and to think of relations as after the fact of the individual's personhood rather than integral to it.

This is to be contrasted with anthropologists who 'in the particular way she/he looks to make "society" visible ... would be scandalized at the idea of a nonrelational definition of persons'.

On the other hand, the use of reciprocity associated with Sahlins (1972), for example, as a basis for understanding the gift economy is more general than the economy of regard and derives from the socially constructed meaning of exchanges. Davis (1992), however, rejects the notion because of its difficulty in handling theft, a sort of negative reciprocity – something is given after all, if unwillingly, and there may be reciprocal action at an uncertain time in the future. He prefers to posit a range of 'repertoires' that might otherwise be associated with the gift. The full list is alms giving, altruism, arbitrage, banking, barter, bribery, burglary, buying/selling, charity, commodity dealing, corruption, donation, employment, exploitation, expropriation, extortion, futures trading, giving, huckstering, insider dealing, insurance, marketing, money lending, mortgaging, mugging, pawning, profiteering, prostitution, reciprocity, renting, retailing, robbery, scrounging, shoplifting, shopping, simony, social wage, swapping, theft, tipping, trading and wholesaling (p. 29). What this illustrates, however, is a detailed empirical filling out of the continuum between gift and commodity, irrespective of the analytical content with which this is done.

There are, however, severe problems with this resolution of the opposition between gift and commodity as can be seen in a number of ways. First, the distinction between the two is fundamentally based on attaching one to use value and the other to exchange value, respectively. Yet, this is extremely misleading. For Carruthers and Babb (2000: 23) correctly observe that:

> Gift giving and gift acceptance are not just about individual likes and dislikes but also about social relationships between individuals. The social meaning of a gift matters much more than its individual utility.

And, as argued in detail by Lapavitsas (2000), the gift often represents entirely useless artefacts and certainly those that are *not* going to be used. They can merely circulate for symbolic purposes in complete contrast to the commodity:

> Unlike the commodity seller, for whom use value does not exist in the product exchanged, for the giver of the gift, the gifted thing might or might not be useful. ... The recipient's perception of the usefulness of the gift ... matters only as far as it affects the giver's assessment of the appropriateness of the gift. The giver alone has to ascertain the right degree of usefulness of the gift for the recipient, while also deciding how appropriately this meshes with the symbolic, sentimental, and moral aspects of the transaction. ... Indeed, for the gift, usefulness might derive exclusively from the act of giving itself, as, for instance, from the prestige and social standing of the giver or past holders of the

gift. There is no imperative on the part of the giver to impart usefulness to the gift.

Of course, some gifts are extremely useful and indispensable to recipients, as in exchange of women in marriage customs, but this is not a universal or necessary property of the gift. Essentially, use value ascribed to the gift can be far removed from its material properties. Indeed, in Mauss's original formulation, spirituality was remarkably perceived to reside within, and circulate with, the gift. On the other hand, the commodity is necessarily marked by its usefulness – it would not be purchased otherwise. By the same token, those uses are attached to social customs or whatever just as they are, if not in exactly the same way, for the gift. As a result, the gift/commodity duality does not match that of use and exchange value.

Second, there is a tendency for an unacceptable essentialism to underpin the gift/commodity duality. Some social relationship or other needs to be expressed and the gift and the commodity have different, but a full range of, capacities for meeting that need. Implicitly, a most powerful illustration is provided by Adam Smith.[9] For him, the propensities to truck, barter and exchange are natural, possibly a consequence of the power of speech. The historical sequence of stages of society, starting with the 'rude' or primitive and ultimately resting in the 'commercial' or capitalism, represent different means of accommodating those propensities as well the tension between self-interest and altruism and between the division of labour and the extent of consumption. The complexity and sophistication of Smith's approach should be emphasised in connecting together underlying propensities, economic forms of organisation for the provision of subsistence, individual and social morality, and a historical teleology. It stands in sharp contrast to Offer's previously discussed account of how gift and commodity accommodate individual needs for well-being and regard. On an even narrower basis, in mainstream economics, gift and commodity are the forms through which utility is realised, with institutions, customs, culture and the like the rational response to market and informational imperfections, see Chapter 7. In such analyses, the commodity, in particular, is perceived to be 'dirty' through its attachment to commercialisation and, thereby, its diminished capacity to express certain social relations that can only be taken up by the gift. The previous point, however, establishes that there is very little in principle that cannot be interpreted by the commodity as use value. As Carruthers and Babb (2000: 26) suggest, 'When used as gifts, commodities also enable people to express their feelings about relationships with others.' Of course, it might be argued that the commodity as gift allows the recipient to measure the monetary worth in the eyes of the giver. But there is always something else involved, as revealed in Finn's (2000: 144) account from Thomas Turner's diaries:

> His habit of recording the cash values of goods he proffered to friends and neighbours in return for their gifts to him demonstrates his ability

to navigate between and across systems of economic, social and moral calculation. When Thomas Tester's wife gave him 'two carp for a present' in July 1755, Turner thus noted that he had reciprocated with '1 lb of sugar and 6 fish hooks, value about 9d' ... of a gift received from his father-in-law in 1760 ... he commented shortly before his wife's death, 'so that I look upon it as a thing of greater value than barely [i.e. only] the worth of the present'.

The intermingling of gift and commodity *par excellence* is, however, deemed to be found in contemporary Japan where, for Clammer (1997: 165):

> These gift relationships today take place within the commodity form, utilizing commodities in some sense to transcend the commodity.

But it is important not to exaggerate the extent to which the Japanese culture of gift giving is in opposition to the quantification attached to the commodity and money. For Brumann (2000: 224):

> Social roads in Japan are paved with gifts. ... From a Western point of view this should give material culture an opportunity to flourish. ... But when it comes to important social events involving people close to oneself, Japanese do not make much use of the refinement of their famous material culture. Instead they give, of all things, money, and the recipients of the gifts prepare detailed lists of how much they received and from whom.

Brumann suggests that this would be seen as impersonal and second best in the west, the difference in Japan being due to 'concern for measuring and comparing social relations' (p. 225).

More generally, there is a false presumption that money impersonalises, especially when it comes to gifts.[10] Paradoxically, though, those closest within the family may give money as a present since the personal and the intimate is secure and, within capitalism, the nature of what can be purchased is appreciated and is left open. Cash gifts are also common at marriages in 'traditional' societies as opposed to the impersonality of the gifts arranged through the wedding lists of contemporary capitalism. On the other hand, the extensive exchange of non-monetary gifts at Christmas can often take on an impersonal and purely token nature as the giving of the gift as such becomes more significant than what the gift is. Even money, despite or even because of being measured by quantity rather than quality, can acquire a personal quality. For Indian Parsis, it is customary to give money in round figures plus one in order to distinguish the transaction from commerce which is perceived to deal in large, whole figures.[11]

Third, and drawing upon the previous two points, the gift/commodity polarity has forced itself into a position of seemingly getting the analysis the wrong way round, neatly summarised in Miller's (2001) notion of 'Alienable Gifts and Inalienable Commodities'. For the goal should be to understand the social relations that give rise to different forms of social exchange, inappropriately summarised as lying along the gift/commodity continuum. Instead, two ideal types of exchange are being imposed as the filter through which to comprehend those relations. The latter are so diverse and complex that confusion necessarily prevails over the distinction between gift and commodity. Consequently, Strathern (1988), for example, correctly perceives the contrast between gift and commodity as at best a heuristic device with certain strengths in illuminating the differences in relations amongst people and objects. The emphasis is on social relations for (p. 161):

> The difference between gift exchange and commodity exchange is systemic; it is hardly admissible to decide that this particular transaction results in alienation, while that particular one does not. One cannot tell by inspection.

Similarly, although Appadurai's (1986a) concern is predominantly with the commodity, this leaves him to comment on the gift by way of comparison. He understands the commodity in terms of the wide variety of social use values that it can carry. Thus (p. 3):

> Focusing on the things that are exchanged, rather than simply on the forms or functions of exchange, makes it possible to argue that what creates the link between exchange and value is *politics*, construed broadly. This argument ... justifies the conceit that commodities, like persons, have social lives.

This leads to a correct rejection of the simple opposition between gift and commodity, with 'the exaggeration and reification of the contrast between gift and commodity in anthropological writing', and sees it as 'an oversimplified view of the opposition between Mauss and Marx, which ... misses important aspects of the commonalities between them' (p. 11). But he reaches the right conclusion for entirely the wrong reasons in an inverted form of commodity fetishism, rather than a 'conceit', with the social relations attached to use values seen as the source of value. For, 'this essay took as its starting point Simmel's view that exchange is the source of value and not vice-versa' (p. 56). Thus, gift and commodity are rejected as opposites, not because they reflect different under-lying social relations in different ways but because they are both perceived to be able to reflect the same relations in different ways.[12] In short (p. 13):

> In trying to understand what is distinctive about commodity exchange, it does not make sense to distinguish it sharply from barter on the one hand, or from the exchange of gifts on the other. ... It also means

breaking significantly with the production-dominated Marxian view of the commodity and focusing on its *total* trajectory from production, through exchange/distribution to consumption.

The focus ultimately suggested is correct from the perspective of focusing on an understanding of specific commodities, remarkably anticipating the system of provision approach, but is incorrect in its understanding of the commodity as a category. Consequently, we are then conducted on an exercise of purely speculative posturing, 'commoditization lies at the complex intersection of temporal, cultural, and social factors' (p. 15), as do most things!

Further the relationship between the gift and commodity has not been one of equality in difference. Gift began as the 'other', what the commodity is not, embracing the new territory of the primitive, before being reflected back upon its *alter ego*, the modern or the advanced. The parallel between gift and commodity as dissolving extremes has been taken up in Carrier's (1992, 1995a) discussion of the relationship between orientalism and occidentalism. He observes that the understanding of the east (orientalism) has often been based upon its otherness from the west, thereby implying an understanding of the west itself (occidentalism), however explicit. Accordingly, there is a dialectical construction of orientalism as the product of the shifting occidental perspective from which it is viewed. Moreover, the opposition between east and west does itself dovetail with a range of other oppositions, not least that of gift and commodity. It follows that there is a tendency to neglect the commodity aspects of the east and, even more important, to neglect or to commodify the gift aspects of the west. Carrier specifically warns against the danger of formalising the evolving distinctions involved in the occidental/oriental coupling and the same applies to the gift/commodity duality. It might allow us to read how the literature has developed but it is a poor guide to what is being read. As Carrier and others have correctly concluded in a third strand of the literature, the gift/commodity distinction is analytically ill-founded. Moreover, just as the key to our understanding of the occident/orient construct is to unravel its starting point in the west, so the commodity should command our attention in the first instance.

From commodities to capital

In loosening some of the tangles around gift and commodity, and use value and exchange value, it has already been argued that: the use value aspect of the commodity has been unduly neglected (except for its postmodernist meaning in isolation from its exchange value, see next chapter); the social relations surrounding its origins and use are subject to commodity fetishism; and one crucial element of that commodity fetishism is the expression of relations between labourers in production as a relationship between things. The last has both a qualitative and a quantitative aspect – incorporating production relations, on the one hand, and the bringing into equivalence of different types of labour, on the other. But can the study of the commodity be taken further at this abstract and general level, and what implications are there for the understanding of the non-commodity production that serves consumption?

First consider the quantitative issue in slightly different terms. If labour is the source of value and different labours are measured against one another through exchange, which labours count or qualify for this purpose? An obvious response is only to count that labour that directly or indirectly contributes to the manufacture of the commodity. By direct is meant the labour of 'finishing', bringing the commodity to its final form before sale, the car assembly worker for example, as opposed to the component manufacturer. By indirect is included the labour that contributes to the raw materials and depreciation of capital equipment that make up the product, the steel, upholstery, rubber and so on. This is a sensible answer but appeal to each of direct and indirect labour is problematic. Take indirect labour. In identifying and in counting the labour, how far back should we trace the process of creating the product? Whilst this could be interpreted as a historical or chronological problem, it is more of a logical issue. Consider the skills of the workforce, for example. Should we count the labour that has gone into teaching or into building schools as part of the labour ultimately embodied in the output of skilled labourers? This conundrum has given rise to a debate over the source of value and what labour should count towards it (e.g. Fine and Harris 1976, 1979, Gough 1975, 1979). In a nutshell, it is a matter of the extent to which the labour of social reproduction should count towards the labour of production and economic reproduction. It has been most fiercely contested in the context of domestic or household labour, that providing for the social reproduction of the workforce, fully surveyed in Fine (1992) but see also debate between Kotz (1994, 1995) and Fine (1995d). Does the housewife's and other such labour count as value – as an analytical not an ethical issue and separate from whether housework should command a 'wage'? For Narotzky (1997: 40–1) for example, in a horribly confused analysis, not least because DIY goods are cheaper for being self-assembly, as is both acknowledged and not at the same time:[13]

> A specific structure of social relations between labour and capital depends on the existence of the DIY consumer market. Capital (that is, furniture firms) extracts surplus value by including future labour in the unfinished goods (a table-kit is sold as a *table*), that is, including as labour costs labour which in fact will be realised by the consumer. Thus, the consumer not only does the work himself without being paid for it, but also pays the firm for the work he will have to do (!!). This, however, allows the firm to lower prices.

The shift in opposition between capital and labour to one between producer and consumer is notable. But, more fundamental is the opening of the floodgates for any labour undertaken in the home or elsewhere to count as unpaid labour for capital. Even more, one could argue not only does labour work for too low a wage for capital or no wage at all, it also uses its spare time to sleep in order to be able to do so. Capital gets our sleep for free! An answer to these puzzles has already been hinted at. For the distinction has been drawn between economic and social reproduction, with Narotzky usefully viewing a variety of types of reproduction as the means to avoid a plethora of unsatisfactory dualisms – between micro and macro, material and cultural, economy and society (p. 1). Yet economic and social reproduction, and the relationship between them, is itself variable according to historical and social circumstances. It is, however, particularly sharp under generalised commodity production. For there, economic reproduction takes place as a distinct sphere of activity in the form of the production of commodities for the market. Social reproduction takes place outside the logic and imperatives of the market although it can be conditioned by it. In short, the problem can be shifted from one of which labour counts to one of which production counts. And the answer is production for the market.

This still leaves us short of the target since very few produce directly for the market. Even, or especially, in the modern factory or service industry, workers have limited direct contact with the market; this is the privilege, or burden, of those handling what inputs come in and what outputs go out. In between, labour and management deal with the production process itself, not with the market. Nonetheless, and this is crucial, if they are engaged in production for the market, they will be subject to its discipline however directly or indirectly. A direct form of discipline will be through those that supervise or reward their work. Indirectly, the competitive process attached to the market will tend to eliminate those producers that do not match its standards.

So far, in taking forward understanding of the commodity, two aspects have been brought to the fore. Commodities are linked to a structural differentiation between economic and social reproduction, and the labour and production that counts towards value is to be found both within economic reproduction and subject to the competitive logic of the market. These conclusions, however, remain too historically and socially general. For there is great variety in how society is structured across economic and social reproduction and what logic is dictated by the market. In particular, at the two extremes stand simple commodity production and capitalist commodity production. For the latter, capitalism is governed by the imperative of profitability, and this makes itself felt throughout the economic sphere – how work is organised, technology developed and adopted, labour rewarded, competitive struggles engaged, and so on. In addition, sharp structural boundaries tend to be drawn within the economy itself, as well as between it and the social. The sphere of production is separated from the sphere of exchange, one concerned with the production of value and the other with its circulation, realisation or buying and selling. Further, with surplus production primarily taking the *monetary* form of profit, a separate sphere for finance also emerges alongside that for trading, each with its own capital.

Matters are very different in the case of simple commodity production, by which is meant independent production for the market, in the absence of wage labour. First, except in the imagination, simple commodity production cannot serve as the sole or main means of livelihood across society as a whole. If everyone could readily produce for the market, then everyone would produce whatever is required for own consumption. There would be little need for commodity exchange. If this is not possible because of the benefits of specialisation, then how that specialisation is created becomes the central issue, and not who produces what. Prior to capitalism, simple commodity production has taken the form of producing and selling a surplus for the market. But it does not and cannot dominate other aspects of slavery or feudalism, for example. Whilst specialised activity in trading and finance also emerges in such societies, the logic underlying competition is different than for capitalism. Producers might, for example, shift from commodity to subsistence production in case of market difficulties and not simply be competitively eliminated.

The point here is not to engage in a discourse on the differences between capitalist and non-capitalist production, as well as the difference between the varieties of non-capitalist commodity production. It is merely to establish that they are very different as commodity production, as the way in which labour counts and is brought to, and measured by, the market mechanism.[14]

Essentially, this is to recognise for the commodity, as much as for the gift, that it reflects underlying social relations and that these are diverse. We have a variety of commodities from the perspective of the relationships, structures and processes through which they are provided. In addition, capitalist commodity production is the most advanced of these in three different senses. First, as recognised in the idea of commodification, capitalist commodity production has a tendency to draw other forms of production into its orbit and convert them to commodity and then to capitalist production – first engagement with the market, followed by creation of, and dependence on, wage labour. The latter is not necessarily realised. In broad historical terms, it depends upon dispossession of peasantry from the land in order to create wage labour in what Marx terms the primitive accumulation of capital (Marx 1976: Part VII). This has been studied under the transition or Brenner debate (Aston and Philpin 1985). Nonetheless, once capitalism has been established, as Gregory (1982: 93) argues in a way reflecting his position on gift and (capitalist) commodity production as lying at two extremes:[15]

> In a gift economy the profit motive is absent: there is no drive to accumulate capital and to increase productive efficiency. The productivity of land and labour is therefore much lower in a gift economy than it is in a capitalist economy.

Yet matters are not quite so simple. For otherwise how is decommodification to be explained? Whilst, first and foremost, capitalism does generate levels of productivity that undermine the viability of other modes of production, it also strengthens the capacity for them to survive since, for example, it cheapens the price of subsistence and of inputs for those engaging in independent production. As Appadurai (1986a: 24) argues:

> Though commodities, by virtue of their exchange destinies and mutual commensurability, tend to dissolve the links between persons and things, such a tendency is always balanced by a countertendency, in all societies, to restrict, control, and channel exchange.

Or, as Gregory (1987: 527) neatly questions in the context of potlatch, as in the giving away or destroying of blankets:[16]

> Today, it is now realized, the problem is not, 'How was the tribal gift economy destroyed?' but rather, 'Why has it flourished under the impact of colonization?'

Second, as a corollary, capitalist commodity production is an appropriate starting point because it provides the space for other forms of production to survive. It does not simply eliminate them but can expand their presence – shells for kula gift exchange become more readily available and 'are still flourishing despite their incorporation into the world capitalist economy' (Gregory 1987: 525). More generally, as already argued, similar outcomes can be the consequence of a simple economic logic. At one extreme, capitalism provides many opportunities for the self-employed to prosper. At the other, pre-capitalist production conditions in the Third World can be promoted by serving world markets. At a more general and abstract level, capitalism depends upon an accumulating core of capital, employing wage labour to generate its profitability. But it also generates a mass of revenue in the form of wages, profits, rents, interest and, in contemporary conditions, government expenditure, all of which can and do support a diverse range of non-capitalist activity.

In short, capitalist commodity production is an excellent testing ground for understanding non-capitalist production. There are, however, two important riders. For such production will be conditioned in some way or other by its insertion within, or interaction with, capitalism. In addition, its presence is indicative of the capacity to resist or evade the superior productivity performance of capitalism – although as Perelman (2000) observes, from Adam Smith onwards, economics has generally ignored the physical force that is used to impose capitalism. Both of these provisos are crucial for, in unravelling the complexities of non-capitalist production, account must be taken both of the conditioning by capitalism *and* the specificity of the social relations, structures and processes that hold it at bay. The nature of non-capitalist production, commodity or otherwise, cannot simply be read off from its dependence upon capitalism and, only rarely, can the latter be set aside as irrelevant and, if so, this needs itself to be explained.

Barter serves as an excellent illustration of these points. It is all too easy, as previously observed in the second section, to view barter as an elementary form of commodity exchange. But this is to commit the error of treating a form of exchange as homogeneous and independent of the social relations underlying it, an error for commodities also. Barters both within and outside capitalism are all very different from one another. Under capitalism, it is rare to find barter at all. This is because of the homogenisation dictated by money and commodities. Most things subject to exchange have a more or less well-known exchange value and, subject to the presence of a market for them, they might just as well be exchanged for money.

Consequently, capitalist barter takes two forms. It can emerge where markets are absent for insufficient weight of, or too costly a discount on, sale and/or purchase. It is extremely unlikely for production to be involved on a continuing basis since, within capitalism, this requires a guaranteed market to cover recurring costs and subsistence of producers. In this case, contact between 'buyer' and 'seller' has to be made through some other informational mechanism than the market – swapping as in a meeting of stamp collectors, or through the advertising services provided by the mass media or, increasingly, the Internet. The 'prices' at which goods exchange are liable to mirror those, however indirectly, that prevail for these items, or similar, on the market. Where bartering becomes well established, as in LETS (local exchange trading systems), a form of money is liable to emerge, such as simple labour-time chits or cigarettes in prisoner of war camps, and exchange ratios for babysitting or gardening are liable to follow closely those that prevail in the commercial world. Further, of course, LETS schemes are heavily dependent both upon some form of exclusion from the capitalist economy and upon the revenue or goods it provides to sustain what is not covered by internal provision.

A very different form of barter under capitalism is between children in the exchange of unwanted toys and the like. Generally they have no knowledge of corresponding prices, and notions of value, if they do enter at all, do not derive from commodity exchange.[17] Barter, then, like the gift and the commodity, has meaning only in the context of the underlying social relations to which it is attached, as emphasised by Humphrey and Hugh-Jones (1992a: 1):

> Attempts to produce a universal definition or model of barter usually involve stripping it from its social context and result in imaginary abstractions that have little or no correspondence to reality.

Barter can more or less be moneyless commodity exchange, conditioned by the reasons for the absence of money, or it can be removed from the dictates of commerce altogether – each case itself requiring explanation. This points to the third rationale for privileging capitalist commodity production as starting point. As already indicated, it incorporates a very complex and full repertoire of economic and social relations, structures and processes in bringing products to the point of consumption, whilst also creating the space for less complex and less advanced forms of provision as this repertoire is drawn upon in piecemeal fashion. For Lapavitsas (2000), 'the transition to capitalism, therefore, can be seen as the process through which exchange value ceases to be a formal property of commodities and becomes rooted in the very structure of the economy'.

Thus, production for consumption within the household, the buying and selling of antiques, the passing on of heirlooms, and so on, all have a relationship to capitalist commodity production but without necessarily emulating or being determined by it. Even the history of consumption is enriched by recognising how provision differs from its capitalist counterpart although, as argued, it should not be gathered into two bundles comprising gifts and commodities. The key analytical element is the bundle of underlying social relations, structures and processes that bring consumption to fruition.

Within contemporary capitalism, two particular forms of non-capitalist access to consumption are worth highlighting. The first is what has previously been designated as 'marooning' (Fine *et al.* 1996: 68). This emulates Cannadine's (1983) use of the term for the survival of the monarchy into contemporary democracies. It does not really belong there but it can persist and even prosper although it is heavily conditioned and transformed by its 'unnatural' environment. Marooning is a form of consumption derived from artefacts that cannot be produced or reproduced by labour. This means they cannot be commodities but they can take the commodity form and be bought and sold. Antiques, heirlooms, etc., readily spring to mind. A theory of consumption that simultaneously seeks to incorporate such marooned items and to chart the oceans of mass production is doomed to sink. Yet, crucially, the value of the marooned is, unlike Robinson Crusoe's sole dependence on his desert island but for marooned items rescued from the shipwreck, heavily influenced by its surrounding seas. This is true both of economic worth as capitalist commodity production seeks, however successfully, to provide 'reproductions', and of subjective worth as the objects' authenticity depends as much upon what they are not as upon what they are.

Second, stretching the nautical metaphor, consumption can be 'hightided' as can other social activity. Marx, for example, controversially clubs all activity in the sphere of exchange as unproductive of value as it deals in the circulation of value alone – whether in merchant or financial dealing. This is despite exchange activities' reliance on capital, profitability and exploited wage labour (see Fine (1985/6, 1988) in debate with Panico (1988), for example). Thus, capitalism itself structures society so that certain activities are precluded from being 'reduced' to (capitalist) commodity production. This is an inevitable consequence of the structural separation of social from economic reproduction. A boundary is drawn between the circulation of capital and commodities and broader social activity, most notably in civil society, the state and the household. Each of these can be a source of consumption, and even of commodity production and the commodity form. The crucial point is that the boundaries do exist and hightide certain elements of production and consumption on the beach lapped by the oceans of commodity production and exchange. Necessarily, some production and consumption remain impenetrable both to commodity production, and even the commodity form is rarely absolutely influential – the examples of love and religion readily spring to mind. Otherwise the boundaries can be fluid as is recognised in the notions of (de)commodification. Thus, as a matter of logic, capitalist commodity production both depends upon non-commodity production and provides for it to prosper. Consequently, Kopytoff (1986) correctly points to what he calls singularisation where even commodity forms are not adopted. But he is wrong to identify the commodity with any act of (pseudo)exchange (pp. 68–9):[18]

> A commodity is a thing that has use value and that can be exchanged in a discrete transaction for a counterpart, the very fact of exchange indicating that the counterpart has, in the immediate context, an equivalent value. The counterpart is by the same token also a commodity at the time of exchange. The exchange can be direct or it can be achieved indirectly by way of money. ... Hence, anything that can be bought for money is at that point a commodity, whatever the fate that is reserved for it after the transaction has been made (it may, thereafter, be decommoditized).

In other words, for Kopytoff, it is exchange itself which makes commodities, a property attached to individual objects rather than social relations and reproduction, for decommodification is the result until an object re-enters exchange if it ever does, as for oriental carpets for example, and

> the only time when the commodity status of a thing is beyond question is the moment of actual exchange. Most of the time, when the commodity is effectively out of the commodity sphere, its status is inevitably ambiguous and open to the push and pull of events and desires, as it is shuffled about in the flux of social life.
>
> (p. 83)

Once again, though, this reveals the need to distinguish rather than to conflate these different types of consumption and to begin with the capitalist commodity to be able to begin to pinpoint the others by way of departure.

Concluding remarks

In her study of women and consumption in the eighteenth century, Kowaleski-Wallace (1996: 25) observes the contradictions of the genteel tea table for, in marking the endpoint of a process of colonial exploitation, 'when a British gentlewoman serves this tea, she also participates in this process of enlightenment, refinement, and civilization'. Such virtues might even be explicitly displayed by the wearing of an anti-slavery brooch as the sugar bowl is offered to a gentleman whose subsequent departure might anticipate an evening with his erstwhile host's *alter ego*, the prostitute. With the increasing availability of commodities, the means of representation of women both shifts and expands. For the upper classes, they become objects for display and leisure, dangerous if too free thinking. For the working class, they are there to serve and provide, not least through careful negotiation and management of the market.

But Kowaleski-Wallace also recognises that the meaning of commodities has undergone a curious inversion. For the commodity previously drew upon the idea of providing rather than of exchanging. She cites a passage from Dr Johnson for whom (p. 1):

> *Commodity* carries its obsolete meaning: 'as a quality or condition of things, in relation to the needs of men, etc: that quality of being "commodious": conveniency, suitability, fitting utility, commodiousness'. That sense of the word *commodity* – as a quality in relation to human need – coexisted during the eighteenth century with another; concurrently, *commodity* was also 'a thing of use or advantage to mankind; esp. in pl. useful products, material advantages, elements of wealth'. The two senses of the word complemented each other, since a thing of no use could not be a commodity, it literally could not be 'commodious'.

Understanding of the commodity/gift duality has tailed upon this shifting meaning of the commodity, focusing on it as an element of wealth at the expense of use value which has been reserved for the gift. In other words, the commodity has been stripped of its connection to use value and the social relations to which they correspond. Not surprisingly, the use value aspect of the commodity has a habit of reasserting itself. The result is either to confuse in insisting that the commodity is gift-like, even though the gift is taken as its negation, or to deny any homogenisation in the exchange value of commodities because of their heterogeneity as use values. So, having taken use value out of the commodity, it is a matter of bringing it back in. However, as will be seen in the following chapter, the commodity is only restored to its full glory if it is understood in both its use and exchange value aspects, and as a product of capital.

4

USE VALUE AND
CONSUMPTION

Introduction

The increasing preoccupation with consumption throughout the advanced capitalist countries during its postwar boom attracted the corresponding attention of the academic world. For consumption easily and positively places on the agenda those issues that have been an increasing focus of attention in the intellectual climate of postmodernist times. Consumption, *par excellence*, concerns the position and activity of the individual in capitalist society. It involves the interpretation of objects, ideologies, culture and identity. Yet consumption is also an immediate economic category. Commodities have to be designed, produced, distributed and marketed before they are sold, bought and, ultimately, consumed.

Interest in consumption, however, faced certain obstacles in entering the academic arena. It became a common complaint, heard especially in history and sociology, that the analysis of consumption had been sorely neglected. For Miller:[1]

> Important are a series of academic trends that have led to an overwhelming concentration on the area of production as the key generative arena for the emergence of the dominant social relations in contemporary societies, and a comparative neglect of consumption.
>
> (Miller 1987: 3)

Within economic history, for example, this has been reflected in a degree of technical determinism – that production and supply make the world what it is over the long term (Fine and Leopold 1993: Chapter 7). For a perspective grounded in the orthodoxy of neo-classical economics, this is justified by the assumption that the market can be assumed to work perfectly in the long run, so that supply rather than demand becomes the determining factor. Paradoxically, this goes hand in hand with a view of the consumer as sovereign in determining the *composition* of what is produced (and how much is saved rather than consumed), even if the *level* of output overall depends upon the dry statistics of the growth in inputs and total factor productivity.

The growing dissatisfaction with methodologies that have given priority to production has led to attempts to redress the balance by focusing on consumption independently of production. The result has been the failure to develop, and a hostility towards, theoretical structures that unite production and consumption. An often scarcely concealed contempt is also understandable, and justified, in the case of neo-classical economics, see Chapter 7. For whilst consumption through utility maximisation is adopted as the ultimate economic determinant, understanding of consumption is thereby severely impoverished. It is confined to demand analysis that, within economics, has essentially remained unchanged over the last century and more since the marginalist revolution of the 1870s. It depends upon assumptions that are false and limited, which have the effect of narrowing the scope of enquiry – that is, that 'rational' consumers should maximise utility subject to price and income constraints on the basis of unchanging and innate preferences.[2] It does not, therefore, provide much more than an easy target for those academics dissatisfied with the traditional emphasis on supply. It is much too unrealistic and narrow an approach to warrant too much attention. Marxism, on the other hand, has proved a more substantive target, given its greater presence within many social sciences besides economics. With its heavy reliance upon the determining role of production, Marxism is well suited to be the scapegoat for the neglect of consumption in the non-economic social sciences, both in itself and for its baneful influence on those who otherwise reject it.[3]

And academia abhors a discovered vacuum. So the attempt has been made to fill the theoretical void surrounding consumption. The apparent lack of a weighty tradition in the area has not proved an insurmountable obstacle. Previously, the ground has been occupied by the intellectual savages of the commercial world – advertisers, marketers, packagers and the media – whose anthropological artefacts are now dug up or, more likely, viewed on a video, and unscrupulously stripped of their hidden meanings and significance. Consumption and its individual and social context are con-, decon- and reconstructed in the light of recent developments in social theory.

For the analytical terrain on which consumption is being discovered is one devoted to the 'post-' rather than to the past. This has been the period of post-Marxism, postmodernism, post-Fordism, in which discourse and semiotics play a vital role, one tending to autonomise consumption.[4] At the extreme, consumption is presumed to have separate, independent and ambiguous effects and content, distinct from other constituent economic (especially production) and social relations. This emerges particularly with the linking of consumption to, or its being enclosed within, the field of cultural studies.

To some extent, there must be some doubts about the originality of these concerns if not the form in which they are posed and the attitude adopted to them. After all, the 1960s witnessed considerable angst about the morality and stability of consumer society, perceived to be one in which manipulated demand for unnecessary goods reflected the combination of the power of advertising and of the individual's psychological need to aspire, conform and surpass. For Galbraith (1962: 135):[5] 'As a society becomes increasingly affluent, wants are increasingly created by the process by which they are satisfied.'

This was the golden age for recognising and spotlighting the role of monopolies and their influence over what is consumed. It was also the period of unprecedented growth of the advanced capitalist economies. Consumers were consuming as never before. How ironic that the current period, of faltering expansion in living standards, especially amongst the worst-off, should witness a critical analysis of consumption of a rather more circumspect variety, based more on understanding as interpretation than as critically hostile and suspicious. Even this posture has a long pedigree. In the history of that most immediate item of consumption, food, Brillat-Savarin could hardly have imagined how popular his idiom would later become amongst the historians, sociologists and nutritionists:[6] his 'Tell me what you eat and I will tell you what you are' has been taken up in the twentieth century and simplified to 'You are what you eat.'[7] Our modern theorists merely have to interrogate what it is that is being eaten. There is more than a plum and a proof to be found in the eating of the pudding, for identity and meaning themselves appear to reside there.

This chapter sets some of these new interpretations of consumption in perspective by re-examining the role played by use value in Marx, not least because it is presumed to have been more or less absent beyond the formality of including it in the definition of the commodity. As consumption depends upon the use value of commodities, the presumption that Marx neglected use value, together with his assigning priority to production, is often thought to explain why there is no theory of consumption in Marx. The next section demonstrates the inadequacy of this view. The conclusion concerning the absence of use value in Marx is shown to be erroneous. Marx's economic analysis treats consumption as contingent upon, if not determined by, the production, distribution and circulation of value. This holds true even in the absence of analysis of the social construction of the meaning of particular commodities. Consequently, such an absence does not justify the rejection of Marx's (value) theory as deficient in understanding consumption, nor for its being incapable of, and incompatible with, construing the significance of use value. The next section also shows that, on the contrary, Marx's political economy has much to contribute to the issue of consumption, although this has more to do with its structural location within the capitalist economy than with concern over particular consumption goods. The third section argues that the idea that Marx had nothing to say about consumption, and could only have nothing to say, derives from a double error, particularly in the work of Baudrillard and his followers, although a powerful and correct insight is their starting point. This is that use values are socially constructed and, as such, cannot be derived from the material properties of the items of consumption. The first error is to take this insight too far and to deny the significance of the material properties of commodities in determining their use value. The second error, not surprising in light of the first, is to presume the corresponding irrelevance of Marx's political economy for the understanding of consumption, not least because of his emphasis on production. The concluding remarks bring out implications for the more constructive analysis to follow.

The use value of Marx

The notion that Marx had very little to say about consumption is based on two closely related, but separate, propositions: first, that Marx was unconcerned about use values as such except in so far as they were a necessary condition for a product to be an exchange value; and, second, that this resulted in a neglect of the activity of consumption itself, except in so far as it was determined by, or reducible to, the chronologically and causally prior act of production.

Both of these propositions contain an element of truth but each is fundamentally misleading. To demonstrate this fully requires a detailed knowledge of, and interest in, Marx's political economy which may be beyond the general reader. For Marx's treatment of use value has to be teased out of his works. As Rosdolsky (1977) has persuasively argued, Marx is far from silent on the matter.[8] Marx's analysis of specific use values emerges when they have already been shown to have a general and major social significance rather than a specific useful property however derived and interpreted. In the first volume of *Capital*, this occurs first of all in the case of money. It is shown to acquire a number of functions which, of course, lead it to be desired by individuals, as a symbol of wealth and status, quite apart from its social functions as means of payment, store of value, etc. Later in Volume III of *Capital*, after the source of surplus value or profitability has been revealed as a consequence of the class relations of production specific to capitalism, the use value of money is elevated to a higher level. Money can function not only as means of payment, for example, but also as capital of a particular type. It can generate a profit if engaged in production, and interest if put to work in the financial sector.

Why is this significant? Before capitalism is established, money has already become a commodity *sui generis* and commands an 'irrational' price for its ability to defer payment. Money can, in a sense, be bought and sold, and the rate of interest is the special price signifying the specific use value of borrowing and loaning money – leading in the extreme to usury, whether for rich or poor. Under capitalism, loans are made both to accelerate purchase in general but also to undertake or expand capitalist enterprise in particular, through use of what Marx calls money capital.[9] It follows that the use value of money depends upon the social relations in which it circulates. In a sense, this is recognised by those who discuss the homogenising power of money – it is only as good as what it can buy, and that depends upon what is available on the market. In a deeper sense, though, the use value of money depends upon the social relations of production that prevail. Under slavery, it can command slaves; under capitalism, it employs wage labour – as well as generating and enabling access to the highly specialised use values attached to the esoteric and complex derivative markets of the financial system. Thus, for both of the commodities, money and money capital, Marx's analysis of *use value* is extremely highly developed (although the matter is not usually seen in this way – he is more thought of as having a sophisticated theory of money and money capital as such).

In short, in Marx's analysis, the use values of money and of money capital are derived specifically from the social relations of production that deploy it and are represented through it. A precondition for this use value analysis, however, is the availability of the commodity labour power that has the use value, not only of producing use values, but also of producing (surplus) value. The use value of labour power is one of the main focuses of Volume I of *Capital*. It is the key to the analytical discovery of capitalist exploitation. This is so in two closely related, but different, senses. It is a relation between the two classes of capital and labour, in which one class buys the other's labour power and coerces surplus labour over and above what is required to produce working-class levels of consumption. And, in the greatest of detail in Volume I of *Capital*, Marx analyses the use value of labour power in the narrow sense of how labour is used; that is, addressing the way production and the labour process develop under capitalism – from domestic industry to the factory system.[10]

In developing his theory of capitalist production, Marx also pinpoints the socially specific use values attached to various commodity types. He distinguishes, for example, between constant and variable capital, one merely passing on its value to commodity as previously expended labour, and the other serving as a source of surplus labour. He also distinguishes between fixed and circulating capital, with the former enduring beyond one turnover time of capitalist production and circulation (manufacture and sale).[11] This is important for the analyses of crises since capital has been advanced but requires accumulation to be sustained to earn a satisfactory return. More generally, the possibility of crises is discussed by Marx on the basis of the distinction between two broad sectors, the means of consumption and the means of production. As demonstrated in the famous reproduction schemes of Volume II of *Capital*, for economic reproduction to be sustained, an appropriate balance must be struck between the two sectors.

In short, Marx does, if only implicitly, substantively analyse the position of a number of specific use values in uncovering the laws of motion of capitalism. But this 'defence' of Marx is liable to call forth the charge of unfairness or 'inadequacy'. Marx does not examine the role of particular commodities, other than in the broad ways specified above. Moreover, those that he does examine are specifically linked to the (expanded) reproduction of the economy as capital rather than as an engine of consumption which, consequently, is confined to a passive or determined moment. We appear to be no closer to restoring Marx's contribution to consumption, even allowing for his treatment of use value.

This is to move to the second charge against Marx, i.e. neglect of consumption. First, consider the standard rejection of Marxist, and classical, political economy by the neo-classical orthodoxy. Lumping a variety of its targets

together as cost of production theory, it suggests that they neglect the importance of demand. Accordingly, it sees itself as remedying this and providing a
more general theory through its demand analysis, based on utility maximisation
and the potential substitution between different goods (use values). Whatever the
merits of this alternative, its claim to provide a theory of demand (and associated consumption) has in a major sense been too readily and too uncritically
accepted, see Chapter 7 for more details. For the theory itself fundamentally
makes no contribution to the understanding of consumption; it is entirely indifferent to the specific use values that are included in the analysis. This is
transparent in mathematical presentation and in the concepts employed, such as
the marginal utility of the unspecified things, A relative to B. In the neoclassical
world, what individuals consume is not specified. Paradoxically, this is not so in
classical political economy, for which the labouring class, in particular, is strongly
identified with the consumption of corn, whose declining productivity, in the
hands of Ricardo for example, leads to falling profitability and a stationary state.

Analytically, the poverty of neo-classical theory of consumption arises out of
two factors. First, as Jevons made clear, his break with the economics of Ricardo
was to reject the labour theory of value as applied to industry and, in its place, to
apply his own marginal theory of rent to the economy as a whole. All production
becomes agriculture-like, although it is called industry. Second, the distinction
between production and consumption is itself extinguished as the latter takes on
the mode of achieving a given level of output (called utility) at a minimum cost
(called income). The chain of activity from initial factor inputs to final utility
makes little conceptual distinction along the way, since all those involved are optimising by setting relative marginal productivities/utilities equal to relative prices.

This failure effectively to distinguish production from consumption is a charge
that cannot be brought against Marx. As discussed in the previous chapter, there
is, for example, the capitalist structure of the economy, distinguishing (or separating) between production and exchange, with final consumption itself lying
outside the realm of the circulation of value, and no longer participating directly
within it. The structured isolation of consumption from production is not necessarily characteristic of other modes of production, and this offers one way of
interpreting Marx's well-known but tortuous analysis of the unity of production,
distribution and consumption in the *Grundrisse* (p. 99):[12]

> The conclusion we reach is not that production, distribution, exchange
> and consumption are identical, but they all form the members of a
> totality, distinctions within a unity. ... A definite production thus deter-
> mines a definite consumption, distribution and exchange as well as
> *definite relations between these different moments*. Admittedly, however, *in its
> one-sided form*, production is itself determined by the other moments.

Further, it is not simply a matter of the nature of the relations between these
three economic moments, in both structure and causation, but also the very defi-

nition of what constitutes each of them that is open to variation between one mode of production and another.

This can be illustrated by comparing consumption under slavery and under capitalism, an example explicitly used by Marx. Under slavery, workers' consumption is indistinguishable from other inputs to production, comparable with the feed for beasts of burden. As far as the slave-owner is concerned, there is a total outlay of corn; feeding workers differs little from feeding the fields with seed. By contrast, one of the civilising effects of capitalism is to sharpen the distinction between human consumption and consumption for production, thereby removing the consumption attached to the production process away from the consumption attached to the worker:[13]

> The worker's productive consumption and his individual consumption are therefore totally distinct. ... In the latter, he belongs to himself, and performs his necessary vital functions outside the production process. ... The fact that the worker performs acts of individual consumption in his own interest, and not to please the capitalist, is something entirely irrelevant to the matter (of social reproduction of labour power) ... *the capitalist may safely leave this to the worker's drive for self-preservation and propagation.*
>
> (Marx 1976: 711, emphasis added)

Thus, the position of (workers') consumption is very different between modes of production. On the other hand, this passage, and others like it, can be viewed as confirming the passive role of consumption within Marx's analysis – it seems, as in the emphasised passage, almost to imply that the social reproduction of labour power becomes automatic under capitalism, not only left off the capitalist's agenda but also disappearing off the theoretical agenda. This interpretation is, however, misleading. For the passage is merely locating the act of consumption of the working class relative to the economy. Just as the economic reproduction schemata of Volume II of *Capital* show how values and use values are reproduced through the circulation of capital, without thereby precluding the possibility of economic crisis, so Marx's analytical siting of consumption does not condemn the working class to the role of an unresisting agent for capital in effecting its own reproduction. Otherwise working-class consumption under capitalism would be treated as comparable with that obtaining under slavery, where reproduction of the workforce includes the raising of children for sale. Indeed, whilst Marx does draw the analogy between capitalism and slavery in this context, it is only in so far as labour's consumption is functional for capital in the reproduction of labour power. Slaves know only too well what will happen to their children as a continuing means of production to their current owners, or as a potential source of exchange value if sold; wage labour can have other aspirations, both in the economic as well as in the civil arena, including consumption.

In short, this abstract discussion around production, consumption and reproduction reveals that each is made up and structured differently between modes of production – even if there are inevitable parallels in the role of consumption in the reproduction of the workforce (which must consume both to work and to breed). But this commentary does not shed light only upon workers' consumption, which under capitalism is isolated from work. *Consumption* of raw materials and other means of production, which are in the monopoly possession of the capitalist class, remains within the economy to form what has already been termed productive, as opposed to final, consumption. Such elements of consumption are, in general, produced and exchanged as commodities under capitalism. They too, like final consumption, are use values whose character is in part defined by their relation to the capitalist economy.[14] This has already been mentioned above in the specific context of constant and fixed capital. As use values in exchange, however, the buying and selling of means of production tend to dominate the process of circulation quantitatively, even if overall a majority of *net* income is consumed through wages. For very little final consumption involves smoking factory chimneys and the use of sheet steel. The weight of *final* consumption, i.e. the removal of use values from the process of circulation, is proportionately limited, the more so if, as Marx argues, capital accumulation is associated with the expulsion of living labour from the production process so that an increasing share of the value of commodities is taken up by constant capital which is exchanged between capitals.

To raise the distinction between final and productive consumption – something structurally specific to capitalism – is to highlight the point that whilst final consumption is driven by the market, it is not uniquely defined as such from an economic point of view. For exactly the same applies to the items of *productive* consumption that are also exchanged as commodities even if they do not, as items of consumption, thereby make their way out of the circuits of capital as final consumption. To base a theory of final consumption on an economic content derived purely from the dependence on the purchase of commodities would unwittingly fail to distinguish between productive and final consumption, as both have these characteristics of exchange and use value in common. But exchange as such is often perceived to be sufficient to specify the economic content of final consumption. And it is much rarer to find analyses of the culture of consumption surrounding those exchanges associated with productive, as opposed to final, consumption, despite considerable attention to the labour process and the culture of production.[15] This will prove significant later in this chapter. Consider for the moment those analyses of consumption that draw propositions from the exchange value of the commodity in general rather than from capitalist (commodity) production and final consumption in particular. This is a major deficiency in that it is the first step in allowing consumption to be more easily autonomised analytically, since it is presumed to be characterised in its economic content purely by virtue of its exchange value alone. This may be appropriate from the immediate perspective of the consumer – all that is of interest is what I get for my money. But, systemically, there is more to the economics of consumption than the act of exchange, the end rather than the totality of a process that begins with production. Otherwise, it is as if commodities only differ, as far as their exchange value is concerned, in how much money is needed to command them as opposed to how they became the use values that they are (through production and other economic processes).

In the often referenced Simmel, for example, exchange value and value are linked to final consumption at the expense of the role of productive consumption, as if the latter were not an essential aspect of the economy. He thereby concludes: 'This is the basis and source of that valuation which finds its expression in economic life and whose consequences represent the meaning of money' (Simmel 1900: 78). This has the effect of distancing both final consumption and the role of money (and value theory) from their *capitalist* foundations, as is observed by Bottomore and Frisby in their introduction to Simmel. Treating consumption as a relationship between economic agents, commodities and money is to strip each of them of their dependence on capitalist production and its associated relations. It is as though consumption, through its origins in exchange via money, were constituted on the foundation of simple commodity production alone. To put it in another way, it is as if consumption is provided through the omnipresent market, not only without capital but also without wage labour. If money is the root of all consumption (evil or otherwise), it is a very shallow root analytically speaking. Whilst final and productive consumption are structured differently within the capitalist economy, they are effectively treated as identical if consumption is only examined as derived from its commodity origins through the expenditure of money. Barthes, however, makes the point well in distinguishing between the different rationalities surrounding productive and final consumption in the context of the planned obsolescence of clothing through fashion: 'Calculating, industrial society is obliged to form consumers who don't calculate; if clothing's producers and consumers had the same consciousness, clothing would be bought (and produced) only at the very slow rate of its dilapidation' (Barthes 1985: xi). Thus, different economic imperatives inform productive and final consumption, and they must be identified in their capitalist origins over and beyond the commodity form taken by use values, and their exchange for money, which is common to both.

Consequently, as the culture and significance of productive and final consumption are quite different because of their different locations *vis-à-vis* the economy, then the relationship between final consumption and the economy has to be established as something more than the provision of use values in the form of commodities. In other words, commodity production as the dominant form taken by final consumption must be recognised to be influential as *capitalist* commodity production. Otherwise, no distinction is made between capitalism's consumption and that derived, possibly ideally, from a system of simple commodity production.

So there are differences in commodities (as means of production and as means of consumption) and in the way they are consumed according to their relative position in the economy. But there are quantitative differences too. These have already been referred to implicitly in the schemata of economic reproduction. Productive consumption and final consumption goods circulate quite differently as values and also have definite quantitative relations to each other in simple and expanded reproduction.

More significantly, because final consumption involves the exit of its value from continuing circulation, its role is no longer defined by the internal logic of capital and its laws. Instead, it has a simple and undifferentiated relation to economic agents as purchasers. It no longer matters what their economic position is – with one proviso, they must have money to pay. As Marx observes:

> [As] *worker* ... as consumer and possessor of exchange values, and that in the form of the *possessor of money*, in the form of money he becomes a simple entry of circulation – one of its infinitely many entries, in which his specificity as worker is extinguished.
>
> (Marx 1969b: 420–1)

In other words, exchange of final consumption goods knows no well-defined class boundaries, a consequence of the homogenisation of commodities as exchange values, in which all can consume anything, at least in principle. Of course, in practice, this is only true in so far as no account is taken of the different spending power of the different classes, their different quantitative access to means of purchase. Here, Marx observes how much this affects the pattern of final consumption. For example, Marx (1969b: 565): 'A large part of the consumption of workers enters into that of capitalists and landlords but not vice-versa.' The latter, as consumers, 'give rise to very considerable modifications in the economy' (p. 493) and for them, a 'reduction in the value of labour power through machinery allows the scope of luxuries to be extended' (p. 572).[16] Further, to highlight the provision of use values in the form of commodities through the material processes attached to capitalist production is important. Doing so, however, does not imply that the nature of the use values themselves is determined exclusively or even primarily by their material properties – any more than the nature of money is determined by the sort of paper or plastic it is printed upon, or the pictures that they display. The material properties of a commodity do derive from production but use value is socially determined in ways that cannot be reduced either to production or the economy alone.

In short, and surely uncontroversially, the structure and dynamics of the capitalist economy do not readily determine the nature and composition of final consumption. The relationship between consumers and the economy, with the former merely as possessors of money, entails that there is no guarantee of stereotypical patterns of consumption. And, even if there were, the distribution of income across consuming groups has first to be determined, before the 'moral and historical' elements that make up workers' consumption can be analysed in terms of socially constructed use values. Yet the qualitative and quantitative elements involved in Marx's value analysis do not preclude the more general social construction of particular commodities and are, indeed, a necessary basis for it.

Consumption as the inversion of the logic of value

Irrespective of the meaning of use values to the (final) consumer, what actually constitutes consumption and how it is structured in the economy and society more generally are specific to particular modes of production. A qualitative, as well as a quantitative, grasp of the relations governing consumption is a precondition for examining who gets to consume what, and this will in turn influence how such consumption is construed over and above the role of other cultural determinants. Marx's theory of commodity fetishism makes the criticism that exchange relations are presented purely as relations between use values – x of commodity X exchanges for y of commodity Y – whereas they also embody (and conceal) the underlying determinants associated with the exploitative relations between producers. X and Y are the consequence of the exercise of human labour organised under definite conditions geared towards production for the market.

This is to begin to address the third charge laid against Marx – that his preoccupation with and priority to production, and his neglect of use value, imply that an appropriate examination of consumption is precluded. The chief proponent of this critique has been Jean Baudrillard. For Baudrillard (1981: 92) understands (or 'reads') Marx as having fetishised the role of commodity fetishism through his single-minded critique of the reification of social relations of *production*. Marx may have revealed production relations but only at the expense of assigning the significance of use value itself to the realm of ideology and superstructure where it can be quietly neglected.[17] Commodities must be seen as created in two senses: they are produced as physical objects but they are also created culturally according to how they are interpreted – as items of consumption, for example.

However, Baudrillard does at least connect the (erroneous) view that Marx neglects use value to a more constructive analysis by correctly recognising, emphasising and exploring the social construction of use value, rather than treating it as a purely physical or natural property (of which Marx is not guilty):

> The whole discourse on consumption, whether learned or lay, is articulated on the mythological sequence of the fable: a man, 'endowed' with needs which 'direct' him towards objects that 'give' him satisfaction. Since man is never really satisfied (for which, by the way, he is reproached), the same history is repeated indefinitely since the time of the ancient fables.
>
> (Baudrillard 1988: 35)

In place of this mythology, Baudrillard (1981: 30) suggests: 'The fundamental conceptual hypothesis for a sociological analysis of "consumption" is *not* use value, the relation to needs, but *symbolic exchange value*, the value of prestation, of rivalry and, at the limit, of class discriminants.' Haug employs the term aesthetic illusion to make the same point: 'In all commodity production a double reality is produced: first the use value; second, *and more importantly*, the *appearance* of use value. ... Appearance becomes just as important and practically more so – than the commodity's being itself' (Haug 1986: 16–17, first emphasis added).

This qualitative conclusion defines the social construction of the meaning of use value in consumption. What is the relationship between the consumer and the consumed in terms of the way in which the latter presents itself to the former, not now, as in commodity fetishism, as a relationship between things, but as a mongrel relationship between the human and the non-human? Not surprisingly, the human partner in the relationship may be endowed with the more active determining role, as in subjective preference theory. More generally, the consumer may be constituted through socially determined cultural relations concerning power, gender, happiness, identity or whatever. But, in either case, this would itself be indicative of commodity fetishism, of setting aside the underlying social (and human) relations that bring the use value to the point of being consumed. These have a quantitative component, comprising the complex determinants of the levels and patterns of what is consumed (usually thought of as economic factors, however broadly defined). These, however, must also influence what is produced and how it is interpreted in consumption.

We take it as uncontroversial, then, that in the extreme, not least in the work of Baudrillard, postmodernism had the effect of detaching consumption from the economy as the former becomes endlessly (X-)constructed as a system of signs. As Kidd and Nicholls (1999: 3) put it, 'in the new formulation the proper study for the historian becomes discourse: human culture is understood as a system of symbolic "signs" to be read as "texts"'. In pursuing this logic to its extreme, the postmodernism of consumption has severed the latter's connection altogether from the material content of the commodities purchased and, thereby, the material processes by which they have been supplied. As Campbell (1993: 42) concludes:[18]

> Consumption communicates social meaning, and is the site of struggles over social distinction. The fulfilling of more concrete needs arising from, say, individual feelings of cold or hunger seems almost an accidental by-product.

Another way of deconstructing such postmodernism is to see it as taking the commodity at the point of purchase as a point of departure. For the analyst, as for the consumer, that the purchase is also a sale for the producer (and an engagement for other economic and social agents) is readily forgotten. A journey is followed from exchange to the individual act of subjective consumption at the expense of social and objective determinants. In this light, although Baudrillard's own point of departure from Marx had been a critique of commodity fetishism,[19] Baudrillard is open to the strongest charge of such fetishism, comprised of two separate but crucial elements. One, as has been readily recognised, is to deny the influence of the economic altogether, in the attempt to circumvent economic reductionism. Thus, Storey (1999: xiii) accepts that the neglect of consumption is no longer valid, and cites Stuart Hall's judgement (p. 23):

> What has resulted from the abandonment of deterministic economism has been, not alternative ways of thinking questions about the economic relations and their effects, as the 'conditions of existence' of other practices ... but instead a massive, gigantic, and eloquent *disavowal*. As if, since the economic in the broadest sense, definitely does *not*, as it was once supposed to do, 'determine' the real movement of history 'in the last instance', it does not exist at all!

The other, less recognised element, is to counterpose consumption and, by implication, culture to the undifferentiated economic, often dubbed production, as if the latter were itself cultureless in content and as a source of culture and meaning in itself and for consumption.

Thus, for Baudrillard, symbolic exchange tends to take on a life of its own, especially in its independence from production.[20] This bias is, however, veiled to some extent by his continuing use of terms such as class, power and productive forces to describe the foundations of consumption. Such determinants do then enter into his analysis. But, crucially, they only do so as external referents, as the given material factors which will be symbolised in or by consumption. They do not enter as determinants of what is consumed or how it is interpreted, only of what is interpreted. Power and so on are only represented or the means of representation and not material factors themselves. Thus, the classic elements of Marxist (or other materialist analysis) are rarely tied to the formal abstract theory around the logic of symbolic exchange, and inevitably act more as the symbolic content of meaning. This represents something of an inversion of Marx's logic, for the layered analysis of use value and exchange is now projected onto productive forces, power and class, rather than these acting as determinants of consumption and its meaning.

It follows that the elements of symbolic exchange are insecure within the analysis. Other symbols are equally possible as externally given referents, as potentially variable as the myriad of (meanings of) available use values. Take power, for example. Whilst Baudrillard argues that consumption distinctions (i.e. who gets to consume what and how) signify, for example, power relations, this is less a logical stance than a lingering influence from his analytical origins from within (and, in breaking with) Marxism. Paradoxically, such power relations, which enable differentiated consumption relations to exist between different classes, might otherwise themselves have no determining influence as far as the social construction of use values is concerned. Power serves to symbolise, not to create, the meanings of consumption.

Baudrillard (1988: 42) does, however, make reference to the determining role of production and power relations: 'The truth is not that "needs are the fruits of production" but *the system of needs* is *the product of the system of production.*' And, historically, 'to socialise the masses (that is to control them) into a force of consumption' is seen as the twentieth-century product of the nineteenth-century's rationalisation of production (p. 50). But these assertions do not move analytically beyond their own level of rhetoric. From here, it is but a short logical step either to excise power relations from what is symbolised or to reinterpret power relations by reference to their meaning within consumption. From a position in which power has been commonly understood as derived from capital and of importance as a symbolic reference, it is liable to evaporate away altogether.

Thus, it can be argued that the connection between the consumption of use values and social relations is inverted. Consumption does act as a class discriminant, but such discrimination has a prior role in making consumption available in the first place. Moreover, the long route to consumption from class relations itself plays a major role in the construction of use values, even if – as revealed by the theory of commodity fetishism – it is more by way of concealment. Few want to be reminded of the world of work and commerce when contemplating consumption. Like Baudrillard in the world of ideas, the point is to escape from the commodity's origins and corresponding material properties and merely inhabit a symbolic world.

In practice, more prominent as symbols in Baudrillard's work than standard categories of Marxist analysis are those of orthodox sociology, dealing with stratification, mobility and aspirations (Baudrillard 1988: 381), and the unusual concept of prestation is understood as a mechanism of discrimination and prestige. Thus, 'it seems that the norm of consumption attitudes is simultaneously distinction and conformity' (p. 36). But this begs more questions than it answers. Why should distinction and conformity derive primarily or exclusively from consumption, and how does it relate to other means of distinguishing or conforming? Why is it possible for consumption to function as a means of conformity or distinction? Is this true of all commodities or more of some than others? Given differences by race, gender, age and so on, what is the nature as well as the depth of the conformities and distinctions that emerge? Answers can only begin to emerge if it is recognised that uniformity and distinction in consumption do not arise spontaneously as sources of social stratification, although they are undoubtedly exploited for that purpose in capitalist as well as other societies.[21] Thus, differences in gender are both a source and a reflection of power. But the nature and content of uniformity and distinction arise out of the particular societies in which they occur and not exclusively, nor necessarily primarily, from the culturally constructed meaning of use values in acts of consumption.

For capitalism in particular, the logical origins of stratification, like other meanings attached to consumption, lie in the system of commodity production itself. Particular class relations induce or constrain the forms through which stratification can occur, both in consumption as well as in other arenas; these forms of stratification then limit the more detailed processes and symbols involved. Such abstract considerations can most easily be brought down to earth through consideration of the daily experience of that most common form of human species, the consumer. Whilst often treated as an interest or socio-economic group, even though all belong, stratification and distinction are heavily influenced by the availability of income. In practice, we all know that those who live by wage revenue (or social security) have different consumption standards than those who live by profit or other unearned income. These are not just signs but realities. We differ in how we eat, how we are clothed, where we live, how we are educated, and so on.

Crucially, however, there is a sense in which this is not logically so. The newspapers love a story in which a common worker is exposed to be living a life of luxury, the better to be able to rationalise a cut in wages for those who are not. For distinctions in the sources of revenue do not determine their levels, so that a worker could, in principle, live like a king or queen and vice versa. As Slater and Tonkiss (2001: 158) neatly put it, the culture of consumption under capitalism seems to offer both a nostalgic escape from commerce and a progressive source of egalitarianism:

> The desire to constitute culture as an autonomous and pure sphere, as a utopian preconfiguration or nostalgic archaism, as an ideal defined *against* market society, has fed the western cultural and political imaginary throughout modernity and produced many romantically starving artists. ... [Yet also] the market emerges – not just in the minds of doctrinaire liberals – as a site of populist pleasures, cultural and political renewal and excitement, and democratic egalitarianism and anti-elitism.

But, even in principle, a worker cannot be a king, nor consume like a king, in a society other than capitalism, in which the monarchy holds a ruling position. For, then, consumption and its symbolic role (including distinction and conformity) have entirely different roots and meanings. Within capitalism, what differentiates the content of the diode, distinction and conformity, is the dependence of consumption on its derivation through exchange. As discussed in the previous chapter, the emergence of money in a system of general commodity production gives *all* the right to consume *everything* – at least in principle. Hence, the basis exists for the process of emulation through consumption – although the detailed paths that it takes other than through the market is not determined. By contrast such emulation cannot occur in non-commodity-producing societies (even the richest peasant cannot buy a way into being a lord).[22] The ideology associated with the potential for uniformity is revealed by Haug:

In the sphere of circulation, only the money in customers' pockets is important to capital irrespective of the customers' class position, and it is precisely in response to this in commodity aesthetics there dominates the illusion through which a particular class culture tends to integrate the workers – the capitalist distortion of a classless culture.

(Haug 1986: 104)

By the same token, the commodity form of consumption implies that *each* (involved in exchange) has the ability to consume *something* in particular. Hence, differentiation in consumption is a necessary product of the commodity form of consumption. Commodity production, entailing a particular form of access to consumption, is the basis for distinction/conformity under capitalism. As such, it appears prior to capitalism, as excessive conspicuous consumption, and early on in capitalism as the elite display of consumption.[23] As Marx argues in the manner of a Victorian novelist:

When a certain stage of development has been reached, a conventional degree of prodigality, which is also an exhibition of wealth, and consequently a source of credit, becomes a business 'necessity' to the 'unfortunate' capitalist. Luxury enters into capital's expenses of representation.

(Marx 1976: 741)

Before commodity production is generalised, the form taken by such conspicuous consumption is necessarily confined to a narrower range of items and may even be focused on one item alone, even the body of the individual to signify wealth, literally, in the capacity to consume. Where the symbol of wealth is accumulated money, as in the cliché of the miser, the capacity to consume is represented by its opposite, the formation of hoards and abstinence from consumption. These casually constructed examples illustrate how material relations govern symbolic exchange value rather than merely serving in the role of what is freely represented.

Thus, as already remarked, there is a curious, usually implicit, inversion of the logic to be found in Marx's treatment of use value. The inversion can only be explicit if use value is recognised to be present in Marx rather than presumed to be absent and/or precluded. For Marx, the use value of commodities, both materially and culturally, is founded on, if not reducible to, the social relations by which they are produced, distributed and exchanged. These relations involve, for example, various aspects of the exercise of power, for which there are symbolic counterparts in the world of consumption, whether it be in bigger cars or richer clothes. But neither the nature, nor the source, nor the role of these symbols in representing and reproducing power can be defined by reference to their consumption alone. For if consumption represents power (or some other attribute), from where does that power come and why does it (or why does

72

conflict over it) not exercise an influence over how it is represented? Failure to address such questions is the inversion of Marx's logic, for which social relations have to be identified before there can be an understanding of how they are represented and what is represented (although this does not allow the reduction of representation to an insignificant epiphenomenon). Otherwise, power and other material relations are taken as given, as external referents, purely employed for the purpose of providing consumers with the targets on which to project their interpretation of what they consume – consumption becomes symbolism, pure and simple.

One consequence of this is that such a use value approach has little place even for the most abstract of historical content, unless it too is derived as symbol.[24] In particular, the laws of development of capitalism and its dynamics are neglected. Even the impact of the simplest, and generally uncontroversial, distinction between *laissez-faire* and *monopoly capitalism* need have no perceptible effect. Haug (1986: 107) points to the difference between a gun used in an imperialist war and one used in a war of freedom. It is the difference between an instrument used to free rather than to oppress. But, 'one cannot tell from the gun itself. ... Its detached and reproduced sensual impression does not reveal the essential difference but serves to disguise it.' Much the same is true of whether an item of clothing has been produced under conditions of monopoly capital, creating relative surplus value through the use of advanced machinery, or whether it has its origins in the backstreet sweatshop dependent upon absolute surplus value.[25]

These breaks, or inversions, of Marx's analysis have profound implications. For the nature of explanation and causation is itself transformed. Marx is usually perceived as employing a simple determinism from production to consumption by which his method is degraded by neglecting, first, the role of contradictory tendencies or laws and, second, the dialectics for which the concrete and the complex are derived from the abstract and simple as the product of many determinants. For Miller:

> The abiding influence of Durkheim and Marx has created a tendency towards a highly objectivist emphasis in much contemporary anthropology. A characteristic feature of much of this tradition is that society is always prior to culture; it is social relations and classifications which are given form in cultural classifications.
>
> (Miller 1987: 64)

The symbolic approach to consumption accepts this dichotomy but places culture prior to society!

Further, as emphasised, such a use value approach itself requires explanatory variables that are arbitrarily embraced as external referents – as has been previously recorded in the case of class and power etc. – although this might be done through the use of abstract categories and theoretical schemata. Sexuality, for example, is extremely prominent (as in its role in advertising), so that gender relations are seen as represented by particular patterns of consumption and their meaning. The content of the analysis depends upon the judicious choice of what is perceived to be most significant in the fetishism of use value. But, for the reasons already outlined, it is inadequate merely to read off changes in the social content of consumption without being able to explain fully why they have occurred. For example, gender representations in advertising do not simply mirror but are determined by changing gender relations, as new products come to be advertised, such as the microwave (to combine work with domestic chores) and video (to combine domestic chores with home entertainment, especially for children) or as old products come to be advertised in new ways to represent the new, independent (usually childless) woman. Further, unless the meaning of consumption is rooted in what is consumed and how it comes to be consumed, the division between the physical and the symbolic content of use values tends to become open to infinitely elastic interpretation – in which case it hardly seems to matter what is consumed, as fantasy can be (better than) the real thing. Coke is a drink, but it is represented as any-(real)-thing.

There are strong parallels here with the limited explanatory content of the longer standing orthodox approaches to consumption to be found in sociology, psychology and anthropology in which it is treated as status, symbol and ritual. Goody (1982) begins by questioning the extent to which so much of significance is hidden in the use values of consumption – after all, advertisers, market researchers, academics and, it might be added, consumers are all too aware of what is going on in their different ways. He puts rather neatly two distinct ways of understanding the hidden meaning of consumption, the one as a purely symbolic fetish which cannot be so, the other as a code of what is so but hidden: 'Do social relations and social structures stand in the same relationship to the bread and wine as the body and blood of Christ, or as a naval cipher does to open speech?' (Goody 1982: 30). It seems that it is only as consumers that we have the wool pulled over our eyes. But when we buy a pullover, what exactly do we know and not know about what it is, and how important is this? Whatever the answer, Goody sees the question as inhibiting the analysis of change:[26] 'The concentration on "meaning" in a specific cultural context ... has tended to push aside studies of long term change' (p. 37). Yet, as Mennell observes of the (structuralist) alternative in which the meaning of consumption is simply determined by social structure:

> The great virtue of the structuralist approach is that it clearly recognises that 'taste' is culturally shaped and socially controlled. Its weakness is that it tends to be static, and has little to say about how tastes change and develop in society over time.
>
> (Mennell 1985: 6)

Ultimately, the result is that little more emerges than the idea that people eat what they like – as presented within an organised framework determined by the academic discipline concerned (p. 13).

From all of this, it follows that the key question is how to link material and cultural factors together, rather than taking them as independent of one another or dependent upon crude determinations in one direction or the other. Those who fall into either the traditional, structuralist camp or the postmodernist camp are liable to read others as doing so and, correspondingly, deserving of praise or criticism depending upon whether ally or foe. Consequently, postmodernists, amongst others, have perpetrated a shallow and inappropriate dismissal of Marx for having concentrated exclusively on (exchange) value at the expense of the social construction of use value.[27] The rejection of Marx has been attached to the demotion of production and, with it, the presumed significance of class for consumption. Yet, it is Marx, amongst others, who is recognised to have established that commodification turns qualitative social relations into quantitative ones of how much money there is to spend. Consequently, consumption patterns cannot be legitimately derived from class relations of production although this does not mean that such class relations in their broader context are irrelevant to consumption.[28] But class, production and exchange value are readily left behind in embracing the pertinence of sign value. Whilst the leading villain in this respect has been Baudrillard, his stance on the rejection of Marx has continued to be readily accepted even though much else of his work has now been rejected as too extreme.[29]

In this respect, Burke's (1996) outstanding study of the consumption of cosmetics in Zimbabwe, from colonial times forward, is instructive, not least because of its strength as an exemplary case study of the relationship between the material and cultural properties of commodities. He investigates how the selling and the meaning of cosmetics has been dependent both upon the strategies of capitalist manufacturers and the intersection of their advertising with shifting meanings of race, gender, cleanliness and so on. In one respect,[30] he appropriately poses the question of the relationship between the material and cultural properties of commodities (p. 8):

> Goods are *not* pure free-floating signifiers; they are not blank slates upon which history and power can write freely. They have concrete material qualities which limit and prescribe their uses and their nature. On some level, food is for eating, soap is for washing, clothes are for wearing.

In seeking an answer, he acknowledges the problematic but useful work of Baudrillard in positing the critical role of sign value in serving 'modern capitalism's ability to generate and control surplus value', and he is particularly appreciative of Haug's 'masterly treatment of "commodity aesthetics"' (p. 6). Much more ambivalence is directed towards Marx and commodity fetishism for he welcomes the idea that 'relations between things … accompany, conceal, or displace the actual state of relations between people' (p. 5). However, he concludes that (p. 6):

Marx's definition of commodity fetishism does not leave sufficient room for the complexity of the relations between things and people, room for the imaginative possibilities and unexpected consequences of commodification, room for the intricate emotional and intellectual investments made by individuals within commodity culture.

Neither evidence nor argument is given for this conclusion. As Carruthers and Babb (2000: 18) put it by way of contrast, 'In Marx's analysis, commodities consist of much more than just a set of useful features: They embody social relationships'.[31] Burke argues, largely correctly, that there has been a Marx-inspired tradition that derives a distinction between met and (bad) false and unmet and (good) real needs, blame for which resides somewhere between commodity fetishism and a conspiracy of the ruling classes. Further, this tradition identifies false needs with appearances rather than realities. But none of this has anything to do with Marx's own understanding of commodity fetishism, for which social relations merely appear as they also are, as relations between things. To emphasise that these appearances are not false, Marx draws the contrast with religious fetishism for which exploitative social relations are expressed as a supposed (false) relationship with the deity.[32]

There is, then, nothing in Marx's definition of commodity fetishism that fails to accommodate Burke's analytical demands. Such a conclusion is subject to one proviso – that the definition should not be confined to the concealment of the social relations of production alone. Burke's case study demonstrates how other relations of domination are concealed (and in a sense, if through reflection, revealed) by the meanings attached to cosmetics, which themselves differ by time, place and consumer. One way of interpreting Burke's criticism of Marx (or some of his followers) is that the notion of commodity fetishism needs to be widened to incorporate those social relations that are reified and veiled through the act of exchange (presence of child labour, environmental degradation, as well as racial and sexual domination). In addition, it is necessary to acknowledge that such social relations structure, without determining, the way in which commodities can be used and understood at the level of the individual – what it is to be clean or beautiful.

In short, Marx's theory of value, of which commodity fetishism is a part or a corollary, sustains an irreducible connection between production (for profit) and exchange (for use). In contrast, postmodernist critics of Marx discount production, depart exchange and (re)construct use value alone. It is worth recalling, however, that Marx's early writings focused heavily on alienation (Miklitsch 1998: 84–5) in the context of consumption. Unfortunately, whatever its veracity, Althusser's notion that Marx broke with this earlier work to embrace political economy has also encouraged the view that Marx had the most simplistic approach to use value, the evidence of his earlier writings, including those on ideology, to the contrary. Certainly, Marx's work revealed a shift of emphasis but, for example, the treatment of commodity fetishism as a concealed relationship between producers expressed as a relationship between things does not necessarily entail the simplistic attitude to the social construction of the use values of commodities that has been attributed to Marx and to Marxist political economy more generally. Miklitsch's account strongly supports the view that Marx's supposed neglect of consumption was a matter of mature choice 'in order to retain the concept of *surplus-value*' (p. 93). In this respect, Haug's (1986) much neglected notion of the aesthetic illusion is instructive as he argues that the shifting products and productions in pursuing profitability create a tension between the material character of commodities and the way they are perceived. Whilst he exaggerates the extent to which that illusion is supported by advertising around sexuality, he forges a close connection between political economy and the culture of consumption, as discussed fully in the next chapter.[33]

Concluding remarks

Much reference has been made to cultural theories of consumption that concentrate on the meaning of use values to the final consumer. Such concern with the interpretation of the objects of consumption is liable to acknowledge the origins of consumption in exchange since, in contemporary capitalist society, a major part of consumption is derived more or less directly from the purchase of commodities. Indeed, the ideological construction of the use value of a commodity, as in advertising and brand image, often explicitly addresses its market origins either to establish a claim to quality – a product is 'the best money can buy' – or otherwise to deny the influence of its commercial origins altogether when presented 'as good as home-made'.

The recognition of the relation between commodities and their exchange value aspect does not, however, suffice to root their interpretation adequately within *capitalist* society. Further, such origins also tend to be set aside in the ideological construction of the commodity's use values. There is an even stronger tendency for the capitalist origins of use values to be obscured and analytically set aside than is the case for their origins in exchange. Companies, for example, project themselves, not their products, as profitable. To do otherwise might suggest overpricing or poor quality. While some of the factors underlying profitability might be incorporated into the meaning of the commodity – for example, the skill or high technology with which it has been manufactured – it is hardly conceivable that 'the best at making a profit' could displace 'the best money can buy' as a favourable attribute of a commodity.

But in practice, even if these attributes of commodities bound for final consumption are ideologically denied, the social construction of commodities as use values, the meaning endowed to them for and by consumers, takes place in the context of both *capitalist* commodity exchange and capitalist commodity *production* (and distribution). This is important in assessing the attempts that have been made to rectify Marx's presumed neglect of use value and of consumption. However, the false charge of neglect is a very different proposition from the one that is often used to criticise Marx; that is, that his political economy essentially *precludes* the possibility of opening up the analysis of use value and consumption. As shown in the previous section, such is the position adopted in the work of Baudrillard. It leads to emphasis upon the social construction of use value from a (false) starting point critical of Marx for having neglected such considerations. It proceeds, however, very little further beyond the confines of interpreting use value as culturally determined by the marriage of final consumption (how the commodity is received) with simple purchase (how it has been obtained). It is an analytical stance guilty of the neglect of the determining influence of capital in production and distribution (as well as through exchange and cultural factors, even if these are more direct influences upon the consumer as such).

By this means, the determination of use value tends to become freed from its material foundations in an even more dramatic fashion. When use values are freed from their capitalist origins, the meaning of consumption is construed as a relation between consumer and consumed. Even though this does not have to be interpreted individualistically and subjectively, there is a tendency to neglect the material content of the commodity itself, i.e. what its physical properties are. Even if culturally determined through society, the meaning of commodities in consumption becomes sufficiently flexible that they are what they mean. They *are* now home-made or the best money can buy since that is what they are believed to be and that is what these expressions themselves come to mean.

In summary, it is crucial to acknowledge that use values are socially constructed, both as products themselves, with material and social origins, and as products with meaning to those that use them (and to those who have produced and sold them). As items of consumption under capitalism, such use values have complex roots in the economy which reach beyond their simply being acquired as commodities in exchange, with their social construction otherwise being a consequence of non-economic factors. Most important is to reject the dichotomy between economy, the material or society and culture. Objects do not arrive through the market as blank sheets after which culture can do its work upon them to create (symbolic) use values. The material processes by which commodities are provided are themselves cultural, reflecting the cultures of work, design, retailing, etc. In short, capital and capitalism are simultaneously economic and cultural categories. How are they to be mutually handled in the context of consumption?

5

CONSUMPTION THROUGH SYSTEMS OF PROVISION

Introduction

This chapter aims to elaborate and, to some extent, to motivate and to justify the central analytical construct that informs my work on consumption. The approach is bound to what is termed systems of provision. But what is a system of provision? An elementary definition is that it is the inclusive chain of activity that attaches consumption to the production that makes it possible. The notion is worryingly familiar in common parlance as reference is readily made to the food system, the housing system, the transport system and, interestingly, the fashion system. The last, usually but not exclusively, is associated with some, but not all, clothing but depends for its name more upon the culture of consumption than upon the object consumed. From our perspective, have these simple understandings of consumption as a system more or less accidentally grasped a deeper analytical content? If so, why, how and what?

An answer begins with acknowledging that the simple definition, once prodded and scratched with the tools of scholarship, raises more problems than it resolves. First, what distinguishes one system of provision from another? Second, as a corollary, is there just one food system, for example, or a number depending upon the categories of food involved – meat, vegetable, fruit, fresh or processed, and so on?[1] Third, what makes up the constituent components of each system of provision along the way from production to consumption? There are the activities of provisioning itself, some more direct than others, such as design, distribution, advertising, marketing and shopping. But what about the gendering of consumption or the other attributes of commodities that are not so obviously commercially 'manufactured'? Quite apart from such definitional conundrums, the system of provision approach raises broader analytical issues. First and foremost, what is meant by 'system'? How does it relate to economic, social and cultural factors? What is its causal significance in explaining how consumption patterns and meanings are reproduced or transformed?

To raise these issues is paramount to situating consumption studies under the broader umbrella of social theory and its continuing enigmas and controversies. It is worth emphasising that our appeal to systems of provision is designated as an *approach*. As such it poses a general analytical framework with considerable leeway about how it should be filled out in both methodological and theoretical content. There may be, for example, those who subscribe to the approach but who reject the way it is applied, whether analytically or in case studies to particular items of consumption.[2]

This chapter seeks to address some of these questions concerning the system of provision approach. The next section draws the distinction between 'horizontal' and 'vertical' analysis, especially as it is applied to consumption. This allows how systems of provision are differentially constructed and distinct from one another to be examined at a general level. In the third section, the relationship between the material and cultural aspects of systems of provision is tentatively broached by interrogating Haug's notion of aesthetic illusion. Despite some weaknesses, his approach focuses usefully on the tensions between the material properties of commodities and how they are perceived – as each is subject to change under the imperatives of profitability. As examined in the fourth section, such tensions are shown to differ across stages of development of capitalism and historically evolved structures and meanings.

From horizontal to vertical

Following classical political economy, it has been common to define the commodity by *two* primary attributes: exchange value and use value. This division has proved the springboard for the elaboration of widely divergent economic analyses. Neo-classical economics sets up a relationship between the two properties: the ultimate (marginal) utility provided by the commodity is the explanation for its price. Marxist economics interrogates exchange and use value dialectically to flush out the concept of value – socially necessary labour time as a relationship between producers – from which is logically derived a critical understanding of capitalist commodity production. As the depository of surplus value, analytical priority is displaced from the commodity as such, and the marketplace, to the world of production, where the origins of exploitation are to be found. Keynesianism assigns paramount importance to the ability of the economic system, if not the state, to generate effective market demand, so that the potential exchange value of the commodity and its ability to command sale become central.

A further distinction flows from the dichotomy between use value and exchange value, that between purchase and sale, reflecting the two sides of a bargain. From this meeting point in the market, the life of the commodity can be traced in two directions, either forward to the buyer and an act of consumption or backward through the seller to the commodity's origins in production. For neo-classical economics, these paths may be seen as harmoniously and efficiently linked through the free play of the market mechanism, unless it be riddled by market imperfections. The priority assigned to individual utility, both as a determining, explanatory factor and as a desirable outcome, gives rise to the idea of consumer sovereignty. The system of production responds as a servant to the needs and wishes of consumers, subject to the availability of resources. In this sense, consumption can be traced back from the individual, through exchange, to act as a determining moment upon production – even if allowance can also be made for distortions in efficiency and competitiveness along the way.

A more radical tradition in economic thought denies the validity of consumer sovereignty, viewing the consumer more as a passive victim of the dictates of production and of producers. The line of causation between production and consumption is perceived to run primarily in the opposite direction: producers decide what is to be made, do not respond to consumers' needs or, worse, they manipulate them through advertising or through the numbness brought on by overfamiliarity with what they make available.

Keynesianism has been less concerned with the opposition between these two positions than with what determines the overall level of effective demand on the market. How well oiled are the wheels of buying in prompting corresponding supply? In particular, the position of money and money markets becomes crucial. Stretching a point for illustrative purposes, this can be thought of as a specific example, in this case drawn from economics, in which (aggregate) consumption is determined by an *intermediate* factor, the operation of money markets, between the two extremes of production and consumption. It has its counterpart in the idea that consumerism is driven by the ready availability of credit. But there are intermediate factors other than the ability to buy (with credit cards), which might be considered to influence the overall level and nature of consumption: marketing (of which advertising is a component) or the psychology of consumption where this is associated with emulation, 'keeping up with the Joneses', for example. In this last case, the jockeying for status assumes greater importance than what is actually consumed (or produced), which is why it can be subject to ridicule or to critical analysis – witness Veblen's theory of conspicuous consumption. Analytically, there is a common element shared between Veblen and Keynes: for one there is the passing on of demand, whilst for the other the overall level of demand is central. But, for both, the nature of that demand in terms of specific commodities is relatively unimportant (although this is historically contingent for Veblen based on items of conspicuous consumption established by the leisure class).

The details of some of these theories have been critically assessed in Fine and Leopold (1993). Here, the intention is more to point to the extent to which such theory relies upon generalities across commodities. Each approach makes only a limited, or purely formal, distinction between different commodities. Some commodities may be more subject to consumer sovereignty and some less so. Emulation may be more important for some artefacts – diamonds for the rich, piano in the parlour for lesser mortals, and so on. But, in general, each theory lumps together great bundles of disparate goods. These are bent collectively to follow the contours set out by that particular theory. Commodities that differ in important respects (from the point of view of consumer behaviour leaving aside how they are provided) are typically subsumed under the catch-all term, 'consumer goods'.

Each approach to consumption also tends to have difficulty reconciling or incorporating the insights offered by the others. This is a separate but not unrelated point. Even if overall demand, method of production, relative power of consumers and producers, emulation, etc., were all taken into account, integration between them might only be effectively achieved at the level of individual commodities rather than as a general theory of consumption (of all commodities). This is the conclusion drawn and adopted in this book.

Theories, then, substantially reflect dependence upon generalisation from archetypal commodities, processes or motives. Consumer sovereignty takes as its model the perfectly competitive industry, with well-informed consumers and rigidly formed or inherited preferences. Its antithesis is highly monopolised capital, with heavy dependence upon manipulative advertising and consumer ignorance. Each approach appears inadequate for two reasons. Both over-generalise from the cases in which each might be thought to have greatest purchase; both are ill-placed to take account of factors associated with the other approach.

Taken together and probed further, these shortcomings are found to be even more serious. For even if, for example, a case is found in which consumer sovereignty or emulation appears to provide a satisfactory explanation for the consumption of a particular commodity, its explanatory power will be illusory. For it would still be necessary to explain why this particular commodity had not been subject, say, to monopolisation and manipulative advertising rather than to the dictates of a well-informed and 'sensible' consuming public. Sealing off individual commodities within the confines of self-contained theories denies not only the complexity of factors involved in the consumption and production of goods but also their relative weight and interaction.

Given the inadequacies of existing theories, it is reasonable to consider an alternative approach, one that is consciously sensitive to the difference between commodities, not so much as items of consumption alone, but in terms of the economic and social processes and structures by which they become such. Even where these economic and social relations are shared, the way in which they interact may well be different across commodities. All tend to be the product of wage labour, but production processes are organised differently, products develop differently, are distributed and sold differently, are consumed and disposed of differently; they serve needs that are themselves socially constructed and satisfied (or not) very differently. These separate processes are not independent of each other, nor is there a rigid one-way line of determination between them.

Consequently, this chapter and, more diffusely, this book argue that each commodity or commodity group is best understood in terms of a unity of economic and social processes which vary significantly from one commodity to another, each creating and reflecting upon what will be referred to as its own system of provision (sop). There is a sense in which this is self-evident. Compared with motor cars, food is produced, sold and consumed differently; yet both may be subject to the factory system, advertising and emulative behaviour. What is gained by emphasising their differences rather than their similarities?

First of all, reordering the world of commodities into sops opens up the possibility for a more dynamic approach to the theory of consumer behaviour. The theories already mentioned, and many others, are essentially static in most respects; whatever the period under investigation, whether at the time of the Industrial Revolution or in the late twentieth century, the typical 'basket' of consumer goods under review is taken as given. Though the composition of this bundle clearly varies from one historical period to the next, existing theories do not adequately explain the mechanisms that lead to the introduction of entirely new commodities, the disappearance or transformation of old ones, or the prolonged survival intact of some inveterate goods. If there is any significance to the relatively recent arrival of the motor car compared with the prehistoric availability of food and the survival of some almost prehistoric foods like bread, it will not be revealed by most theories.

Nor do existing theories explain the consumption of particular goods in particular periods of time, or the processes by which each is made available. Rather, the goods themselves function primarily to illustrate the central argument of the theory; serving in this capacity, they often become interchangeable. Theories based on emulative (trickle-down) behaviour, for example, do not need to distinguish between the consumption of motor cars or food, housing or clothing, to make their point. Nor do they need to distinguish between the eighteenth and the twentieth century. For its purposes, consumption of any of these goods in any period will serve equally well.

The tacit presumption of such theories is that the human propensity to consume is virtually innate and, hence, of much greater importance in itself than any of the individual objects with which it interacts. It also gives primacy to activities or behaviour carried out by individuals, whether rational or irrational, rather than by social agencies, corporate or collective institutions. Such a view underpins much of the theoretical discussion within the disciplines of anthropology, semiotics, psychology and economics.

The sop approach, by contrast, sets the role of consumer choice within a much different perspective, one that views it as determined both historically – and therefore varying over time in strength and influence – and jointly with other variables within separate sops which are themselves subject to significant long-term change, achieved at different rates and with different consequences. This framework encourages the exploration of multiple perspectives, suggesting the possibility that consumer behaviour has played a more determining role in some periods of history and in some commodities than in others.

Such an approach allows theory to accommodate common sense, revealing that consumption over the past 200 years has not proceeded smoothly upwards along a curve of constant slope; that the qualitative and quantitative impact of consumption during a period of labour market (and productive capacity) expansion may be greater than that of periods preceding or following it; that the domestic consumption of coal differs significantly from the consumption of nuclear energy; and so on. Moreover, analysis by sops offers an antidote to what Cannadine (1984) has described as the bias of contemporary events which, in this case, has currently elevated the role of consumption to a more prominent if inadequately differentiated position on the agenda of most social sciences.

So far, the theory referred to has primarily been derived from the various schools of economics and political economy. These offer a particularly powerful example of what can be dubbed 'horizontal' analysis. For mainstream economics, the omnipresent tool of horizontal theorising, especially in the context of consumption, is the idea of a given utility function representing the given preferences of individuals otherwise unspecified apart from their endowments of factor inputs (labour, capital or the like). Theory of consumer behaviour is reduced to that of the demand for goods, itself reduced to the single goal of 'rationality', further reduced to the maximisation of utility subject to the constraints of prices and income. Further, the theory draws no distinction between the goods concerned that are themselves reduced to given material properties that are not specified. Last, understanding the connection between consumption and the remainder of the economy essentially offers little more by way of analytical principle. Rationality as maximisation of utility subject to constraints is carried one step back into the world of production, in which entrepreneurs pursue the same goal, if indirectly, through maximisation of profits on the basis of given production possibilities and prices of factor inputs.

The horizontal nature of such theory, and its generalised application across all consumption, is marked by the formal and technical terms in which it is expressed. Individuals have no identity and so can be designated by a subscript to their utility function, u_i, for the ith individual. Commodities, or goods in general, have no properties and are equally subject to lack of specificity in being denoted by x_j for the jth good. Graphically, supply and demand intersect at equilibrium without reference to time, place or context.

The particularly extreme assumptions that underlie mainstream economics should not blind us to the fact that these endow it with a horizontal approach that is far from being monopolised by it. Indeed, other schools of economics and political economy are generally attached to horizontal approaches to consumption. There are two reasons for this and one consequence.

The first reason is that consumption has often been deployed as a terrain on which to exercise established intra-disciplinary theory. This is especially so with the rapid emergence of consumption to academic prominence over the last twenty years. Whilst working within a discipline, it is realised that there is a chance to address something new. The easiest way in which to do so is to apply existing knowledge. Within sociology, consumption becomes a matter of stratification, of emulation and distinction. For psychology, it is the realisation of underlying propensities. The second reason for the predominance of horizontal approaches is because of the understandable wish to generalise from particular case studies and to draw out wider implications. If fashion, car and housing signify identity, gender and status, let us posit the latter as elements in a theory of consumption.

This account of the prominence of horizontal analysis is far from complete; it is both stylised and neglects the equally important processes by which scholars reflect back upon and transform what they have previously collectively created. In this respect, the predominance of horizontal analyses has had the consequence of impeding satisfactory integration across the various approaches. This is true of interdisciplinarity as well as of different explanatory variables. For the latter, at a general level, there is the now increasingly recognised difficulty of integrating the material with the cultural. But the same applies to the constituent elements that make up sops – the relationship between production, design, retailing and, ultimately, consumption itself. Those who have sought a synthesis across various intra-disciplinary, but horizontal, contributions to consumption have inevitably been unsuccessful. Stacking horizontal theories on top of, or alongside, each other, throwing in all the relevant variables, is simply more of the same, not much better in any other sense. Fine and Leopold (1993: Chapter 3) demonstrate this through the valiant but vain attempt of the, predominantly US, discipline of consumer studies to provide both coherence and an identity for itself. Instead, it has self-confessedly been in a chronic state of disarray. We have an accumulating mass of case studies, and an equally significant if less numerous portfolio of theories drawn from the social sciences. The more the portfolio expands, the more it feeds upon itself, creating space for new studies on the basis of the rationale provided by the old. Overall, the discipline thrives but lacks coherence. Much the same has occurred across the more scholarly following but generally less market-oriented study of consumption across the social sciences.

Such disorder can be addressed by substituting 'vertical' for horizontal analysis and addressing consumption through sops.[3] In order to articulate the different horizontal theories, and the explanatory factors that they incorporate, it is both necessary to trace the path from production through to consumption and to 'descend' to the level of particular commodities so that the appropriate degree of specificity can be addressed across the material and cultural factors underlying consumption. This is necessary both for those seeking to move from the material to the cultural and vice versa. For those who wish to rectify the cultural turn attached to postmodernism, it is first necessary to recognise that it departs the moment of exchange by journeying to, and focusing upon, the act of consumption. The world left behind is variously described as the economy, or even reduced to production, as opposed to culture and consumption. Far from being a dark, unseen and unknown world, it is presumed to have been unduly privileged as determinant and object of study. Yet its corresponding literature has not stood still as postmodernist accounts of consumption have prospered and become dominant. Indeed, considerable attention has been devoted to how consumption is provided, tracing a route back from the moment of exchange in the opposite direction to consumption.[4] Even so, it does include some account of the culture of consumption since those involved in supply do seek to address this themselves in order to promote sales successfully.[5] Consequently, attention is drawn not only to production but also to the range of activities that connect it with consumption and how these condition one another. In this respect, another obstacle, of a horizontal character, to the study of consumption has been exposed and, to some extent, overcome in the literature. This has been the over-reliance upon ideal types, initially focusing on mass production/consumption, Fordism or whatever and, subsequently, setting it against the alternative of flexible specialisation, or neo- or post-Fordism.[6] Scranton (1998), in particular, has offered the most sophisticated account of the development of different forms of production. Whilst wishing to redress the balance against the notion of an historically rampant Fordism, he is equally convincing on the heterogeneity of the organisation of production where it departs from the archetype feedstock for mass, or niche, consumption.[7] In an explicit discussion around consumer society, Scranton (1994: 505) concludes:

> Unpacking the category 'consumer goods' to reveal the variety of production systems involved in provisioning a public could have a useful result in acclimatizing scholars of consumer societies to the complexity of the networks of design, technology, labor process, and distribution involved in the historical mutations of manufacturing.

There are three important aspects to Scranton's contributions. First, he covers a very wide range of factors – even a partial list would include technology, labour process, market and skills, design, management and organisation, finance, product diversity and differentiation, (sub)contracting, advertising, distribution and retailing, quite apart from the role of the state and regulation, on the one hand, and the significance of particular geographical locations, especially cities, on the other.[8] Second, these separate elements cannot be put together randomly but neither are they in a fixed relationship to one another. In addition, there are relations across the diverse forms of production – mass production, for example, can be a source of cheap inputs, of demand for other types of products and production as well as providing a source of entrepreneurs, who would otherwise be deskilled, or of unskilled labour arising out of productivity increase and rationalisation. Third, Scranton (1998: 10) suggests these factors resolve themselves into 'four broad approaches to the business of making goods and meeting needs – custom, batch, bulk, and mass production'.

However valid the apparent reliance upon four ideal types in place of two, the crucial point from Scranton's analysis remains the diversity not only in production and products but in the whole sequence and structure of activities through which commodities are delivered to the consumer. A similar conclusion can be drawn from those studies that have taken aspects of the delivery of consumption apart from production as their starting point, with diversity across both product and time. This is true of retailing, marketing and advertising, for example, as illustrated by the studies of Corley (1987) for DIY goods, brewers and tied houses, and product differentiation within Lever Brothers, by Westall (1994) for insurance, and for the retailing of tobacco products by Hilton (1998).

Three important conclusions can be drawn from this cursory review. First, the production of commodities is heavily dependent upon a multiplicity of factors, which lie outside the immediate domain of production itself. Few outside mainstream economics would reduce production to the optimal choice from available technology in light of input prices and demand conditions. Yet, equally, many may have neglected the extent to which production depends upon design, marketing, retailing, etc. It is, in other words, not only consumption that has been neglected in the analysis of production. Second, it is not only a matter of a multiplicity of factors but also how they are integrated with one another. As recognised in the sop approach, the outcome is distinctive sops for consumption which are set apart from one another and incorporate structures and dynamics of their own. Third, such sops, whether accepted as such or not, are dependent upon particular patterns of vertical integration and disintegration, since the activities concerned are generally sequenced (design, production, sale, etc.) with their being more or less incorporated under common or separate organisational forms (Langlois and Cosgel 1998).

Here, once again, mainstream industrial economics is particularly weak, even by its own account. Formal deterministic models are entirely ambiguous in predicting outcomes. As argued in Fine (1999d), in a critical review of Sutton's (1991) treatment of competition and market structure, the mainstream's approach to vertical integration is essentially to see it as modifying or as a modified form of horizontal competition.[9] This is a consequence of the failure to confront the dynamic factors and tensions underlying the restructuring of the economy in general as well as of particular sectors.

In contrast, in this context, Marx's theory of production has much to offer, both in method and substance. He argues that the accumulation of capital is subject to two contradictory tendencies attached to its development of the division of labour (how work is organised and done within and between places of production as defined by the market). On the one hand, separate trades are brought together to exploit what would in modern parlance be termed the economies of scope. On the other hand, production processes can be subdivided and form the basis for new sectors, thereby accruing economies of scale. Consequently, the drive for productivity increase depends upon the outcome of a competitive process. It cannot be predetermined as it depends upon the combination of factors attached to production and outlined above and which condition the competitive process. Further, the tension between these underlying tendencies and the socio-economic conditions that accompany them provides a sound basis on which to comprehend the diversity of production revealed by Scranton. It is not a prediction of inevitable trend for the incorporation of production into a single Fordist form, or other numbers of ideal types.[10]

Locating the aesthetic illusion

The rest of this chapter extends the theoretical groundwork for the exploration of sops by returning to the earlier discussion of the two basic properties of commodities: use value and exchange value. Despite their being common to all goods, even simple and abstract analyses in the context of capitalism tend to cut them off from one another, concentrating exclusively on one property or the other. This produces a limited and skewed view of commodities, although it can also stimulate fruitful debate and furnish empirical insights. The work of Haug (1986) is in part an exception, since he confronts the relationship between the commodity as use value and exchange value, exploring their dialectical interaction and how they can be made compatible with one another. Although far from prominent, his ideas warrant close attention.

Haug has focused on the way in which the imperatives of capitalist production create a tension between the changing material content of the commodity and its meaning as a purchased item of consumption. Although the scope of his analysis is too restrictive, limited to the disguise of product degradation through the endowment of commodities with a degree of sexuality, it does provide an introduction to other critical elements of analysis taken up in the next section. These elements include the broad issues of periodising capitalism (into stages with corresponding structures of consumption) and the role of historical contingency (the continuing influence into the present of constructions of consumption carried over from the past). Whilst a variety of capitalist imperatives, structures and processes apply *across* the economy and society which vary between one stage of capitalism and another, their incidence and mutual interaction for particular commodities give rise to historically contingent sops that differ one from another.

Subject to income and availability, individuals exercise choice over what they consume. In exploring this activity, a great deal of emphasis has been placed on those influences that lead the individual consumer to choose in a particular way. Within economics, choice is governed by the maximisation of utility, derived from given (unexamined) preferences. Psychology endows the individual with a wider variety of motivations, some of which are partially intrinsic, like appetite, while others are extrinsic or socially derived, like emulation of those in higher income groups. This duality is mirrored on the other side of the transaction: commodities themselves also combine intrinsic, physical properties of use value (flavour, texture, etc.) with some perception of this use value, which is extrinsic to the commodity itself and socially constructed. The sweetness of chocolate, for example, is both a physical and a psychological property; the latter is intricately and intimately conflated with the human characteristics of sweetness.

Consequently, choice must be seen as a relationship between the individual and the commodity. This has sometimes inappropriately been cast as a relationship between equals; in this context, either the commodity takes on human attributes or the individual is dehumanised, reduced to the status of calculating machine or animal, as in economics and psychology. But, leaving aside this reification and anthropomorphism, other pertinent questions surrounding the commodity's use value need to be addressed. Going behind immediate physical properties, how do the economic origins of a commodity affect the way in which it is perceived as a use value for consumption? This is the mirror image of the question that asks what the individual consumer brings to the act of consumption.

First, there is a relationship between the commodity's physical properties and how it is perceived. At the most basic level, this implies that given commodities are interpreted as use values within what are definite limits, although these might be remarkably elastic. A motor car cannot literally satisfy a hunger, other than metaphorically speaking. Most notably, advertising attempts to endow commodities with properties over and above their capacity to achieve them – even in the imagination. More generally, the elasticity of the meaning of commodities in consumption is tied to the changing physical content of the commodities themselves. If the origin of the commodity is traced back to production, then as production processes change, so can the nature of the products. Thus, elasticity in the meaning of commodities derives both from the changing interpretation of given physical use values and from unchanging interpretation of potentially changing use values.

An example of the latter is provided by the technical changes that have facilitated the preparation and packaging of whole meals rather than of individual foods. Eating out in a restaurant, or buying bread from the 'local' baker, creates the impression of a more personalised service than that associated with a fast-food outlet or shopping in a supermarket. Yet the restaurant may simply be concealing a growing dependence on the delivery of mass-produced or pre-prepared meals ready for its kitchen's microwave, just as the local baker may depend on the delivery of mass-produced frozen dough. Supermarkets, with in-store bakeries to satisfy as wide a range of shopping needs as possible, may artificially generate the smell of freshly baked bread.

This raises a second question – how does the changing meaning of commodities in turn affect the physical content of the commodities themselves? The question goes beyond the issue of consumer sovereignty, which assumes that given preferences are satisfied by given commodities or not, but does not question the derivation or transformation of preferences themselves. Rather, it concerns the dialectic between the changing meaning of commodities and their changing content, irrespective of consumer sovereignty. To give a simple example, the recent fashion for healthy foods has led to a variety of products claiming to be 'natural', accompanied by an equally variable change of both meaning and content. Any food that advertises itself as only containing natural ingredients is liable to be full of sugar – true but misleading from the point of view of associating healthy with natural, see Chapter 11 for further discussion.

There is then a complex and shifting relation between the two aspects of the use value of a commodity – its physical content and its interpretation. Too often this complex relationship has been treated too one-sidedly. Those focusing narrowly on consumption alone tend to examine the meaning of commodities to consumers (i.e. what it is sold as); little attention is paid to the tension between this image of the commodity and what it actually is. On the other hand, there are those whose concern is primarily with the quality and cost of the commodity, at the expense of how it is perceived by the consumer. Haug (1986) has made an attempt to bring these issues together. His discussion of what he calls the 'aesthetic illusion' draws the distinction between what is produced and how it is presented and perceived and examines how they interact.

His starting point is that the need for the capitalist to guarantee sale makes it necessary to present the commodity as desirable: 'The lust for money is the reason why, under capitalist production, the commodity is presented in the image of the consumer's desires' (Haug 1986: 24). But this does not go far enough; it might also apply to non-capitalist commodity production and it also still leaves the consumer's desires undetermined. To supply a plausible source for the latter, Haug emphasises the role of sexuality in the formation of an illusory content in commodities – although sexuality also has a history that would need to be elaborated and explained. Beginning with the exchange process, Haug suggests that commodities borrow their aesthetic language from human courtship.[11] Its attributes are then universally projected onto all commodities: 'It is not the sexual object which takes on the commodity form, but the tendency of all objects of use in commodity-form to assume a sexual form to some extent ... exchange value transforms itself into sexuality' (Haug 1986: 55). Of course, at times, sexuality itself takes on a commodity form as in prostitution – but also more generally in pornography.

The commodity as an object of consumption may become endowed in modern parlance with the properties of a sex object, although the term is usually associated with the sexual reification of women rather than with the eroticising of objects. These properties then become desirable aspects of the commodity. Cars must appear to incorporate a sex drive, although they are not a sex drive in themselves. For Haug, the attempt to bridge the gap between what the commodity is and the preferred use value is undertaken by advertising.

No doubt the roles of sexuality and of advertising are exaggerated. There are plenty of other social relations on offer to form the illusory content of commodities, and the gap between these illusions and the real thing is not only, nor necessarily predominantly, determined and filled by advertising. The media, the state and the family are, for example, primary sites for the creation, reproduction and the satisfaction of needs, although the balance between the commodity and non-commodity forms of provision has a different and shifting balance for each, as does the nature and role of advertising.[12] But, once advertising is itself recognised as a factor influencing sexuality, the structure of the analysis is compelling because it offers and draws upon a dynamic and contradictory relationship between the commodity as a use value and the commodity as an exchange value.

There is always a potential gap between the commodity's (physical) use value and its imputed use value, and this gap varies both with the product itself and its endowed sexuality. Moreover, the determining motive behind this structured gap, and its dynamic as its jaws open and close, is the wish to guarantee sale. This is a competitive process within and across the various sectors of the economy. If, for the sake of argument alone, it is presumed that the levels and nature of advertising vary with the size distribution of firms within a sector, then the aesthetic illusion (and its real effects on the commodity over time) will differ between one sector and another. More generally, the dialectic between the material and illusory content of commodities will vary from one to another, according to how the competitive process works out in practice. The endowed sexuality of each product will be as distinct as its material properties. Indeed, some, if not all, products are liable to be divided by gendering, partly as a consequence of advertising even if in conjunction with other sources of gender roles – it does not, for example, need advertising to make kitchen products primarily female.

Already the relationship between commodity, sexuality, advertising and competition in this analysis reveals that different commodities are ideologically constructed according to a logic that is not uniform across them. Cars are gendered as male. Chocolates are gendered as feminine in a way that differs from the gendering of household items employed in domestic chores. However these sex types are constructed and assigned to commodities, capital is stretched between ensuring sale through widening the illusory gap (and getting away with the illusion) or, potentially, attempting to close it through modification of the material content of the commodity itself. Chocolate can be made sweeter, motor cars more powerful; the aesthetic illusion is not simply the commercially led misrepresentation of given use values. The latter themselves change in response to the dialectic surrounding their reconstructed and illusory properties.

Haug also locates the analysis within the realm of *capitalist* commodity production. He associates the movement from luxury to mass consumption with the transition from *laissez-faire* to monopoly capitalism: 'From now on it is no longer primarily expensive luxury commodities that determine big business but relatively cheap mass-produced articles' (Haug 1986: 22–3). The imperative of profitability is seen to have a number of effects in the era of monopoly capitalism. First, there is the attempt to reduce the cost of production (irrespective of the productivity increase through the use of machinery) through taking less time to bring the commodities to market, by including less labour within them and by cheapening and reducing the quantity of raw materials that are used. For Haug, since this inevitably worsens the quality of the product, it leads to a widening of the gap to be bridged by the aesthetic illusion (p. 23).

Second, in order to sustain demand, there is an attempt to build obsolescence into commodities so that replacement consumption is essential. This can either come from qualitative obsolescence (as dictated by the fashion system, which makes use values irrelevant before they are physically exhausted) or it can come through quantitative obsolescence (the use of defective design with no gain in cost reduction in order to guarantee replacement demand). As Lefebvre comments:

> Obsolescence … experts are well acquainted with the life-expectancy of objects … such statistics are part of the demography of objects and are correlated to the cost of production and profit. … To this familiar theory we add two observations; first, the *obsolescence of needs* … secondly … an extreme *fluidity* of existence.
>
> (Lefebvre 1971: 81–2)

What is the significance of these two factors, lower cost at the expense of quality and obsolescence, planned or otherwise? They certainly correspond to our casual, empirical experience as consumers. Appliances, especially motor cars, do wear out unnecessarily quickly. On the other hand, consumers (and producers in turn) do become aware of this and require (at least the illusion of) longer lasting products. Much the same is true of product quality. So, once again, the forces acting upon the aesthetic illusion are both complex and subject to a wide set of varied influences and outcomes. In the case of the automobile, for example, the illusion of masculinity entailed not just obsolescence of the product by model change (and status by changing with it). There was also the *addition* of unnecessarily heavy and dangerous bodywork to represent speed, power and strength – the issue that prompted the emergence of Ralph Nader and the modern US consumer movement.

In short, Haug has provided some theoretical insights for examining the dynamic, social reconstruction of use value, although his analysis is over-generalised, exaggerating certain tendencies and excluding others. But a crucial general conclusion can, nonetheless, be drawn. The commodity as a use value bound for consumption and as an exchange value deriving from capitalist production necessarily across each of these facets exhibits a potential diversity of development. How these two aspects are bound together and mutually change or support each other is key to the understanding of consumption. But even at this abstract level, imperatives of profitability and of sexuality give rise to outcomes that are distinct between commodities. Consequently, even before consumption is explored more deeply through the imperative of profitability and for ideological determinants across a wider terrain than sexuality alone, it already follows that the sop of each commodity is potentially unique.

There is, however, a serious problem with Haug's notion of aesthetic illusion. He poses the illusion in terms of bridging the gap between the shifting material properties of the commodity and how it is perceived. Sale must be guaranteed even though the material properties change, and culture, especially through advertising and sexuality, does the trick. This involves much too sharp a separation between the origins of the material and cultural properties of the commodity. This can be seen in two ways.

First, the idea of aesthetic illusion as 'gap' between material properties and perception is questionable. An objection might legitimately be based on ontological grounds with an apparent assumption of a falsely perceived but given world of objects of consumption. This is not what is of immediate concern. Rather, the idea of an aesthetic illusion leaves unexplained how the original aesthetic arises; we only know that it must be transformed with shifting material properties, motivated by profitability.

Of course, it could be argued that the original aesthetic is historically given, contingent upon whatever illusions have been perpetrated in the past. This is, however, to shift to the second way of exposing the weakness in Haug's account. For him, it is as if the (shifting) material and cultural properties of the commodity are produced independently of one another, although some intimacy must be established between them. It is almost like a game of ping-pong with the material and cultural taking turns to bat the ball to one another. We can take any shot in the game as starting point. But what if both players are on both sides of the net, and the game changes faster than they play it?! In short, matters look very different if the same processes that produce the material properties of the commodity also contribute to its cultural content. As Slater and Tonkiss (2001: 180) put it:[13]

> Aestheticization features in all stages of a commodity's life cycle and indeed draws together processual moments – production, circulation and consumption – which have been regarded as separate by earlier economic and social thought.

So the aesthetic illusion is inevitably more deeply rooted than a form of deceit at the point of sale and purchase. Advertising and design are inextricably and often deliberately linked, as are design and production. These are all cultural as well as material activities and, as such, influence, however indirectly, the cultural properties of the commodity as item of consumption. For this reason, Haug's aesthetic illusion is inadequate not simply or primarily because of the limited focus upon advertising and sexuality to which other aspects can be added. He is also insufficiently attentive to the systemic character of the culture of consumption, how it derives from points and factors throughout the sop. This will be taken up in the next chapter.

Stages, structures and contingency

As observed in the previous section, Haug dates the growing significance of the aesthetic illusion from the time of the transition from luxury to mass consumption, which can be alternatively identified with the transition from *laissez-faire* to monopoly capitalism. Such analysis needs to be taken further both in its depth and in its historical specificity. Within *laissez-faire* capitalism, for example, the defining characteristic is less the dominant mode of the illusory consumption of the rich as the mode of exploitation of the poor. Productivity increase is less important than the extension of the working day for men, women and children. In Marx's terms, there is greater dependence upon the production of absolute surplus value. Such extensive exploitation of labour implies that there are limits to the transformation of the production process[14] and, as a result, there are also limits on the displacement of one type of raw material by another as a consequence of changes in production methods.

The same is not necessarily true of the content of products. Because competition tends to be across fragmented, small-scale producers, intense market competition leads, on the one hand, to the imperative by producers to adulterate their products and, on the other hand, to the need for consumers to discriminate between the good, the bad and the ugly. Inevitably, competitive survival dictates that those who refuse to adulterate their products will be competitively eliminated (just as, by analogy, there is no choice but to employ child labour whatever the benevolent intentions of the employer).[15]

Further, in order to associate the aesthetic illusion with the rise of advertising, Haug neglects its place in the earlier period of capitalism, perhaps because the potential for such illusion was constrained by the very limited consumption of the poor, often bordering on the edge of physical survival. There are, for example, two competing or complementary explanations for the development of the habit of tea drinking amongst the British working class, neither of which owes much, if anything, to the aesthetic illusion. One is emulation of the upper classes; the other is to create the illusion of a hot and satisfying meal when diet is otherwise confined to lumps of bread, cheese and dripping. Nevertheless, there are always some illusions around consumption, and these are not necessarily the poorer for belonging to those poor in consumption – otherwise anthropologists and ethnography would long have been rendered redundant. However, as Haug suggests, under capitalism in its early stages, the preferred focus for the aesthetic illusion is to be found more in the luxury consumption of the wealthy. This itself often depends upon commodities produced by highly labour-intensive and skilled methods or through self-employed, 'unproductive' labour directly employed outside the control of capital.

The arrival of monopoly capitalism is accompanied by substantial differences, which go well beyond those identified by Haug. This is the age of the factory and of large-scale machinery. First of all, competition works primarily through the cheapening of commodities, fought through productivity increase rather than through a decline in product quality. Nonetheless, monopolisation does create the potential for formal or informal collusion (without thereby eliminating competition). Not only may this take the form of price-fixing cartels; it may also be conducive to the creation of particular norms in the aesthetic illusion surrounding the mass consumption of the working class – through, for example, an expansion in goods falling sway to the fashion system or through the failure to provide long-lasting products. The provision of high-quality goods, whether embodying extra or even lower levels of costs, may be subordinated to other non-material aspects of the commodity. For example, Haug (1986: 26) highlights the illusory status value of some commodities by pointing to the 'same' goods being sold at different prices; the higher priced goods enjoy the illusion of higher quality (in a neat inversion of the laws of political economy, for which price is an index of cost of production). A general mechanism through which this is achieved is branding. Often, of course, created by advertising, branding works in part precisely by 'enhancing' the quality of a product merely by virtue of its name and irrespective of its immediate material content.

It would, however, be wrong to presume that there is no consumer reaction against the widening gap between the commodity and its image, which the brand name is intended to fill. Consumers can be sceptical about the quality of what they buy and can initiate a counterculture, expressed in one form as the desire for the 'real thing' or its equivalent. This has been particularly prominent in the success of unbranded goods, especially in US supermarkets or, significantly, in retailers developing their own brands, although these may be sourced from the very same producers as the branded product. It cannot be presumed that the reaction against illusion is purely the product of a restless consumer movement rather than a lever in the competitive struggle within retailing and between retailers and producers; nor that what is 'real' is not itself subject to illusion – as evidenced by the 'Real Thing' (Coca-Cola), the so-called ploughman's lunch, or by the seizure of the 'natural' or 'traditional' in foods, used as a selling point for the mass product serving the health craze.[16]

Adulteration and contamination are also transformed under the sway of monopoly capitalism. Certainly, the occasional wine is still laced with poison to preserve or to mature it. But, contemporary with the protective legislation on behalf of the working class (Marx's discussion is primarily concerned with the length of the working day), so the crudest forms of adulteration have long been legally proscribed. This serves to reduce the cost of reproducing labour power – other capitalists do not benefit from fellow grocers selling chalk as cheese. It also diminishes the competitive position of small-scale producers, who tend to depend on the poorest quality, in product as well as labour conditions, in order to survive.

Adulteration, however, does take on a new form and new names, as revealed by Haug. It is the displacement of existing raw materials rather than their reduction (or veiled replacement). The machine age is one in which both production processes and products are revolutionised. Most notably, fresh – dare one say natural? – ingredients are displaced by the artificial, perhaps most often in the case of food. For bread, the preference for the use of white flour has been motivated by its keeping longer, holding more air and water, requiring less skill in baking, and facilitating the sale of the bran and germ extracted as animal feed (Cannon 1987). More generally, chemical additives reduce costs, add colour for presentation (so that orange flavour really does become artificial in colour) and act as preservatives. An equally important development is the rise of convenience foods. This is strongly linked to the growing labour market participation of women with children and, consequently, cannot be read off either from the needs of the economy or from the illusion of preserving whilst transforming the nature of, and need for, 'home cooking'. It is heavily determined by the changing nature of the family, following the demographic transition in the fifty years around the turn of the last century (Fine 1992).

Nor can it be presumed that the modern form of adulteration is exclusively an issue of less and different (cheaper) inputs, as has already been illustrated by the history of the US automobile. Here, the extraordinary growth in the dimensions of the models – even to the extent of their becoming grossly inefficient and unsafe – reflected in part the monopolisation of the industry in which more cars could be sold by adding costly features. And cartel collusion prevented the emergence of small-scale, long-lasting alternatives. But the industry was also a reflection of the power of US imperialism with its global command of raw materials and ability to source inputs, to manufacture and to drive these domestic 'tanks'.

This is not a simple matter of tension between the aesthetic illusion and the so-called 'adulteration' of the motor car. It depended upon a range of forces derived from twentieth-century capitalism and from the US hegemony within it at a global level, demonstrated by the subsequent decline of these monster automobile models. Whilst the consumer movement's role in undermining the market for 'gas-guzzlers' should not be underestimated, attention should also be drawn to the eventual emergence of competition from smaller scale imports (not least the VW 'Beetle' as a Trojan horse for the Japanese) and the increasing price of oil.

Thus, there are systematic differences in the formation and the resolution of the aesthetic illusion between *laissez-faire* and monopoly capitalism arising from the different imperatives by which profitability is pursued. Such differences extend more generally to other aspects of economic organisation, not only through advertising, but also through cartelisation, finance, distribution and marketing more generally. These are all transformed between the two stages of capitalism with potential significance for the location and intensity of the aesthetic illusion. And there are also pertinent differences in the non-economic arena in the social reproduction of the workforce, the nature of the family, etc. The transition to mass production is associated with shifts in a variety of other relations, apart from that in consumption, as denoted by the transport, communications, demographic and domestic revolutions – each of which has a general and detailed impact upon the reconstruction of consumption in thought and deed. In addition, the separate elements of provisioning tend to become distinguished from one another, with separate professions emerging for design, advertising and marketing etc.

As important as the differences *between* stages of capitalism in the determination of consumption are the tensions *within* a stage between its various determinants. A number of these have already been identified for monopoly capitalism, not least Haug's conflict between the material degradation of the product and its ideological enhancement, whether by sexuality or by other means. Further, monopoly capitalism also pits modern forms of adulteration against *improvements* in materials, production processes and products. To some extent, Haug has fallen prey to the illusion that traditional products are superior to their modern equivalents or replacements. But the marked advances in the material quality of many products are, in fact, no mere illusion despite the occasionally deceptive use of scientific or technological wizardry as a selling point.

How are the various influences derived from production or otherwise on the formation of consumption to be integrated? First, each contributing factor (production etc.) may obtain across the economy as a whole or, as in the case of sexuality, across society. The imperatives associated with profitability or with disguising the commodity apply in principle to each sector embracing, for example, cars as well as food and clothing. For this reason, their use as explanatory variables has previously been termed 'horizontal' as they are interpreted broadly across all consumption items.

Horizontal influences should be seen as tendencies whose strength varies between one commodity and another. Variations might reflect differences in the material composition of the commodity itself, differences which will affect the potential scope for adulteration, productivity increase, etc., and will themselves be influenced by competition between capitals and the conflicts over the conditions of the manufacturing system.

The interaction of these determinants will give rise to specific structures of provision that vary from one commodity to the next, partly because of the different strengths of the tendencies concerned and partly because their interaction can be different. Does it lead, for example, to structured degradation, obsolescence or even quality enhancement? The term 'vertical' has been used to distinguish between specific structures of provision of consumption goods that result from the interaction of horizontal factors. Consequently, vertically there is potentially a different *system of provision* associated with each commodity. Whilst the logical foundation for this approach has been provided through the elementary anatomy of the commodity, with Haug's analysis as entry point through profitability, sexuality, advertising and the aesthetic illusion, these factors neither suffice nor are necessarily the most decisive in any one sop.

Consequently, a sop (in, for example, housing, food or fashion) is taken to denote the articulation of economic and social factors that give rise both to the level and composition of consumption (quantitative aspect) and the meanings with which it is endowed (qualitative aspect). Inevitably, different authors who are engaged in this field approach their subject area with a wider or narrower analytical and historical scope. Haug describes the transport system thus: 'the private car, together with the running-down of public transport, carves up the towns no less effectively than saturation bombing, and creates distances that can no longer be crossed without a car' (Haug 1986: 54). For Ball (1983) housing is discussed in terms of a structure of provision which runs from the plot of building land, through the many aspects of the production process with its associated agencies, to the housing market itself (rather than as a system of differing forms of tenancy); Goody (1982: 37) sees food in terms of the five phases of production, distribution, preparation, consumption and disposal.

Initially, the analytical focus of academic work has been predominantly upon the relation between production and consumption and between the material and ideological content of the commodity. In practice, a sop entails a more comprehensive chain of activities between the two extremes of production and consumption, each link of which plays a potentially significant role in the social construction of the commodity both in its material and cultural aspects. This has increasingly been recognised in the study of consumption. In other words, distribution, finance and marketing are all important components of provision. Advertising, after all, is only one component itself of marketing; sexuality only one component of the ideological content of commodities.

Finally, the role of historical contingency must also be acknowledged. Each structure of provision contains developmental tensions within it but these must be sufficiently compatible or articulated to enable the system to deliver the goods. They must also, for the commodity to survive, be able to accommodate change over time. How change occurs and how extensive it is will be contingent upon the extent and relative strength of persisting elements along the chain of provision and, to some degree, on the internal or external mechanisms that trigger change.

A simple example will illustrate the point. It is well known, as documented by Noble (1985), that the needs of the military have been highly important in accelerating the development of some consumer goods through the transfer from the military to the civilian arena of technology, production, innovative organisations of work and the products themselves. Historically, the supply of military uniforms acted as a stimulus to the mass production of civilian clothing, just as government provision of biscuits and canned goods hastened the pace of innovation in the preservation of foods.[17] The first system of standardised clothing sizes, for example, was introduced in the American Civil War in response to the sudden large-scale demand for soldiers' uniforms. After the war, the ready availability of standard sizes gave a spur to the mechanised development of men's clothing, particularly men's work clothes. This stimulus was not transferable to the production of women's clothing, which continued to lag behind that of men's well into the twentieth century.

Some war-triggered innovations fail to have a lasting effect; in the UK, witness the postwar displacement of women workers from factories, the corresponding disappearance of full-time workplace nurseries, and the closure of subsidised restaurants serving nutritionally balanced meals at cost. Other innovations, however, did take hold: workplace canteens became commonplace, as did the provision of school meals. The survival of some government-sponsored interventions but not others points to the multiplicity of often competing factors at work that determine, at the end of a long chain, the goods and services available at any one time.

In another sector, the history of sugar offers a different illustration of the impact of historical contingency on the pattern of consumption, Fine *et al.* (1996: Chapters 5 and 6). The fact that the UK still maintains one of the highest per capita consumptions of sugar in the world testifies to the enduring effects of its imperial past (Mintz 1985); the patterns of the UK's cultural and economic domination remain visible in the British diet today. The reality of slavery is lost in an illusion of sweetness (much as a diamond is for ever if not the apartheid system that produced it). Historically, sugar served as a luxury item of consumption – as a medicine, a decoration or a spice (accompanying 'all things nice'). With colonisation and the proletarianisation of the British workforce, it became a cheap source of energy in the hot meal provided by a cup of tea. In the modern period, its association with dental decay and heart disease has led to a drop in the consumption of sugar direct from the bowl. But the level of two pounds (0.9 kg) per head per week has been maintained, much to the advantage of capital's productive capacity, through the increasing use of sugar as an additive to preserve and sweeten manufactured foods. As such, it has the added advantage of being a 'natural' ingredient for advertising purposes.[18] In this way, the earlier dependence upon sugar as a part of the British diet has been preserved in line with the interests of the sugar industry.

Even so, sugar's structured continuity with its past has been subject to erosion. The British refining industry has been associated with cane sugar, predominantly from the Commonwealth, whereas its new ties are with the European Union, which has depended exclusively on home-grown sugar beet. Sugar is also vulnerable to overproduction and the rise of corn syrup and artificial sweeteners. In these and other respects, the consumption of sugar bears the markings of influences not shared by the consumption of other foods like cheese and milk. Yet these distinctions tend to disappear in discussions of food advertising, for example, where the meaning of a product as presented is divorced from the meaning derived from its origins so that the cases of both sugar and cheese may inappropriately be used as generalisable examples to support broader cultural or economic arguments.

Differentiating and identifying those critical factors that have profoundly influenced the character of consumption (public sector purchasing and imperialism in the cases of clothing and sugar cited above) emphasises the heterogeneity of factors at work, and opens up the possibility of a much richer discussion of consumption. The vertical approach applied here, concerned with the linkages along the chain from production to consumption, does not refute the presence and importance of horizontal factors that may be common to more than one sop. But it suggests that these are liable to play a different role within each sop. This is true both of cultural and material factors; products are advertised *and* produced differently, and these differences apply equally to distribution, marketing and consumption itself. But there must also be some overall coherence in how these elements are integrated and developed, even if subject to contradictory forces.

Such is the subject of Fine and Leopold (1993: Part III), where the approach based on sops is illustrated by analyses of retailing, advertising, food, clothing and the role of consumption in the Industrial Revolution. Their content is far from comprehensive, even within their selected vertical and horizontal areas of focus. Hopefully, they serve to demonstrate what can and needs to be done in understanding consumption and in moving beyond those half-serious maxims of consumerism – 'When the going gets tough, the tough go shopping'; 'I shop, therefore I am' – which have informed the latest fashions in the study of material culture.

6

SYSTEMS OF PROVISION AND CULTURAL SYSTEMS

Introduction

This chapter builds upon the groundwork of the previous one by positing a cultural system as being attached to each system of provision (sop). It does so by examining how cultural and material analyses can be integrated or, more exactly, integral, specifically rejecting the idea of a *circuit* of culture in favour of a cultural *system*. The second section reviews a number of approaches to the culture of consumption, examining how some have broached the task by bringing culture back into the economy and others vice versa. This allows the idea of a circuit of culture to be identified as a sort of parody of the circuit of capital. It is shown to form the basis for a useful but limited approach to the relationship between culture and economy, for which the relations and structures attached to capitalism are incorporated as well as the sites to and from which culture purportedly moves. The third section revisits some of the material from the previous chapter in light of the now enriched understanding of culture, re-examining the material basis of structures, tendencies and periodisation in the context of consumption. Finally, in the fourth section, the sop approach is clarified by responding to a range of criticisms that it has attracted and by providing illustrations of the approach from the literature. These complement the case studies previously presented in Fine and Leopold (1993), Fine *et al.* (1996) and Fine (1998c).

Cultural systems

As is apparent from the previous chapter, the attempt to integrate material and cultural studies is far from new. Such endeavour has strengthened over the past decade or so, as consumption studies have taken the issue more seriously. In particular, with postmodernism on the wane, for consumption as more generally, it is a matter of bringing the economy back in, a theme that recurs throughout the literature from a variety of perspectives. Sayer (1997) denies the separation between culture and economy, Carrier and Heyman (1997: 369) 'use the realm of class to point out that consumption strategies cannot be analysed solely in terms of the meanings of objects', and Leslie (1998) locates consumer subjectivity (and

101

advertising) within the context of place and space. For Blomley (1996: 238), 'a retail geography worthy of its name ... must take both its economic and its cultural geographies seriously'. Fardon (1999: 402) bemoans that '"hard" social science produces the discourse on making things, while "soft" social science specializes in studies of using them'. Livingston (1994: xv) observes 'fields that stopped talking to each other around twenty years ago, when the "new economic history" and the "new social history" partitioned the discipline and encouraged the settlement of their respective territories'. Beng-Huat (2000b: 199) concludes a study of Singaporeans ingesting McDonald's with the judgement that, 'in the selling of McDonald's, as in any imported goods, economic interest is strategic while its cultural representation to achieve this interest is always simply tactical'. Warde and Martens (2000: 10) draw the following implication from a broader menu for eating out:

> Despite some significant theoretical developments like Featherstone's nuanced incorporation of insights from postmodernist speculation within a cultural studies tradition and Fine and Leopold's exposition of a 'systems of provision' approach deriving from political economy, there remains a need to develop more fully and integrated understanding of the relationship between consumption and production.

But bringing the economy back in with culture (as well as vice versa) is easier said than done or, rather too easily done in view of the double fetishism perpetrated by Baudrillard, previously elaborated in Chapter 4. For how the economy is to be brought back in and, as important, what it is, are far from certain. Consider, for example, the defensiveness exhibited by Morley (1998: 492) in quoting Grossberg's (1995: 80) response to Garnham (1995) who bemoans the divorce between cultural studies and political economy:[1]

> 'Cultural studies did not reject political economy, it simply rejected certain versions of political economy as inadequate' because of their 'reduction of economics to the technological and institutional contexts of capitalist manufacturing ... their reduction of the market to the site of commodified and alienated exchange and (their) ahistorical and consequently oversimplified notions of capitalism'.

Significantly, the issue is not one of whether political economy should engage with the study of culture but what political economy and how, and exactly the same applies to related issues such as class and power, as well as production itself. For Morley (1998: 480) himself, there is a need to strike a balance between conjuncturalism and particularity and between categorisation and generalisation, 'to complement that perspective on the "vertical" dimension of media power, with a simultaneous address to its "horizontal/ritual dimension" (p. 487), and to find a defence against 'the eternal verities of political economy and the sociology of mass consumption' (p. 489). Bermingham (1995: 13) comes to a similar view:

> It is impossible to understand the history of consumption without also examining our conceptions of culture, the workings of culture, and ultimately subjectivity. In fact it has been the failure to do this which has resulted in the purely economistic accounts of consumption which see it in a secondary role after production or which focus on commodities rather than consumers.

The only general agreement, then, concerns antipathy to restoration of the (stylised) *ex ante* predominance of economy/production over, or at the expense of, consumption as most easily represented by the (equally stylised) Frankfurt School. Storey (1999: 22–3), for example, sees the latter in terms of privileging 'access' over 'use' and 'meaning', and asserts that 'political economy's idea of cultural analysis seems to involve very little more than detailing access to, and availability of, cultural texts and practices'. So, 'by reducing cultural consumption to simple questions of "access", the political-economy-of-culture approach threatens, despite its admirable intentions, to collapse everything back into the economic'. No one wants this but there is even doubt over whether there is a distinction between economy and culture, the denial of which leads Sayer (1997) to criticise Stuart Hall and his followers. And the flight from Baudrillard also raises the issues of the nature and content of causation and explanation.

Interestingly, much of the foregoing discussion draws upon the consumption of cultural products themselves particularly following the era of modernism (and the Frankfurt School) for which such artefacts have first become identified historically with high art and then come under threat as such from mass consumption (Bermingham 1995: 2–3).[2] Clearly, the culture attached to consumption has shifting meanings as we move across time, place and goods. Consequently, it is necessary to examine what cultures become attached to what goods, as well as those cultures that are not called upon, irrespective of whether the goods are defined as 'cultural' or not.[3] Thus, it is not surprising that the tension between political economy and culture should be especially taut when cultural goods are under consideration, for it is more or less unavoidable given the notion that commercialisation modifies the nature of the product, how it is produced and how it is received. Further, the cultural turn of consumption has motivated the notion that cultural commodities as a whole are distinct from others, as in the bringing together, for example, of the collection edited by Bermingham and Brewer (1995) concerned with 'The Consumption of Culture' and set apart from the earlier volume of Brewer and Porter (1993) attached to 'Consumption and the World of Goods'. Yet, there can be no presumption that the latter have any more in common with one another than the former's attention to 'Image, Object, Text' – nor that culture is any less important to the world of goods than it is to image, object and text.

103

Put in qualitative terms and subject to the vagaries of the meaning of culture, it is to be suspected that these conclusions are fully acceptable in principle to all other than those dedicated to some form of ahistoricism. The same applies to the inescapable implication for the future study of consumption: that it must seek to address the tension between economic and cultural factors, with consumption understood as the social construction and use of both things and ideas about those things. As Lee (1993: xi) puts it more specifically for the contemporary world of capitalism:

> The essence of all consumer goods can be found in the fact that they are, first and foremost, commodities ... produced in order to be exchanged for profit. ... Consumer goods have a social meaning, and that social meaning is, in the first instance, always contingent upon their status as commodities.

Further, he identifies the need to address economy and culture simultaneously 'for consumption is *the* social activity which, above all others, unites economy and culture' (p. xiii).[4]

It is, however, one thing to accept such conclusions in principle, quite another to put them into practice. Whilst much of the literature referenced above has been extraordinarily disparaging about the economics and political economy they have rejected, it can certainly be claimed that very little has been offered in its place (Lee 1993: 147). As a result, the reintroduction of the economy to the study of (the culture of) consumption is conducive to collective, if ordered, chaos. Indicative of the latter is the overview provided by Crang (1997: 3), for example, for whom there has been 'no single cultural turn'. Consequently, 'the economic and the cultural have long been cast as "self" and "other", each defined as what the other is not' (p. 4). He observes five aspects of the cultural turn in economic geography: the continuing opposition between economic and cultural; economic applied directly to cultural analysis; the economic as embedded in the cultural; the economic represented through the cultural; and the cultural (products) as increasingly economised (commodified). On the other hand, order is explicitly provided and eagerly grasped by many through the extremely influential notion of circuit of culture. This has been popularised in a series of Open University teaching texts (du Gay *et al.* 1996, du Gay 1997b, MacKay 1997b). These take a simple diagram for expositional purposes in which consumption, production, identity, representation and regulation are the five mutually conditioning and interconnected nodal points around which culture circulates. One immediate result is that culture is not the product of consumption but is generated, distributed and transformed or reconstituted along its entire circuit. As du Gay (1997a: 10) suggests, 'Our "circuit of culture" suggests that, in fact, meanings are produced at several different sites and circulated through several different processes and practices (the cultural circuit)'. The remainder of this section undertakes a critical dialogue with the idea of cultural circuits both to draw upon its rich contribution as well as to move to an alternative approach based on cultural systems (see Figure 1).

Whilst culture is structured by its circuit, it is not thereby unduly determined. As argued by Negus (1997: 73), culture is not derived exclusively from production as in 'the production of consumption perspective' since there is no 'neat fit (or fusion) between production and consumption' and we cannot 'explain the activities of consumers … simply from the way in which they [particular products] are produced'. And MacKay (1997a) offers a number of themes to explore in the journey around the circuit: creativity versus constraint; the distinct nature of consumption and production practices; the situated nature of everyday practices; the broad range of consumption practices; the need for qualitative and ethnographic research; and a spatial dimension.

A number of points need to be emphasised about this approach, not least because it has remained remarkably free of criticism.[5] First, as is acknowledged, it owes its origins to Johnson (1986), where a similar, if different, diagram is displayed.[6] This suggests, second, that the five nodal points are arbitrary in number and content. Why not others, especially through disaggregation and refinement?[7] Third, and in this Johnson bears a close (re)reading, answers to the questions that he poses, especially those concerning causation across nodes, have not been progressed. In this light, it is hardly surprising that Harrington and Bielby (2001a: 11) remain neutral on such issues: 'In analyzing the circuit one can

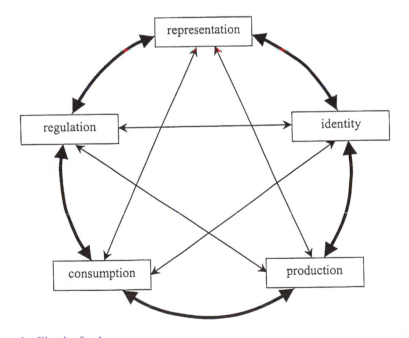

Figure 1   Circuit of culture

Source: From du Gay *et al.* (1996: 3)

begin with any moment or site that one chooses; while they might appear to be distinct categories, they overlap and articulate with one another in myriad ways'.

Fourth, it is apparent then that the notion of circuit(s) of culture is little more than metaphor, an organised recognition of the different sites at which culture is generated and mutually determined. Thus, in reality there is no genuine, certainly not exclusive, structured movement of culture in the way represented. Culture is not, for example, a commodity in which production must occur before sale can be realised, although it is suspected that the model for the circuit of culture is the commercial production of cultural products in which this is the case, see below. More generally there is no chronological or sequential movement between the posited nodes.

Last, and most important for consumption studies more generally, there has been a conflation between the (real or material) circulation of commodities and the (in a sense, imagined) circuit of culture. As a result, whether explicitly or not, much of the recent turn to culture has, in consumption studies, invested sites along the circuit of *commodities* with a cultural content. The point is that such sites, with the exception of production and consumption, cut across the nodes that have been used in practice to represent the circuit of *culture*. As the commodity moves through its sop, so it picks up and transforms culture along the way. This offers the opportunity to examine cultural content in a piecemeal fashion, with more or less acknowledgement of the interrelationship between the various participating moments – what contribution has been made by advertising, marketing, design, retailing or whatever.

Such observations point to a weakness in taking the cultural as starting point for confronting the economy, most notably through the circuit of culture. For a prominent form taken by economic analysis within consumption studies has been what has been termed 'mimetics' by Goodman and Watts (1994) in an entirely different context, the idea that agriculture develops as if a reflection of industry (or not). Similarly, the cultural has been perceived to be distinct from, but a pastiche of, the economic. Such is already inscribed in the idea of *circuit* of culture, suggesting movement akin to that of capital or commodity production and circulation. Fine (2001a: Chapters 2 and 3) has argued in detail how such mimetics has informed the cultural and consumption studies associated with Bourdieu. It is not simply that the terms such as cultural, symbolic and social capital are freely deployed but also that they are incorporated into a framework of analysis endowing them with an economic (and capital-like) content. Most important, they are perceived to be fluid or convertible into other forms, like money and commodities. Here is perpetrated a most paradoxical illusion. For all that is solid not only melts into air but exactly the opposite pertains, as all social relations become as if a form of capital. Most significantly, this is reflected in the 'plethora of capitals'[8] that have found their way into social theory, inspired by Bourdieu's lead by example through cultural, symbolic, social capital, etc.

As evidence of mimetics, consider Goldman and Papson (1996: 79), for whom, in the production of commodity signs, the origin of surplus value lies in the structure of the fetishized communicative exchange set up by ads. Viewers habitually perform this exchange as an unequal exchange, giving value to the signs when they permit themselves to be positioned.

Constantly deployed is the image of movement, 'the velocity of this process of meaning circulation has accelerated … [a] ceaseless repetition of this circuit' (p. 10). Further, 'difference drives the sign machine. The dynamic between differentiation and imitation drives the circulation of sign values' (p. 27), with 'acceleration of commodities, signs, and people through the circuits of production, distribution, and consumption' (p. 115), so that 'meanings rooted in history are thus dislodged and made to join the endless circulation of signs, where they become limitlessly sequenced and resequenced according to the logic (or whim) of the market' (p. 116). Ultimately, 'the logic of commodity sign production drives an accelerating circuit of cultural appropriation and waste' (p. 139), with 'the relentless circulation of meaning' (p. 190), an 'accelerating circulation of sign values' (p. 257), and with the result that 'the circuit between commodity images and the appropriation of rebellious subcultural expressions of style has become nearly seamless' (p. 259). All of this conversion of culture into sign value is fuelled by the wish to overcome the slow pace of real circulation or demand (p. 273):

> By turning to culture to expand the range of exchange values, capital has exported its crisis tendencies into the cultural sphere. The capitalist ideal of overcoming barriers to capital circulation has bred a commodity culture driven by an amazingly rapid turnover of signifiers and signifieds.

Similarly, for Carruthers and Babb (2000: 27), the meaningfulness or symbolism of commodities is sufficient to overcome what would otherwise be satiated levels of demand:

> The 'meaningfulness' of commodities therefore serves a very useful purpose. If consumers acquire commodities only because of their physical utility, before too long the consumer has had enough. Demand is capped by a person's finite demands for whatever the commodity provides. The situation is rather like sitting down to dinner and eating: The capacity of a stomach sets a fixed limit on how much even a hungry person can eat. But if commodities instead offer symbolism and meaning, consumer appetites become nearly insatiable.

A number of errors are committed here. Commodities (and goods) always have symbolism and meaning, and it makes little sense to compare worlds with and without them. Leaving this aside by accepting, for example, that in some sense commodities can become more endowed with symbolism, this does not suffice to resolve the problem of insufficient demand for commodities. The monetary form taken by goods (and the need to generate a profit) creates the problem in the form of economic crises that can prevail irrespective of the extent of symbolism. This is not to deny the importance of symbolism in the competition for success around particular commodities, as is evident in growing advertising costs for some but not all of them. It is unhelpful, however, to see this as creating demands that would not otherwise exist, and wrong to see this as resolving problems of deficient demand across the economy as a whole.

Other crude attempts to integrate the economic and the cultural often draw equally casually upon discredited economic analysis – simple acceptance, for example, of the invalid distinctions between Fordism and post-Fordism, and of globalisation and, ultimately, glocalisation. More specifically, if invidiously and arbitrarily picking victims, Gottdiener (1997: 46) relies upon underconsumption in the context of theming as the 'mirror of production'. Accordingly, 'the issue for the continued expansion of capital is no longer so much the problem of production, or capital valorization in commodities at the factory, but of consumption, or capital realization at the market'; hence he agrees 'with Baudrillard that symbolic processes solve the realization problem of capital' (p. 48). Perhaps this should be told to those who have suffered the (symbolic) effects of the East Asian or other crises and recessions with corresponding loss of capacities to consumer, or perhaps, like the Gulf War, these did not happen![9]

These are all examples drawn at a highly general and abstract level, with equally grand conclusions. There are more modest and more detailed studies. For Nixon (1997), advertising agencies are the intermediaries in circulation of culture between production and consumption. But there are others, such as management-inspired corporate culture as in Salaman (1997). Advertising is also covered by Messaris (1997), perceived as allowing consumers to fill in subjective detail without loss of producers' purpose, the sale; by Garvey (1996: 5) for whom, 'readers' interaction with advertising has never been a passive process of absorbing advertising messages';[10] and Moeran (1996) who finds, 'orientalism' aside, how similar is a Japanese ad agency to others around the world. Especially in the context of food, Marsden et al. (2000) see regulatory culture as increasingly being driven by large-scale private retailers. For Valentine (1999), consumption (eating) at home involves multiple identities within the household but these can only be defined in relation to other sites. Calder (1999: 26) focuses on consumer credit, departing from what were found to be two myths:

> before consumer credit people 'rarely went into debt and always lived within their means'; and second, that consumer credit destabilized traditional moral values by make it easier for people to live lives devoted to instant gratification and consumer hedonism.
>
> (p. 26)

There have always been moral panics around consumer credit. In contrast to such ideology, the conclusion is reached that, 'the developments in consumer credit over the years since the credit revolution only reinforce my argument ... that the principal significance of consumer credit is the way it regulates and ultimately limits the hedonistic qualities of consumer culture' (p. 294). In particular, far from allowing hedonism to float free, it reinforces a work ethic, work and play hard, with 95.5 per cent of consumers paying off their debts (p. 302). The book closes by citing a bumper sticker – 'I owe, I owe; it's off to work I go!' (p. 303).

Humphery (1998) points to 'retail culture', including the creation of retail space and contemporary one-stop shopping, and distinguishes the new from the familiar. How does one become the other through history? Crossick and Jaumain (1999a: 27), in their edited collection (1999b), note a paradox at the heart of the representation of the department store as cathedral of consumption: 'the goods offered to the aspirant consumer market were often mass-produced and aggressively priced, yet the culture being sold with it was one of luxury, indulgence and good taste'. More generally, they significantly draw the apt conclusion that (p. 35):

> The department store is a complex phenomenon which interlocks with so many themes ... that its emergence as a major subject of historical research is not surprising. It is however striking that this emergence does not come primarily from an examination of the department store itself as a phenomenon is retailing history ... [but] from historians wrestling with the concepts of modernity, consumption and gender. One sometimes wonders whether the department store – even with the solidity of its iron frame and plate-glass windows – is capable of taking the weight of analytical expectations heaped upon it ... at times one feels that one is learning more about the place of the department store in contemporary discourse than about what went on in the department store itself, more about its role in the culture of consumption than about the practices of purchasing and using goods in ordinary bourgeois lives.

As if to illustrate the point, Lowe and Wrigley (1996) see the contribution of retail capital to consumption in terms of sites, chains, spaces and places plus gender, play and landscapes.[11]

The studies just discussed do not necessarily make explicit reference to the circuit of culture but they are compatible with it,[12] thereby reflecting how an initial cultural turn has led to the bringing back in of the economy. Essentially, the circuit offers the prospect of unity between its various moments, justifying a more or less self-contained analysis of each individual moment. In other words, despite commitment to examine both the economic and the cultural in a spirit of interdisciplinary endeavour, the result often has been a consolidation of intradisciplinary or topic-based (retail, advertising, etc.) studies. In short, the circuit of culture approach has advanced little beyond the content originally offered by Johnson other than to fragment it into more or different elements. Moreover, the strait-jacket imposed by traditional analytical boundaries leads to an, as yet, continuing weakness in economic analysis itself, hardly surprising in so far as it depends upon a return ticket from the economics-less, cultural approach to consumption.

This is to revisit the conundrum that Haug sought to resolve through the notion of aesthetic illusion. As observed, he neglects that production and other moments do not simply strain the bounds of the received notions of commodities, they are also positively constitutive of consumer culture. The circuit of culture does not make this error but nor does it tend to recognise sufficiently the stresses placed upon (circuit of) culture by the circuit of capital. As observed, much concern has been directed at how activity away from the act of consumption itself is significant for the culture of consumption. For Lee (1993: 39):

> Goods have already been given potential meaning and symbolic value prior to their introduction as the symbolic goods of lived culture … advertising and marketing do not have the ability to achieve a total symbolic closure around the goods that they promote, [but] the power of such agencies cannot be ignored.

The same conclusion can be drawn from Leach's (1993) study of corporate influence on the culture of consumption. He argues (p. 147):

> After 1890 the institutions of production and consumption were, in effect, taken over by corporate businesses. … At the same time, merchants, brokers, and manufacturers did everything they could, both ideologically and in reality, to *separate* the world of production from the world of consumption.

But, he insists, production and consumption remain inextricably bound together despite the wish of commerce to conceal, for example, any connection to work and working conditions in peddling their wares (p. 149):

> All of this served to give to consumption its independent character, communicating a sense that, in the world of goods at least, men and women could find transformation, liberation, a paradise free from pain and suffering, a new eternity in time. … But this was illusory. It was illusory because the world of consumption, however seemingly severed from the world of production, was always dependent on and always vulnerable to the capitalist forces that created it.

In addition, Leach focuses on the creation of corporate culture away from the point of sale, not so much in design and product as in public relations, corporate image, and the support solicited from outside direct corporate control, in institutions specifically set up for, or adopting, such a role albeit in the context of formal autonomy and incorporation of other purposes and activities (p. 382):

> An immense legacy was passed on, an institutional legacy of corporations, investment and commercial banks, business schools, commercial art schools, museums, universities, and the federal government. These institutions and the services they performed grew dramatically, especially after 1950.

A similar, if less wide-ranging account, is given by Marchand (1998a: 4–5) who also observes diversity across corporations and their strategies:[13]

> As we trace the quest for a corporate soul over the first half of the twentieth century, we will encounter a great variety of stratagems and initiatives as one major company after another discovered the need for a more favorable and distinct corporate image and more self-conscious public relations. No two companies faced exactly the same needs and circumstances; each defined its purposes and strategies in different ways. The striking diversity of these many case studies enriches this story of emerging corporate cultures and public relations strategies.

In short, consumption and its associated sops are conduits for cultural influences that are both diverse and originate and evolve, often purposefully, away from point of sale and use and corresponding commercial activity.

Yet surely all of this account of non-consumer sources of consumer culture is merely to revisit the material covered by the circuit of culture? At one level, the sites to be visited, this is correct. But there is one major difference from much that has gone before as a result of the perspective from which culture is perceived, from the side of sale as opposed to purchase, for which the structures and imperatives of the capitalist economy are unavoidable, both as material and cultural determinants. Such insights can be illustrated and extended by earlier work on food (Fine and Leopold 1993: Chapter 12 and 13, Fine 1998c: Chapter 4). Against received wisdoms of the trickle-down of information in healthy eating campaigns, it is argued that information about food (or the knowledge that consumers deploy in the context of adopting a healthy or unhealthy diet) is attached to a food information *system*. This is distinct from, but integrated with, the food system as a whole which generates information, consciously or otherwise, just as it generates food, see Chapter 11. Five features are characteristic of the food information system – it is construed, chaotic, constructed, contradictory and contested[14] – all well illustrated by eating disorders and many other aspects of food culture.[15] In a similar vein, Cook *et al.* (1998) have examined what they term the circuits of knowledge in the UK food business,[16] building upon Lien's (1997: 19) suggestion that 'the social production of foods for sale is closely linked to the social production of knowledge'.[17]

Although information, knowledge and culture are by no means synonymous even if they could be analytically pinned down, they do have much in common. Consequently, it is appropriate to examine cultural systems for consumption alongside the integral chains of activities that correspond to their sops. Although liable to be more fluid, they can be structured like sops, especially with the professionalisation of design and marketing, for example, which can adopt a distinctive content and dynamic of their own.[18] Further, an important implication of this proposed focus on cultural systems attached to consumption is the rejection of a simple opposition between production and consumption or producers and consumers. Carrier and Heyman (1997: 370) reveal why this is important:

> Construing people as consumers rather than workers is a local manifestation of a larger public shift in perception that ignores the fact that almost all Westerners work or depend upon a worker for their consumption. The interests of people-as-consumers, however, are presented as more uniform, universal and just than the interests of people-as-workers, presented as unjust, sectional self-interests. ... The result, as is shown in the history of labour relations in Britain and the United States since 1980, is the overriding of workers in particular firms, in the name of the common interest, one at a time, and their interests as people (as both workers and consumers) being seriously damaged. Construing people as workers or as dependent upon them would make this process of serial immiseration much harder.

Studies of consumption as opposed to production have previously proceeded along such lines in sufficiently diverse ways that their shared framework has tended to remain unexamined. Models of consumer sovereignty suggest harmonious interaction with producer ultimately serving consumer. This conclusion is inverted in models of corporate manipulation of consumer tastes and wants. Postmodernist accounts, drawing upon the construction of identity, consolidate the focus on the consumer in relation to a world of signs as opposed to material culture and provision.

The last refuge along the circuit of culture is always that rascal, the consumer. In this respect, one of the achievements of the literature is not only to have moved beyond consumerism or consumer society as an explanatory concept, see Chapter 8, but also beyond whether consumer society is good or bad, meeting real or false needs, and so on. The intellectual and ethical record of how consumption has been interpreted, like its practices themselves, is undoubtedly mixed and complex. Much of the recent literature has begun to see itself as rejecting a traditional neglect of the pleasure principle, as if Veblen, Packard, Galbraith and the like are the only past commentators, and this is all that they had to say. This is especially so for Livingston (1994, 1998), and for Pendergast (2000: 6)[19] who, in periodising the switch from Victorian to modern masculinity as represented in the printed media, disputes the interpretation of the rise of culture of corporate capitalism as a two-act tragedy. Act one is marked by the decline of popular and labour movements, and act two by the reification of all social relations and the rise of individualised consumerism. He defies the 'conventional wisdom' he himself posits: 'Thus the rise of consumer culture led to the degraded individual and cultural life we are stuck with today'. Lears (1998) appeals for ambiguity in reconsidering the impact of abundance,[20] but Wyrwa (1998) provides a history of the idea of consumption as primarily incorporating a critical element.[21]

Surely, though, Gronow (1997: 11) is correct to emphasise that consumption has always been enjoyed, 'full of social interaction', not only 'oriented towards obtaining a profit' and 'also governed by a "useless" etiquette and numerous "irrational" habits and customs'? This has inspired Fine's (1997c) treatment of consumption as play. Equally, it defies belief that it has taken the rise of post-modernism for consumers and its observers to have recognised that enjoyment might be involved. But with postmodernism, that pleasure miraculously floats free of an evaporating material world, for one welcoming the opportunities offered by reflexive modernisation. For Lash and Urry (1994), 'with an ever quickening turnover time, objects as well as cultural artefacts become disposable and depleted of meaning' (pp. 2–3). Further, 'what is increasingly being produced are not material objects, but signs' (p. 15). And, presumably, signs of signs, leaving one wondering how it is possible that profits are ever made lest it be through the full gamut of academic clichés of contemporary capitalism – the global, the local, the informational, flexibility (post)modernity, time–space, bodies, and so on.

Sops revisited

Be all this as it may, whatever the historical record of how we perceive our own consumption, and how others have perceived it at the time or in retrospect, it is an another achievement of consumption studies to have understood the multidimensional content and sources of the culture, or cultures, attached to consumption. The issue to be addressed is whether such diversity can be appropriately accommodated within a circuit, as opposed to a system. Posing a cultural system as attached to consumption is a break with a focus on the active or passive consumer as can be acknowledged by drawing a parallel with the political system, not least because it and consumption are often used as metaphors for one another. Just as politicians try to persuade voters to spend their vote on them, so consumers are perceived as voting for their purchases.[22] Yet few would seriously consider reducing the political system, or take as analytical starting point, the confrontation of the voter with the ballot box. The act of voting, and its meaning and significance, are highly contextual according to the political system in which they take place. Why should consumption be different? And why should it be seen culturally as a circuit as opposed to a system, like the economic, the political, the ideological or the social systems?

It is also necessary to go beyond a change in terminology, from cultural circuit to cultural system. The previous discussion of the culture of consumption from the economic side primarily focused upon vertically integrated activity within the commercial sphere. It has to go much further in dealing with the culture of consumption. For, as recognised by the new household economics, it is necessary to consider the shifting relationship between commercial and non-commercial forms of provision and shifts within, and transformation of, these broad categories. Here, however, because of its lack of historical specificity, the new household economics tends to assume what it has to prove or investigate – that activities shift seamlessly across boundaries according to exogenously given but evolving comparative advantage. Many who would reject such reductionism do so by bringing in socio-cultural factors but only as impediments to the forward march of narrowly conceived rational choice.[23] Schor (1991: 85), for example, suggests, 'there are big differences between household labor and the experience of being "on the job". The two do not share the same structures of pay, accountability, control, or technology.' Nonetheless she deploys a comparative advantage argument, combining low wages for women and, to a lesser extent, low evaluation of domestic labour itself, arguing that there has been

> too much stress on this cultural imperative [of the role of women], and that the more important culprit has been the devaluation of the housewife's labor. … The devaluation of household labor has made a less efficient technology cheaper. The labor-saving potential of socialized housework will be chosen only when women's time is highly valued.
>
> (pp. 102–3)

To this is added the insidious cycle of work-and-spend arising from the interwar watershed that witnessed a shift from the psychology of scarcity to the psychology of abundance. Further, employers wanted longer hours, and workers wanted what they could get rather than getting what they wanted.

What is the alternative to such arguments that fit a stylised history to equally stylised economic and social factors? First, as discussed in Chapter 3, there needs to be precision about what constitutes a commodity proper. There is an enormous difference between the mass consumption items produced under conditions of twentieth-century capitalism and those goods that have been held in ownership and then sold for whatever reason (and which should not be classified as commodities since they are not systematically produced for the market). For these, and for the range of 'commodities' in between which are to be found to a greater or lesser extent throughout the history of consumption, the nature and impact of commercial pressure are very different depending on the socio-economic conditions to which they are attached. Thus, when Brewer (1995) restricts his discussion of culture to 'works of imagination and the elegant arts', because these take the form of commodities and are commercialised, they do not constitute commodities at all in the same sense even as the Hogarth engravings, reproduced for the wider audience both qualitatively and quantitatively as examined by Paulson (1995).[24]

Second, there is a presumption that the commercial sphere is liable to generate higher levels of productivity and incorporate the non-commercial. Such a tendency, however, as in the discussion of vertical (dis)integration, is associated with countervailing tendencies, not least the provision of cheaper inputs for those forms of production that are not directly commercially oriented. This is apparent in the case of the household where, for example, the sewing machine and haberdashery can reinforce the viability of home production, quite apart from providing opportunities for informal earnings. Once again, the resolution of these opposing factors cannot be simply reduced to a netting out of overall comparative advantage. The outcome is highly dependent, less on the competitive process as such as on the socio-economic relations governing non-commercial provision.

Third, the foregoing implies that the distribution of different forms of production for consumption should not be reduced to simple comparative advantage, with the requirement, for example, that mass production or whatever be matched in some sense by some other compensating factor to retain viability. It is necessary to determine how different forms of production for consumption are reproduced and transformed despite their possible lack of a commercial logic and their interaction with it. Both the nature and viability of such non-commercial production and consumption are liable to be heavily influenced, if not eliminated, by the predominance of commercial alternatives. These can even present themselves in the form of a commercial counterculture, as in the contemporary desire for the home-made or the customised (which can, of course, often be supplied *en masse* in practice).

Such considerations reinforce the conclusions of the previous chapter that periodisation is essential for the study of consumption even if not in the form of a sequence of consumer revolutions and despite the disdain with which such periodisations have otherwise often been greeted. In the case of Tedlow (1990), for example, who has chosen to focus on the rise of mass production in order to address shifting forms of marketing, there are charges of lack of representativeness across the United States as well as lack of generalisation to other countries. To some extent, however, this is to miss the point of periodisation which is intended to identify distinct stages in the development of consumption and their dominant, not universal nor determining, characteristics.[25] Earlier work on consumption, for example, was initially prompted by the wish to explore the relationship between the rise of mass consumption and the increase in female labour market participation (Fine 1992). It was found necessary to examine the periodisation not only of production but also of the family (in the light of the demographic transition) and the role of the state. But there is no presumption that such periodisations have neat and tight correspondences with one another, either chronologically or in each and every instance of production, consumption, family size and female labour market participation.

This is the result of the previously identified resolution of tensions between conflicting tendencies. Reliance upon the latter is well established in the study of consumption, in ways that combine material and cultural factors. Ritzer (1993, 1998), for example, has put forward the McDonaldisation thesis, and perceives it to be a consequence of a Weberian drive for modernist rationality, although his later work tempers this with considerations of postmodernist aspects. Critics of Ritzer, as in Smart (1999), almost universally perceive a need for a more sustained political economy and lesser generalisation as if to anticipate the need for consumption and McDonald's itself to be understood in light of specific sops and cultural systems. Otherwise, together with the even more demanding Alfino *et al.* (1998) in critique of Ritzer, the humble hamburger is simply being asked to bear too much social analysis, like the department stores as cathedrals of consumption, covered in the earlier discussion of Crossick and Jaumain. Bryman (1999) offers a complementary alternative in the form of Disneyisation based on theming, dedifferentiating (items of consumption), merchandising, and requiring emotional labour.[26] Postmodernism can be understood in terms of the tendency to the consumption of the sign. Last, but not least, globalisation (and localisation and their interaction as glocalisation) have been significant in the study of consumption.

Studies of the food chain have emphasised the tendency for the industrialisation of agriculture and the displacement of activity and control to manufacturing and, ultimately, retailing, see Chapter 11. In doing so, such studies initially settled comfortably into a theory of internationalised agro-food complexes (Friedmann 1993, 1994). Prompted in part by the biotechnology revolution, the influence of post-Fordism, and the empirical diversity revealed by a fuller range of foods, this gave way to a swing to the opposite extreme and to analytical agnosticism.[27] Most recently (e.g. Goodman and Watts 1997), a less extreme approach has been adopted, emphasising the impact of globalisation, interaction all along the food chain, diversity and specificity by crop and country, and the need to avoid 'mimetics' and address food as such rather than extrapolating from theory developed, however appropriately for industrial production systems.[28] This has now given way to actor–network theory to avoid science–nature dualisms (Goodman 1999, 2001).

The analytical use of tendencies has, however, to be treated with some caution. There is a danger of identifying an empirical trend, possibly over-generalising, designating it as tendency and even allowing for countertendency so that the theory accommodates all empirical outcomes including counterexamples. Whilst this may reflect sound empirical judgement, tendencies should be analytically grounded in the socio-economic imperatives of capitalism and be shown to underpin more complex outcomes. Previous work on eating disorders, for example, has attempted to show how they arise in a multiplicity of forms and severity as a result of the imperatives both to eat and to diet which are themselves possible because of the paradoxical co-existence and symbiosis of eating and dieting industries.[29] For Shammas (1990: 8):

There are two tendencies in the writings on consumption in the past. One is to view consumers as alienated from the means of production, pushed into the market-place, and force-fed market goods until, through merchandizing and advertisements, they become hooked on a culture of consumption. The other tendency is to interpret the accumulation of all new commodities as an unequivocal sign of general societal advancement and well-being. ... [In contrast] ... one has to leave open the possibility that trends over a long period of time may be other than linear and that not all types of consumption change in the same way.

In short, structures, tendencies, relations and reproduction are recognisably imperative to the provision of commodities for consumption and to their cultural attributes. In addition, they are the consequences of capital and of capitalism. The study of the culture of consumption needs to take this more seriously than a symbolic reification of various non-economic factors as cultural, symbolic or other forms of capital!

The approach examined and applied

The understanding of consumption in terms of sops and culture represents the position from and not to which the sop approach has evolved. Crewe (2000: 281) comments:

> The importance of this approach is that it points to the possibility of 'a more balanced treatment of the relationship between production and consumption' (Leslie and Reimer 1999: 402), one which also acknowledges the symbolic significance of commodities.

To some extent then, the approach has previously been recognised as such and has even been followed by others. Hansen (2000) understands the international provision of second-hand clothing to Zambia in these terms. Lemire (1992, 1997) deals in both first- and second-hand clothing around the UK Industrial Revolution, and suggests in her second study of the sop approach that 'no category of goods better illustrates this hypothesis than does dress'. A similar view is to be found in the edited collection of Burman (1999a) in the context of the sewing machine, for which the complex relationship between (de)commodification and fashionability is central. As previously observed, the study of eating out by Warde and Martens (2000) seeks to add and integrate cultural studies to the sop approach, an issue returned to below noting, for the moment, the (false) presumption that culture was previously absent. Narotzky (1997: 102) finds the perspective wanting only in so far as it does not address non-commodified consumption and its relationship to the commodified. Similarly, although otherwise supportive of the approach, Pennell (1999: 553–4) suggests: 'Fine and Leopold leave unquestioned a further, related assumption; their analysis is dependent upon an understanding of consumed objects as *always being* commodities'. This is a reasonable observation of Fine and Leopold (1993) but the deficiency has been addressed, hopefully redressed, in earlier chapters. Even so, the original contribution reflects two, possibly implicit, stances, now made explicit: the heavy dependence of contemporary consumption (and study of it) upon (capitalist) commodity production and the need to understand the latter in comprehending the distinctiveness of non-commodity consumption.[30]

As quoted above, Leslie and Reimer (1999) are also generally favourable to sops in assessing the relative merits of three approaches – the others being commodity chains, associated with Gereffi (1998, 1999, 2001) and Gereffi and Korzeniewicz (eds) (1994), discussed below, and the circuits of (culinary) culture of Cook *et al.* (1998). The last's concern as geographers is the proper inclusion of the social construction of space. Lury (1996: 229) perceives the sop approach as being insufficiently developed to consider the emergence of consumer culture adequately, to which this book is a response. Further, like Leslie and Reimer, there is concern that 'it is not entirely clear how Fine and Leopold establish the basis on which vertical systems of provision come to be isolated from each other'.

This issue is crucial and was explicitly addressed in debate: Fine (1993a) with Glennie and Thrift (1992, 1993) and, subsequently, in Fine *et al.* (1996) and Fine (1998c). Is it possible that horizontal factors are so important that they inextricably leak, even flood, across sops, preventing them from constituting themselves as distinct from one another? Significantly, to raise the question in this way is to accept the prior existence of sops. Otherwise, how could they contaminate one another, however much they do so? If the horizontal leakage is sufficiently serious, then the sops involved will have been merged into one another. A further, related element in the case against sops is the idea that consumption is so fluid in meanings and practices, especially in light of postmodernist interpretations, that no sop, and associated cultural system, is sufficiently stable to be able to be identifiable, irrespective of its attachment to others.[31] To some extent, this is an empirical question but not entirely so. For, as is carefully argued in the debate, sops are defined by the integral nature of their structures, relations and practices, by elements located *away* from consumption itself. The culture of consumption is so inventive and flexible that any two objects can be brought into contact with one another (their mutual contribution to utility, for example, as far as less imaginative economists are concerned).[32] Sops cannot be defined as more inclusive nor as wider in scope simply because two commodities (or the idea of them) are consumed together. Rather, it is precisely at distant sites that sops are formed because of the imperatives of capital and capitalism – the need to finance, design, sell, produce, etc., in ways that are consistent with one another and continued profitability. This is not deny the logical possibility that provision can become so fluid that no settled system of furnishing consumption arises. But this is liable to be on the margins of the advanced capitalist economy rather than at its core as tends to be suggested by those, wedded to postmodernism, who project the subjectivities and fluidities of consumption back onto its material sources. That is if these are considered at all.

Another element in the case against the sop approach is in questioning how sops are to be defined or identified. The previous paragraph offers some indication, the most important point in addition being that outcomes are contingent, not predetermined. It is a matter of identifying the structure and dynamics of the provision concerned. Case studies have been offered in earlier work, especially for foods but also for clothing. An interesting, if unwitting example, is provided by Negus's (1997) postscript to the Walkman study. Here, it is shown that a complex commercial struggle took place in which Sony attempted to use its power in hardware to tie down and incorporate artistic control. It failed. But if it had succeeded, and that success had been generalised, the sop(s) around the production and reproduction of music would have turned out differently. At a grander methodological level, other than reasonably to criticise him for universalising and generalising the concepts involved,[33] Bourdieu's notions of habitus and field have been generally accepted without criticism.[34] They are expressly designed to allow for structured practices to develop a logic and content of their own making. Exactly the same applies to sops.

The previous two reservations about the sop approach are mutually inconsistent in so far as the first suggests it is too deterministic when set against the fluidity of consumption and the second that it is not deterministic enough since sops are deemed to be historically and socially specific. Essentially, this inconsistency is equivalent to a third objection, that the approach is inappropriately structured as a framework. The argument is that 'horizontal' are as important as 'vertical' factors. The latter comprise variables such as gender, for example, or practices such as retailing. That the horizontal is important, however, is not in dispute. Rather, it is posited that the relationship between gender or retailing and consumption is complex and varied, and differentiated by sop. By the same token, the notion that gender or other horizontal factors represent fluidity *across* sops is to accept the prior presence of those systems.[35] The conclusion is not to deny the pertinence of horizontal study,[36] but to claim that it does not provide an appropriate framework for the study of consumption.[37] Gender, race, retailing, etc., and consumption have to be disaggregated as objects of study. The question is how, and the sop is an appropriate approach.

Far more extensive than direct reference to the sop approach are those studies that can be interpreted as having contributed to it, necessarily unwittingly and possibly unwillingly. At the very general level, the necessity of addressing vertical specificity can be illustrated by three different examples.[38] James (1993) is essentially a mainstream economist, seeking to break in a marginal way with the orthodoxy by allowing for a dichotomy between preferences and values, with the divergence between the two differing between developed and developing countries. His book covers a range of topics on this basis,[39] not least whether the adoption of western practices in developing countries is advantageous or not. He allows for a number of different mechanisms – the search for modernity, the social learning of tastes (through school and factory), positional values, advertising, colonialism, status, cognitive dissonance and that preference change may follow upon behavioural change. Otherwise, he is blissfully unaware of the social construction of the meaning of the objects of consumption. Yet, he is capable of concluding, even on this limited basis that 'the impact of new products ... will depend on the particular circumstances and will need to be assessed separately for each product and for each country' (p. 31).

Equally from the economic side, Gereffi and Korzeniewizc (1994) and Gereffi (1998, 1999, 2001) have posited the idea of global commodity chains within world systems theory (the developed and undeveloped worlds are necessary complements of one another), although these controversial analytical origins have increasingly been displaced by analytical eclecticism.[40] Concern is less with consumption as such than with the prospects of Third World producers either escaping or, at least, benefiting from attachment to world markets controlled by globally organised capitalism. The approach is too narrow in a number of respects, primarily because of the over-generality of the world systems approach from which it originates. It unduly presumes that commodity chains are necessarily global (although some technological developments have allowed some commodity chains to become more national or local); it reduces these global chains to two ideal types – producer or buyer driven – and it totally neglects the cultural circuit altogether.[41] These points are well illustrated by Gibbon's (2001) attempt to defend and to extend the global commodity chain approach against the criticism of Cramer (1999) that it fails to accommodate the Mozambique cashew sector. First, he argues that it serves as a heuristic device for case study purposes, with such chains potentially obstructing as well as promoting value-added upgrading as far as low-income, Third World producers are concerned. He accepts that the approach has primarily been confined to clothing, and that the world systems framework poses more questions around concepts and methodology than it resolves. Indeed, his defence borders upon tautology for the applicability of the approach is limited to instances of its empirical incidence. For, with respect to the fruit, food and vegetable sector that is used in seeking to identify chains other than clothing (p. 349):

> With regard to generalizability, the perspective claims to be addressing only those GCCs where Northern merchandizers/retailers play a leading role.

Ultimately, the presence of such chains is not questioned and explained – why some commodities and not others, for example. Rather, the issue is which particular agent coordinates the chain in linking production to sale, as if the only alternative is a free or uncoordinated market. Not surprisingly, the scope of the approach is widened by adding potential coordinators other than producers or buyers as the drivers of the chain. Gibbon specifically adds the model of international-trader-driven chains. In short, the global commodity chain approach is a partial and simpler version of the sop approach. It painfully slowly evolves by recognising the limitations imposed by its initial model of buyer- and producer-driven chains. Other, intermediate agents are necessarily introduced. Analytically, it is an organised framework for empirical typology, focusing upon structures, agents and process, these corresponding, respectively, to the commodity chain itself, the coordinator and coordinated, and upgrading value added or not.

Despite its lack of finesse around the constituent elements and the nature and the generality of global commodity chains, the approach is explicitly organised around the empirical presence or otherwise of vertically organised commodity chains. On the other hand, from the cultural side, as will be observed of Appadurai's (1997) treatment of consumer society, see Chapter 8, its different genealogies and histories lead him to adopt a commodity-specific stance for entirely different reasons. This is a consequence of his general habit of appearing, in retrospect, to take empirical and concrete observations and generalising them to the abstract, thereby allowing an incontestable reimposition upon the starting point.[42] Thus, for him, consumption is self-effacing, habituated and highly specific to the individual: 'in all social contexts, [consumption] is centered around ... the body [that] calls for disciplines that are repetitious, or at least periodic' (p. 24). As a result, 'all socially organized forms of consumption seem to revolve around some combination of the following three patterns: interdiction, sumptuary law, and fashion' (p. 29), not least in consumption, as the pursuit of pleasure, the tensions between nostalgia and fantasy as opposed to fantasy and utility (as an interpretation of Campbell's romantic ethic) and between individual desire and collective disciplines (as for Rojek). These are all thrown in, together with consumption as work in the household, and as the commodification of time (with reference to E. P. Thompson and the impact of industrialisation). As Moeran (1996: 284) perceptively observes of Appadurai, 'like others in sociology and anthropology ... he is concerned not so much with the way in which commodities form a *system* but with the meaning of different elements in the "cultural construction of value"'. Yet, Appadurai is drawn to commodity-specific analysis, as is Moeran (1996) himself for whom there are six types of value – use value (use however subjectively or socially constructed), technical (its physical or design properties), appreciative (aesthetic or cultural), and social (ethical, status, etc.). These four are perceived as encapsulating Bourdieu's social and cultural capital. They coalesce to form the two other kinds of exchange value – commodity and symbolic. With respect to Appadurai, is this not a case of the pot calling the kettle black? As far as conclusions are concerned, they do end up in the same commodity-specific pot:

> It is, then, by taking account of these six types of value, by analysing how *specific objects or commodities* are given particular values over and

above their material properties, that we can begin to understand consumption practices throughout the world.

(p. 296, emphasis added)

Similarly, Carruthers and Babb (2000: 44) judge that the differences in the ways that meaning is attributed to commodities suffice to warrant a commodity-specific approach:

> The kinds of meanings that get attached to commodities draw on a small set of recurrent themes: social status, attractiveness, gender, age, social relationships, ethnicity, group membership. These core meanings get deployed in different ways as they are connected to different commodities.

Such commodity-specificity is necessarily notable of the highly diverse case study literature. Rogers' (1998) account of the Barbie doll constructs it as icon, as a collector's item, as glocalisation (as Americanisation), the fortunes of corporate Mattel Inc., the tensions around race, class and gender, as deplored for stereotyping and praised for socialising, as experienced, remembered and socially and subjectively reconstructed. It is rooted in (doll) history, fantasy, bodies, intellectual property rights, Disneyisation, the social reproduction of children, domestic production (of clothes for grandchildren), etc., and theming with 100 different Barbie dolls around three themes – hair, life-style and glamour – each with corresponding accessories.[43] But Barbie is only made possible through its dependence on the international division of (child and slave) labour, for which Rogers provides telling insights (pp. 102–8).[44] No less harrowing is the account by Bishop and Robinson (1998) of the Thai sex industry as an unacknowledged system of production, with attached cultural systems on both sides of the commercial divide, western tourist and eastern sex worker. Arce and Fisher (1999) examine how totally different narratives are attached to Bolivian coca and Tanzanian honey, as illegal drugs and fair trading, respectively, through the global chains of meanings and provision, albeit locally integrated.

Beng-Huat (2000a) focuses on clothing as an illustration for

> the 'idea' of consumption as a phenomenon. Visually it is ubiquitous and indubitable, but conceptually its 'unity' is highly problematic. Each item in the constantly expanding array of goods and services which modern urban individuals and households have to consume routinely in order to reproduce their daily life is surrounded by its own systems of production, distribution, marketing, procurement and, finally, consumption. Each of these systems is in turn constituted by its own multifaceted and segmental economies in an increasingly globalised capitalism.

Equally, in the context of clothing, Jirousek (2000: 234) observes that a mass fashion system is a result of economic factors relating to the development of the textile industry … substantial means of production, an effective distribution system that includes the ability to disseminate rapidly changing fashion ideal, and a mass consumer public that has both the income and the social mobility to support such a system.

Crane (1999) demonstrates how the fashion system is no longer subject to trickle-up or down (if it ever were) because of its dependence upon multiple sourcing in supply and targeting in demand. As a result, elite fashion creates clothes that are not designed to be worn – relief all round[45] – but to raise commercial publicity so that profit can be made both from segmented and mass markets.

For the rise of yuppie (reimagined specialty) coffees and the reimagination of class in the United States, Roseberry (1996: 763) traces the material and cultural systems involved to conclude:

Proper understanding of the proliferation of specialty coffees requires consideration of the experiences and choices of the consumer in the coffee shop and at the dinner table, but it also requires consideration of the methods, networks, and relations of coffee production, processing and distribution, and sale in the 1980s, as well as placement of those methods, networks, and relations within a wider history.

Auslander's (1996a) study of French furniture is exemplary in allowing for (p. 33)[46]

a dialectic between analysis of stylistic change, on the one hand, and of political and economic changes, on the other. The specific use of materials, the historical repertoire of forms, and the products of distance culture emerged out of a set of perpetual dialogues between the culture of production, the system of distribution, and the culture of the court.

In her study of the sewing machine, Coffin (1994: 751) admits:[47]

I deliberately bring together subjects that are usually treated separately: family incomes and credit payment, construction of femininity and methods of marketing, and advertising, sexology, and models of the female body.

Miles (1998) is one amongst many who follows the need to concretise general or abstract features of consumerism through specific commodities, as is the case with the even grander approach of Roche (2000). Further, the attempt to address horizontal factors such as gendering can also be interpreted as needing to descend to sops as in Mort's (1996, 1997) study of clothing and masculinity (although he is explicitly concerned about leakage across sops). Yet the weight of consumption studies as a whole is to reject universal and oversimplified assumptions concerning consumption, decoration and the mundane chores of women. Further, in recognising variation across time, product and space, de Grazia (1996: 3) concludes:

> To make sense of the accretion of sexual meanings and gender identities around practices of consumption the authors could not be wedded to any single definition of the polymorphous term consumption.

For Auslander (1996a: 277):

> All acts of consumption were also acts of production, but some modes of consumption were defined as almost exclusively masculine. This gendering of forms of consumption was not stable across the century, however, nor were the boundaries between the masculine and the feminine impermeable at any given moment.

This is an appropriate conclusion to draw from a historical study of French furniture; it should provide a lesson for future studies.

7

ECONOMICS AND CONSUMPTION

Introduction

At the heart of mainstream economics lies a striking paradox. For, on the one hand, the whole discipline rests on its analysis of consumption. Even where the topic does nor arise directly and explicitly, the theoretical framework deployed depends upon individual motivation to consume as a means of maximising utility. Everything is organised towards that end. On the other hand, despite its inescapable importance, the understanding of consumption by mainstream economics is shallow to the point of being paper thin. It has already been indicated in full by the idea of utility maximisation – automated subjects relating hedonistically to unspecified objects, with little context and content other than the constraints imposed by prices and incomes.

How and why this should be so is covered in the next section. It offers a conceptual critique of the contribution that economics has made to the understanding of consumer behaviour. Overall, demand theory within economics has changed very little over time and so has not been a source of innovative thinking. First, economics has been confined to a narrow behavioural and motivational calculus – individual utility maximisation. Second, in formal theoretical terms, and contrary to immediate impressions, economics does not effectively have a distinct theory of consumption – either to confront the specific nature of what is consumed or to distinguish consumption from production. In short, economics is the most extreme version of a horizontal theory of consumption. It takes a simple and single idea, utility maximisation, and generalises it across all commodities simultaneously, whilst keeping all other factors constant, not least through unchanging preferences and products.

Some economists seek to resolve the paradox mentioned at the outset by warmly embracing it. The leading representative is Gary Becker who believes that utility maximisation should be allowed to explain every aspect of society. As argued in the third section, he sets an extreme standard against which others can appear to be more tempered in allowing for other motivations as well. Nonetheless, complementing one universal standard of human behaviour, and there are many from which to choose, with another merely compounds the

125

problems as is illustrated by a close examination of the work of Bowden and Offer on consumer durables.

Whatever its theoretical and conceptual deficiencies, mainstream economics has always prided itself on its empirical work claiming that, alongside its mathematical models, this renders it uniquely rigorous and scientific across the social sciences.[1] This is challenged in the fourth section. Starting by taking the example of cars, it demonstrates how, in practice if not in principle, the individualistic demand-based approach to consumption is susceptible to neglect of one of the most obvious determining factors, gender. This is indicative of a major stumbling block for empirical work by mainstream economists: their taking the individual consumer as starting point. The social rather than the individual should provide the basis for identifying norms of consumption. These themselves need to be explained by a combination of material and cultural factors. Otherwise, as suggested in the closing remarks, material and cultural analyses will reside side by side, at best dysfunctionally joined at the hip.

The isolated poverty of economics

Consumer theory within economics has remained essentially unchanged since the end of the last century. Today's students of economics are still required to match relative marginal utilities to relative prices in a way that would be recognisable to the students of Alfred Marshall. Not only has postmodernism failed to make its presence felt within economics,[2] the discipline has itself internally generated no shift in conceptual content. Indeed, the basis for understanding consumption has remained essentially unchanged since the marginalist revolution of the 1870s which witnessed the demise of classical political economy associated with Ricardo and Smith and the establishment of neo-classical economics, organised around supply and demand, which has survived and prospered until the present day.[3] This is all the remarkable given the disdain with which other social scientists have long perceived the assumptions made by economists.[4] It is worth exploring how and why economics should be so immune to revision when addressing consumption.

Mainstream economics has been built upon the central notion of the rational economic individual,[5] who optimises subject to constraints. For the firm, there is given technology and, in conditions of perfect competition, given prices for both inputs and outputs. The object is to maximise profits, and those firms that fail to do so are eliminated by competition. For the individual consumer, there are given tastes or preferences and the individual's motivation is to extract as much utility as possible from the given income available. Consumers are deemed to do so by choosing between a mix of goods whose enduring ability to satisfy utility is set against the price that each commands.[6] In this presentation, consumer theory has been reduced to demand theory with no substantive adjustments to allow for the limitations of treating the behaviour of the individual consumer, as optimiser, as analogous with the behaviour of the firm, a matter returned to below.

For the moment, it is worth emphasising that economics only has a theory of consumption in the limited sense of a theory of (market) demand for goods.[7]

As observed, the theory has scarcely advanced conceptually. But the mathematical presentation of its results and the econometrics for estimating their implications empirically have increased significantly in sophistication.[8] But the idea that consumption is predominantly determined by the maximisation of utility subject to the prevailing budget and price constraints has been the undeviating focus throughout. The conceptual poverty of this approach has been noticed from early on, if habitually confined to the margins of the discipline, like the twitching of an unwanted but unavoidable guilty conscience. Kryk observed this narrow-mindedness, criticising 'economists adopting utilitarianism even as it is being rejected by other social scientists' (Kryk 1923: 138). In an introduction to a survey article, Brown and Deaton assert:

> In particular we are interested in the effects (on consumption) of changes in real income per head, the structure of relative prices and the distribution of income, and we should like to have a means of allowing for the introduction of new commodities and changes in taste.
>
> (Brown and Deaton 1972: 1150)

The last wish has rarely been acknowledged let alone fulfilled. Scitovsky (1976: xii) has been blunt in reflecting the state of the art: 'People's tastes, the way they spend their money and arrange their lives, are matters economists have always regarded as something they should observe, but must not poke their noses into.' While for Waller (1988), the role of 'habit' in economics is found to fall outside orthodox economics, essentially because of its departure from purposeful, reflective behaviour and the inconvenience it creates for models of general equilibrium theory. Endogenous behaviour is most damaging to general equilibrium theory since it tends to yield multiple and indeterminate equilibria. Further, Mason (1981, 1984, 1998), for example, on conspicuous consumption, might just as well not exist as far as economists are concerned. And so the list could run on to include economists such as Veblen and Galbraith who might, in the past, have been observed before passing on. Now they are simply ignored.

Consequently, partly because economics has tended to be sealed off from other social sciences, those economists that do criticise demand theory have usually had some other axe to grind, having found the orthodoxy too blunt a tool for their particular purpose. Scitovsky, for example, was concerned with what appears a simple enough problem – why people did not seem to be happier with increased affluence. To raise such problems and others like them, especially in the context of non-economic factors and theory, is to court the label of idiosyncrasy as far as economics is concerned – both by stepping outside economics to embrace the considerations of other disciplines and by breaching the conventional assumptions within economics.[9]

Thus, consumption is reduced to the theory of the demand for goods. In turn, this is equivalent to the cost-minimising behaviour of the individual in meeting a given level of utility when prices are fixed for the goods involved. There is a formal identity between this analysis and that for the entrepreneur attempting to minimise the cost of producing a given level of output in the light of input prices. For those who have struggled through a first year of economic principles, this ought to be transparent either in the correspondence between the associated optimising conditions – relative marginal utilities (products) or marginal rates of substitution between consumption goods (factor inputs) should equal relative prices – or in the correspondence between indifference (isoquant) curves and the tangential budget lines. Essentially, the consumer is treated as a self-employed firm that seeks to produce utility as cheaply as possible and makes demands for inputs according to their prices.

Conceptually, the economic approach to consumer behaviour is justified on the grounds that it extracts the rational and systematic part of the determinants of demand, thereby separating them from and discarding other motives or behavioural characteristics. The latter, then, are presumed to be of secondary importance and, more in hope than expectation, to cancel each other out when aggregating over all individuals to obtain total demand. Economics has traditionally considered all other aspects of consumer behaviour to be the subject matter of other disciplines, despite occasional concern with the origins of initial preferences or with breaches from 'rational' behaviour. On the extremely rare occasions when these appear in the literature, they are treated as deviations from standard optimising behaviour – in this sense, the 'irrational' or 'non-rational' being determined by the previously conceived 'rational'.[10] By homogenising and setting aside all non-utility-maximising behaviour as 'irrational', economics effectively eliminates itself from the possible development of an *interdisciplinary* theory of consumer behaviour and heavily discourages even a *multidisciplinary* approach.

In addition, economic theory depends upon axiomatic model building and equilibrium in which many important determinants are taken not only to be exogenous, indeed to be explained on its behalf by other disciplines, but also often to be fixed. This is particularly so of consumer preferences which are pegged to a given utility function. Formally utility equals $u_i(q_1, q_2, ..., q_i, ..., q_n)$ where consumer, or often household, i derives utility u from consuming quantities x_j of the n available goods. This assumption concerning the exogeneity and the fixed nature of individual utility, and hence preferences over consumption goods, is so powerful that economic theory often proceeds on the basis of one or other of two extremes – either that all individuals can be treated as if each has the same preferences which can then be subsumed under a single representative consumer or that each and every individual is uniquely different with no commonality in underlying preferences. Of course, these assumptions are anathema to other social sciences concerned with the causal origins of preferences and the social processes by which they are either shared or distinct.

Further, not only is the economy built up from the atomised behaviour of individuals, but even this methodological reductionism is undertaken within the narrowest analytical scope. For the behavioural assumption underlying the theory of consumption is that the individual is motivated exclusively by the desire to maximise the previously assumed utility. The ability to do this is centrally a function of income available and the prices of consumption goods. Again, to other social scientists, this approach must appear uninviting because of its extraordinarily narrow analytical boundaries, in terms of both the motivational assumptions (confined to self-satisfaction) and the behavioural assumptions (pursued with ruthless efficiency). In effect, rational economic 'man' combines the basest instincts of a selfish beast with the highest forms of commercial calculation![11]

Thus, the economic theory of consumer behaviour focuses attention away from individual acts of exchange around specific commodities. These become of no interest in their own right, since each is meaningless in isolation from the others. Only 'bundles' of commodities give utility, so that the individual acts of obtaining and enjoying individual purchases become irrelevant. This results in a form of reification around the act of consumption. For it is now the commodities rather than individuals that take on the attributes of commanding pleasure. This is formally made clear by expressing underlying preferences as relations between the goods themselves. As Deaton and Muellbauer (1980: 27) unquestioningly proceed in the leading text on the economics of consumer behaviour, 'we write $q_1 \sim q_2$ and say "q_1 is indifferent to q_2"', where the qs are different bundles of goods over which *individuals* have preferences. Effectively, the economics of consumption can be seen in terms of goods actively moving themselves to satisfy passive consumers – the allocation of scarce resources to competing ends in Lionel Robbins' (in)famous definition of the discipline at the height of the Great Depression!

Leaving aside these polemics around commodity fetishism, a term that would not be recognised by mainstream economists in word even if pervasive in deed, consumer as demand theory concerns itself with the interdependent totality of sales and purchases undertaken by the individual. In theory, this would include all acts of sale and purchase over a lifetime – incorporating initial assets, not least ability to labour or human capital, and intertemporal discounting of present as against future consumption (plus account of the disutility of labour and the utility of leisure). Aside from these factors and acknowledging the role of transactions costs and imperfect information, little attention is paid to the necessity for consumer behaviour to take place over time, combining together a number of discrete activities, not least the carrying out of purchases and their consumption, as well as the process of decision making itself. On these issues, economic theory tends to be silent.

An example will help to illustrate why these various features of the neoclassical orthodoxy hang together and render economics fragile to any innovative incursion around consumption. In the wake of the Keynesian revolution, in which the macroeconomy is perceived to depend upon the overall level of demand, it became necessary to specify the overall level of consumer expenditure. This has given rise to the theory of the consumption function to complement other macroeconomic aggregates such as the investment function or the demand for money. In exploring the consumption function, an anomaly was discovered. Whilst it was expected that those who were richer would save proportionately more (and hence consume proportionately less) – what Keynes referred to as a psychological law – it was also found that the increase in consumption out of a given increase in income was different in the short run than in the long run. Duesenberry (1967) put forward the relative income hypothesis to explain this. Basically, consumers are stratified and in the short run have a lower propensity to consume because it takes them some time to adapt to being in the higher strata associated with their higher income over time. Obviously, this endogenises consumption[12] since preferences to consume become dependent upon economic stratification and paths of social mobility. Whilst providing a neat explanation for the empirical anomaly around the short- and long-run propensities to consume, the relative income hypothesis was noted for a time but has fallen out of favour, essentially because it would have been associated with multiple equilibria, endogeneity of preferences and social processes. Instead, a preferred explanation has been the permanent income hypothesis, associated with Milton Friedman (1957), in which short-run changes of income are seen as windfalls around a norm and are consumed thinly over the remainder of a lifetime.[13] This approach can be made consistent with the optimising behaviour of individuals with given preferences.

With few exceptions, economics has constructed a self-contained and narrow notion of consumer behaviour, both in terms of its objects of analysis and in terms of its associated causal factors. It has been concerned with regular empirical laws, theoretical regularities derived from demand systems, and the connection between these two.[14] For example, empirically, Engel's law hypothesises that the poorer a family, the greater the proportion of income spent on food; theoretically there is the fixed requirement that the substitution effect of good i for good j must equal that of good j for good i. In recent times, axiomatic consistency through mathematical modelling has been used to give rise to powerful parametric constraints that prove important in estimating demand curves or, more exactly, demand systems, and this serves the supportive function of linking the theory to empirical enquiry. For Blundell, 'Perhaps the most appealing feature of economic research into consumer behaviour is the close relationship between theoretical specification and appropriate estimation technique' (Blundell 1988: 16). This allows Deaton and Muellbauer (1980: 80) to reject casual reliance upon, and neglect of, theory and to call for: 'careful theoretical analysis. … The real challenge is one of intellectual honesty; we must construct models that are fundamentally credible as representations of the behaviour and phenomenon we are trying to understand.'

Yet by credibility, they mean mathematical consistency in obtaining parametric constraints from neo-classical demand analysis. This might be considered careful only along a very narrow and well-worn path, with no account taken of what economists tend to dismiss as irrational or outside their compass – they ignore behaviour other than individual utility maximisation and they refuse to explore the origins of (changing) preferences. Thus the only concession made by Deaton and Muellbauer to violation of rationality in consumer behaviour is to consider the possibility of money illusion (under which individuals falsely feel themselves to be better off because they have more money but do not take sufficient account of higher prices).

Moreover, the idea that consumers make decisions independently of one another is so deeply ingrained that the aggregation problem in demand theory (the relation between the collection of individual demands and of overall demand) takes on an almost perverse logic. Initially, a single consumer is taken as representative of society as a whole as if society were a single rational consumer. This has been found to be excessively restrictive, both theoretically and empirically, for even if each individual (household) has the same preferences, aggregation over them is not simple given the impact of differing distributions of income. Accordingly, Blundell argues:

> The most persuasive level of analysis must be at the individual consumer or household level ... and some form of aggregation prior to empirical analysis is often inevitable. ... The clear attraction of individual level data is that they avoid aggregation bias. Such bias can result both because of the complex interactions between individual characteristics and price/income effects and also because of nonlinearities in consumption behaviour due to non-linear Engel curves, corner solutions, rationing, non-linear taxation and imperfect credit markets.
>
> (Blundell 1988: 18)

Though this quotation points to some specialised economic concepts, most important to note is the theoretical and empirical detail that is embraced in respecting the independence of individual consumers. No account is taken of social factors that might lead consumers to behave in similar or even identical ways. Though to do so would not in itself resolve the aggregation problem, the absence of social factors in aggregating reflects the way in which this problem is conceived, and the treatment of consumption more generally. Exposed is the refusal to acknowledge anything other than the narrowest of determinants. Except, in practice, Blundell (1988) typically presents estimates on individual households grouped according to their type – with or without children, by level of income, etc. This involves an implicit assumption that certain types of households behave in the same way and that others do not. This is never justified nor explained; it is simply taken for granted just as previously it was assumed that all households determined consumption independently of each other.

Such token acknowledgement of the social in terms of socio-economic characteristics is, in part, a consequence of the availability of greater, desktop computing power. It has enabled large data sets with information on households to be used to estimate demand functions rather than the previously more common practice of treating the aggregate level of demand as if it were the result of a single representative individual's chosen consumption patterns. Significantly, such data do allow estimation to distinguish between household types by variables such as age, composition, class, etc. It is common, and sensible, to employ such proxies to represent household differences. This again enhances the scope for estimating the demand functions but only by importing the unexamined assumption that the proxy variables give rise to unexplained distinctions and conformities in underlying utility functions. As already questioned, given the underlying presumption that all (household) preferences are exogenous and fixed, and so potentially equally diverse, why should some groups be treated as sharing tastes as distinct from others? Once again is reflected the imperative of pushing aside the issues of what consumption is and why other than along unexamined and limited conceptual lines.

It is precisely the narrowness of this approach to consumer behaviour by economics that sets the points of departure for contributions to consumer behaviour from the other social sciences. These are concerned with the formation of preferences, with information processing by the individual, the activity of purchase, the activity of consumption, and the feedback mechanisms between these – although no particular structure and sequential division of these processes is sacrosanct.

In pinpointing this non-intersecting duality between the approach of economics and that of other disciplines to consumer behaviour, it is crucial to recognise that they all tend to have one central factor in common, the focus on the individual in and around the act of exchange. Within economics, this is usually taken as a focus for criticism by radical theories, with their emphasis on social relations and behaviour, such as class and conflict. In response, neo-classical theory, especially in contrasting itself favourably with classical political economy or Marxism, prides itself on having provided a theory of demand to complement the theory of supply.

Even this is misleading in anything other than a formal sense. True, the theory of utility maximisation subject to a budget constraint does lead to the derivation of demand curves in which the relative marginal utilities are equated to relative prices. But, significantly, this is completely independent of the specific use values of the consumption goods concerned. It is crucial that the goods be distinguishable from each other in their capacity to enhance utility, but the specific reasons for their differences are quite irrelevant – hence the nomenclature in the simplest textbook case of the existence of just two goods labelled as q_1 and q_2 in order that indifference curves can be drawn to illustrate substitution between them. The goods might be labelled bread and cheese to add some readership interest. But the economic theory that prides itself on incorporating demand does not in effect do so, since the nature, causes and motivation of that demand remain absent – except in the broadest sense of satisfying utility.[15]

Indeed, consumption within economics is almost always treated abstractly without reference to specified items of consumption. It involves pure formalism in which any number of consumption goods are given algebraic symbols to represent them – as in the utility function above. In this light, it is hardly surprising that the nature of consumption goods and of consumption activity cannot be addressed. As Slater and Tonkiss (2001: 50) recognise:[16]

> The theory of utility can only explain the formation of price given the demand for particular products (water, camomile tea, espresso coffee). It cannot explain the demand for these products in themselves. In this sense, utility theory is not a theory of 'usefulness'; it does not explain why people subjectively value certain goods, only how value comes to be expressed as price. The subjective reasons why I might prefer tea to coffee are, in this economic model, unknowable.

This is as true for broad categories of consumption, such as food and clothing, as it is for specific items. Paradoxically, this is brought out most sharply in the particular functional form for utility associated with Geary-Stone (Deaton and Muellbauer 1980: 65). It hypothesises a minimum standard of living necessary to obtain positive utility, signifying some concession to physical and even social survival. But even this can be specified abstractly as an undefined vector of goods, $(g_1, g_2, ..., g_n)$. Indeed, the exact nature of the consumption goods under consideration is only specified once empirical studies are broached.[17] The motivation for this is less to examine, let alone to explain, the physiological or socio-historical basis of subsistence than to provide particular functional or mathematical forms under which econometric methods can be used to specify demand functions statistically. This leads to speculations like Engel's law which, once formulated, are then translated back into what must have been an appropriate form of the utility function in the first place. The causal content of such theory is extremely limited, since it essentially seeks merely to discover those utility functions that would generate the empirically revealed expenditure patterns – and under a set of assumptions that are far from realistic. There is also the assumption that given preferences extend not only across populations but also across time.

In short, neo-classical consumer theory is not only self-contained relative to other social sciences, but also akin to a sealed unit within economics itself. It is partly for this reason that there has been negligible advance in the economics of consumer behaviour over the past century. The poverty of the economic theory of consumption is, however, not simply confined to its inability to deal with the nature of the goods consumed. There is also a deficiency in conceptually distinguishing the theory of consumption (treated as demand) from the theory of production (treated as supply). For between the two, there is an exact parallel: the demand theory is essentially identical to the axiomatic theory of supply. The maximisation of utility subject to price and income constraints creates an identical mathematical problem to the minimisation of cost subject to output constraints and factor input prices. Conceptually, individual consumers can be interpreted as if they were entrepreneurs producing utility, rather than output, as efficiently as possible. The strict parallel highlights the extent to which neo-classical economics lacks a distinct theory of consumption – for the equality of marginal rates of substitution with relative prices applies indiscriminately both to ratios of marginal productivities and to ratios of marginal utilities.[18] The duality theory associated with cost functions, which applies equally to supply (produc-tion) and to demand (utility), is an explicit acknowledgement of theoretical duality/identity between production and consumption. In the orthodoxy, the merging of consumption and production takes place explicitly in the analysis of the household – which becomes both a site of consumption and of production, most notably in the work of Becker. Deaton and Muellbauer (1980: 245) state, for example: 'Household production theory is an integration of theory of the consumer with that of the firm.' This tends to conceal, however, that the theory of the firm and the theory of the consumer are already almost identical.

Interestingly, the traditional radical critique of neo-classical economics is that it does not have a distinct theory of production – by which is meant that it cannot explain the source of a surplus through some form of exploitation and/or that it treats the production process in narrow technical terms alone rather than as a relation of conflict between workers and bosses at the factory. On the other hand, radical theories have been charged with the reverse weak-ness, that of failing to offer their own theory of demand, depending upon cost of production alone. Putting radical theories on the defensive over demand has allowed the poverty of neo-classical economics' own demand theory to go largely unnoticed. The exception has been the critique of the concept of consumer sovereignty and all that this entails in pointing to the powerful role of producers in determining, first, what our preferences are and, second, what the goods are that are made available to satisfy them (Mohun 1977).

The manipulation of preferences returns analysis to the traditional concerns of non-economic consumer behaviour theory, as in investigating the impact of advertising. Significantly, as discussed in Fine and Leopold (1993: Chapter 14), advertising in economics is more at home within the field of industrial economics, as part of the theory of the firm or industry rather than that of the consumer. This is indicative of the greater depth and variety of economic anal-ysis around issues of supply as opposed to demand. Within orthodox economics, control over supply concerns the exercise, for example, of monopoly power, for which the theory of supply does have a richer and more changing content than the theory of demand. The poverty of the latter follows from the passive role played by consumers as the depositories of the utility that is ultimately created by the economic system. Central to this is the concept of competitive equilibrium in which, for example, a size structure of industry is ground out that is endogenous to the system (although it depends upon the parameters of supply that determine least average cost of production). So the number of firms is analytically deter-mined, unlike the number of consumers which is given as a datum (unless demographic factors are incorporated). In mainstream economics, there are competitive mechanisms at work that can transform the system of production. The same is not true of the system of consumption.

The divergence between the analytical content devoted to supply and demand does not, however, rest there. For the notion of competitive equilibrium forms a key concept from which potential divergencies are identified as a means of understanding the real world. Almost inevitably, these divergencies focus upon the conditions of supply, although externalities and monopolisation are equally possible, in principle, for both supply and demand. The simplest example is provided by the model of pure monopoly in which consumers suffer higher prices and lower output. But the incorporation of other causal factors or behavioural assumptions, around oligopoly theory and managerial motivation, has led to a rich set of models within the economics of supply, even though these tend to be limited by the continuing assumption of exogenously given technology.[19]

The same does not apply to the economics of consumption or, more exactly, demand. Yet matters are not quite so simple. For, within economics, developments in the theory of supply have been highly relevant to the determination of consumption. Even so, such exceptions tend to prove the rule, exposing the limitations of the orthodoxy only at most to be acknowledged before being set aside. To return to the example of the economics of advertising, the main approach has been to link it to industrial economics and construe advertising expenditure as part of, or akin to, an accumulated fixed cost. It can act as a potential barrier to entry. Assessing the effects of advertising in this context has been primarily carried out within the discipline of marketing, or economics itself, as distinct from the discipline of consumer behaviour. For it has been closely linked to modification of demand curves (through the addition of an advertising variable) and their interaction with supply, with emphasis on econometrics and the associated problems of modelling, sampling and statistical techniques (Malhotra 1988).

So, first and foremost, progress within economics around consumption has primarily been confined to econometrics, or the statistical application of formal models. If a case is to be made for successful development within neo-classical demand theory, it is in the finer specification of the mathematics of the analysis as a means of making empirical estimation more consistent in particular ways.[20] It is worth dwelling on this matter in two revealing aspects. First, essentially the goal is to estimate elasticities – how responsive demand for consumption goods is to price and income changes. The success of the estimates in the statistical terms of 'goodness of fit' can in part be interpreted as a test of whether underlying preferences are fixed and exogenous. For example, the National Food Survey is used to estimate income and price elasticities for particular foods. Where these estimates do not perform well statistically, this is put down to the separate factor of shifting tastes. However, and transparently, from a causal point of view, this is sheer tautology since whatever happens empirically can be interpreted as reflecting an appropriate balance between shifts with given preferences and shifts

135

between preferences. And, because shifts in preferences are taken as the residual explanatory factor if, in accepting this approach, there were shifts in preferences alone, they would be explained as far as possible in terms of elasticities (Fine *et al.* 1996: Chapter 7).

Recent developments within the economics of consumer theory have, however, been both theoretically and empirically extensive, despite the narrow terrain on which they have been constructed. For, rather than addressing what is consumed (other than in a quantitative sense) and how preferences are formed and exercised, attention has been confined to pushing forward theory as the technical basis on which statistical estimation can be further honed. For example, consumer durables pose particular problems because choice is discrete, and they are considered as capital goods providing a stream of consumer services over time. This has posed the problem of what economists term 'corner solutions'. For, when working with aggregate data or the representative consumer, it can be presumed that some amount of everything will be purchased. This assumption cannot be maintained when working with data at an individual household level, so that models involving frequency of purchase – as well as whether items are purchased or not – have to be developed to fit the data statistically.[21]

The previous paragraph has been primarily concerned with consumer theory at the microeconomic level of demand for particular goods. In estimating aggregate consumer expenditure for macroeconomic modelling purposes, the role of the representative consumer has become more sophisticated. Where previously a behavioural assumption was made, such as a fixed proportion of income being spent, the representative consumer in more recent theoretical developments is presumed to optimise over a lifetime, thereby needing to undertake sophisticated intertemporal decisions and to form expectations about the future path of the economy itself. Again, in so far as this has been associated with theoretical innovation, it is entirely in response to the needs of statistical estimation rather than in any deepening of the understanding of consumption itself. Thus, there is a division between the study of consumption from a macro (overall expenditure) and micro perspective, in spite of 'a common theoretical structure'[22] based on the representative consumer with fixed preferences and motivation as previously outlined.

Economics, then, has always been flush with a wealth of empirical studies, and the development of the study of consumption has even flourished on the continuing basis of a dialogue between the empirical evidence and the theoretical techniques for handling it. There is always room to re-estimate price and income elasticities of individual or aggregate consumption whether because additional data are necessarily generated with the passage of time or because some new theoretical nicety can be incorporated – whether as a result of computer-enhanced statistical capability or through some incremental concession to the realities of consumption as in the recognition of corner solutions. But these advances in techniques and empirical estimation are both prodigious and in extreme disproportion to the conceptual core that has remained both narrow and unchanging. Whatever the validity and use of these studies, in macroeconomic forecasting or in designing tax proposals, for example, the persisting weakness of economics in consumption theory is illustrated by the ways in which it has *not* been used. Whilst manufacturers and retailers are well aware of the dependence of demand for their products upon the prices they charge and the income of their potential consumers, they are acutely conscious of other factors and positively seek both to identify them through psychographics etc. and to manipulate them by changing preferences through advertising. Further, the weakness of consumer theory within economics is demonstrated by the limited space it commands in the *New Palgrave Dictionary of Economics*. This runs to four volumes and over 4,000 pages, but the space devoted to consumption-related topics, depending upon how broadly these are interpreted, is probably less than 100 pages. A topic such as conspicuous consumption warrants an entry of only half of a page![23]

From unendurables to durables

The preceding discussion has laid out some of the causes for the limited contribution made by the discipline of economics to the theory of consumer behaviour. First, its notion of rationality excludes the concerns of other social sciences. Second, it does not have a specific theory of what is consumed, with utility created in the abstract through optimisation like any other 'production' process (cost minimisation for a given level of utility/output). Third, as a generalisation of the two previous points, the substance of the consumer as subject and of the consumed as object are simply left unexamined. And, fourth, developments within economics tend to focus upon supply and are, thereby, removed from a concern with consumption.[24]

These features go a long way towards explaining why economics has been so uninfluential in the other social sciences when it comes to consumption. As already apparent, economics unacceptably takes as given what other treatments seek to explain, not least the nature of consumer and consumed over and beyond fixed individuals defined by their preferences and utility maximisation and fixed goods defined by their physical properties. For this reason, whilst economics imperialism has made considerable headway in some areas in encroaching upon the traditional terrain of the other social sciences, its progress has been extremely limited for consumption.

But it is far from non-existent as will be revealed in two ways that serve, in part, as generic illustrations. First recall, for mainstream economics, that there is presumed to be a core range of 'rational', i.e. utility-maximising, behaviour. This raises the issue of how extensive is that range. Where does it end so that the 'irrational', or other motivations, can take over, and to what objects or activities does it apply (Zafirovski 2000)?

One extreme in this respect is provided by Gary Becker, a Nobel Prize winner in economics for economics imperialism. He pushes out indefinitely the boundaries of what he terms the 'economic approach'. He has set himself the task of explaining as many economic and social phenomena as possible on the basis of individuals optimising from given preferences. This is the basis for a number of contributions: the theory of human capital, for which Becker is most renowned – that we seek training and work experience on the basis of the extra returns that they provide in the form of higher wages; the new household economics uses given preferences to determine whether women take waged work or not and how many children are desired in light of the opportunity cost of childcare; and the manipulative content of advertising is dismissed in favour of its informational role, with apparent changes in preferences being due to better informed consumers.[25]

Here, focus will be on a more recent contribution from the Becker stable, concerned with addictive behaviour. The topic is taken to be a considerable challenge to the orthodoxy, possibly lying outside its analytical scope, because addiction would appear to indicate both irrational and shifting preferences. Thus, Becker and Murphy (1988: 675) open:[26]

> Rational consumers maximize utility from stable preferences as they try to anticipate the future consequences of their choices. Addictions would seen to be the antithesis of rational behaviour. Does an alcoholic or heroin user maximize or weigh the future? Surely his preferences shift rapidly over times as his mood changes?

Interestingly, addictive behaviour is perceived to be extremely pervasive, so that orthodox theory would be the poorer if unable to accommodate it (pp. 675–6):

> People get addicted not only to alcohol, cocaine, and cigarettes but also to work, eating, music, television, their standard of living, other people, religion, and many other activities. Therefore, much behaviour would be excluded from the rational choice framework if addictions have to be explained in another way.

This is then followed by the astonishing claim that as long as rationality, as understood by the orthodoxy, is able to 'explain' (i.e. produce a model in which what is taken to be addictive behaviour is a possible outcome), then there is no need for any other theory (p. 676):

> Fortunately, a separate theory is not necessary since rational choice theory can explain a wide variety of addictive behavior.

The way in which the model works is to allow an addictive good to affect current utility positively and future utility negatively. Rational consumers, maximising utility over all time, take this into account in deciding simultaneously at the outset on whether to consume the addictive product in the present and in the future given anticipated prices and incomes. You may be rational in choosing addiction if the present pleasures outweigh the fully anticipated and discounted drawbacks of the relatively distant future. On the basis of such a model, it is possible to yield what are claimed to be 'new insights into addictive behavior' (p. 675), around binges, cold turkey, limited impacts of temporary price increases, and the role of anxiety and stress in bringing about addiction. Further, in a subsequent paper, Becker *et al.* (1994) estimate the demand for cigarettes on this basis (also taking account of the role of potential monopoly pricing, if not advertising and the impact of smoking on earnings and life expectancy).

The main point to be made here is that, methodologically, it is presumed that if rational behaviour can explain any form of consumption empirically then no other explanation is necessary.[27] Thus, with sufficient ingenuity, it is unnecessary to address the issue of how preferences are formed and what constitutes the nature of the goods over which they are exercised. One implication of the theory is that high enough prices, now and in the future, will ultimately eliminate addiction since the costs of generating utility through consumption of addictive goods becomes prohibitively expensive. This, however, points to one aspect of consumption with which the orthodoxy is unable to deal. This is the rejection of rationality by consumers, whether in counterculture generally or, more specifically, in the desire to consume items more just because they are more expensive (as in conspicuous consumption) or harder to obtain (if illegal, for example).

This highlights a particular feature of the economic theory of the consumer, whether addressed to addiction or not. It is general, in being derived from the maximisation of given individual utility, without specifying differences in consumption goods themselves. Indeed, it is common only to specify one good as opposed to another in abstract mathematical terminology (just as supply and demand curves, more generally, are deemed to apply to all goods and markets). This is why addiction is seen as a common phenomenon, without distinction, across the range of activities listed above from alcohol to religion and many other activities.[28] The nature of addictions as differentiated social constructs is entirely obliterated. They are simply understood and explained on the basis of rational, optimising individuals.

In later work, Becker (1996) has widened the scope of his economic approach even further. He argues that individuals have given utility and preferences at any moment in time as the basis for the goods they then consume. But such instantaneous utility is embedded in an underlying and shifting 'extended' utility function. This adds other variables that shift over time. They themselves divide into two categories, personal and social, and are perceived as forms of capital. This is because one standard interpretation of capital within neo-classical economics is the productivity of time – how waiting for consumption (and utility) potentially enlarges the amount available, sowing corn that might otherwise be eaten, allowing a tree to grow for wood rather than chop it immediately, or saving and investing resources rather than consuming them.

For personal capital, of which human capital is the leading example, individuals gain over time through learning or experience. But, as already indicated, personal capital can apply to skills and sophistication in making and benefiting from decisions around consumption directly. Social capital derives from interaction with others. Becker's motivating example is the long queue at one restaurant and none at another that otherwise appears identical. The queue at the popular restaurant, it can be deduced, signals something we do not know but that others do. So you learn and benefit from such interaction with others and, in principle, all *social* phenomena can be reduced to individual choices over goods, personal and social capital (Becker 1996: 25):

> We assert that this traditional approach of the economist offers guidance in tackling these problems – and that no other approach of remotely comparable generality and power is available.

For Becker, the assumption of differences in underlying preferences is simply arbitrary and weak, and nothing is to be expected from the other social sciences in explaining them (p. 49):[29]

> No significant behavior has been illuminated by assumption of differences in tastes ... (which) along with assumptions of unstable tastes, have been a convenient crutch to lean on ... ad hoc arguments that disguise analytical failures.

In short, for Becker, in taking the economic approach to its logical conclusion, social science (and history) become reducible to optimising behaviour around an extended utility function, $u(q, p, s)$, where q, p and s represent, respectively, quantities of goods, personal capital and social capital, each strategically chosen by consumers in light of constraints. Moreover, with the major exception of the differences between the genders, the logic of parsimonious use of factors in explanation leads to the assumption that all humans have the same biologically given extended utility function. The idea is that apparent differences in individuals can be explained entirely by different external circumstances and hence choices of, and outcomes for, personal and social capital. Consider the treatment of the extended utility function.

First, it is invariant across individuals (p. 25):

> The establishment of the proposition that one may usefully treat tastes as stable over time and similar among people is the central task.

Second, the extended utility function should be invariant across time (p. 5):

> The utility function itself is independent of time, so that it is a stable function over time of the goods consumed and also of the (personal and

social) capital goods ... the extended utility function ... is stable only
because it includes measures of past experience and social forces.

Third, then, as previously indicated, apparent differences in individuals' current
tastes may be the consequence of identical underlying extended utility functions
but differences in experiences and opportunities, across time, place and a whole
range of other socio-economic factors (p. 6):

> The influence of childhood and other experiences on choice can
> explain why rich and poor, whites and blacks, less and more educated
> persons, or persons who live in countries with totally different traditions
> have subutility functions that are radically different.

Fourth, with minor qualification, there is an appeal to biological determinism, at
least as a starting point at birth (p. 126):[30]

> Each person is born perhaps not as a *tabula rasa* – an empty slate – but
> with limited experiences that get filled in by childhood and later experi-
> ences.

Finally, with a breathtaking and unjustified leap of faith, we are informed that
the economic approach extends not only to the other social sciences but to the
natural sciences also (p. 9):

> I believe the main reason habitual behavior permeates most aspects of
> life is that habits have an advantage in the biological evolution of
> human traits. For as long as habits are not too powerful they have social
> as well as personal advantages.

So Becker lies at one extreme in applying the economic approach; he recognises no bounds. His fellow economists border on the contemptuous for his lack
of finesse in demarcating territories for the other social sciences and in reducing
the social to the economic and, as has been seen, the economics to the biological
(Swedberg 1990b). Akerlof (1990: 73) lampoons Becker as having learnt to spell
banana but not knowing when to stop!

The alternative for those still wedded to mainstream economics is to delimit
the scope of economic analysis and to complement it with that drawn from the
other social sciences if seeking interdisciplinarity. This then creates a divide
between the rational (and economic) and the irrational (and social), as elaborated
at length by Zafirovski (2000) in his account of the relations between economics
and sociology. Inevitably, the line between the two is subject to movement.
Initially, with the marginalist revolution of the 1870s, prior to which much classical political economy drew no rigid boundary between the economic and the
social, economics established itself as the science of the market – supply and

demand. In addition, as Velthuis (1999) observes for Talcott Parsons, sociology and economics should not overlap since one concerned the social and the other the individual, respectively, whatever subject matter they addressed, economic or otherwise.[31]

Such simple dichotomies are no longer respected. They have never been accepted by the likes of Becker, and the current phase of economics imperialism, as outlined in Chapter 2, is rampant, drawing upon the notion of the social as the non-market response to market, especially informational, imperfections. But, Becker aside, if the division between rational and irrational is accepted, alongside economic and social, this raises three questions. First, where does the boundary lie; second, what constitutes and determines the irrational; and, third, how do the two broad spheres of behaviour and activity interact with one another?

There can be no general answer to these questions although a general observation can be offered. This is that, especially in the current intellectual climate, the outcome is liable to promote economics imperialism. It will not be entirely of the Becker type – the social reduced to the as if perfect market. Instead, the concepts and theories of the other social sciences will be recast in a form, usually mutually inconsistent, in which a core element of neo-classical economics can command a place. The leading example of this from the past, in the Becker mould, is human capital. It is now used widely and uncritically across the social sciences, without regard to its origins in Becker's methodology. Quite apart from its reification of the processes by which education is gained and deployed, ironically, human capital is used as a means of stratifying although its definition is grounded in methodological individualism.

A similar, if far less prominent and extensive, application is to be found in the work of Bowden and Offer (1994, 1996) on consumer durables.[32] It is taken as illustration for a number of reasons. First, it is an overt attempt to extend mainstream economics in order to examine specific items of consumption. Indeed, their work is self-confessedly inspired by Becker (Bowden and Offer 1994: 278). Second, the approach of Bowden and Offer, B&O, is laid out in a number of contributions that allow it to be clearly understood. Third, in addition, they have debated with the sop approach, offering a spirited riposte.[33]

Specifically, B&O appeal to Becker for his work on the family and the use of time.[34] Time is particularly important for B&O since they do not refer to personal and social capital, the terms now preferred by Becker himself. Instead, B&O essentially proxy such capitals in two different ways – as time itself and as the materialised productivity of time or physically durable (consumer) equipment.[35]

Significantly, both concepts are ahistorical, although used to explain historically specific outcomes – diffusion of household appliances in the twentieth century. Inevitably, the historical content – in both the use and meaning of goods – has to be added on, as will be seen, in potentially arbitrary and inconsistent ways. Observe, however, that far from challenging these charges, B&O clarify and, remarkably, fully embrace them (Bowden and Offer 1999: 563):

> Economic categories (and the economic notions of rationality and
> motivation) are indeed timeless, but not in the sense that they stand
> outside historical time. Rather, economists assume that they apply
> throughout historical time. This is merely a way of saying that human
> nature remains constant in history, while environments, prices, and
> cultures change.

Initially, a distinction is drawn between time spent on work or domestic obligations and discretionary time. This is so that Bowden and Offer (1994) can
distinguish between those household appliances that are *time saving* in enhancing
the productivity of housework, so allowing for more discretionary time, and
those that are *time using* in requiring discretionary time in consumption. The
duality between time saving and time using is seen as corresponding to
producing and consuming within the household, the latter as a source of entertainment. Representative goods are the vacuum cleaner and the television,
respectively.

The distinction between these different times has resonance with an extrapolation from the world of capitalist work, where (labour) time is apparently sold
and, in employment, is primarily governed by commercial considerations. As is
evident from the domestic labour debate (Fine 1992: Appendix), there is no
corresponding discipline governing time spent outside work. Consequently,
distinguishing between time-saving and time-using appliances has limited
systematic social basis. Nor is it even rooted in individual decision making. B&O
admit 'it is sometimes difficult to disentangle the time-saving and time-using
attributes of goods', referring to television, motor cars and bicycles (p. 743).
Inverting their own definitional logic and descriptive hypothesis, for example,
they classify the telephone as a time-saving appliance because its diffusion follows
the pattern that is typical for them of the appliances delineated as time saving (p.
744).[36] In short, whether derived by analogy with employment or not, the
distinction between time saving and time using does not apply readily to the
household where a discipline of time is neither enforced nor liable to be
adopted.[37]

Ambiguity also arises in addressing time devoted to *housework*. As B&O
observe, this has stagnated until falling slightly in the recent period of greater
female labour market participation. How is this possible given the adoption,
however slowly, of *time-saving* appliances? The answer is in the shifting relative
weight of household standards, productivity and other demands on time. Yet, if
standards increase above home productivity, in cleaning and washing for
example, raising time devoted to them, this is indistinguishable other than in
name of activity, from time using for entertainment through use of leisure appliances. Explanation has become tautological in attaching time saving and time
using to housework and leisure/entertainment, respectively. Why do we not say

that the standards of domestic entertainment have risen rather than that the appliances involved are time using? For B&O (p. 728):

> 'Time-saving' goods reduce the time required to complete a specific household task. An electric washing machine reduces the time required to clean a tubful of laundry, compared with manual methods. … Time-saving goods can increase the quantity of discretionary time, whereas time-using goods enhance its perceived quality.

But redefining time using as enhancing the quality of time does not offer a resolution. Is not the *time* spent in cleaner houses or clothes of higher quality, at least subjectively?[38] How do we distinguish between the quality of time as opposed to the quality of the appliances or their output?

The last point concerning new, higher quality, services is an important point for empirical reasons. B&O do suggest that the time-using, leisure appliances may have diffused faster because they needed to displace alternative equipment for cooking, cleaning, etc., particularly in view of other claims that might be made on household income. Once again, however, there is a distinct atmosphere of tautology and self-selection. If something new becomes available which is not provided by any other means, generally affordable at going prices and incomes, there is surely a distinct possibility that it is going to diffuse relatively rapidly. A fuller analysis would surely need to look at some such goods that did not diffuse rapidly or which failed altogether and, consequently, disappeared from a retrospective investigation of later patterns of ownership.[39]

There are two possibilities, leaving aside the availability of entirely novel services. Either an appliance saves time per unit of output, but may be used to provide a proportionately higher or lower level of output so that the actual time commanded can be higher or lower than before. If the household introduces an appliance that is not time saving in this sense, it would appear to be behaving inefficiently, since it is paying for a durable without increased labour productivity. Or, scarcely addressed by B&O, the appliance can be a source of utility in and of itself without the use of time at all, as acknowledged by them for cars (pp. 743–4). The most important example, however, is household accommodation. Presumably the same applies to furniture which is intriguingly associated with appliances because of their close income elasticities of demand (p. 733):[40]

> The priority for acquiring time-saving durables was similar to that of furnishing a home, and indeed it is likely that the two activities were related.

But are housing and furnishing time saving, time using or time enhancing? These ahistorical categories create more conundrums than they resolve![41]

Thus, within the Becker framework itself, the simple division of time between using and saving is fractured by a variety of complications that undermine corresponding categorisation of household appliances. In addition, attention has shifted to demand, equally complex, on which B&O introduce two further influences. One is the low value placed upon women, whether as consumers or as workers. Their priorities as consumers are deemed to be low for time-saving appliances compared with what are deemed to be non-gendered appliances such as lighting and radio. Leaving aside ambiguity in the gendering of goods as male or female – would food be considered non-gendered because all have to eat? Such an argument is insufficiently tight. Even within a patriarchal framework, appliances that save women's working time within the household could, subject to price, still be adopted.[42] For they could be used efficiently to serve men indirectly in other ways, as is evident from the limited reductions in the amounts of female domestic labour when time-saving appliances are adopted.

As workers, women are deemed to be unable to command a sufficiently high wage in the formal economy to warrant substituting for their time in the domestic economy with bought-out appliances. As it is observed that women were often responsible for producing the very goods that could allow, or make it economically viable for, them to work,[43] some sort of balance is required in determining how much they worked out of the home to allow them to purchase the appliances that made waged work a viable and adopted choice. For, presumably, the lower are women's wages, the cheaper will be the appliances that they produce. Consequently, it is worth highlighting the way in which patriarchy, although never termed as such, is being used as a residual explanatory factor in an implicitly extensive way and one which is not necessarily consistent with the underlying neo-classical economics employed. For, treating women's time and needs as of low value involves complex issues of conflict between efficiency and distribution both within the household and between the household and the (male?) formal economy. Who controls and gains the advantage from women's work?

Once again, elements of tautological reasoning appear to be involved, with patriarchy relied upon when required but otherwise set aside.[44] Goods are labelled as gendered, or not, according to who might benefit from consuming them.[45] But how, then, in a world of patriarchy are we to explain that women's, girls' and children's clothing accounted in the UK in 1936 for a larger share of consumer expenditure (37 per cent) than that of men and boys (26 per cent) (Bowden and Offer 1996: 257)?[46] A separate point in the context of clothing is that the virtues of a washing machine depend upon having sufficient dirty laundry to wash to make it worthwhile. If the fabric of household consumption, including hardware and hollowware, as well as clothing, have yet to be purchased in sufficient quantities, it is hardly surprising that appliances that use them as raw materials are less attractive.

The other factor influencing demand is what can be called *access*. This has two components. On the one hand, differential access to household appliances is dependent on public policy, not least on whether and on what conditions electricity and gas are provided, for example. On the other hand, capacity to purchase, over and above income and price, depends upon availability of credit to smooth expenditure. There is a tendency to see credit as promoting diffusion; it makes possible in advance what would otherwise be impossible by outright purchase (p. 246):

> Desire is stoked by advertising and facilitated by credit.

This may be so for individuals *ceteris paribus*, i.e. for manipulable preferences and given cash prices for goods.[47] But, as is apparent, purchase on credit is extremely expensive when taking account of the excessive levels of interest payments.[48] Consequently, the particular conditions governing the availability of credit can also be considered to have *impeded* the diffusion of ownership by virtue of the high prices effectively charged. In addition, the targeting of advertising to those elite households which could more readily purchase appliances can have an impact upon the quality of the goods made available, making them unduly costly at the expense of higher volume, lower quality, or less heavily designed, products serving uniform mass markets.[49]

This is a specific example of a more general argument concerning how product differentiation, oligopoly, advertising, availability of credit, etc., can influence the structure of demand, and hence productivity, cost and diffusion. Ironically, each of Bowden and Offer in separate contributions recognises this possibility in their respective studies of the demand for cars. Thus, Bowden and Turner (1993: 256–7) close their contribution on interwar British car demand as follows, arguing from market structure to pricing, and from pricing to low scale and high cost undermining mass markets:[50]

> The policies pursued by British manufacturers also acted to confirm and compound the existing structure of the market. ... There was thus no reason to follow Ford into a price war. ... This could be justified – insofar as short-term profitability could be – and was ensured by a policy that concentrated on extending the existing middle-class market.

Similarly, for Offer (1998: 318), for the United States in the 1950s, 'the Big Three avoided competition on price, which could eliminate profits and even drive the weakest out of business'. Instead, a major form of competition was through shortening model cycles from three to even two years, with heavy implications for costs (pp. 328–9):

> Each of the Big Three had scores of model variants. All of them received a face-lift every year. ... Each design emerged from an array of false starts. At such a pace of styling change, product planning and approval became a big drain on management effort. ... Frequent styling played havoc with quality. ... The Edsel acquired a poor reputation for

quality; partly because it was a new design, but also because it rolled down the lines intermixed sparsely with other Ford cars, and workers never had a chance to learn to assemble it properly.

A further effect was to intensify the costs of selling the car through dealers, a factor that Offer points to as explaining the sharp fall in price of a car from new to one year old, curiously neglecting the planned obsolescence built into rapid change in models.

In short, the structure of provision, and how its separate components interact and function, are crucial to pricing, demand and diffusion. This is to be drawn to the sop approach. But most of the foregoing is concerned with critical discussion of the factors that *influence* demand without, as yet, breaking fundamentally with the chosen inspiration provided by Becker. But what exactly is *demand* itself? This has essentially been taken for granted by B&O, with one exception provided by their discussion of 'arousal', in which the natural preference for goods is moved back one step biologically from utility (Bowden and Offer 1994: 735ff.).[51] The demand for time-using entertainment appliances is explained in terms of the natural human need attached to sensual stimulus, the ease with which these can be consumed, and the pace of technological progress in providing them cheaply. It is even argued by B&O that television viewing has, unwittingly echoing Becker, addictive power.

Significantly, Becker's own theory of consumption is similarly based on biological considerations, presuming that all individuals have the same underlying preferences but that they learn differently what to enjoy through the differential accumulation of personal and social consumer capital. Consequently, for Becker, consumption paths, including addiction, are chosen in order to optimise. Having surveyed the options, we would choose to be a telly addict or not. Consequently, it becomes arbitrary, if not again tautological, to explain TV viewing as (arousal) irrational, especially when it is considered as a deliberate pre-commitment to pay excessive credit charges to become addicted to it (Bowden and Offer 1994: 742–3).

The demand for TV suggests a further questionable illustration of extrapolating from the discipline of time imposed by waged employment, for which time is usually seen as one dimensional and activities are mutually exclusive of one another. In contrast, within the home, one is not at work or at play. In terms of the radio, for example, women are liable to have been listening whilst doing the housework and, indeed, programmes have been so designed. Similarly, the TV (and video) are essential for time saving as far as childcare is concerned.[52] In some respects, the TV and radio can be considered as comparable to lighting, liable to household multiple ownership and to be on as long as someone is in the house.

In this light, note how tautological the arguments become. Once a good, such as a TV, is purchased, even if on hire purchase, insatiable demand would suggest it would always be in use as running costs are extremely low. As this is not so,

B&O introduce the value of time to explain the outcome. For TV watching is given up, once the individual's sensual capacities have been worked sufficiently far down the marginal utility curve (p. 732):[53]

> Our explanation is cast in terms of the marginal cost of discretionary time, and its marginal utility. Consumers have apparently given greater priority to enhancing the quality of discretionary time than to increase its quantity. This reflects the uneven pace of technological change, which has found it easier to increase the attractions of leisure time than to reduce the burden of housework.

No doubt, with different empirical outcomes, the priorities would be judged to be otherwise, indicating that the analysis has no explanatory content.

Apart from treating activities as mutually exclusive as far as time is concerned, a further deficiency in the account of demand by B&O is the notion of appliance itself. So far, the discussion here has been careful, with a few necessary exceptions, only to refer to (domestic and household) appliances, although B&O tend to alternate without thinking between the terms 'appliance' and 'durables'. But the two are very different, although B&O probably intend one to be a subset of the other, respectively. Without wishing to be pedantic, a durable is simply something that lasts for what is an ill-defined length of time. It is a universal category without historical content. The household enjoys a very wide range of durables, from plastic buckets, fixtures and fittings, clothing, food stores, other household effects, through to the putative categories of time-saving and time-using appliances themselves. An immediate issue is why B&O's approach should not apply to all of these 'durables'.[54]

Appliances, on the other hand, especially with the terms 'domestic' or 'household' appended, are a different kettle of fish. As a subcategory of durables they are socially and historically specific. They simply did not exist prior to the twentieth century – there were Elizabethan durables if not domestic appliances. The notion of appliances is a socially constructed category, not only in the sense that electricity and the white goods have to have been invented and made, but in what counts as an appliance in practice. This is variable – does it now include an electric kettle or an iron? – and, without going into detail, it depends upon how the goods concerned are designed, produced, sold, used and construed as objects – do antique carpets or old masters count as household durables?

Yet again, it is to be suspected that the notion of appliance as durable has been gleaned by extrapolation from the economic theory of the market economy. In this context, the parallel durable is fixed capital. As such, it is tied both conceptually and chronologically to a more precise, however satisfactory, definition. Fixed capital is durable in the sense that it cannot be changed in the short run during which employment and output decisions are presumed to be made. By the same token, it lasts beyond the period of a single cycle of production for output. For convenience, in constructing national and corporate accounts, fixed capital is also presumed to depreciate at a definite rate so that it lasts for a particular period of time.

Such considerations cannot apply to the household because, unlike the capitalist enterprise, it is not motivated by a profit *rate*, which is necessarily tied to time. What would constitute the length of time of the production period for the household beyond which an appliance qualifies as a durable? Should it be daily or annual, by the regularity of wage or other payment, or even intergenerational? There can be no answer and, as a result, a slightly separate consideration has been brought into play concerning how goods are purchased. Fixed capital and household appliances are both heavily associated with use of credit. Consequently, appliances usually constitute a high expenditure relative to income, with goods losing the status of appliance as income increases relative to their price. But this need not be the case, and how and whether goods are treated as appliances or not inevitably depends upon the commercial strategy of those providing them rather than exclusively upon their physical properties of durability and service to the optimising consumer.

From individual demand to social norms

The foregoing meticulous conceptual examination of B&O is motivated by the wish to reveal how wedding the economic approach to other approaches (arousal, economy of time, durables, gender, etc.) gives rise to irresolvable conundrums, readily revealed but equally easily overlooked. By contrast, there is a consistent if uncompelling logic underlying the work of Becker and those followers who confine themselves to the 'economic approach' in its pure form. For Becker, the optimising behaviour of individuals as an explanatory tool prevails without bounds in terms of its scope of application, from the market far beyond. Ultimately, he is forced to regress back to biological determinism. But, in pressing forward, to appropriate the world within the prism of the economic approach, Becker is forced to acknowledge a cascade of empirical phenomena that appear to violate his approach: those associated with social behaviour and outcomes. As a result, the theory is refined and extended, most notably through the extended utility function. At the last, in moving through consumption goods and human, personal and social capital, the social itself is incorporated, albeit as the accumulated experiences of individual interactions.

One alternative to Becker's extremeness, as illustrated by the work of B&O, is not to reject his reductionism but to complement it by supplementary factors, thereby illuminating, however weakly, the richness of individuals and their objects of consumption. For B&O, a start is made with the notion of arousal. But it would be a very blunt instrument even if, as they claim, it can broadly distinguish between the motives for engaging in watching TV rather than cleaning the floor. Offer (1998) himself begins the process of taking a few more steps along this road of exploring the consumer psyche in his explanation for the US 'automobile frenzy' of the 1950s. He closes (p. 341):

149

The 1958 downturn was the first expression of doubt about affluence as comfort, luxury, and sensual gratification ... an early stirring of post-material discontent with *mass* consumption, a rejection of the uniformity that it seemed to require, an expression of intelligence, rationality, and prudence in consumption, a quest for more sophisticated form of distinction and self-expression ... that consumption was not a mere quantitative corollary of growth in which affluence is a reliable proxy for satisfaction. Rather, it portended a more dynamic experience of consumption, as a psychic balancing act which oscillates between comfort and pleasure, between gratification and prudence.

Thus to arousal is added comfort, luxury, sensual gratification, dynamic experience, psychic balancing and prudence. Further, recall as discussed in Chapter 2, Offer (1997) also seeks to complement utility with the economy of 'regard' in order to explain non-market behaviour and its interaction with the market. Where does this road of adding factors lead? In the commercial world of marketing, of which the passage just cited from Offer might serve as a pastiche, the avenues to be explored and criss-crossed are as multifarious as the products being peddled. The counterpart in the academic world is the theory of consumer behaviour. It draws heavily upon the psychology of consumer behaviour (Fine and Leopold 1993: Chapter 3). In doing so, it confesses itself to have formed a 'theory of the month' club. Psychology provides a rich vein of factors for explaining why consumers want goods or might be persuaded to buy them. As reported in Fine and Leopold (1993: Chapter 5), casual perusal yields the following, by no means comprehensive, collection of club members:

High or low involvement, arousal, attitude, affect, attributes, intention, reaction, learning, satisfaction, expectation, atmospherics, environment, context, convenience, memory, familiarity, judgement, choice, impulse, generics, cues, status, brand, impression, class, time, age, inference, endorsement, stereotypes, community, socialisation, norms, knowledge, lifestyle, enthusiasm, materialism, culture, self-perception, routinisation, stimulus, sentiment, role-playing, psychographics, mood, encoding, focus, situation, adaptivity, opinion, leadership, imagination, variety, scripts, vividness, disconfirmation, precipitation, persuasion, reinforcement, reminder, seduction, aesthetics, humour, etc.

In addition, as is already apparent, such underlying psychological propensities can be supplemented by more or less surreptitious introduction of institutions, such as the state, social relations, gender, or the weight of history, customs and culture. The gap in practice from Becker can appear to be enormous but, in principle, it is not so great. He takes as endogenous and ingeniously to be explained by optimisation what others take as exogenous. Whilst the Becker version displays an unyielding logic – one principle serves all – the alternative is more palatable to non-economists (and many economists as well). However inconsistently, it allows each and every factor to be accommodated, revealing a capacity to draw upon traditional approaches from the other social sciences as well as displaying a certain distance from the unacceptably reductionist extremes of the economic approach.

As previously discussed in Chapter 2 more generally than for consumption, the most virulent form in which mainstream economics is influencing the other social sciences is through the information-theoretic as opposed to the economic approach. One emphasises that the world should be seen as if it were the consequence of market (especially informational) imperfections and the non-market response to these. The other constructs the virtual world of the market and non-market as if market. The information-theoretic approach has been far more successful in colonising the other social sciences than its predecessors, not least because: it includes it as a special case (some markets might approximate perfection); it is more capable of disguising its dependence upon methodological individualism in the form of utility maximisation; and, reflecting the latter, it is more open in accepting the presence of institutions, customs and the impact of history, albeit as response to, or outcome of, market imperfections.

Yet, despite successes elsewhere, economics imperialism of both varieties has made remarkably little headway in influencing the growth in attention that other disciplines have dedicated to consumption. This is so even for the field of consumer behaviour itself that shares a focus upon the motivation of the individual. Typically, the standard textbook for consumer behaviour theory, such as Mahatoo (1985), starts out with the simplest model of attributes and motivations as far as the individual is concerned. This is then built up into a more complex model which ultimately allows society to have an effect in the final pages of the text. Through sociology, variables such as the family, class, status and life-style enter into the explanation. More on the research than the textbook agenda, anthropology provides a ritualistic account of consumption, and semiotics deals with its symbolic content. The dull compulsion of prices, incomes and given preferences rapidly becomes buried under the weight of variables introduced from psychology and marketing.

If narrowness in realism turns the discipline of consumer behaviour away from economics, a different unworldliness turns off the more scholarly social sciences. At a methodological level, once revealed, the extraordinary reductionism of both economic and information-theoretic approaches are entirely alien to social theory and its traditions. Further, especially in the wake of post-modernism, contemporary studies of consumption are inevitably concerned with context and the social construction of meaning. Despite its claims of dealing in history, culture and custom, as the non-market response to market imperfections, mainstream economics is incapable of addressing the meaning of consumption other than as something that resides in the physical properties of the objects themselves.[55] This, more than anything, explains the extent to which economics and the other social sciences have remained at arm's length when it comes to consumption.

Yet, the last refuge of economics as an intellectual scoundrel is in its claims as a predictive and/or quantitative science. It deals in formal mathematical models with corresponding statistical techniques that allow patterns of consumption to be forecast or 'explained' in contrast to interpretative approaches. Such claims need to be taken with a heavy dose of salts. First, as is apparent from the theory of consumer behaviour, economics is extremely limited in the range of factors that it considers in examining demand. Marketing departments and consumer research do well to steer clear of economics.

Second, as previously argued, the depth of explanation offered by economics is extremely limited. With preferences taken as given, for all but a minusscule set of studies that are entirely marginalised, changes in demand due to changes in prices and incomes are deemed to be independent of unexplained changes in tastes. Further, little or no account is taken of the way in which consumer tastes are served and moulded systemically, through product development and advertising, for example.

Third, however, the main problem with quantitative work inspired by economics is that it is demonstrably both methodologically and empirically ill-conceived. It starts from the question – why does an individual choose to have this good, that one, or this bundle of goods? It is more appropriate to eschew the individual for social patterns of norms of consumption, differentiated by socio-economic variables. Why do different strata of people – by age, gender, class, household composition, ethnicity, as well as income – consume in similar patterns or not?

This different starting point has informed earlier work on consumption norms, which should be understood as systematic patterns of consumption subject to various socio-economic variables (Fine 1983, Fine et al. 1992a–e, 1993, 1996, Fine and Simister 1995). Consumer choice is liable to trace out definite patterns across the population, in which variables such as social class and household composition in terms of gender and age will be of importance. The various patterns of consumption that do or do not arise by different socio-economic classifications give rise to corresponding norms of consumption. Crucially, a consumption norm in this sense is not to be interpreted as a common level, whether some measure of average or not, although this is what one aspect of a norm can be. Rather, the norm is supposed to reflect the presence or not of patterns of consumption that differ systematically across the population. For some goods, a TV or a lottery ticket for example, consumption is so common as to represent a norm in the sense that more or less everybody has one. For other, luxury goods, the norm is for those to have them only if they are wealthy and of a particular socio-economic class – as in a country estate. It is even possible to perceive the norm for a consumption good to be what might be termed null, one of random distribution across the population – speculatively, whether hair is short or long, for example.

Initially, the empirical work listed at the beginning of the previous paragraph focused on consumer 'durables',[56] motivated by the wish to explore the relationship between their purchase and increasing female labour market participation. In line with other research in this area, it was found that (married) women working more did not, *ceteris paribus*, lead to higher levels of ownership of what are deemed to be labour-saving devices.[57] Whilst paradoxical, rather than logically inconsistent with the new household economics, such evidence suggests that norms are established for consumption to which individuals conform rather than exercising demand independently of one another.

Consider cars for example (Fine *et al.* 1992c). Until recently, with some exaggeration, it could be claimed that the single most important factor in determining how highly ranked a car is to a household is the presence of a male of working age.[58] This certainly is a gendered durable as is well recognised in the literature on the culture of the car (Moorhouse 1988, O'Connell 1998, Miller 2001b). Yet gender has, until recently, scarcely entered the literature on the demand for cars. For Bowden and Turner (1993), for example, not a word, and only one or two in passing for Offer (1998). No doubt, with the growth of single women purchasing cars and households taking a second car – and corresponding targeting of advertising and marketing – and the greater prominence of gender issues generally, the situation has begun to change.[59] Nonetheless, Whipp and Grieco (1989: 13) are able to report that:

> The first official UK survey explicitly concerned with gender and transport did not take place until the mid-1980s.

This is despite two ways in which inequality between men and women is structured as cause and effect through transport. First, men and women have different transport *needs* given their division of responsibilities. Second, men and women have unequal *access* to transport itself. In terms of transport needs, Hamilton and Jenkins (1989) find that men and women make about the same number of journeys. But more men (68 per cent) than women (31 per cent) are qualified to drive a car; more men (88 per cent of those with licences in the Greater London Council area) than women (two-thirds of those with a licence) had primary access to a car; and shopping accounts for 25 per cent of women's journeys. Thus (p. 33):

> While the male breadwinner, who has traditionally had first call on 'the car', has enjoyed the benefits of massive investment in road construction, women have borne the brunt of diminished investment in public transport.

The advantages of greater access through travel are illustrated to some extent by the premium in earnings of 27 per cent for those women commuting distances between one and two miles (1.6 to 3.2 km) to work as compared to those who travel less than one mile (1.6 km) (Pickup 1989: 214).[60] It is also crucial to recognise how the tendency to subordinate women's employment to that of a male partner leads to the location of residence and the timing of mobility between them to suit his and not her career or employment prospects.[61] Significantly, as far as most work on the demand for cars is concerned, public transport might just as well not exist!

Concluding remarks

The previous section outlined in the briefest of sketches how an alternative approach to the empirical analysis of consumer demand might be undertaken. Whilst it will also be associated with different statistical techniques,[62] this is not the main point at issue. Rather it is one of motivation in switching focus from the internally generated demands of the individual to the externally evolving norms of society to which individuals do or do not conform.

In this light, the empirical results will also be interpreted differently. For mainstream economics, regressions on consumption data, in aggregate over time or cross-section by households, constitute explanation in and of themselves and close the analysis that will have begun with a model. The depth with which the theory is being explored is minimal, at most worrying over the test statistics attached to the estimated parameters or the model as a whole or in parts. By contrast, the norm approach merely sets itself the task of identifying common or distinctive patterns of consumption by socio-economic strata. As such it opens up two questions. First, what are the material and cultural processes by which social norms are or are not ground out? Second, how do they give rise to the empirical patterns of consumption that have been identified?

Not surprisingly, the answer suggested here is through the sop approach (and cultural systems) as previously laid out. Whilst this chapter has been highly dismissive of the treatment of consumption by mainstream economists, this is despite the importance of the economic itself. The weakness of the dismal science should not be considered an invitation to neglect its subject matter for more pleasurable cultural pursuits, isolated from their material, in part economic, foundations. Economic determinism/reductionism and cultural subjectivism/relativism are not the only options but they are one another's *alter egos*, already highly influential in pure as well as impure forms as a result of interdisciplinary boundaries. Whilst the inroads of economics imperialism have been limited in the study of consumption, certainly in comparison with other fields and topics, there are no guarantees for the future. Scholars of consumption not only have a duty to progress together the material and cultural aspects of their understanding, but are particularly well positioned to contribute more generally to resisting economics imperialism and to provide alternatives.

8

WHAT IS CONSUMER SOCIE

Introduction

In the modern world, it has become a cliché to suggest that we inhabit, are even victims of, a 'consumer society'; that 'consumerism'[1] is rampant; that we are dominated by 'consumer culture', having passed through a 'consumer revolution'. Such a focus on the consumption associated with affluence is remarkably blinkered, not only for its neglect of those who live on the margins in advanced capitalist economies, but also more strikingly for those in the Third World for whom consumption remains a matter of life or death – whether through starvation, disease or homelessness. No doubt, it is the general relief from such hardship in the developed world, some would say at the expense of the Third World, and also the recent historical origins of such affluence, that renders possible a preoccupation with levels and patterns of popular consumption beyond the mere minimum.

But what precisely is it that makes up consumer society? A flood of images immediately suggests itself: the opulent megastores that occupy the centres, and increasingly the fringes, of our cities, the rows of houses packed with both consumer durables and the more immediate items of gratification to the five senses. Whether the sixth sense of inner well-being is any more satisfied, however, remains a moot point, to which critical reference is often made.

In short, the notion of consumer society has a powerful hold; it releases an array of ideas and associations as wide as the range of possessions to which they correspond. Yet it lacks a coherent analytical content by which is meant a reasonably precise definition with an associated explanatory role, whether in terms of cause or effect. In fact, precise and meaningful definitions of consumer society are extremely hard to come by; they are as rare as the use of the term is common.

One reason for this is that consumption itself previously has played a minor role in the social sciences, with the notable exception of economics where it occupies an important position but remains conceptually underdeveloped for any purpose other than statistical estimation. Rather, production has traditionally served as an analytical starting point with a corresponding neglect or subordination of consumption. Again and again, it has been argued within each

155

particular social science, particularly by those that react against the orthodoxy of supply-side dominance, that consumption has been set aside or is simply perceived to be a passive reflection of production.

But such neglect of consumption belongs to the past. Now the various social sciences have much to say about consumption. Even so, theories of consumption have been less systematic than for production and less easily coordinated across the social sciences. No doubt this reflects the relative lack of uniformity in consumption as compared with production relations – there appears to be a wide choice of what to consume, less on whether to work or not and how. Consequently, the notion of consumer society has served as an umbrella, indeed a middle-range concept, under which consumption has been examined, seeking to provide order and generality across the disparate and the particular. This has been done by drawing selectively upon what is presumed, but is not demonstrated, to be a coherent set of analytical insights, most of which derive from immediate casual and empirical origins.

In this light, the second section of this chapter presents a selective review of various uses of the term 'consumer society', revealing how elastic it has become in its application across time and place. The third section suggests that underlying the notion is an informal and unsatisfactory appeal to supply and demand as explanatory devices, with an inevitable emphasis on the multifarious factors that feed through demand. To a large extent, this has been recognised in the literature which, as shown in the fourth section, has sought an explanation for consumerism in the system of supply to which it is attached, especially the mass production of the modern era. The final section concludes by arguing that such systemic analysis does not go far enough and remains too general. An alternative method for examining the concerns raised by the notions attached to consumer society is to be found in the sop approach.

In search of consumer society

It is impossible to provide a satisfactory review of the literature on consumer society for two related reasons. First, it is a concept so widely used that searching out a comprehensive overview would be an endless task. The problem is aggravated by the common use of consumer society in a supporting rather than a centre-stage role – the background against which some other theme is played out, such as the mores or the manipulated possessiveness of modern society. Second, where the term is used, its meaning and significance are often taken for granted. For the notion of consumer revolution has proven to be definitionally and historically elusive, see Glennie (1995: 181) and various contributions in Brewer and Porter (1993). There is very little analytical literature spotlighting consumer society as such.

Here an attempt is made to isolate and explore certain themes that have been employed in the notion of consumer society. An obvious starting point is that of timing. When did the consumer society arrive historically? McCracken (1987) provides a useful survey of literature on the history of consumption. In doing so, he freely uses the term 'consumer society' without ever explaining what he means by it. However, one condition does appear to be irreducibly necessary – that consumption should be served by exchange through market forces. There may have been certain systems of production which were well provided for by self-sufficiency and which enabled the few to lead luxurious lives at the expense of the many. But this would not fall under the rubric of consumerism, even allowing that the variety of what could be consumed would be constrained by the absence of commodity exchange.

Given this basic ground rule of provision through the market, consumerism has historically been allowed a free range, subject to the empirical identification of the growth in the market for one or more consumption goods. Much of the history of consumption references, and takes as its point of departure, the volume of McKendrick *et al.* (1982). It initiated recent interest in the topic both within and outside the discipline (Hansen 2000: 13). Of necessity, McKendrick *et al.* could not draw upon the wealth of theoretical and empirical literature on consumption that has appeared subsequently. As a result, and certainly in retrospect, it might have been preferable if the literature had benefited from a different starting point. McKendrick *et al.* pose the issue of a consumer revolution complementing that of an industrial revolution in eighteenth-century England. Whilst profoundly historical in its intent, the underlying implicit theory and approach is remarkably ahistorical and underdeveloped.

McKendrick *et al.* depend upon a scarcely concealed projection from an idealised celebration of twentieth-century living standards and mores.[2] It has encouraged others to journey through time and space in search of appropriate definitions and corresponding examples of consumer societies and revolutions, inevitably forcing the highly heterogeneous under a common terminological umbrella. Thus, D. Davis (2000) examines diverse consumer revolutions across Asia, including China. Glickman's (1999a) annotated review of consumer society in the United States runs to fifteen pages. Purdy (1998) seeks to apply McKendrick *et al.* to Germany. Pendergast (2000) charts the rise of consumer culture in the shifting notions of masculinity. Carter (1997) examines the emergence and the changing nature of the female consumer–citizen in Germany.

Weatherill focuses on the growth of the pottery trade in the period before 1780: 'The mechanics of the trade – the business, the travellers, the shops – bound producers, traders and consumers together into a composite whole. A consumer society would not have been possible without them' (Weatherill 1986a: 72). Equally, she argues that: 'Increasing demand for a wide range of goods and clothing was as important in industrialisation as the invention of new methods of production' (Weatherill 1988: 2). For Lemire, the period 1750–1800 witnessed the development of consumerism in the ready-made clothing industry. She concludes: 'Consumerism had developed apace under the combined influence of popularised fashions, a growing British cotton industry and a small but impressive trade in ready-made clothes' (Lemire 1984: 41). Breen extends the influence of early British consumerism to colonial US imitators: 'this consumer revolution affected the lives of all Americans' (Breen 1986: 487), with the result that, 'without too much exaggeration, Staffordshire pottery might be seen as the Coca-Cola of the eighteenth century' (p. 496). Interestingly, whilst elsewhere Breen argues again that 'the eighteenth century witnessed the birth of an Anglo-American "consumer society"' (Breen 1988: 77), this 'vast consumer society' is then seen as reacting against the consumption of British goods as a form of protest during the War of Independence, following events in Boston.

Stretching a point, Stuard (1985), in reporting upon a collection of studies by medieval historians, traces the effects of consumption on the economy back to the thirteenth century. More specifically, Mukerji (1983) identifies consumerism with the rise of capitalism and with the innovations that it is able to provide in consumption goods in response to a materialist world of thought (so that reproduced maps become a popular item of display, depicting and reflecting colonial discovery and conquest). Thirsk's (1978) book *Economic Policy and Projects* carries the subtitle *The Development of a Consumer Society in Early Modern England* to connote the growth of consumer goods in the seventeenth century; some of the goods remain familiar today, such as pins, vinegar, tobacco and starch (now disappearing), while others are now less familiar or unknown, such as woad, aulnage, hand-knitted stockings and copperas. My favourite example, though, is provided by Adshead (1997), with consumerism identified in both Europe and China between 1400 and 1800.

Not surprisingly, with the passage of time and use, the uncritical and casual use of consumer society has not gone unremarked. Pennell (1999: 549) tartly asks of the concept:[3]

> At once atemporal in its purchase, but also culturally and economically specific in its causes and consequences. What then can be made of such a chameleon analytic tool, one which has carried the baggage of so many societal shifts, not the least of which is the advent of 'modern' culture itself?

In short, sampling from the literature reveals that the notion of consumer revolution, consumerism, or whatever, is like a towel which gets wet as it dries! For the more it is used, the more its own credibility is undermined. This is unwittingly revealed by a correspondingly guilty Appadurai (1997: 33) for whom it is necessary to be careful, in the context of consumer revolutions, to distinguish genealogies and histories. For:

> Multiple processual flows that underwrite any given conjuncture ... [result in] the processes implied by history and genealogy creating multiple temporalities for any given practice. It further follows that in studying the consumption practices of distinct societies, we must be prepared to encounter a host of different histories and genealogies

present at the same 'moment'. Thus, in France, the consumption of perfume may, in 1880, be underpinned by one kind of history of bodily discipline and aesthetics, while the consumption of meat may respond to wholly other histories and genealogies.

In less obscure language, this is accepting that consumer revolutions are different in principle and practice across time, place and commodity. As a result, the term cannot be deployed to mark one stage of (consumer) society from another. In addition, as emphasised by Beng-Huat (2000a) in the context of Asia, the determinants of consumption, including those highlighted by those who wish to rely upon the idea of consumer revolution, depend upon stages and nature of economic development and organisation, quite apart from a range of other factors. The same is apparent from the distinctions drawn between modern and postmodern consumption, even in the absence of the economic, as revealed by Muggleton's (2000) comparison between the two, incorporating shifts in the creation of identity, differentiation, authenticity, style, and so on. In short, history cannot be readily periodised by consumption as such and, even if it were so periodised, it would require reference to determinants other and 'heavier' than the proximate practices of consumption itself.

In general terms, then, analytical endeavours around the notion of a consumer revolution inevitably depend upon a more or less sophisticated version of supply and demand, an explicit point of reference for McKendrick *et al.* which identifies industrial with supply and consumer with demand in making an eighteenth-century revolution for each. The underlying, if informal, logic is one of shifting supply and demand curves, leading to an outcome, if not equilibrium, at quantitatively and qualitatively higher levels. The idea of consumer revolution inevitably emphasises the significance of shifts in demand curves as an explanatory device, associated with consumer-led revolution and presuming that attention to them has lagged behind supply. Not surprisingly, the imbalance in historical analysis has been redressed by a revisionist school which seeks to place emphasis on long-term change as the consequence of demand as well as of supply. Gilboy is frequently cited as an early exception to supply-side hegemony, arguing that 'in the field of economic history as well as that of economic theory there has been a tendency to overemphasize the factor of supply' (Gilboy 1932). Later historians have reiterated Gilboy's lament, bringing the role of demand into greater prominence (Breen 1986, Jones 1973, Weatherill 1988).

McKendrick argues most forcibly that the birth of the Industrial Revolution owes as much to demand or, more exactly, to consumption as it does to supply. What is more, demand may even have been the midwife of the shift in supply. With respect to consumption, he talks of a 'revolution' (McKendrick 1982: 1); changes 'of lifestyle' (p. 3); 'consumer boom', 'men, and in particular women, bought as never before' (p. 9); so that 'the first of the world's consumer societies had unmistakably emerged by 1800 ... (if not) *all* the features of modern consumer society' (p. 13). In sum, 'the consumer revolution was the necessary analogue to the industrial revolution, the necessary convulsion on the demand side of the equation to match the convulsion on the supply side' (p. 9).

For orthodox historians, especially those leaning to the right across the intellectual spectrum, this demand-side approach has certain attractions. First, it is an open invitation for detailed study of the changing patterns of consumption. As these expand, they are perceived as the motive force of economic progress – neatly combining the welfare theorems of static *laissez-faire* economics with consumer satisfaction as the source of growth. Second, as consumption is increasingly confined to those with direct or indirect access to income, so economic progress is associated with the history of the rich or *nouveau riche*. Accordingly, for McKendrick, an important ideological accompaniment of the consumer revolution of the eighteenth century is the overcoming of the puritan ethic against consumption. Unfortunately, this development has been seen too readily as a reaction against a blanket ban on all consumption or enjoyment rather than against the moral outrage at its unequal distribution. Third, the preoccupation with consumption diverts attention away from supply, production and work, which all too readily carry a connotation of Marxist and class analysis. Consumption, by contrast, is primarily a private affair for the individual concerned.

Finally, there are resonances between the approach of McKendrick and his followers and the then parallel revival of contemporary monetarism and neoliberalism. Those that have reacted against Keynesian policy making eschew state intervention to manipulate effective demand and, instead, rely upon supply-side factors to provide full employment in the short run. In doing so, they tend to embrace the role of demand in the long run. And that demand will be sustained by activities from the *nouveau riche* at the turn of the millennium, driving consumption which becomes a kind of *de*industrialised revolution. In this respect, the idea of consumer revolution neatly, if unwittingly, complements those of post-industrial society and even the 'end of history'.

Supply and/or demand?

The analytical framework around supply and demand, however well recognised and understood, raises a number of problems in theory and practice. First, whatever its validity, the consumer revolution argument is located at, and motivated by, *micro*(economic) arguments, most notably by reference to Wedgwood and pottery in the case of McKendrick. It is simply presumed that such is sufficiently representative of the economy as a whole and that, a related but different point, the sum of the parts is indicative of the whole. Significantly, detailed studies such as those of Berg (1998) and Berg and Clifford (1999) are much less grand in their claims and more concerned with the changing consumption patterns across classes as the idea and the boundaries of necessities and luxuries are transformed in principle and practice. Associated expansion of demand can lead to productivity increase in the sector concerned as well as spin-offs to other sectors. For

Cole, 'a substantial literature has begun to appear on the subject, and the growth of demand is now widely regarded as one of the essential elements in the transformation of the economy' (Cole 1981: 36). For Crafts:

> In the short run supply does not create its own demand ... the level of output depends on the level of aggregate demand, which may not be that which achieves full employment in the short run. Levels of demand that push the economy towards full employment in the short run might elicit greater investment and productivity increase, thereby enhancing the growth rate of the productive potential.
>
> (Crafts 1981: 131)

Even McCloskey (1981: 120–2), who generally denies significant impact from role of demand for the economy as a whole, makes three exceptions – in case of foreign trade, high unemployment and demand-induced technical progress – all of which she dismisses on empirical grounds. However, the orthodoxy not only takes account of demand; embracing it within a multicausal explanation is taken one distinct step further by incorporating the variety of explanatory factors into a system of demand and supply, through which all analysis is filtered. Crafts continues:

> The long-run rate is made up of a large number of these short-run spells, and so the economy's rate of growth will depend on levels of demand. The majority of recent English economic historians of the eighteenth century have (*possibly unconsciously*) written in this vein.
>
> (Crafts 1981: 131, emphasis added)

This is to have anticipated endogenous or new growth theory, in which technological change is generated within the analysis rather than taken, as is traditional in mainstream economics, as exogenous.[4] The new growth theory emerged in the mid-1980s and has itself witnessed a miraculous expansion of contributions. Without going into details, a multitude of factors have been used to explain productivity increase – learning by doing, human capital, economies of scale and scope, R&D, and so on. However, consumption as an impulse to productivity increase has rarely figured (except negatively in dampening saving, investment and, hence, whatever promotes growth). Even so, its potential has a long pedigree. Adam Smith argued in his *Wealth of Nations* that economic progress depended upon how far the productivity associated with a growing division of labour would be constrained by the extent of the market or demand.[5] Crudely, the larger the market, the greater is the scope for economies of scale with existing technology. In addition, larger markets will provide greater inducements to innovate, since the potential returns will be so much greater.[6]

Such an approach appears to be the most favoured explanation of those who seriously consider the matter of the effect of demand in the long term.[7] It is a sort of infant industry argument, only to be applied in the absence of any grown-ups. But the effect of protection, or larger and more certain demand, is subject to dispute – does it lead to featherbedding and higher prices or to dynamic accrual of scale economies? Quite clearly, this cannot be answered by reference to demand alone. Which of these two responses occurs depends upon other conditions for which the structure of supply is most important, as well as the level and distribution of income.

Probing this further reveals problems for the consumerist approach. For, to put it in extreme form, the idea of firms straining to revolutionise supply but held back by deficient demand presupposes either a monopoly having mopped up the available markets, or a fragmented industrial structure operating in the absence of competition. Otherwise firms would compete with each other for the available demand and rationalise where scale economies warranted it. All of this appears highly improbable for the period of the Industrial Revolution, where large numbers of small firms in competition with each other seem to have been more the order of the day for at least a century. Of course, greater demand would help any firm or industry but whether this leads to cushioning or to inno-vation is conditioned by factors surrounding supply – availability of finance, for example, or market restrictions – most of which are studiously ignored by those relying upon the direct or indirect impact of demand upon supply.

In short, even if endogenous growth can translate consumption into higher demand, and higher demand into higher productivity and growth, matters are not so simple. For, why does this occur at some times and not at others, and in some sectors and places and not others? As argued in Fine and Leopold (1990, 1993: Chapter 11), anticipating a formal argument of Atkinson (1995a), it is also possible for elite or luxury consumption to lead to fragmentation of production and unduly high (possibly false) quality at the expense of productivity and the serving of mass production and markets.[8]

Interestingly, McKendrick implicitly rejects the demand-led theory of trans-forming supply. His emphasis, for pottery and clothing and fashion more generally, concerns the entrepreneurial and social creation of a differentiated demand in conformity with status enhancement. Accordingly, limitations upon demand, especially where they affect economies of scale, are irrelevant since capital itself is fragmenting demand as a marketing strategy – changing the design, colours and articles of the pottery manufactured to serve and to sustain changing fashion.

McKendrick's analysis of the pottery industry, with its focus on the entrepreneurial activities of Josiah Wedgwood, has not escaped criticism, espe-cially from Weatherill (1986b). She argues that Wedgwood was neither a typical representative of the industry, nor its leader, so that he cannot be taken to be the exemplar of its specific success; nor can the potteries exemplify the economy as a whole. And, even *within* this one industry, different sectors need to be acknowl-edged based on differences both in quality of raw materials employed and of markets served. It is far from clear, for example, why a decorative piece of

Wedgwood display should give rise to a functional demand for coarse tea-drinking ware. In any case, even after a period of rapid expansion, the sector still employed only 1 per cent of all industrial workers and just half of 1 per cent of all workers (Weatherill 1986b: 299). This cuts the impact of the Wedgwood enterprise down to size.

But even if this is set aside, and Wedgwood is granted the status of leading entrepreneur in setting an example followed by others, does the type of role he played in the creation of demand necessarily lead to an industrial revolution through a consumer revolution? The answer is ambiguous. For the Wedgwood characteristics that McKendrick describes are ones that are usually associated with inefficiency, even within orthodox economic analysis. By employing fashion to charge a high price on a new piece and then dropping the price to reach a wider market, Wedgwood is essentially operating as a discriminating monopolist for 'he had accomplished, in fact, the most spectacular example of a successful policy of product differentiation in the history of British pottery'.[9] Nor is charging prices well above marginal cost to give goods a snob value a recipe for economic efficiency. Indeed, modern consumerist society is more accustomed to the introduction of goods at lower prices initially in order to gain acceptance for mass-produced goods.

These factors point to static inefficiencies in Wedgwood's activities which would have had the further effect of fragmenting the market for pottery, thereby potentially *delaying*, not hastening, the availability of the demand for, and the supply of, a less fashionable but cheaper and more generally available product to serve more of the 'lower orders'. It is at least as plausible to see the luxury market of the eighteenth century as an obstacle to the development of mass production for the lower classes in the nineteenth century, as it is to view it as a stimulus to emulation from below.

In short, on theoretical grounds, the argument that demand as such can play a significant role in long-run economic change is extremely weak, and the theoretical analysis presented here suggests that the conditions under which it could play a role are not typical of the period of the Industrial Revolution. The consumerist approach tends to presume that if the consumption of the lower classes chronologically follows that of the upper classes, then this is evidence of trickle-down (and of a sort of multiplier demand effect from a higher level stimulus). There is a simple fallacy in this. Without necessarily presuming that the growth of consumption habits is naturally determined or that it is uniform across a population, exactly the same sort of observations could occur even if there were no emulative effects. This is so if consumption is simply expanding across the population in line with rising incomes – you eat beef once you can afford it!

The substantial increase in the domestic consumption of coal illustrates this process. Flinn (1984: 252) estimates it rose from between 1 and 2 million tons in 1700 to over 5 million tons in 1800. Distribution and marketing of the coal required the development of a highly sophisticated and complex set of activities, especially in the run from the mines of Newcastle down to the hearths of

London.[10] And different grades of coal, in terms of both burning capacity and associated toxins, influenced consumption in the domestic and the industrial markets. Indeed, Weatherill (1986b: 384) observes that Wedgwood himself used at least five different grades of coal.

Not surprisingly, growth of domestic consumption has tended to be overshadowed by the dramatic rise in the use of coal for the production of iron from the last quarter of the century onwards and for its presumed role as an energy source in the Industrial Revolution. As far as domestic consumption is concerned, however, there are considerable parallels with the economics of the pottery industry – even if the Wedgwoods of coal do not readily present themselves. Yet it would be far-fetched to view the rise in coal consumption as originating out of the emulative behaviour of the lower classes (with fashion emanating from London as the major domestic market). More important was the availability and cost of transport, the price of coal, its potential substitutes, and the levels of income, together with overall population size and housing conditions (given the weather).

Two further differences between coal and pottery are relevant here. First, coal was more important in quantitative terms, contributing about 60,000 to total employment in 1800 (Flinn 1984: 365), roughly six times the level of employment in the potteries (Weatherill 1986b: 453). Second, its ability to expand demand had been heavily circumscribed both by monopoly and by taxation. Though the effects of monopoly control on final prices may have been small, taxation may have raised them to a level at least twice the costs of production, especially in the London market (Hausmann 1984a, b). This is evidence of the driving force of income even in the context of *restricted* demand.

If the first problem for consumerism is in assigning an independent role to demand in explaining major changes in economic performance, the second is in addressing the corresponding major transformations in society more generally. For, beyond the informalities of the supply and demand analysis attached to consumerism, its theoretical origins are rooted in a particularly simple version of mainstream neo-classical economics whose even more sophisticated version would be unacceptable, as discussed in Chapter 7. This has been made explicit in the response to consumerism by those economic historians wedded to the mainstream, such as McCloskey (1981) and Mokyr (1977). For them, major change can only come from a supply-side revolution, narrowly conceived. With given technology and endowments, shifts in demand can do very little to bring about fundamental change other than in the composition of supply. It follows that there can be no demand without supply revolution.[11] McCloskey (1981) reminds us of this by referring to the isolated, closed and atomised economy of Robinson Crusoe when arguing that aggregate demand cannot shift output. Indeed, it is far from clear how supply and demand analysis can do anything other than chart the change in economic and social relations (and the relation between the two) when discussing the Industrial Revolution or other such sustained periods of economic and social change. There are two exceptions –

either for some form of endogenous growth,[12] as previously discussed, or through some demand-induced shift in the availability of marketable resources. For the latter, the consumer revolution has been associated with the rise in demand for commodities inducing a shift of resources (or supply) out of the household. This is discussed later.

Third, the supply and demand approach to socio-economic change, including consumption, suffers from being conceptually ahistorical. Those simple diagrams for supply and demand are notably lacking specificity in time, place and commodity. Indeed, there is an element of tautology in such reasoning. Irrespective of the difficulties of assigning responsibility to supply or to demand as prime mover, formally the identification problem in econometrics, whatever happened can be disaggregated into shifts along a curve together with shifts of the curve. In general, shifts along the curve are taken as prior and whatever residual remains can be explained by shifts of the curve.

Fourth, whatever the technical niceties of the foregoing, which might test the patience of those untrained formally in economics, a deeper methodological point is involved. Essentially, supply and demand take the history out of the study of consumption as a theoretical starting point. Having done so, it can be brought back in again to explain the shifts in supply and demand. Characteristically, whatever the sophistication of the initial confrontation with supply and demand, this second stage is attached to more informal analysis in which more or less anything can be incorporated as any number of supply- and demand-side factors and theories are addressed. McKendrick *et al.* present an early illustration, especially around the shenanigans of Wedgwood together with emulation, distinction, advertising, etc. Such factors, however, are precisely the ones that are necessarily assumed to be constant or non-existent (or irrational) in drawing up the supply and demand curves that, thereafter, are taken to shift!

The attraction in drawing upon supply and demand lies less then in their capacity for, and a knowledge of, their explanatory purchase than in providing an informal framework for organising the factors that are to be addressed. For Benson (1994: 51) for example:

> The growth and redirection of consumer demand can be understood only when set alongside the growth and redistribution of supply.

Each variable can be assigned to either or both of the sides of the market scissors. Such a framework, however, is itself questionable, especially within a historical context. The decisive conceptual moment is the sale and purchase by producer and consumer, *ex ante* and *ex post* activity constituting supply and demand, respectively, although it is not purely a chronological distinction since, for example, producers advertise in order to influence consumers (and can design products accordingly). Put in these terms, the analysis is simply bizarre. If supply and demand, aggregating over all economic agents, are tied to equilibrium, then historical change cannot be broached. If, however, purchase and consumption are perceived to be followed by subsequent rounds of supply and demand, then this year's demand feeds as a factor into next year's supply and the distinction between the two evaporates.[13] In other words, a framework of supply and demand precludes consideration both of the reproduction and transformation of the conditions that underpin them.[14]

Much of the literature, usually implicitly, has contributed significantly to undermining the supply and demand approach to consumption, seeking instead, from different perspectives and emphases, to understand how consumption has been socially (re)constructed. A limited version of this by way of partial departure from supply and demand is to be found in alternatives to utility maximisation as explanation for individual behaviour. The classic starting points are Veblen and Simmel, with their views on distinction and emulation, and the separate but closely related issue of the gendering of consumption. These have been shown to be limited in scope both theoretically and empirically.[15] Trickle-down has been complemented by trickle-up, and it is a simple step to go for trickle-across, indeed trickle in any direction by cross-cutting social stratifications. Trickling is, after all, only a mechanism not an explanation. Accordingly, if rarely explicitly, the trick of emulation and distinction has increasingly been displaced by the treat of attention to social relations, structures and meanings, as typically in Miller *et al.* (1998) whose study of shopping boasts an approach that deals in a network of everyday reflective activities, embedded in social relations and attached to commodities, place and identity.

Nonetheless, the use of ahistorical theory, of which supply and demand is the most general type, persists. De Vries (1993), for example, draws explicitly upon the new household economics, most closely associated with Becker. Utility maximisation by individuals across and within the commercial and non-commercial sectors (the household) are used to explain the consumer revolution in terms of an exogenously shifting comparative advantage in favour of commerce, inducing a corresponding shift of labour out of the household.[16] Voth (1998) adopts a similar approach, drawing upon ideal notions of the household, the market, consumption, and the interaction between them across stages of history separated by 300 years in time and, possibly, even longer in socio-economic and cultural context and determinants.[17] As argued in Chapter 7, it is worth emphasising that such theories ultimately depend upon an assumption of preordained human rationality, translated into biologically determined consumer preferences which remain immutable across generations however much they may be conditioned by bringing in historical and social contingency. The underlying assumptions upon which such analyses rest are rarely made explicit by their proponents outside the esoterica of their origins in mainstream economics, and are rendered more palatable for consumption by more informal presentation and inconsistent, hybrid integration with other material.

As is apparent, then, putative consumer revolutions as demand-led breaks, and advances, involve the theoretical omission of historical specificity in order to bring it back in, often on an inconsistent basis with the original supply and demand framework. Once these historical floodgates are open, more or less anything can pass through them, with a greater or lesser historical content. This means that studies of consumer society rarely reduce its historical manifestations to a simple growth in the consumption of marketed goods. Each links it to particular causal factors whether they be ideological, distributional, technological or based on marketing. The marker for such studies was fully laid out, both analytically and, to a large extent, historically, in the work of McKendrick *et al.* (1982). These authors bring together a complex range of formative influences on the development of consumption which is deemed to operate favourably for the economy. Locating their study around the end of the eighteenth century, they present its consumerism as not simply analogous to the present day's but as providing its foundation or birth (whereas other studies of earlier periods see it as, at best, an abortive model).[18]

From consumption back to production

The work of McKendrick and his colleagues is critically assessed in Fine and Leopold (1990, 1993: Chapters 7, 10 and 11). It provides a benchmark for studies dealing with later periods, since these are generally situated in (or beyond) the era of consumerism in which mass production is presumed to have taken hold. Here then, there is a sense of history in defining the consumer society – it is defined as the modern period of mass consumption, based on mass production, and thereby sets itself apart from the past. Consequently, the analysis of consumer society tends to have a greater economic content. Indeed, production tends to be restored as the key causal factor, diverging from most of the historical analysis of earlier periods which argues against the predominance of supply/production over demand/consumption.

Put most simply, consumer society is perceived to be the consequence of mass production (of uniform goods through the factory system, particularly during the twentieth century). Thus, Westley and Westley link the creation of working-class norms of consumption – 'there is a tendency for everyone to want the same things and even to buy the same things' (Westley and Westley 1971: 14) – with factory production in 'the age of automation and mass consumption' (p. 43). For Alt (1976: 72, 80), the interwar period

> is precisely the period of the transition from competitive to monopoly capitalism, from limited production to planned mass production, from the occupational communities of the early industrial working class to the consumer leisure of the mass industrial laborer. ... The transition to monopoly capitalist society tends to shift the source of social relations, culture and ideology from a class culture of work to a mass culture of consumption.

Most significant in perceiving consumer society as deriving from production is Hudson's (1983) *Archaeology of the Consumer Society: The Second Industrial Revolution in Britain*. Like many other studies, the evolution of consumer society is transformed into the history of mass production. An appendix, for example, lists 100 or more key inventions or innovations, all of which are to do with the technology of production (even if this has been directed to the creation of new consumer goods).

If the notion of consumerism that informs studies dealing with the period of the nineteenth century onwards is firmly based on the centrality of mass production, a diversity of approach is still made possible through distinguishing the *mechanism* by which mass production is translated into mass consumption. This mechanism can then be taken to be an important causal factor which can itself influence the timing of the arrival of the consumer revolution.

The earliest candidates, put forward to undermine the primacy of production in this way, are retailing and distribution. Logically, and to a large extent historically, a wedge can be driven between mass production and mass consumption. For the latter can exist without the former, with standardised goods being sourced from a fragmented industrial structure and serving a widely dispersed market. Mass consumption then precedes and paves the way for mass production through the distribution and marketing system (see Fraser 1981). Further, through display forms of retailing, demand for consumption goods can itself be stimulated. As and when sufficient mass markets are created, then mass production can displace fragmented production.[19] In this way, the development of retailing takes on a prominent role in transforming mass consumption into mass production and in forging a continuing link between the two.[20] Consequently, the transition to a consumer society is one charting the rise of mass and multiple retailing and its subsequent subordination of retailers to producers and their branded goods (see Jefferys 1954).

Advertising is a related but chronologically later mechanism which has also been put forward as translating mass production into mass consumption. It is argued that the arrival of mass production in the United States, typified by Ford, required producers to create markets for their goods by breaking down traditional working-class consumption habits. This is deemed to have occurred during the interwar period in the United States, concurrent with the rise of the advertising industry. The most prominent exponent of this view is Ewen (1976) who points to the need to manufacture consumers as well as products. Similarly for Lasch:

> In the early days of industrial capitalism, employers saw the working man as no more than a beast of burden. ... Only a handful of employers at this time understood that the worker might be useful to the capitalist as a consumer; that he needed to be imbued with a taste for higher things; that an economy based on mass production required not only the capitalistic organisation of production but the organisation of consumption and leisure as well. ... In a simpler time, advertising

merely called attention to the product and extolled its advantages. Now it manufactures a product of its own: the consumer, perpetually unsatisfied, restless, anxious, and bored. Advertising serves not so much to advertise products as to promote consumption as a way of life.

(Lasch 1979: 135–7)

Ewen's argument rests on the questionable presumption that, prior to the introduction of widespread advertising after the First World War, the US working class had somehow resisted the invasion of capitalist products into their working and domestic lives. Nevertheless, the attention devoted analytically to Fordism as a mode of production is complemented by its necessary significance as a manufactured mode of consumption.

In many ways, in identifying the interwar years as the period which witnessed the manufacturing of consent to consumerism through advertising, Ewen's contribution brought to a close what might be termed the psychological approach to understanding consumer society. Before him, there had been a generation of social commentators arguing that US society had been employing advertising, or depending upon psychological influences more generally, to create false or undesirable needs. These were only to be satisfied by a process that reproduced them at a higher level. Packard (1957) refers to the eight hidden needs preyed upon by advertising – emotional security, reassurance of worth, ego-gratification, creative outlets, love objects, sense of power, a sense of roots and immortality. For him, advertising is less about selling products and more about buying customers. Similar sentiments were to be popularised by Galbraith (1962, 1969, 1973) and Lefebvre:

Needs are seen as clearly defined gaps, neatly outlined hollows to be stopped up or filled in by consumption and the consumer until satiety is achieved, when the need is promptly solicited by devices identical to those that led to satiety; needs are thus incessantly re-stimulated by well-tried methods until they begin to become rentable once again.

(Lefebvre 1971: 79)

In this light, consumer society becomes one dominated by the imperatives of profitability which, in pursuit of markets through psychological manipulations, creates and serves false needs without necessarily generating greater happiness, satisfaction or harmony. In addition, such critical stances (the guilty conscience of affluence), whilst tied to an economic analysis, were also concerned with the ethics of consumer society, with its vulgar materialism and possessiveness – summarised by Marcuse in his work *One Dimensional Man*. Marcuse acknowledged his intellectual debt to Packard whilst also distinguishing between true and false needs and the general failure to recognise the disease of 'toil, aggressiveness, misery and injustice' (Marcuse 1964: 4–5).

Such analyses tend to have a close affinity with those that understand consumerism by reference to the idealised ethics of an earlier age and its corresponding way of life. It borders on what has been the most commonly used context for the idea of a consumer society, a moral critique of the life-styles and ethics of modern capitalism. Of course, throughout history, consumption has always fallen between being condemned and being pursued:[21]

> The definition of consumption as a social problem is an old story and not an exclusively American one. Concern about the moral consequences of new patterns of consumption has persisted with remarkable tenacity from early in our history. ... By the late 1600s in the Anglo-American world there emerged the ideological origins of an economic theory emphasising the beneficial effects upon production of a free market, acquisitive instincts, and a rising standard of living. ... Materialistic and individualistic ideologies found legitimisation. ... From 1880 through 1920 the shift from a producer to a consumer culture gained new momentum. ... This change from the sanctions of religion to those of personality involved the increasing identification of happiness with pleasure.
>
> (Horowitz 1985: xvii–xxvii)

Since the mid-1970s, however, and coinciding with the end of the postwar boom, the theory of real and false needs has been legitimately brought into disrepute. Beyond the bare minimum of physical survival,[22] all needs are socially determined and it is arbitrary to divide them into those that are genuine and those that are not. Interestingly, more recent literature concerning deprivation has recognised this by defining it in terms of a capacity to participate in society, which immediately construes needs in terms of access to socially agreed norms of consumption.[23]

The move away from the notion of consumer society as a psychology of spiralling and artificial needs has led to much more emphasis being placed on consumption itself rather than its being treated as a confined response to the imperatives of mass production. This has given rise to the new urban sociology in which consumption is seen as a major factor in creating rather than simply reflecting social stratification, previously assessed in detail in Fine and Leopold (1993: Chapter 17). It is perceived as bringing into question the idea that work and production, as opposed to consumption, are the crucial existential spheres (see Moorhouse 1988).

Shifting the site of analysis in response to consumerism has not been entirely novel. The analytical amalgam of Fordism as motive force and advertising as transmission belt moved the locus of attention away from the factory into the pages of magazines and on to (the intervals between) the programmes of radio and TV. But, most importantly, an interest developed in the home, expressed in two ways. First, the consumer revolution is identified with a domestic revolution, in the making of the modern home:

The change, for example, from the laundry to the washing machine is no less profound than the change from the hand loom to the power loom; that the change from pumping water to turning on a faucet is no less destructive of traditional habits than the change from manual to electronic calculating.

(Cowan 1982: 223)

Not only is self-sufficiency eroded within the home as commodities are bought in place of home-made goods, but also the home itself becomes a temple to consumer society. Filled, and surrounded, by the artefacts of mass production, if rarely itself such a product, the home and activities within it become transformed (see Hardyment 1988, Hayden 1982). Out go servants and in come mechanical devices, intensifying and extending the housework to be done and creating the modern nuclear family with the dedicated housewife at its centre. The discovery of the 'household germ' goes hand in hand with the standardisation, if not fixedness, of kitchen, bedrooms, living rooms and bathrooms: 'The bathroom evolved more quickly than any other room of the house; its standardised form was accomplished in just over a decade (the 1920s in the United States)' (Cowan 1982: 227).

Second, then, the analytical focus (and material direct responsibility) for consumption fell upon the housewife (although by no means the chief beneficiary of expanding levels of consumption). With the major exception of the motor car, consumerism has always been heavily associated with the female, particularly in its early forms when tied to luxury, display and distinction. The gendering of consumerism has also occurred in the modern period but, for quite the opposite reason, i.e. because of the close identification of women in the household, serving as mundane and unobserved providers (and purchasers).[24] This is certainly true of the interwar period in which the housewife was no longer to be perceived as a cook but as a can-opener (Ewen (1976: 171), quoting C. Frederick, *Selling Mrs. Consumer*, New York, 1929). From the same source, Hayden quotes: 'Consumptionism ... the greatest idea that America has to give to the world; the idea that the workman and the masses be looked upon not simply as workers or producers, but as consumers' (Hayden 1982: 280).

It is important, however, not to exaggerate the extent to which notions of consumer society have been constructed on the basis of divisions between men and women. More significant have been the divisions between rich and poor (although the focus for consumerism has at times also shifted to those of different age groups). Historically, consumerism has inevitably been associated with the expenditure of the wealthy, for it is only recently that the majority of the population, at least in advanced countries, has had a sufficiently weighty level of expenditure to be included in what has previously been a highly exclusive society. Walton (1986), for example, argues that bourgeois women in mid-nineteenth-century Paris had a decisive influence on industrial development through their taste for hand-made items. On the other hand, Rostow (1967) characterises his fifth stage of economic growth as the age of high mass consumption with the emphasis on the new middle class, a suburbanised population, durables, and higher grades of manufactured food and drink – all from the 1920s onwards in the United States.

Initially, then, consumerism is associated with the elite. The patterns that they set are presumed to be emulated through time and with the growing income of the lower orders, giving rise to a 'democratisation' of consumption (Boorstin 1973) – a sort of universal franchise to consume.[25] In this way, the notion of consumer society is necessarily moved away from the privileges of the few, at least within advanced countries. With or without trickle-down effects, it is mass consumption of mass-produced commodities by the mass of the population which comes to the fore. Recognition of this is best illustrated by the work of Katona (1964). He understands *The Mass Consumption Society* as unique in the general degree of affluence and the high share of consumer expenditure in national income. Consequently, mass consumer psychology is able to influence the course of the economy through the availability of, and fluctuations in, general discretionary spending power.

No sooner has this theoretical state of affairs been reached than its presuppositions are thrown into doubt. First, there is in the theory of post-Fordism, the notion that mass production can potentially be displaced by cooperating firms, using small-scale but flexible production processes and serving market niches.[26] Second, mass consumption is perceived to have attained its limits as consumers have become satiated with standardised goods. Thus, for Leiss *et al.* (1986: 49), consumer society becomes an enormous assortment of goods also subject to rapid change. Third, and following upon the rejection of the distinction between real and false needs, all products are endowed with a highly variable content in terms of what they represent or signify (what they mean to those who consume them). Fourth, advertising does not merely act to endow products with false attributes; it becomes part and parcel of a more general articulation of the economy together with the media, communications and culture. In short, consumption becomes one, if not *the*, leading activity within postmodernist society (Miller 1995b). Far from clarifying our understanding, these more recent considerations unleash a conceptual chaos. Jameson, a leading exponent of postmodernism in an article entitled 'Postmodernism and Consumer Society', points to:

> a periodizing concept whose function is to correlate the emergence of new formal features in culture with the emergence of a new type of social life and a new economic order – what is often called moderniza-tion, postindustrial or consumer society, the society of the media or the spectacle, or multinational capital. This new moment of capital can be dated from the postwar boom in the United States in the late 1940s and early '50s or, in France, from the establishment of the Fifth Republic in 1958. The 1960s are in many ways the key transitional period, a period in which the new international order (neocolonialism, the Green

Revolution, computerisation and electronic information) is at one and the same time set in place and is swept and shaken by its own internal contradictions and by external resistance.

(Jameson 1985: 112–13)

So far, this is a disorganised and unweighted bundle of the many features that make up contemporary capitalism and its history. However, it continues as follows:

I want here to sketch a few of the ways in which the new postmodernism expresses the inner truth of that newly emergent social order of late capitalism, but will have to limit the description to only two of its significant features, which I will call pastiche and schizophrenia: they will give us a chance to sense the specificity of the postmodernist experience of space and time respectively.

(Jameson 1985: 112–13)

One can but speculate that the second quotation is but a schizophrenic pastiche of the first; it adds little order to our understanding of consumer society (whilst saying much about the concept of postmodernism – at least in this area of application!).[27]

Towards a critical alternative

In a review of McKendrick *et al.* (1982), Williams (1984: 337) asks: 'How valid is the concept "consumer society"?' The previous sections have provided some considerable support in favour of posing this question. By briefly re-examining the reasons for this, a rather different and, hopefully, more analytically rigorous approach will be suggested to explain the significance and sources of changing patterns of consumption.

First, paradoxically because it seeks to periodise history by its presence or not, consumer society has problems dealing with historical specificity. Under its rubric, the affinities between any two acts of consumption are forced to be accommodated, even in as diverse episodes in history as the expanding consumption of luxuries in the thirteenth century and the mass consumption associated with contemporary advanced societies. Scientific enquiry does prosper by discovering regularities across apparently diverse phenomena, but the uniformities here are both superficial and questionable. Once account is taken of wider economic and social factors, acts of consumption cannot be legitimately identified as different species of the same genus. Consequently, consumption is not to be understood by reference to itself, alone, in isolation from anything other than its proximate causes and accompaniments (such as what is consumed and by whom).

Production is the most obvious factor to link with consumption even if, in the context of consumer society, this has often been shunned because of the belief that the supply side has already commanded too great an analytical attention. The major exception is in notions of consumer society which draw upon the determining role played by mass production. From this there follows, almost automatically, the predominance of mass consumption, with its accompanying relishes of manipulative advertising, unsatiated appetites, and a generalised individualistic and materialistic ethic.

But, on close examination, the simple and general linkage between mass production and consumption founders on its narrowness; it provides at best only a partial model of what is consumed. Even today, more than half a century after the classic development phase of mass production, many other models of production/consumption abound; many commodities fall outside the framework of the classic model. This is especially so of the increasingly important service sector and of housing – paradoxically so for the latter, which has been perceived as the primary site of mass consumption.

In short, accepting the centrality of mass production as the leading edge of industrial society does not provide an adequate explanation of what is consumed and why. There are differences in the methods of development of mass production across different commodities and across different countries (despite some trends towards the globalisation of both production processes and products). There is sufficient diversity in production itself, through technology and design, labour processes, etc., to allow for diversity in consumption even if it were the passive reflection of production, see Chapter 5.

Of course, consumption is not simply a passive reflection of production even if one were to embrace fully the heaviest criticisms of the notion of consumer sovereignty. Whilst an interest in consumption alone might focus on the slip twixt cup and lip, there is equally a wide variety of slippage between the factory and the cup and its contents. The link between production and consumption is not a simple unity of opposites – as often presented both in a simplistic Marxist model of contradictions between exchange value and use value and in the simultaneous model of supply and demand in the orthodoxy of neo-classical economics. Before production can be translated into consumption, income has to be generated and distributed across different socio-economic groups, their preferences and habits have to be formed and (re)acted upon, and products have to be packaged, distributed and marketed. These chains in the link between production and consumption confirm the problems of defining a single model, either for the dependence of consumption upon production (what has been termed here a vertical approach) or for the suggestion of the uniform significance of factors (such as advertising or emulation) on consumption across a range of diverse commodities (what has been termed a horizontal approach).

Briefly summarising, the analysis of consumption should not seek to deny the pervasive influence of the characteristics that have been associated with consumer society, revolution or culture. Nor must it neglect the immanence of trends acting indirectly upon consumption – through mass production and modes of retailing and distribution. But the impact of these factors must be

studied in relation to each other in anticipation of diverse outcomes for particular commodities or groups of commodities, according to their specific
interaction in combining different economic and non-economic factors. In other
words, a sop approach (as developed in Chapters 5 and 6) opens up the possibilities for a much richer discussion. The distinct set of imperatives governing
different sets of commodities is implicit in the use of terms that describe them –
namely, the food system, the energy system, the housing system, the fashion
system, the transport system, etc. The use of the term 'system' signifies the idea
that certain structures and dynamics have been set in place for each separate
group of commodities. Whilst these are not cast in stone, nor without affinities at
least in part across commodity groups (sharing technical, marketing or other
features), the presumption must be that there is a stronger vertical link in the
process from production to consumption within each of the sops than there is
between them.

9

WHATEVER HAPPENED TO PUBLIC CONSUMPTION?

Introduction

The 'new' wave of consumption across the social sciences is now in its third decade. Inspired by postmodernism, the literature has been heavily skewed, especially initially, towards a cultural turn, preoccupied with the subjectivities and identities of consumers and the meanings of the objects of consumption. With culture perceived to open up a realm of conditional freedom for the individual consumer, the role of the state has slipped into the background, if not altogether out of sight, in studying consumption. At one level, this is surprising since, in other areas, social sciences have concentrated on the role of the state, not least in its clash with the market, and in the need for 'Bringing the State Back In', Evans *et al.* (1985). On the other hand, by way of remarkable symbiosis with neo-liberalism, the state has often been perceived to be anti-cultural and, in this respect, anti-consumption. Inspired by the image of an army of Mao suits, or of bureaucracy stifling talent, individuality and initiative, the state is perceived to corrupt the social, the cultural and consumption, just as it putatively corrupts the market and economic efficiency. By this means, although their two virtual worlds are rarely brought together, postmodernism and neo-liberalism complement one another in their anti-statism.

Yet, even if the state's contribution to consumption is only, and unreasonably, recognised to be negative in some sense, the case for examining its impact remains strong. Neo-liberals, in arguing for the withdrawal of the state from the economy, need to demonstrate its baneful effects. Surely the same applies to the impact of the state upon the content and the nature of consumption? However, this chapter takes as its starting point the continuing *omission* of the state in consumption studies. Indeed, it is a startling point since, either directly or indirectly, the state can be associated directly or indirectly with as much as 50 per cent or more of consumption. We refer, of course, to public as opposed to private consumption, leaving aside definitional and conceptual conundrums around the public/private divide. Despite the heavy presence of public consumption, the literature has almost remained exclusively preoccupied with private consumption, sourced by the commercial sector. Where public consumption has been to the fore, it is very much a case of exceptions that prove the rule, by-products of passing debates as in Burrows and Marsh (1992) and Keat *et al.* (1994). The main example has been concern with 'consumption classes', as posited by Peter Saunders (1984, 1988). For him, public consumption, especially in the form of council housing, has represented a lower level of class.[1] Otherwise, the contrast between private and public consumption has been high-lighted by the attack on the one by the other, by means of the various forms of privatisation. Nonetheless, despite the prominence of issues such as the quality, spread and price of service delivery, the attention of consumption studies to privatisation and to continuing public consumption remains limited. Indeed, where departing its emphasis on private (commodity) consumption, scholarly attention has been inclined to switch to more or less commercial and/or excep-tional forms of consumption, as with the arts, collecting heirlooms, self-provisioning or whatever.

Whilst exaggerated, if limited, interest in the commercial is less surprising in a postmodernist world, given the wealth of interpretative material furnished by sophisticated advertisements, it is surprising how little the retreat from postmod-ernism has as yet diverted attention to *public* consumption. Nor is this explained by a leftist antipathy to consumption as such, in deference to the analytical priority of production. For a continuing feature of consumption studies is the notion that production has been and remains unduly privileged.

In this light, this chapter seeks to settle a debt, or at least pay some interest on a debt, that was left on the debit side in the closing chapter of the first edition of *The World of Consumption* (Fine and Leopold 1993). There, with a strong tinge of guilt, it was recognised that the book had conformed to the overwhelming feature of the explosively growing literature on consumption that had just been critically assessed – its almost exclusive preoccupation with private consumption as realised through the purchase of commodities. This represented a double omission; for, not only does it neglect public consumption, it also leaves unchal-lenged the notion attached to neo-liberal ideology, that public consumption is merely an alternative form of private consumption, and liable to be inferior in efficiency and quality of delivery. Even those rejecting the presumed inferiority of public provision, on efficiency and/or equity grounds, have been subject to an assault of making the public more like, or more meeting the standards set by, the private sector. Quite apart from various forms and extents of privatisation of public services, this is most notable in the way in which the practices and termi-nology of the private sector have been aped as public consumption is attached to commercial criteria and the serving of clients and customers etc. With neo-liberalism also on the retreat, at least in the academic world, is it not appropriate to examine the difference in nature between public and private consumption, lest the public become embroiled in the Third Wayism that primarily assigns it a residual, if extensive, role of social protection?

So it is opportune to redress the analytical balance between public and private consumption, especially in order to bring out their respective distinctive-ness. This is easier said than done. For we all have a fully formed and daily personal and individual experience of private consumption. We buy and we consume. But, in the case of public provision, we may buy or not depending upon the extent and depth of commercialisation, and then we also consume. What is the difference? Is it a matter of who provides, as in the case of nation-alised industries, for example? But then a publicly owned steel industry would provide for public consumption – possibly acceptable according to intuition in so far as steel-users are perceived to consume on behalf of the public. Yet steel-users are liable to be in the private even if supplied by the public sector. Does it then have to do with the nature of the *product*, cutting across the public/private divide in *provision*? Health and education might be designated as public consumption but not electricity and gas. But, then, what about water? This would seem to require us somewhat arbitrarily to allocate products on a case-by-case basis, and the notion of (public) utilities is merely to rename the problem. Is it the nature of the consumption process itself, undertaken collectively in some sense, as opposed to being individual and in isolation – the park as public good or the football crowd and concert?[2] But is this not an inappropriate identification of the private with the home? For we drive *private* cars as individuals on *public* highways (provided by the state or paid upon individual use by tolls)? Consumption is no exception when it comes to the blur across the public/private divided once closely examined.

Not surprisingly, these conundrums reflect a much more general and histor-ical process of a shift in meaning of what constitutes the private and the public and, equally, the private as opposed to the social. The distinction is immanently both materially and ideologically reconstructed. It can even lead to complete reversals of meaning – as in the British notion of public schools, which are conventionally thought of as private in other countries, in the announcement of companies going public when private ownership in them becomes available in the form of buying shares, and (a personal favourite) the payment of royalties to individuals as opposed to the crown. The next section seeks to set these conun-drums aside by arguing that the dichotomy between public and private consumption is analytically questionable. In reaching this conclusion, it is suggested that in shifting attention from notions of private to public consump-tion, the latter tends to be associated with a broader set of issues and concerns so that the initiating attachment to consumption is diluted or lost altogether. This process offers an explanation for the neglect of public consumption in the litera-ture. In the third section, these points will be illustrated by a selective and superficial dip into a number of historical attempts to bridge the divide between public and private consumption. The concluding remarks draw out some strategic implications.

Addressing consumption socially

As already observed, the private/public divide is far from well defined. Does this explain the difficulty, if not impossibility, of pinning down public as opposed to private consumption? To some extent it does. But more progress can be made by examining the specifics of consumption rather than the fuzzy boundaries of the public/private divide in general. Here the advantages of the sop approach come to the fore, with its emphasis upon differentiated chains of activity from production to consumption, corresponding cultural systems, and the interaction between the two.

What are the implications of these perspectives for the distinction between public and private consumption? First, and most important, the distinction between public and private consumption is analytically invalid, certainly as a generalised starting point for each is socially and historically constructed – in relation to one another and, almost inevitably, chaotically across different sops and cultural systems. In reaching out to the latter, it is apparent that private consumption is attached to social or public determinants whether materially or ideologically. Such are the insights yielded, respectively, for example, by Marx's commodity fetishism and Foucault's domination of body and mind. Relations between private consumers and objects of consumption are deeply embedded in the social domain despite the appearances and, to some extent, the reality of the opposite. For the young Baudrillard (1998: 193), culture is such that 'Consumption is a myth ... *a statement of contemporary society about itself*, the way our society speaks itself. And, in a sense, the only objective reality of consumption is the *idea* of consumption'. On a more material level, Sack (1992: 104) comments, especially with mass production, that 'the consumer's world includes only the front stage of mass consumption and relegates extraction, production, distribution, waste, and pollution to a hidden backstage'.[3] Or, in more abstract terms, underlying every act of private consumption are material and cultural systems, both making it possible and endowing it with meaning or, more exactly, a milieu for creating meaning. Public and private consumption are inextricably linked to one another with ill-defined and variable boundaries.

Second, in this light, when the distinction between public and private consumption is deployed, for whatever purpose, it tends, respectively, to implode upon the individual or to explode upon society. Here the contrast is between (the older, yet less mature) Baudrillard and Marx. For one, postmodernist subjectivity floats free even from the constraints imposed by bodily survival. As Warde (1994: 231) puts it, referring especially to the work of Zygmunt Bauman, the construction of the 'heroic consumer'

> prevents us from appreciating the constraints people face in their consumption practices. ... The use of the term 'the consumer' signifies an undersocialised actor; it exaggerates the scope and capacity for individual action.

Or, in more down-to-earth fashion, Corrigan (1997: 32) concludes of postmodernism: 'consumption communicates social meaning, and is the site of struggles over social distinction. The fulfilling of more concrete needs arising from, say, individual feelings of cold or hunger seems almost an accidental by-product.'

In the case of Marx, as argued in Chapters 3 and 4, much of the literature on consumption is (falsely) motivated or justified by the presumption that his chief analytical concern – to root out the social and material origins of the commodity in capitalist production – has precluded consideration of consumption in defer-ence to a focus upon class (conflict) and uncovering the laws of production. In short, if Baudrillard unduly focuses upon the subjectivity of the individual consumer, Marx is drawn away from consumption altogether to the presumed objectivity of production.

Third, if attention is drawn to public consumption, as something beyond the market, then it necessarily reaches for a systemic understanding to uncover one or more fetishisms that are attached to commodities whether as material or cultural objects. What is it that underlies and is not revealed by the private rela-tionship between consumer and object of consumption that may be (made) more overt in the case of public consumption? For Marx, it is the social relationship between producers as opposed to these (being treated as relations) between things. For (critical) notions of consumer society, it tends to be about the hidden persuaders, false as opposed to real needs, public squalor and private affluence, emulation and distinction, and so on.[4] Most recently, private consumption has been most markedly rendered public or social by concerns about the environ-ment – how our consumption leads to global warming, to destruction of Brazilian forests, to excessive use of chemicals, and so on.[5] More generally, many other public issues may be attached to private consumption, such as boycotts as in sanctions against apartheid, child labour and for improvement in wages and working conditions.[6] In each case, the core of what is involved cannot be discov-ered directly or adequately addressed in the (private) relationship between consumer and consumed.

Fourth, an immediate implication is that as private becomes understood as public consumption so it is translated into something else other than consump-tion itself.[7] Even with the narrowest of consumer concerns, for quality of product and absence of price fixing for example, there is a focus upon the regu-latory and legal environment, quite apart from a systemic understanding of the economy itself.[8] In its most limited and ideological form is the idea that the economy should conform to some sort of ideal competitiveness and integrity between buyers and sellers. By shifting focus from private to public consumption, there is a simultaneous shift from the narrow confines of consumption itself. At least, other broader issues are incorporated, not least the morality of the market and what are presumed to be distortions in or of its practices as well as the legiti-macy of capitalism itself. As Damer (2000: 71) eloquently argues of the Glasgow Rent Strike of 1915, such events are '*essential* aspects of the class struggle', in contrast to the interpretations of Manuel Castells and Peter Saunders for whom the struggle is confined to the 'sphere of consumption'. The point is less to adju-dicate on this debate by deciding or defining where the sphere of consumption ends and class struggle begins. Rather, as recognised in Lavalette and Mooney (2000) more generally, struggles around consumption have the potential to shift from private to public domains and, in doing so, to question and challenge the conditions governing provision.

The chequered history of public consumption?

There is, then, a sense in which opening the distinction between private and public consumption is to unravel commodity fetishism and more – to reveal the social relations that underpin purportedly private acts. For capitalism creates a structural separation not only between the economy and society but also, within the economy, between production and exchange. In this respect, it forges a particularly powerful disconnection between private consumption and society more generally, for there is a double distance between it and production – reflecting the journey from household to exchange and from exchange to production. Thus, Miller (1995a) sees one aspect of modern consumption as the 'rupture' arising out of our no longer producing the majority of what we consume so that consumption is a derived relationship to distantly produced objects with which we have to come to terms.[9] In addition, it creates a corresponding dialectic between tradition and modernity, respectively, as the consumed is no longer the produced. As a result, one ploy in advertising commodities is to play upon their origins, in an attempt to claim authenticity, not least in how or where they are produced. In advanced capitalism, authenticity can also derive from other stages in the sop, in design or quality of ingredients.

Not surprisingly, though, early understandings of collective consumption are liable to take an idealised construction of more direct access to consumption as their critical point of departure, whether drawing upon the supposedly authentic experience of pre-capitalist societies or not. In particular, the Ricardian socialists attempted to forge a direct link between consumption and work.[10] As such, they employed a labour theory of value in order to demonstrate that the working class does not fully consume what it produces. Profits arise out of labour being purchased at below its value.

The issue then arises of how to eliminate profit and restore the full value of labour to those who contribute it. A number of solutions have been posited. One of the earliest was for the issuing of money only in the form of labour chits, designating how much labour had been contributed and, consequently, representing a claim on consumption according to the labour time required, by others, to produce goods. Such schemes are seen as essential in order to restore the connection between how much you work and how much you consume in a world in which no one any longer works to provide subsistence directly. Marx's analytical contempt for the Ricardian socialists is well known. Its most important features include the failure to understand both that capitalism is based on fair, not unequal, exchange, with labour power becoming a commodity that sells at a value below labour time contributed or coerced, and that money can only represent labour time (or value) indirectly, following a multiplicity of mediations.[11] Nonetheless, Ricardian socialism and the Ricardian labour theory of value remain powerful systemic indictments of consumption under capitalism. Those who do not work should not consume; that they do so, in the extreme as far as the rich and powerful are concerned, is indicative of exploitation of those that do work.[12]

Significantly, such insights as are derived from Ricardian socialism do not depend upon a labour theory of value – the availability of consumption for those who do not work in the physical form of goods suffices to demonstrate the presence of exploitation. Consequently, the modern version of Ricardian socialism, derived from the work of Sraffa, rejects the labour theory of value on analytical grounds as being incapable of explaining prices satisfactorily. The Ricardian socialists themselves, and their immediate followers, however, were less concerned with such esoteric issues and puzzled over how capitalists could get away with it. One answer was sought in the preferential access to money which, in and of itself, appeared capable of accruing a return to those who possessed it in sufficient quantities for a sufficient length of time. Accordingly, as the counterpart to labour in production, money in exchange seemed to offer a systemic explanation for the inability of the working class (and petty producers) to consume the total output collectively. It led to schemes either for the abolition of money altogether or for making it freely available without payment of interest, as in the social credit movement.[13] Of course, such ventures continue to survive, if more out of necessity on the margins than as a putative critical assault upon capitalism, in the form of local exchange trading systems (LETS), ranging from mutual babysitting groups to more ambitious schemes.[14]

The cooperation movement focused on the avoidance of profit out of the employment of distribution workers (other than in the form of a dividend).[15] As Furlough (1991: 136) suggests, it deployed a systemic notion of workers as doubly exploited, both as producers and consumers. Whilst both could be tackled simultaneously, the movement was inevitably subject to shifts in, and conflicts over, relative emphasis. The First International, with Marx's blessing, perceived cooperation as serving three purposes: providing monies for politics and strikes; a legal basis for propaganda and activity; and as a concretisation of working-class values (p. 51). With the growth of commodity consumption, however, competition emerged between the radical and reformist wings of the movement (pp. 65–6), so that 'the cooperative movement ... sought a very delicate balance between rectifying the worst abuses of capitalism and incorporating certain goals of socialism' (p. 117). Ultimately, the cooperatives became a more distinct arm of the labour movement, a third pillar of socialism alongside trade unions and the Labour Party. By the same token, the cultural substituted for an economic critique of capitalism (p. 9):

> Consumer cooperation expressed and channeled a significant critique
> of capitalism, specifically capitalist consumer culture, at the same time

that it offered resources and space within which to organize political activities. To neglect that critique is to miss the richness and depth of that historical moment and to mute the extent of people's visions, aspirations, and struggles within that particular political culture. Such neglect also erases an important radical critique of consumer society that had concrete, grass-roots form as a working-class institution.

Thus, the goal was to seek honest and moral commerce and cultural activity (including education) beyond commercial activities *per se* that were themselves associated with false luxury and seduction (pp. 98–9), thereby incorporating a moral critique of consumerism as alienating, inauthentic, manipulative and anti-revolutionary (p. 9). In short, despite the containment of the activities and the systemic critique of capitalism associated with cooperatives, it would be a mistake to see it as essentially the same as private commerce (p. 71):

> To characterize cooperatives and capitalist chain stores as variants of the same commercial form mutes the intensity of the struggles between the two forms over the strategies, purposes, and meanings of consumption.

In addition, the cooperation movement also disproportionately involved women through their daily lives as shoppers responsible for household consumption. Exactly the same is true of the US National Consumers' League and its White Label campaign, begun in 1898 and ending in 1918, which 'drew women into public life in ways that validated what might be termed their "social citizenship" almost twenty years before the passage of the women's suffrage amendment to the Constitution' (Sklar 1998: 34). More generally, the movement illustrates the earlier commentary concerning the conundrums across the private/public consumption divide. For, as Sklar argues, it sought to connect apparently private consumption with the conditions under which goods were provided, shifting and forging a link between concern over the quality of goods and the conditions under which they were produced.[16] It constructed an imagined community of interest between consumers and workers, empowering consumers to speak for the community as a whole. Not surprisingly, as an outlet for otherwise politically disenfranchised middle-class women, this had effects on who represented what, with a wish to play down a tension between the quality of the products and the quality of the working conditions under which they were produced. Especially for clothing, in the context of new theories concerning the spread of disease, it was convenient to suggest that healthy workers and working conditions were necessary for healthy products. But, whatever compromises were reached, the movement was sufficiently influential that 'in state after state factory laws were strengthened, factory inspections encouraged, hours laws enforced, and child labor discouraged' (p. 21).[17]

Significantly, the illustrations so far considered have represented the pursuit of the interests of workers in tracing private consumption to its public or social origins. But nor is capital idle in straddling and defining the divide between the public and the private where consumption is concerned. As Sklar reports, larger scale manufacturers even welcomed the White Label campaign as a means of both promoting their own goods through seals of approval and beating out competition from sweatshop competitors. On a more pro-active basis, US corporations from the 1930s onwards have been concerned about their public image and the process of consumption as a public activity. This is the theme of work by Marchand (1998a, b), Clarke (1999a) and Leach (1993). The last argues, in an unremarked contrast with the intent of the Consumers' League, that (p. 147):

> After 1890 the institutions of production and consumption were, in effect, taken over by corporate businesses. Business, not ordinary men and women, did most to establish the value and the cultural character of goods. ... At the same time, merchants, brokers, and manufacturers did everything they could, both ideologically and in reality, to *separate* the world of production from the world of consumption (and, in the process, the men, women, and children, were also divided up).

Leach's emphasis is upon the battery of institutions seeking to sustain the 'awesome creation' of this illusory separation of commercial from consumer culture (p. 150), involving 'schools, colleges, and universities ... the great urban museums ... federal and municipal governments' (p. 154). For Marchand and Clarke, attention is more focused upon the projection of a variety of aspects of public consumption, more or less removed from products themselves, as in the promotion of scientific values and community life.[18]

Once, however, the world of private consumption is opened up for interpretation in a wider public role, it has the capacity to assume more or less any mantle, just as the notion of private consumption has free range over the construction of personal identity. Thus, McGovern (1998) points to the parallels and connections that have been drawn between citizenship, and democracy, and consumption – with advertising, for example, perceived as analogous to politicians seeking to persuade consumers to vote with their money, and a presumed republicanism of classless equality before the market (although some have many more votes than others!). Nationalism and patriotism are also closely associated and promoted with consumption, not only for the United States with its culture of consumption but also, for example, in Nazi Germany and support for domestic produce (Reagin 1998, Möser 1998).[19]

Many more examples could be brought forward to illustrate how attention to public consumption leads to its being attached to other social issues and, hence, transformed into something else. But there are two pervasive examples, one quantitative and the other qualitative. For the quantitative, under capitalism, private consumption is primarily a matter of individual choice albeit constrained by income. Consequently, public consumption can be detached from particular commodities and associated with consumption in general, as access to consumption through transfers of income other than through the market. The 'divi' after all is not paid in kind, although this is certainly one way of targeting public consumption, as in use of food vouchers. Significantly, in the case of income transfers other than through the market, an inversion is involved. Whilst they are often calculated in order to enable the public to attain minimum levels of consumption of particular items, what is actually consumed remains subject to individual discretion. Child benefit may not be spent on children; housing itself or housing benefit as income may be provided; in case of welfare benefits, such as old-age pensions, a standard of living may well be targeted without the presumption that it will always be spent in corresponding ways. In short, consumption and income become increasingly associated with one another at the expense of the specificity of consumption itself. This is true of measures of standards of living and of poverty, and in economics where the term consumption is usually reserved for aggregate expenditure and demand independent of its particular composition.[20]

Such is the banality around how public consumption is provided as an income, thereby detaching it from consumption as such. Qualitatively, the mix of provision associated with income transfers (whether and how designated for specific items of consumption) and consumption in kind is so varied that it can only come under a common umbrella by being designated as something else. There is also the potential to incorporate elements that do not have a foundation in private consumption. Thus is constituted the welfare state, the most developed and general form both of social consumption and of its transformation into something else. It has the capacity to provide income, consumption in kind and other aspects of social reproduction that are not associated with consumption even if previously understood as private, as in care of children, for example.[21] In short, the rise of private consumption and the transformation of its *alter ego*, public consumption, into the welfare state is a historical product of advanced capitalism in the second half of the twentieth century. Symbolically, with the extremes of postmodernism, as Sulkunen (1997) observes, the public morality of consumption associated with distributive equity becomes displaced by concern with individual freedom from control. Yet, it is a world which, according to Lyotard and Baudrillard, is too chaotic to allow for adequate representation of the *individual* let alone the social (Holmwood 1997).[22] We beg to differ or, at least, to shift ground from exclusive preoccupation with 'representation' by addressing them through the sops to which they are attached.

Concluding remarks

Neither surprisingly nor accidentally, the journey across the public/private consumption divide has ultimately arrived at the welfare state. This notion itself is an exemplary illustration of the main analytical proposition offered here. As private becomes public consumption, so it ceases to be consumption and is transformed into something else. This is not exclusively nor primarily an intellectual or ideological transition, although both are involved and contested. Changes are involved in the structure, nature, processes and relations of provision. In many ways, not least with 'consumption' substituted for 'property', and in light of what is often strong commitment to welfarism, Marx's tart remark on bourgeois society in the *Economic and Philosophical Manuscripts* of 1844 is refuted:[23]

> Private property has made us so stupid and one-sided that we think a thing is *ours* only when we have it.

For the commitment to the welfare state as 'ours' can be very strong.

Yet, to some extent, the logic underlying Marx's position remains valid, although it must be qualified not least because the politicisation or whatever that accompanies the shift from private to public consumption is ambiguous in its implications and impact. For, on the one hand, in setting the issue of private consumption within the domain of public issues, very powerful and wide-ranging discursive and material pressures are potentially brought to bear, around welfare, the environment, working conditions, etc. On the other hand, however, there is a corresponding displacement from focus upon the private and upon consumption. This means that bourgeois notions of private consumption may remain resilient, can prosper and may not be contested. There can be no better illustration than the rise to prominence of the postmodernist preoccupation with consumption and identity under which notions of public consumption have at best been precarious.

In short, the goal of public consumption is sustained only by becoming translated into something else that is broader in scope and content. Otherwise, at best, it is liable to be confined to the dictates of what constitutes private consumption by other means. Here, an analogy can be drawn with the classical notion of the shift from the economism of trade unionism to revolutionary consciousness, for which the raising of economic demands within capitalism is not perceived to be at the expense of moving to the political struggle to overthrow the system. As has been shown, both theoretically and by illustration, the radicalisation of struggles around consumption exhibits similar features, although the organisational basis for mounting struggle and for moving from one level to another are very different. In common, there is a broadening and shifting of meaning and content as well as conflicts over what issues are to be contested and by and for whom.[24] Whilst the preoccupation of scholars remains focused on private consumption, it makes no small contribution to constraining the meaning placed on public consumption and the nature and extent of its provision.

10

WELFARISM IN LIGHT OF GLOBALISATION

Introduction

In the previous chapter, it has been shown that as private becomes recognised as public consumption, so the consumption aspect of provision is tempered and even displaced by other considerations. The prime example is the welfare state with which this chapter is concerned. More exactly, the focus is upon how the theory of the welfare state has shifted. The next section observes the recent emergence of the new welfare economics, in which welfare is perceived in terms of the behaviour of optimising but imperfectly informed individuals. It ultimately leads to the idea of the welfare state as collective risk management on behalf of its citizens. This is the political economy of the welfare state as economics imperialism, as discussed in Chapter 2. As such, it is a far cry from the political economy of the welfare state that understood the latter in terms of the contradictions and conflicts of capitalism as a system of economic and social reproduction, as laid out in the third section. Over the past decade, as critically detailed in the fourth section, this has given way to the welfare regimes approach. It argues that different welfare states are attached to different ideal types. This approach has, however, been subject to contradictory pressures. On the one hand, as also discussed in more general terms in Chapter 2, globalisation is perceived to be homogenising welfare systems, forcing them to comply with one another in the competition between nations for economic success. On the other hand, the empirical evidence suggests increasingly diverse outcomes in welfare policy by programmes and by country. The result has been an uncomfortable accommodation both with the evidence and with the new welfare economics. In contrast, in the fifth section, an alternative approach is suggested. Like that for private consumption, it argues for a sop approach in which welfare provision is explicitly tied to the economic and social reproduction of capitalism.

Thus, this and the previous chapter have been motivated by the wish to shift the balance of the literature away from an almost exclusive preoccupation with private consumption. Despite the continuing commitment to the sop approach to public as well as private consumption, much more is involved than a simple shift in focus. For, as argued in the previous chapter, the nature and meaning as well as the material organisation of public consumption is distinct from that of private consumption and, as such, is socially, historically and programme specific. Although, in this respect, we do not provide case studies ourselves, they are abundant in the literature precisely because of the importance and prominence of health, education, social security and so on. Hopefully, the sop approach will help both in the reading and construction of such studies.[1]

The new welfare economics

Until its demise at the end of the 1960s, the postwar boom was primarily understood as the era of Keynesian welfarism (and modernisation in its image for the developing world). Interest in government expenditure as far as mainstream economics was concerned focused on its overall level, and hence impact on aggregate effective demand. Keynesianism provided a rationale for government intervention, and expenditure, to correct macroeconomic malfunctions. Whilst such government expenditure could be wasteful (digging and refilling holes), its major components, other than for defence, have been implicitly presumed to finance welfare programmes of one sort or another. From a macroeconomic perspective, however, the composition of that expenditure has been of lesser significance than its quantity. Consequently, the details of welfare provision were left either to the lesser mortals dedicated to applied microeconomics or to other disciplines. In part, this also reflected a different division with economics apart from macro/micro, one between the short and long runs. Macroeconomics addressed short-run fluctuations around a given and unexamined long-run path. Otherwise, welfare expenditure primarily served to correct static market imperfections. Paradoxically, the secular growth in welfare expenditure, and the more general increase in state economic intervention, remained largely unobserved by economic theory, not least because Keynesianism in principle at most required a short-run stimulus to aggregate demand as opposed to ever-expanding expenditure (Fine and Murfin 1984).

These intellectual divisions have recently been cast aside by general developments within economics as well as by the specific emergence of a new welfare economics based on information-theoretic market imperfections. To illustrate the latter by way of a typical example, consider a government that wishes to guarantee each of its citizens a certain level of income, and hence consumption and welfare, at the cheapest possible cost by providing a subsidy where choosing to do so by whatever citizen criteria. A problem is that the government does not know the earning capacity of its individual citizens, although it does possibly know how these are distributed across the economy as a whole. It might be thought that government ought simply to make up income to the desired minimum for those earning nothing or below the minimum. However, there are what are termed incentive compatibility problems. For a citizen earning just below (or even just above) the minimum through working long hours at low wages, such a subsidy scheme would provide an incentive not to work at all and realise, instead, the minimum income and full leisure time. It turns out that it is optimal for the government to offer a subsidy even to those whose income will rise above the minimum as a result, thereby avoiding its citizens being caught in a poverty trap. For, otherwise, it might find itself laying out even more income subsidy to such individuals as they lower their own income by choosing not to work. As a result, the workforce is structured into those working or not and receiving minimum income, those with subsidy taking them above the minimum, and those above minimum without subsidy.[2]

In this example, the state's objectives have been taken as given, and it plays a strategic game with its citizens to ensure that each has at least a minimum income. But now suppose that the minimum income itself is set by popular vote with expenditure financed out of taxation. Too high a minimum would not be feasible since insufficient numbers would work and provide adequate taxable income. Too low a minimum would be voted against by a majority of potential low-wage workers and shirkers.[3] In such extremes, there must be an equilibrium in which a median voter is most satisfied.

The details of the example need not detain us unduly. What is important is the nature of the analysis. On the one hand, the economics of the welfare state is reduced to a problem of informational imperfections and incentive compatibility. As a result, Taylor-Gooby (1998a) offers what is an appropriate critique of rational choice as an approach to public policy. He concludes (Taylor-Gooby 1998b: 221):[4]

> The intellectual position that underlies the new directions in public policy is based on a view of economic choice that sees behaviour as ultimately motivated by instrumental rationality.

On the other hand, its politics is subject to the dictates of the median voter, although this can be complemented by a theory of political activity in which costs of acquiring influence are set against the gains of doing so.[5] Thus, as the Swedish economist Asar Lindbeck (1995: 9) puts it:[6]

> The basic dilemma of the welfare state, however, is that the more generous the benefits, the greater will be not only the tax distortions but also, because of moral hazard and benefit cheating, the number of beneficiaries.

Further, this is all subject to complex and dynamic factors 'reflecting the interacting adjustment over time of basic behavior patterns of households, firms, interest-group organizations, politician and public-sector administrators'.

Now, whilst the discussion has been set up in terms of work and income, is it confined to such? It could apply equally, like the information-theoretic approach itself, to any market or targeted need, to specific items of consumption such as health, housing and education or for income maintenance during involuntary unemployment or retirement. In this context, the economist's handling of 'risk' does not so much concern vulnerability as the probability distribution of know-able but unknown outcomes. Reducing such risk can even be counterproductive! For, with guarantees across income, education or health, individuals have lower incentives to save, thereby reducing investment and economic performance. It is all a matter of whether the correction of market imperfections is better or not than the consequences of the original distortion. The logic underlying the understanding is always the same – it is simply a matter of importing the specific risks or informational or other market failures characteristic of the item under consideration.[7] With such a universal theory, a marriage with designated concerns from whatever source is more or less automatic. For the welfare state, as Dilnot's (1995) 'assessment' reveals, it is a matter of incentives to work, to save, and to form or break up families, together with affordability and willingness to pay. More specifically, Snower (1996) proposes vouchers for health and education in order to accrue benefits of the free market and yet to handle the informational asymmetries for credit in these sectors. Similarly Phelps (1996a, b) sees the welfare state as a system of entitlements and benefits, justified by the presence of asymmetric information and market imperfections but still does not see why there should not be private insurance. He further suggests this leads to a sort of prisoners' dilemma situation in which incentives and the ethos to work are being undermined, thereby raising unemployment. This is all due to a sequence of lobby groups winning influence one after another.

In addition, Lindbeck *et al.* (1999) incorporate consideration of the influence of social norms by which they mean a mechanical demonstration effect (or, more exactly, stigma or negative conspicuous consumption)[8] in which the more who take benefits the more the incentive (or less disutility) from doing so (p. 3):

> It is likely that an increase in the number of people who receive welfare benefits weakens the social norms to live off one's own work. Moreover, individuals who live off public transfers may over time come to value their leisure more.

Whilst their formal model, in the vein previously outlined, guarantees a single equilibrium, it is particularly sensitive to small changes in underlying exogenous conditions (p. 30):

> When social norms are introduced into an analysis, one might fear a plethora of possible outcomes – that 'anything can happen'. However, in the present simple model, this fear turns out to be unjustified. The range of possible outcomes is in fact highly restricted. Essentially, there are only two alternatives: a low-tax society supported by a majority of taxpayers or a high-tax society supported by a majority of transfer recipients. Which of these two potential equilibria will materialize depends on preferences and on the wage distribution.

The economist's apparent fear of multiple equilibria reflects a lingering distaste for indeterminacy. For in the absence of uniqueness, subject to random shock, an economy/society will not necessarily return to its known starting point. As Lindbeck *et al.* make clear, their model does benefit from uniqueness of equilibrium, albeit with one or other of two sorts of outcomes – a scroungers welfare state with many potentially low-skilled workers on benefits funded by relatively few and highly taxed high-skill workers, as opposed to a highly skilled workforce, with high levels of employment and low levels of taxation. However, it is a simple matter to endogenise the exogenous factors that determine which sort of equilibrium arises for the Lindbeck *et al.* model, thereby providing for multiple equilibria. One obvious option, for example, is to allow the wage distribution to be subject to state expenditure on education. Depending on how this is done, it might be expected that either equilibrium is possible with the result depending on whether the economy started off with relatively high skills and the capacity to sustain them through taxation. Such indeterminacy can then even be transformed from a source of fear into a virtue. For it enables the welfare state to be understood as a system (as comprising one equilibrium as opposed to another) in which 'history' matters.[9]

Thus, Freeman (1995), for example, takes such theorising one stage further by interpreting interaction between labour markets and welfare provision as a *system* ('by analogy with models of fitness landscapes in biology'! (p. 16)). He argues that high taxation in Sweden allowed for an egalitarian wage structure (since high-skill workers had relatively little incentive to pursue wider differentials since these would be taxed away) and for high levels of public sector expenditure, and hence full employment. Wage compression also reduces labour turnover, induces lower hours of work, commitment to work sharing, and enables competitiveness in sectors based on high skills (until these come under short supply because of low rewards). He concludes that this all fits together, and that marginal changes in different parts of the system (such as reduced benefits, lower taxation or public sector cuts in response to neo-liberal pressures) would render the system dysfunctional.[10]

From the perspective of other social sciences, the idiosyncrasies of this selection of contributions is less significant than the limited principles deployed when set against the scope or potential scope of application. The welfare state is ultimately reduced to a structured system for handling or, if endogenising politics, for responding to efficiency and equity issues in the context of informational and other market imperfections. It might seem churlish to be so cold about developments within and around economics that at least relax some of the earlier bonds and bounds attached to rationality and market harmony. And there is much to welcome, not least for example, in the work of Amartya Sen and others who have popularised the capability approach to welfare, and other aspects of the human condition.[11] Sen (1993: 30) has applied the capability approach in his own work to well-being and poverty, liberty and freedom, living standards and development, gender bias and sexual divisions, and justice and social ethics. Yet, he does acknowledge that (p. 33):[12]

> A full accounting of individual freedom must, of course, go beyond the capabilities of personal living and pay attention to the person's other objectives (e.g. social goals not directly related to one's own life).

The demise of O'Goffe's tale

To recognise that individuals have goals other than those directly serving their own needs is a far from satisfactory step in determining what those goals are and the extent to which they are served. From an analytical point of view, a considerable tension plays between how to understand society and how to focus upon individual capabilities,[13] one that has often been resolved by engaging with moral philosophers and their traditions of hypothetical argument concerning ethical, distributional and other such issues. The net effect, whatever the intent, may be to consolidate methodological individualism and the colonisation of other social sciences by economics. In other words, is the welfare state about the capabilities of individuals or the political economy of capitalism?

The answer was the latter for a decade or more, from the end of the postwar boom, with the sociology of the welfare state dominated by those offering an approach attaching itself to Marxist political economy.[14] The work of O'Connor (1973), Gough (1979), Offe (1984) and, to a lesser extent, Ginsburg (1979) was most prominent.[15] It had a number of appealing features, even apart from its radicalism. First, it posed a systemic analysis based upon the imperatives of capitalism, with attention both to its economic and to its non-economic needs as a system. Second, a political economy is posited. In the case of O'Connor, this led to an analytical approach to state expenditure which bordered on parody of Marx's understanding of (private) capital. For the state was understood to advance social capital,[16] itself made up of the two components of social investment and social consumption. Both of these are considered to be 'indirectly' productive for capital by providing infrastructure and a compliant and educated working class, but social consumption can also include social expenses on warfare and welfare which do not necessarily support profitability and accumulation. O'Connor essentially relies upon the underconsumptionist theory of Baran and Sweezy, in which monopoly capitalism is stagflationary and not self-sustaining. As a result (p. 41):

> Monopoly capital and organized labor have, in effect, 'exported' their conflicts to the competitive and state sectors.

Gough (1979) deployed a more general political economy which is essentially distributional/functional in content. As Torfing (1998: 178–9) succinctly puts it:[17]

Gough deliberately seeks to avoid a functionalist explanation of the modern welfare state ... by explaining [it] ... as a result of class struggles fought within the structural limits of capitalism. ... [Do not] overlook the fact that he does not pay much attention to the nature of the structures of capitalism and how they are translated into constraints of actions. His real contribution is that he invokes an action theory which is not based on methodological individualism. However, the problem with Gough's action-based theory of the development of the modern welfare state is its class reductionism etc.

In economic terms, profit is higher the lower are the money and social wages, each of which is subject to class conflict. The difference in the social wage is that the conflict not only is distributional over its level, but also concerns its goals and forms. Thus, the welfare state (Gough 1979: 12):

simultaneously embodies tendencies to enhance social welfare, to develop the powers of individuals, to exert social control over blind play of market forces; and tendencies to repress and control people, to adapt them to the requirements of the capitalist economy. Each tendency will generate counter-tendencies in the opposite direction; indeed, this is precisely why we refer to it as a contradictory process through time.

Third, then, for both O'Connor and Gough, but especially Offe (1984), the welfare state is caught between the needs of accumulation and those of social reproduction and legitimisation. The contradictions of capitalism are both reflected in and intensified by the welfare state, not least as a fiscal crisis, as expenditure tends to outstrip revenue. Nonetheless, specific outcomes within the welfare state and its particular programmes and policies are conditional upon how the balance between accumulation, legitimisation and reproduction is resolved.

In effect, then, this approach involved an understanding of the welfare state in terms of the economy's inability to sustain both itself and the social conditions necessary for its reproduction; these in turn derived from a fundamental antagonism between capital and labour over distribution. To some extent, such conflict (and its attachment to crisis in general and to that of the welfare state in particular) could be tempered by productivity increase through which competing claims on output could be accommodated, but such considerations tended to be pushed into the background, and presumed to be overwhelmed by demands for wages, profits and state expenditure (on working-class welfare or otherwise functional for capital). Over the past decade, the approach has not been rejected so much as modified to incorporate economic and political interests other than those of capital and labour, and also to incorporate the impact of globalisation. Consider the latter first.

As already observed in Chapter 2, the notion of globalisation can be caricatured as having drawn on two models – one derived from the realm of culture and the other from finance. In each case, the speed and power of internationalisation is perceived to overwhelm and homogenise national differences. To a large extent, in the case of culture etc. such crudity has been modified, if not rejected, by acknowledging that the local influences and transforms the global in highly specific ways giving rise to 'glocalisation'. But the same is not true of finance, with the dual images to the fore of instantaneous communication through computer-based trading and perfectly mobile and rootless capital.

Not surprisingly, issues apart from culture and finance are perceived to lie somewhere between these two extremes. The welfare state is no exception. The literature has moved away from considering its inner, national crises to focus upon the limits to change imposed by globalisation. The continuing work of Gough is indicative.[18] In Pfaller *et al.* (1991a), it is argued that welfare statism is under challenge by exposure to international competition and mobility of capital.[19] In the short run, capital will seek out the lowest levels of taxation and other burdens in seeking to maximise returns.[20] On the other hand, long-term competitiveness depends upon the services provided by the welfare state which generate increases in productivity. Further, quite apart from the squeeze on policy imposed by the dictates of internationally mobile capital, internal national conditions also impose constraints on policy implementation (p. 8):

> It is not unlikely that society will have difficulties in setting priorities at all, because each avenue of adjustment is blocked by vested interests.

Beck (2000: 2), in typical fashion, offers the most extreme form of the withering away of the (welfare) nation-state, deploying a parallel with Marx from the Communist Manifesto:

> 'All fixed, fast-frozen relations, with their train of ancient and venerable prejudices and opinions, are swept away'. … Today the 'fixed and fast-frozen' is the welfare state and trade-union organization of labour, while the 'ancient and venerable' are the bureaucratic prescriptions and fiscal extractions of the (national) state.

His emphasis is on the ability of multinationals to export jobs to where wages are lowest (p. 3). The problem is that there is no international state to provide a new social contract arising out of 'the fact that capitalism produces more and more with less and less labour' (p. 63) – although the knock-on effect of cheaper goods is not considered other than in reducing employment.

In this light, it should be apparent that the profit–welfare-squeeze hypothesis has simply been raised to a global level with internationally mobile capital functioning *externally* as the working class previously did *internally*. Outcomes depend upon the balance of forces, and the institutions and policies through which they are expressed, but they are heavily circumscribed by (unspecified) limits. As O'Connor and Olsen (1998a: 21) put it:

> In the new, more global environment, financial capital, transnational corporations, and other actors play a significantly greater role in determining what is desirable, or even possible, with little if any regard for 'strong' labour movements. This may be done purposefully or, as with the actions of bond traders, currency speculators, credit-rating agencies, and others who buy, sell, and deal in capital markets, more unintentionally. Keynesian policies, protective regulations, social programs, and other progressive distributional policies associated with the 'golden age of welfare capitalism', thus soon were defined as market 'rigidities'. They have given way to deregulation, massively regressive shifts in taxation policy, balanced budget legislation, and the dismantling or downgrading of welfare states. In this global environment, all governments – even incumbent social-democratic or labour governments ... – have much less room for manoeuvre.

There is, however, one shift in emphasis which is to give much greater prominence to longer term competitiveness to which the welfare state is understood as a major contributor in promoting higher productivity. As observed, it is perceived that the capacity to adopt corresponding policies is highly circumscribed both internally and externally, leading to two responses, one national and one international, but each tied to the notion that, in practice, there are losses from what is not a zero-sum game. At the international level, long-term productivity slowdown is the consequence of seeking short-run competitiveness through lower levels of funding of the welfare state. Consequently, as suggested by Mishra (1998), there is a need for internationally recognised welfare standards to preclude a race to the bottom – if generalised, an appeal for an internationalised Keynesian/welfarism – especially if domestic restructuring of economy and welfare will be resisted by those who suffer and have formed social norms around living standards (Rodrik 1997).[21] In this vein, in considering globalisation, unemployment, flexibility, and ageing, Mishra (1999: 33) argues:

> We therefore reach a paradoxical conclusion. Increasing globalization and competitiveness create economic conditions which require the state or the public sector to play a *more*, not less, important role in social protection.

Otherwise, at the national level, the failure to accommodate appropriately to international realities can lead to even higher levels of unemployment and lower levels of welfare expenditure as capital exerts its market discipline.

In short, globalisation has been deployed to reinforce the notion of crisis or restructuring of the welfare state that previously derived from national consider-ations alone.[22] As Pierson (1998a: 785) puts it:

> Few serious commentators on social policy accept the globalization story in its simplest form. … Nonetheless, there is a good deal of support for the view that states have been obliged to recast their social policies under the imperatives of global economic forces.

This has given rise to a literature on whether, to what extent and how the welfare state is being dismantled or subject to retrenchment.[23] In this vein, Powell and Hewitt (1998: 11) conclude that 'the welfare state is being redefined, but reports of its death have been much exaggerated'.[24]

To stand back and reflect on the latest literature on the welfare state is to catch sight of several degrees of irony. First, whilst much of the previous work within the tradition of Marxist political economy is rejected as being too deter-ministic and reductionist to class and the economy, these are features which have been fully embraced, albeit with limits imposed by the (internationalised) economy with which welfare interacts to grind out more or less favourable outcomes according to a more refined disaggregation of political forms, processes and institutions. Second, what was previously seen in O'Goffe as an unduly pessimistic prognosis for the welfare state in view of extrapolation from the close of the postwar boom, is now taken for granted. Third, whilst the profit-squeeze approach has always been influential, with Gough (1979) for example often serving as a teaching text, it has been complemented by consideration of more mainstream concerns, especially trade-offs between short and long runs, and between welfare and short-run competitiveness. This is, however, just one example of a more general and sophisticated application of the new informa-tion-theoretic economics in which market imperfections are readily translated into differences in growth performance over time. The new or endogenous growth theory has sought to explain why growth rates have *not* converged, why globalisation of finance and technology for example does not lead to common outcomes.[25] Drawing upon a more or less indefinite range of market imperfec-tions, including welfare expenditure and political variables, market imperfections are used to explain why growth rates *differ*. In addition, these are incorporated into growth regressions with a degree of sophistication which, whilst still highly problematic, totally dominate the amateurish efforts of the welfare state litera-ture where statistical techniques are deployed. Paradoxically, just as non-economists are using economic arguments to explain why the welfare state is doomed to be confined within highly restrictive limits, so economists are using the welfare state (and other non-economic variables) to explain why such limits are far from predetermined. At best, in the non-economic literature, this is usually recognised by reference to internal political and/or institutional factors, see Scharpf (2000) for example. The idea is that these filter the impact of economic globalisation, correctly drawing the implication of differentiated outcomes, but with limited and stereotyped understanding of the economy, as demonstrated for example by Korpi and Palme (1998).

From welfare state to welfare regimes

Thus is set globalisation against the welfare state as the free flow of investment is presumed to undermine, if not to eliminate, the state's room for manoeuvre. But as Fine and Harris (1979) observed for the earlier debate inspired by Murray (1971), the state often promotes, rather than reluctantly accepts, globalisation (or internationalisation). Much the same is true of the stance towards welfare, not least with the privatisation to international corporations (Whitfield 2001). This points to the need to reject a framework of state versus globalisation and to examine how underlying economic and political interests are represented nationally and internationally. Instead, in its economic analysis, non-economic literature on the welfare state is caught between the two worlds of political economy and (new) mainstream economics. But it is not suspended without motion. It has a dynamic, which increasingly sees it drawn to the latter's seductive charms.[26] For, over the past decade, certainly since the appearance of Esping-Andersen's (1990) *The Three Worlds of Welfare Capitalism*, his approach has become a, if not the, central influence on the understanding of the welfare state by social theory. For Headey *et al.* (1997: 332), for example:[27]

> Suffice it to say that, for better or worse, Esping-Andersen's 1990 book is now a well-established landmark in relation to which any subsequent work must situate itself.

There is now a huge literature both deploying and criticising Esping-Andersen's approach. Usefully, he has published a restatement and refinement of his framework of analysis and the rationale for it (Esping-Andersen 1999).[28] At its core remains the notion that welfare provision is typically attached to one of three different types of regime. Gornick and Jacobs (1998: 692) provide a useful, if incomplete, summary of what is involved:

> Esping-Andersen's typology includes: the *social democratic welfare states*, which primarily include the Nordic countries ... the *conservative (or corporatist) welfare states*, which are dominated by the continental European countries (represented ... by Belgium, Germany, and the Netherlands); and the *liberal (or residual) welfare states* (represented ... by Canada, the United Kingdom, and the United States). In the social democratic regime, entitlements draw on the principle of universal rights of social citizenship; in the conservative regime, entitlements are based on work performance; in the liberal countries, entitlements derive primarily from assessments of individual need.

As a result of focus upon such regimes, the approach can in part be perceived as heavily descriptive in the particular focus it has upon regime types as 'clusters' of characteristics. The idea is that particular policies or forms of provision tend to be associated with one another, thereby structurally distinguishing welfare regimes. Whilst this can be understood informally, cluster analysis is also a formal statistical technique with the capacity to determine whether a sample population can be partitioned according to its variation over a number of characteristics. The parallel is with those who sit a number of examinations across the disciplines and deciding over which sorts of topics students tend to be good or bad. We come up with student types and corresponding subject types.

Now much of the literature has been concerned to question the legitimacy of Esping-Andersen's typology, both for the countries that he does include as well as for those that he does not and, by the same token, for the characteristics that are or are not included.[29] From a statistical point of view, throw in one or more students and/or one or more exams, and you can find that there are more or less regimes, even a different typology, as well as a potential reallocation of subjects across regimes. Thus, in which regime to place the Netherlands is problematic 'as it includes features of both social democratic and conservative-corporatist welfare states' (Gornick and Jacobs 1998: 692). For their empirical work on public sector employment, the Netherlands is placed in the latter regime but, in studying redistributive policies, Headey *et al.* (1997: 333) assign it to the social democratic camp![30]

Esping-Andersen (1999: 73) does not, however, consider such conundrums to be a problem since they derive from too partial or too comprehensive an understanding of what is to be analytically incorporated:

> The bases for typology construction ... are welfare *regimes*, not welfare *states* nor individual social policies. 'Regimes' refers to the ways in which welfare production is allocated between state, market, and households. Some confusion may arise because the word 'regime' is often applied to all kinds of phenomena: 'poverty regimes', 'pension regimes', or 'male bread-winner regimes'. ... Some criticisms of 'the three worlds' are ... irrelevant because they are not addressing welfare regimes but individual programmes. ... It is unquestionably relevant to compare 'bread-winner models', and it goes without saying that this has direct relevance for welfare regime comparisons but, again, a welfare regime typology does not stand or fall solely on one social dimension; and, again, 'bread-winner regimes' and 'welfare regimes' are two distinct dependent variables.

In short, in the cluster analysis, all policy programmes should be included. Or should they? In his definition of welfare capitalism, Esping-Andersen (1999: 7) refers to the presence of universal citizenship, social solidarity, full democracy, recognition of trade unionism, and educational provision. But health provision, for example, does not warrant a mention (although it is addressed in the context of the United States as a liberal regime). Neither does housing even though the form and level of provision is highly variable across different welfare regimes. Of course, the more such policy programmes are incorporated, the greater the potential for divergence across the three identified regimes and for others to be posited. As P. Davis (2000: 13) observes, with corresponding relevance to the developed world:

> Esping-Andersen's approach tends to sideline the role of health, education and many other policies within the welfare regime. His original work focuses on income maintenance and labour market practices. In Bangladesh, however, the range of health, education, housing, land policy and financial services has a greater impact on poor people's livelihoods than the meagre cash transfers available.

One conundrum that Esping-Andersen (1999: 75) does acknowledge is provided by Castles and Mitchell (1992) in their consideration of Australia, New Zealand and the UK. Here, low levels of government expenditure attached to its more egalitarian use lead to an understanding of these liberal regimes in Esping-Andersen's classification to be dubbed as a fourth 'radical' regime. For Esping-Andersen, however, this is merely to mistake the historical means by which the liberal regime is formed from its continuing features.[31] It is also perceived as a potential historical aberration, subject to erosion (Esping-Andersen 1999: 89–90). Another case of regime proliferation acknowledged by Esping-Andersen (1997, 1999: 90–92) and discussed at length is provided by Japan, and Kwon (1997) more generally has pointed to the need for different regimes to characterise East Asian welfare systems. In this case, Japan is seen as a 'hybrid case' (Esping-Andersen 1999: 92), possibly 'a uniquely synthetic expression of liberalism and conservatism' (Esping-Andersen 1997: 187). Alternatively, 'it is arguably the case that the Japanese welfare system is still in the process of evolution; that it has not yet arrived at the point of crystallization' (Esping-Andersen 1997: 187).[32] Finally, there is the potential for a Mediterranean model which Esping-Andersen (1999) dismisses through an inconsistent procedure; first, he rejects it as depending on a single programme (social assistance) (p. 90), then he does so on the basis of a simple statistical test for differences in 'familialism' which is not a full range of programmes. Trifiletti (1999), for example, suggests a Mediterranean regime because of the particular combination of labour market and familial policies, not least for their impact upon women.[33] Sainsbury (1999a) also argues that adding a gender dimension to welfare regimes has mixed consequences across them. Do trade unions, for example, consolidate the male-worker model or support women at work, and more generally for social provision, labour markets and taxation?

Trifiletti's critique is merely the latest in a long line of contributions that have pointed to Esping-Andersen's neglect of the gendering of welfare capitalism, both in its constituent elements and, frequently, in his formulation of a typology of regimes. In particular, emphasis has been placed on the role of women outside of the labour market, and the relationship between household and welfare provision. However, Esping-Andersen (1999: 12) sees himself as having fully embraced this criticism by placing greater emphasis on the household than previously.[34] This is taken up later.

As a descriptive typology, the positing of three regimes by Esping-Andersen leaves much to be desired. On the grounds of hybrids across the regimes, a total of seven are logically possible (singles, doubles or all three together!). Divergence by individual programme or policy from regime assignation can be dismissed as neglect of the overall picture. Gender is incorporated after the event by paying more attention to the family. In addition, there is unlimited capacity for claiming history has yet to do its work in moulding an appropriate regime into shape should it appear to present anomalies. Indeed, there are even hints that the system of welfare regimes is a highly historical specific product, 'institutionalized ... during the 1960s and 1970s ... when strong worker protection and labour market regulation emerged, when social citizenship was fully affirmed ... when the core features of welfare states crystallized ... [and] essential differences between ... welfare states were affirmed'. Further, 'the timing was auspicious: the consolidation and maturation of post-war welfare capitalism coincided with the onset of the new, post-OPEC economic realities of slow growth and rising structural unemployment ... with accelerating economic globalization and rising structural unemployment' (Esping-Andersen 1999: 4). Thus, welfare regimes derive from a historically peculiar window of opportunity for countries at appropriate stages of development. Finally, the empirical rationale for identifying the three regimes and assigning countries to them depends upon a mix of superficial and arbitrary statistical techniques.[35]

But, in part by way of summary, the most comprehensive critique of Esping-Andersen's welfare regimes approach is, ironically, provided by Gough (2000a, b) in his seeking to adapt the approach to developing countries. He lists the following: failure of some countries and programmes to fit the typology; neglect of health, education and housing; narrow notion of decommodification; overemphasis on class at expense of other forms of stratification such as ethnicity, gender (especially through households and division of labour) and religion; and insufficient attention to the constraints imposed by globalisation. As Gough acknowledges, some of these issues have been taken on board by Esping-Andersen in his later work. Gough's own approach is to offer more of the same – to add an extra (southern European) regime and more factors and processes, Gough (2000a: 8):

> Despite outstanding problems, I conclude ... that there is life left in the concept of welfare regimes – enough to make it worthwhile trying to apply it to understand the social policies emerging in developing societies. The essential truths behind the concept are that institutions,

interests and even ideas cluster together in persistent cross-national patterns which, second, reproduce through time. In this way clusters of similar nation states can be discerned, and comparative analysis can be conducted at a meso-level between the global and the national.

The result is a remarkable conflation of the various approaches to the welfare state – welfare regimes, new welfare economics, globalisation as constraint, and his own, decreasingly influential, political economy. Gough's (1999: 4) inaugural lecture at the University of Bath poses the needs of capital against the needs of the people, 'roughly' defining the welfare state in these terms:

> Public rights or entitlements to the means to human welfare in general and to minimum standards of well-being in particular, independent of rights based on property or income.

He also seeks positive-sum outcomes in simplistic terms, with capital seduced into a stance of greater humanity through the long-term competitiveness that can derive from welfarism (p. 9):

> The fundamental argument is two-fold. First, that welfare states ... can enhance the competitiveness of national capitals. Second, that in the process this changes the way that private capitals interpret *their* needs. In an increasingly competitive world welfare states can provide a competitive advantage to private capital and at the same time encourage different forms of capitalism with different moral underpinnings and welfare outcomes.

Thus, Gough's motivation, like Esping-Andersen, is essentially to discover empirical regularities and to supplement them with case-specific investigation. Consequently, theory takes a secondary and far from coherent and transparent role.[36]

So consider the theory deployed by Esping-Andersen. Initially, it is primarily structural and relational in content, in the sense of positing relations between structures.[37] As Esping-Andersen (1990: 19) himself puts it, he deploys the 'sociological notion that power, democracy, or welfare are relational and structured phenomena'. The welfare regimes are simply structurally distinct clusters of welfare programmes. What are the other structures to which they are connected? Again, there are three, which are taken to be causal (Esping-Andersen 1990: 29). The class structure, particularly the working class, is important as the basis for political mobilisation. Second, however, there is the structure of political coalition in which the position of the middle classes is crucial, depending on how and whether they are wooed by, and form an alliance with, the working class (Sweden) or not (the UK). Finally, historically inherited institutions are of significance as in the case of Germany. The relations between the two sets of structures are mediated by three processes, decommodification, stratification and employment generation. Decommodification is the extent to which individuals are able to exist independently of the labour market (as a result of welfare policies), stratification reflects the impact of welfare provision on social differentiation, and employment is concerned with its compositional structure, the organisation of the labour market, working conditions and degree of commitment to full employment.

More recently, Esping-Andersen (2000d) has distanced himself from theory, questionably claiming that sociology from Weber to Parsons is essentially theoryless and more concerned with classifications and typologies. These depend upon historical benchmarks having come to fruition. In this respect, he places his own welfare regimes in the same tradition as Marx's *Capital* and Lipset's notion of postwar settlement, each conceptually incorporating material historical developments. As such he is concerned to identify key aspects of any particular society (p. 61):

> Principally, we rally around grand questions and suggestive *Leitmotifs*. The grand question which gave the social sciences their identity was how social order, democracy, equality, or solidarity could be compatible with an urban, industrial capitalist economy: the tension between efficiency and solidarities.

In this respect, it is easier to discern what he theoretically disavows. He is scathingly contemptuous of postmodernism for its lack of touch with reality and the problems that it poses (p. 61):

> The anything-goes, all-inclusive thrust of sociology is now pushing it towards issues ever more removed from central 'trade-offs', from the workings of capitalist democracies. The move is towards psychologistic concerns with social identities, towards anthropologizing, historicism, semantics. The heroes of *fin de siècle* sociology are blasé postmodernists, 'deep historians', and savage 'deconstructionists', none of whom appear especially inclined to maintain an ongoing dialogue with say Weber. Today, there are probably more books on sexual identities than on power or social class; more debates on language than on how to conduct good empirical analysis.

He is also unimpressed by the failure of Manuel Castells to finesse the relationship between abstract and concrete levels in that, within his work, the two inevitably conform to one another without illumination of either (p. 74):

> My impression is that he began with an imagined holistic gestalt and then proceeded to examine all the minutiae of all its component parts in order to fit them into his imagined whole.

202

Esping-Andersen sarcastically rejects mainstream economics for its intolerance towards alternatives (p. 61):

> Economics would crash if there were no free choice. Paradoxically, economists espouse a theory that is profoundly monopolistic. Respectable economists are condemned to do their shopping in an academic equivalent to the Soviet *komsomol* store: choice is restricted to one brand only of the same basic ware. ... As the joke goes, the definition of an economist is someone with a PhD in laissez-faire ideology.

Yet this is to work with an old model of mainstream economics that has already been superseded. And Esping-Andersen seems unaware that the new model offers a multiplicity of choices over the incidence and impact of market imperfections and their implications for non-market relations. Indeed, where he does indirectly notice such developments, it is to welcome them, finding that economics is more interested in classical 'trade-offs' than sociology, and that economic sociology is undergoing a renaissance.

Ultimately, Esping-Andersen opts for a theoretically informed cross-section and time-series mode of investigation. Despite his sharp critique of Castells and mainstream economics, Esping-Andersen's sociology has considerable affinities with them, and there is a suspicion that his general methodology follows from his welfare regime approach rather than vice versa – with much other theory discounted as typology. As is and will be increasingly apparent, this renders the theory adopted open to an arbitrary and potentially contradictory content irrespective of the strains placed upon sought-for empirical realities, themselves stripped of postmodernist meaning and grand theoretical roots.

Yet the shifting analytical content of Esping-Andersen's work is far from arbitrary, reflecting both conformity to, and reaction against, the shifting intellectual environment in which it resides. With sacrosanct loyalty to the welfare regime approach, postmodernism and grand theory are both rejected. But, as already observed, Esping-Andersen (1999), in response to criticism, places much more emphasis on the family and, consequently, defamilialisation which is reduction of individual dependence on the family, as women work or their fertility drops, for example. Defamilialisation is the household counterpart and mirror image to labour market decommodification. Consequently, there is an explanatory shift to the 'intercausal triad of state, [labour] market and family'. But, despite its lesser prominence, this is not at the expense of the earlier triad of class, political coalition and institutional inheritance. For, as has been argued by Kemeny (1995), criticism of Esping-Andersen has tended to focus on his male-centredness, the neglect of women's wider, especially non-market, roles, and the constraints imposed by his three-regime typology. It has neglected his theory of power which Kemeny suggests is implicit but central. With this insight, it is relatively easy to see how significantly Esping-Andersen is influenced by the power resources thesis (PRT) and, in particular, how the structure of class interests become differentially translated into welfare regimes through the mediation of political coalitions, and other institutions such as the state, family and trade unions. Significantly, the book by O'Connor and Olsen (1998b) comprises a collection of essays that extend rather than criticise the Esping-Andersen approach, under the umbrella of PRT, its introduction making clear that it offers a compromise between structuralism and pluralism.[38] The criticisms take the form of extending structures and interest groups to include gender and race and globalisation. It becomes increasingly to look like a descriptive framework in which outcomes are explained by the interests and actions behind them, generalised and refined as required by inclusion of more case studies and issues – as O'Connor and Olsen (1998a: 19) put it, 'Power Resources Theory in an Era of Globalization: Identifying Actors and Structures'.[39] Not surprisingly, the issue of gender alone, its many dimensions and outcomes across issues and nations, is liable to blow the welfare regime approach apart.[40]

Nonetheless, the focus on the family does represent a methodological shift for Esping-Andersen. In his earlier work, he is 'focused on the state's larger role in managing and organizing the economy', determined to 'follow the broad approach ... [and] understand the "big picture" ... making grand comparisons' (Esping-Andersen 1990: 2). Emphasis is also placed on the comparative approach as against one based on 'laws of societal motion' which 'nearly always posit similar and convergent evolutionary paths' (p. 3). In Esping-Andersen (1999), he explicitly states his intention of rejecting public and rational choice theory for its 'disembodied treatment of economic life' and also Marxist political economy for its reductionism to class struggle (pp. 10–11). Instead, with one reservation, he embraces the comparative institutional method for, 'its great asset lies in its sensitivity to historical transformation and cross-national variation' (p. 11). No doubt, with some sense of a dual *mea culpa* (rather than display of knowledge of the literature), his dissatisfaction concerns exclusive focus on *macro-relations*, for which the importance of the *family* is overlooked (p. 11):

> My reservation has to do with the blindness of virtually all comparative political economy to the world of families. It is, and always has been, inordinately macro-oriented. It occupies itself with macroscopic constructions, such as welfare states, world trade, international finance, or trade unions, and with similarly huge outcomes, such as inflation, employment, inequality, or growth ... a sound understanding of postindustrial society must be anchored in the household economy.

Yet, what exactly is the political economy that Esping-Andersen deploys both to address the macroscopic and what is now a descent to the microscopic of the family? Across his work as a whole, despite his antipathy to O'Goffe, there is heavy reliance upon a distributional/Keynesian approach. The economic theory is identical; it is only the crude reductionism to ruling-class legitimacy that is rejected. Explicit reference is made to Kalecki's concern with the political consequences of full employment and whether a profitable capitalist economy could be sustained in face of the growing strength of the working class (Esping-Andersen 1990: 162). Within this framework, there are considerable nuances, with some limited potential for trade-offs between employment, money wage and real wage, and with outcomes dependent, not surprisingly, on the welfare regime adopted. Nonetheless (p. 164):

> The pursuit of full-employment policy objectives presumes the preservation of private entrepreneurial discretionary powers ... social policy became the chief arena within which distributional solutions were sought. However, this has come to place the welfare state in a double bind: it is given responsibility for both full employment performance *and* distributional harmony. The two functions ... are inherently incompatible.

Considerable emphasis is placed on the changing composition of the workforce, both by gender and occupation (public/private and industrial/services), and on demographics, especially the burdens of retirement.

Little further refinement is evident in the later work as far as the macroeconomic is concerned. Indeed, there is an inclination to shift the earlier macroscopic elements out of explanatory consideration. This is reflected in the debate over (de)commodification with Room (2000) (Esping-Andersen 2000c). Room's critique is both telling and limited. For it is usefully interpreted in two distinct but closely related senses. First, Esping-Andersen is interpreted as one dimensional, as reducing the issue of labour market dependence to that of access to subsistence income or consumption. Room's own response, drawing upon Marx's *Economic and Philosophical Manuscripts*, is to add another dimension, alienated work. This amendment is most favourably seen as symbolic of the much wider range of factors that bind workers to the labour market in a variety of ways, from status to ideology (quite apart from the more mature economic analysis developed by Marx himself in his later work, most notably *Capital*).

Second, though, the nature of these bonds cannot be reduced to a matter of income replacement alone. As for consumption, so for work. The relations, structures, processes and cultures associated with the labour markets straddle the articulation between economic and social reproduction in complex, varied and shifting ways (Fine 1998a). In short, Esping-Andersen is one dimensional both in focusing upon access to income and in his understanding of access itself. This allows him to retain his notion of welfare regimes without regard to the differentiation between welfare programmes and how they are provided. Indeed, Esping-Andersen (2000c) accepts Room's criticisms in terms of having been too one dimensional but indicates his own approach in the following terms (p. 351): 'To a welfare researcher, like myself, decommodification signals a citizen's relative independence from pure market forces; it captures one important dimension of freedom and constraint in everyday life of advanced capitalism'. What this indicates is a shift in the understanding of welfare from power, resources and classes to one of 'citizen' in face of the 'pure market', as if this could be a single dimension. Of course, each of these terms is highly contentious and ambiguous.

In this vein, in his later work, Esping-Andersen's understanding of welfare regimes has undergone a far from subtle transformation. In their first phase, the newly formed welfare states are in some respects seen as marginal (Esping-Andersen 1999: 31):

> The post-war achievement of less inequality with, typically, full employment and rising prosperity was probably more due to well-functioning labour markets and fortunate demographics than to the coming of the welfare state itself. As far as the first two post-war decades are concerned, the chief impact of welfare states on equality and employment was limited mainly to the consolidation of social citizenship rights. Where welfare states made a huge difference was their ability to guarantee against social risks.

Consequently, crises of the welfare state in that earlier period are perceived to be '*endogenous* ... it was doing things badly or bringing about unwelcome consequences'. By contrast, the current crisis is seen as deriving from '*exogenous* shocks that put into question the longer-term viability of the welfare state' (p. 3). The welfare state is perceived as a Trojan horse from which these exogenous shocks burst onto society, for 'the warriors inside the Trojan horse of our times are globalization, ageing, and family instability; a simultaneous market and family failure' (p. 148). As before, the result is 'a severe trade-off between welfare and jobs, equality, and full employment' (p. 173).[41]

In a nutshell, the macroscopic analysis now suggests that welfare capitalism is dysfunctional within limits that are variable according to the institutional and political accommodations that are reached. Those limits have been narrowed by the superimposition of globalisation and demographics. For the former, all of the emphasis is upon its negative implications – higher productivity and international competitiveness entail loss of jobs in manufacturing. No mention is made of the cheaper availability of goods and corresponding rise in incomes from competitive productivity increase. Rather, attention is drawn in part to the growing inequality that accompanies post-industrial economies, 'full employment implies more wage inequality' (Esping-Andersen 2000a: 10). This entails a need for service sector employment to grow and compensate for job losses in manufacturing. This cannot be automatic since

> families could not themselves assemble refrigerators, let alone an automobile ... [whereas] households are perfectly capable of preparing their own dinner, tending to their own children, or washing their own car. Globalization may punish our low-skilled workers, but if families decide to lunch out they will stimulate various low-skilled jobs in restau-

rants. In brief, how does it all add up? What is the connection between global pressures, household behaviour, and employment?

(p. 97)

A mainstream neo-classical economist would ask such questions, and Esping-Andersen's movement to the microscopic represents an informal appropriation of the new household economics, especially associated with Becker, in which families optimise through trade-offs over gender distribution over domestic and waged work according to external constraints. As Esping-Andersen (1999: 58) observes in a self-parody:[42]

> The intensity of the trade-off depends on several factors: number and age of children, whether mothers work part-time or full-time, and whether husbands help. ... Lamentable as this may be, it is perfectly consistent with a standard neoclassical joint-decision model of house-hold behaviour.

But such flirtations with mainstream economics are not confined to the new household economics. For, the household derives its welfare from the state, the market and its own activities. It is 'the ultimate destination of welfare consumption and allocation. It is the unit "at risk"' (Esping-Andersen 1999: 36). This leads to the following section heading, 'THE FOUNDATIONS OF WELFARE REGIMES: RISK MANAGEMENT', with opening sentence 'social policy means public management of social risks'.[43] This then leads to the standard account for the welfare state that is associated with mainstream economics, not least in terms of market failures including reference to information failure.[44] It is all a far cry from the alternative previously examined (Esping-Andersen 1990: 11):[45]

> The central question, not only for Marxism but for the entire contem-porary debate on the welfare state, is whether, and under what conditions, the class divisions and social inequalities produced under capitalism can be undone by parliamentary democracy.

Only time will tell whether what Taylor-Gooby (1997) has ironically termed the 'second-best' theory of class, state and capital will survive[46] and how much, as an alternative, the political economy of the welfare state will be colonised as risk management.

Towards an alternative

But what should form the content of a political economy of the welfare state? For reasons that will become apparent, it is not appropriate to pose an alterna-tive *general* theory. For *the* welfare state is a misnomer in the sense that welfare provision is distinctive not only across countries but also across its separate constituent elements within each country. For, first, the welfare state is *programme* specific. In other words, housing, education, health programmes, etc., have to do with housing, education and health as previously elaborated and justified in this book for private consumption. The rationale for the sop approach does not evaporate simply because of a greater or lesser involvement of the (welfare) state. It also follows that the cultural and ideological aspects of welfare provision will be programme specific, depending for example upon how the different components of welfare beliefs are reproduced or transformed.[47] These differ whether they concern health, education, work ethic or gender, over time and by socio-economic strata. This is not to suggest that the different programmes, and their cultures, are independent of one another, nor that they do not share common determinants. However, how and to whom welfare is delivered are structurally interdependent with, in principle, a whole range of factors interacting in different ways with different and shifting effects. But how housing, for example, is provided – land, other inputs, construction, finance, tenure, etc. – is as important as, and dovetails with, social custom, welfare principles, political and economic pressures in ways that are unique to housing itself and distinct from health, education or whatever. Paradoxically, if the globalisation thesis were applicable to the welfare state, we would expect programmes to become more similar not only in the levels and composition of expenditure but also in the details of provision itself. One model for public housing, one for education, and so on, to conform to the principle of most competitive nation. Evidence suggests otherwise than this *reductio ad absurdum*.[48]

Second, differentiation of the welfare state by country as well as by programme is a consequence of each country being at its own stage of development, and subject to its own structure and dynamic of economic, political and ideological forces. These will interact with, or be concretised through, the provision attached to particular programmes. This conclusion draws negatively from Esping-Andersen, and the literature it has inspired, whereby his three welfare regimes have increasingly proven to be an analytical and empirical strait-jacket as far as mounting evidence from case studies by programmes and countries is concerned, more observed in the breach as more welfare states are encompassed and each is more carefully disaggregated. To some extent, this collective reaction against the welfare regime approach is being directed towards an alternative in which path dependence, institutional sclerosis and the like are to the fore. This has been particularly promoted by the 'failure of retrenchment' literature, especially Pierson (2000).[49] As the welfare state has not been rolled back as far as is warranted by neoliberalism and globalisation, so the previous rounds of expansion must have incorporated material and ideological barriers to cuts in programmes. The weakness of this alternative is its failure to address adequately how and the reasons why some programmes and policies are reproduced and expanded and others are not.

Such a conclusion is particularly apt for the rapidly expanding work on welfare in East Asia. A range of writers have pointed to the paradox of welfare provision expanding in response to the financial crisis of 1997, especially in

South Korea, namely Yang (2000), Kwon (2000), Tang (2000) and Mishra and Asher (2000). For Shin (2000: 104–5):

> The changes to the social security system in Korea in the wake of the financial crisis are paradoxical from the perspective of globalism enthusiasts. The reforms have proceeded as a crucial measure in coping with soaring unemployment as well as alleviating the insecurities associated with structural adjustment. They have not been limited to the establishment of a social safety net. Rather, they have been developing towards a more redistributive and comprehensive welfare system. All these reforms have taken place at the same time as the Korean economy has been fully integrated into world markets. ... [There are] some clear implications for the understanding of the relationship between globalization and the social security system. The impacts of globalization on policy will not necessarily be harmful and rather will be dependent on the structure of the domestic institutions. Indeed, politics do still matter in the development of the welfare state even in an era of globalization.

But the more general, often implicit, point to be drawn from this literature is the variability of welfare provision across welfare programmes and countries. As White and Goodman (1998: 19–20) put it:

> While they share certain common features, East Asian welfare systems are not homogeneous ... have relied heavily on distinctive social, demographic, political and economic conditions which may not be present elsewhere and are in any case under threat in East Asia itself. The East Asian experience may have greater relevance to other societies in the early stages of economic development as a recipe for 'developmental welfare'. But there are serious issues of transferability/feasibility even in these cases.

Their edited collection ranges over pensions, housing and various components of social security, drawing out the heterogeneity both across countries and programmes. As White (1998: 176) appropriately concludes more generally even if, for him, in the context of China:

> Welfare reform cannot be seen merely in terms of choices between alternative policy options or directions; rather, the range, nature and feasibility of these choices are heavily determined by deeper dynamics which are propelled not only by broad structural changes in the social, economic and political spheres, but also by the particular constellation of interests and perspectives which cluster around welfare issues like iron filings round a magnet.

Third, then, the welfare state concerns the relationship between social and economic reproduction, and the fluidity between them as processes are moved across the 'public/private' divide. To some extent, the (re)drawing of this divide can be captured by the notions of commodification and decommodification. These are, however, totally inadequate as used in the welfare regimes approach. For, each goes much deeper than a simple understanding based on more or less (labour) market dependence. Whilst capitalism has a tendency to commodify, this also creates a countertendency, for the very same process of undermining non-capitalist provision also strengthens it, not least through the provision of cheap means of production and consumption. For the new household economics, this is simply a matter of reading off outcomes in terms of a more or less socially sticky comparative advantage. By contrast, outcomes both in the division of labour between commercial and non-commercial, and in the formation of labour market structures and dynamics, are highly contradictory and contingent.

Fourth, provision through the welfare state can, and has been, understood in terms of the creation and meeting of social norms. But these have to be understood in a sophisticated and complex analytical framework. As a customary standard of living – of which the wage bundle is a major factor – such norms are differentiated both by different sections of the population and by the consumption goods themselves (as suggested for social policy programmes in the first point above). Consumption norms are not simply an average as such, even with some above and some below the 'norm'. The latter is more appropriately understood as the outcome of continuing socio-economic processes which grind out customary patterns of consumption. What those patterns are and how they are determined is very different from one commodity to another. Food, housing, clothing, etc., are not only differentially consumed but the patterns and levels of consumption are the consequences of very different structures and processes of causation, see Fine *et al.* (1996) for food, for example.

Fifth, similar considerations apply to the distribution of (wage) income from which social policy in part takes its point of departure. Labour markets are not simply structured and differentiated, with correspondingly different wages and conditions and access by socio-economic status. Each labour market is itself structured and functions in an integral way, depending upon deskilling, reskilling, presence of trade unions, public or private, casualised or secure, competitiveness in product markets, and so on, as argued in detail in Fine (1998a). As there are socio-economic processes that match income levels to consumption norms (and vice versa), the homogenising influence of monetary remuneration is far from absolute. In other words, both the determination of the distribution of (wage) income and the potential for its effective redistribution have to be firmly rooted in an appropriately wide range of suitably integrated considerations. Thus, in so far as labour markets are a key element straddling economic and social reproduction, as they are under capitalism, and are themselves differentiated, this reinforces the conclusion that the welfare state is subject to a dual differentiation both by country and by programme.

11

WHITHER CONSUMPTION
STUDIES?

Introduction

The closing chapter of the first edition sought a move of focus from private to public consumption. In content, if not intent, the opposite is the case here. The following section is organised around issues raised by food studies, predominantly if not exclusively served by the private sector. The purpose is to display affinities with, if not detailed illustrations of, the themes raised earlier in the book as well as to comment upon a number of food-specific issues.[1]

The closing section returns to generalities. It reiterates that, in contrast to many other instances, the study of consumption, especially in view of postmodern 'traditions', has remained mercifully free of a colonising economics. However, postmodernism's own version of individual subjectivity (the negative image of an optimising individual with given preferences) has strengthened both the longstanding divide between cultural and economic analysis, and weakened knowledge and use of political economy. This reflects a neat and unfortunate complementary role with mainstream economics that has itself become increasingly intolerant and ignorant of alternatives to its received methods and techniques.

In short, neo-liberalism and postmodernism have co-existed in parallel, complementing one another through inhabiting mutually exclusive worlds that have discouraged alternatives. As their reign has waned, their influence remains in passing on a potential for genuine analytical integration of the economic and the cultural that remains as weak as it is necessary.

From land to lip

The literature on food that addresses consumption whether directly or indirectly, explicitly and consciously or otherwise, is longstanding, diverse and extraordinarily rich in scope and content. At a number of levels, this is hardly surprising. As one of the most basic of basic needs, it necessarily commands attention from antiquity to the present day. And, like other basic needs such as housing and clothing, it spans the primitive and minimum of necessities to the luxurious, refined, sophisticated and wasteful. Nor is this dualism necessarily mutually exclusive across its two extremes. For, in some sense, the 'primitive' nature of food can be perceived to survive along a thread that runs from cannibalism to postmodern preoccupations with the body and whatever is eaten, how and by whom. For Probyn (2000: 14), 'food goes in, and then, broken down, it comes out of the body, and every time this happens our bodies are affected'. Whatever else food is about, it is always ingested, digested and excreted through the act of consumption.

One result is to have popularised Brillat-Savarin's aphorism, 'Tell me what you eat and I will tell you what you are'. Interestingly, this is often misleadingly shortened to the quip 'you are what you eat'. But, what exactly is it that you eat? Answers are as plentiful as the interpretative imagination, ranging over the biscuit-like flesh of Christ to the 'Real Thing' of Coca-Cola. No less than for other items of consumption, food has served as a wealthy source of raw material for the study of symbolism, from family values to romantic fantasy. But scholarly interpretation of the meaning of food scarcely originated with postmodernism. Anthropology, in particular, has been built upon assigning different meanings to food, from taboo to feast, from Mauss' gifts to Levi-Strauss' structuralism and beyond. With Douglas and Isherwood (1980), the anthropological is projected forward (or is it sideways?) from primitive to advanced societies. Here, anthropology and sociology merge, adding to the analytical tools that can be brought to bear. Food involves stratification, sociability, socialisation, and so on, Mennell *et al.* (1992).[2]

The same applies to other objects of study such as marriage, kinship, death and burial. But, in one respect, food is different. Even if decreasingly so for the First World, food has remained a major sector of the economy. Consequently, it has given rise to a subdiscipline within economics dedicated to agriculture. This has so much confined itself to drawing parasitically upon the mainstream that it has scarcely commanded an audience beyond its practitioners within economics itself, let alone more broadly. Strikingly, if unwittingly, confirming the analyses of Chapters 2 and 6, Antle's (1999) Presidential Address to the American Agricultural Economics Association on the 'New Economics of Agriculture' is replete with references to market imperfections, informational asymmetries and the like.[3]

The poverty of food economics, for consumption as demand as well as for agricultural supply, has vacated the field to political economy. It remains stronger in this area than any other.[4] There are good reasons for this, over and above the opportunity offered by the absence of the mainstream, arising out of the nature of food itself. First, supply is attached to the land, thereby requiring a theory of landed property, its associated social relations and rent. Such is imperative once departing the idea of mainstream economics – that land is a resource like any other, only in fixed supply, with rent determined by naturally given differentials in fertility. Second, the food and agrarian questions have inevitably dovetailed with one another. On the one hand, what is the relationship between industry and agriculture? On the other hand, how does that relationship shift over time, particularly in the context of developmental transition? Here food and political economy necessarily confront one another across a much broader terrain, incorporating history through, for example, the problem of the transition from agrarian to industrial society, and rural sociology and its concerns with the distinctiveness, survival and transformation of agricultural and rural communities. From small farm to big business, the politics of food has also been prominent although, of late, the issues of lobbies and subsidies have been supplemented by those of the environment, biotechnology and food scares.

This alarmingly brief and superficial overview of the presence of food across the social sciences serves its intended purpose if it suggests why food occupies a leading position in the study of consumption. It is not so much the weight of study, impressive though this is, as the scope of issues and intellectual traditions with which they have been confronted. Admittedly, much of the literature has run along parallel lines, with different emphases and methods co-existing without necessarily contesting or complementing one another. Certainly, until recently, this has been especially true of the distance between the study of food as agriculture and the cultural turn in the study of food as consumption.

Yet, in other respects, food studies have been in the vanguard as far as the implications for consumption are concerned. It is worth dwelling on five instances. First, by the early 1990s, in advance of the more general literature, the globalisation approach to what was termed food regimes had already been established. Essentially, particularly drawing upon a few key commodities, such as grains, sugar and beef, Fordist agriculture was perceived to have been rampant on a global scale, with common technologies being deployed for mass production of uniform commodities for multinational traders serving homogenised consumers, food regimes for Friedmann and McMichael (1989), Friedmann (1993) and McMichael (1994).

Second, that foodies should have keyed into globalisation so quickly and readily is explained more by their preoccupation with agriculture than a reaction against the McDonaldisation of consumption. For rural sociology had been concerned with the barriers to capitalist development of agriculture. This itself reflected two issues – what is different between agriculture and industry and what prevents agriculture from becoming more industry-like. Initially, an answer to both questions was offered in terms of agriculture's backwardness because of its undue dependence upon the pace, rhythm and uncertainties of the seasons. Against this, Goodman et al. (1987) put forward the thesis of increasing displacement of agriculture by industry through what they termed appropriationism and substitutionism, correspondingly the replacement of natural with manufactured inputs and the shift of agricultural activity to industry. Irrespective of the merits of such analysis,[5] Goodman and Redclift squarely placed on the analytical agenda the issue of the vertical connections between the consumption of food and its supply, albeit skewed towards the agriculture/industry as opposed to the industry/consumption divide.

213

This would have been of more significance as a drawback but for two further precious elements in food studies from the perspective of consumption more generally. For, third, precisely because of its preoccupation with grand historical questions and the transition from agrarian feudalism to capitalist industry, and yet the survival to whatever degree of non-capitalist farming (the peasantry or, more exactly, peasantries, for example), the associated literature has focused on the nature of ((non)-capitalist) commodity production, the differences between the various () combinations and how they interact with one another. As a result, the analytical issues addressed in the opening chapters of this book have long formed part and parcel of food studies.

Fourth, in parallel with attention to vertical relations between agriculture and industry as essential to changes in production, the sociology of agriculture has reached outside the rural community itself to locate the sources of power over it. The new rural sociology has acknowledged how absentee landlords, banks, wholesalers, retailers, property and labour markets, governments at national and international levels and, ultimately, consumers exercise leverage over rural sustainability, restructuring, transformation or destruction.

Fifth, no sooner was all of this achieved and consolidated in the mid-1990s that it was immediately thrown into disarray, often by those who had put it in place. Goodman and Watts (1994) offer a particularly insightful critique in terms of what they term mimetics. For them, agriculture has unduly been understood by comparison with models of industry and how it does or does not conform to them – its failure for example, for whatever reason, to be sufficiently (neo-) Fordist. As argued in Chapter 5, this begs the question of the nature of industrial organisation itself, with one or more models of industry being unduly deterministic of complex, socially and historically rooted features underlying industrial reorganisation. At the same time, the global food regime approach rapidly proved to be incompatible with the empirical evidence for a wide range of products including the exemplars at its core. Homogenisation had been greatly exaggerated in light of differentiation in organisation by crop, both within agriculture itself and in wider economic and social relations around it.[6] In this respect, food studies were again in the vanguard in reacting against the globalisation hypothesis and emphasising heterogeneity at the international as well as the national and other levels.

Thus, by the mid-1990s, there was a sense in which the globalisation hypothesis was already being killed off in food studies before it had even been established elsewhere. One of the thrusts of the debate with Fine (1994a, b) in *Review of International Political Economy* was to suggest that food systems could be reorganised so quickly and variously that systemic or structured analysis had been rendered redundant. No doubt, apart from representing a guilty reaction against earlier commitment to the overdetermination of food regime analysis, this signified an early, if equally exaggerated, response to the prospective impact of biotechnology. One response has been to examine how a proliferation of factors interact with one another, possibly leading to a multiplicity of models (or mimes). This is most notable in the global commodity chain literature, discussed in Chapter 5.[7] As Friedland (1997: 231) has put it:[8]

> Thus, there are commodity systems where producing corporations are globalised and others where merchandisers are globalised, although production is local, regional, or national ... What is needed is a typology of globalisation.

As hard evidence was hard to come by at this early stage in the life of GM food, the reaction against mimetics/globalisation was primarily methodological – apart from case studies for or against globalisation/industrialisation hypotheses. Actor–network theory (ANT) has proven most attractive. Originally designed to explore the relationship between science and society, ANT's main concern was critically to break down what was perceived to be an artificial distinction between the natural and the social. The critique goes beyond postmodern recognition that the *understanding* of nature is socially constructed to incorporate the idea that human and non-human agencies are integral and symmetrical (if not necessarily symmetrically placed and capable). Humans act on nature and nature reacts and vice versa, and neither should be analytically privileged.

The appeal of this for the world of food in the context of global warming, mad cow disease and biodiversity is immediate, see Goodman (1999, 2001) and Murdoch (1997, 1998) for more general accounts. The ANT approach also offers the following features. It claims to question all (unacceptable) dualisms. Nature/society evaporates alongside macro/micro, for example. For individual agents are irreducibly situated within their shifting networks of relations (both human and non-human) with others. No agent without network and vice versa. In addition, ANT has been enabled to exercise its own version of what I term '-ismitis'. As it claims to have abolished (all) illegitimate dualisms, so it can read off all other contributions through the prism of having failed to do so. Anyone who explores the distinction between nature and society, even to discover how they are integrated, is liable to be found guilty of dualism. The parallel is with accusations of functionalism, structuralism, instrumentalism, economism, etc., against those who dare to suggest that function, structure, instrument, causation and economic factors prevail in society. It is as if the answer 'none' to the question of how many times do you beat your wife means being guilty of being a wife-beater on zero occasions. Further, as the dualism critique itself depends on recognising duality if only for it to be dismissed, it can be turned back upon itself with accuser turned accused, see Lockie and Kitto (2000) on Goodman (1999) for example.

The intention here is not to offer a thorough critique of ANT in general nor in the context of food.[9] Suffice to observe that, apart from its self-fulfilling critique and misreadings of others, its proposition of symmetry between human and non-human is highly questionable. To lampoon, man eats shark and shark eats man are different order of events. In addition, as is explicitly recognised, the

ANT approach is entirely descriptive and, otherwise, without causal content (Murdoch 1997: 747). In short, in raising and putatively abolishing the dualism between society and nature, ANT offers a salutary reminder of certain factors that might otherwise be overlooked (especially those concerning the social connections between agents and feedback mechanisms between social and material worlds). These are, however, arbitrary in the sense of being subject to analytical choice because they are unguided by socially and historically rooted theory, not least the nature of capital and capitalism for the contemporary world.

This is not to deny that fallacious divisions between nature and society are commonly to be found. The Ricardian theory of rent is an outstanding illustration, with rent derived as a physical property of the land in terms of differential fertility. Marx's theory, however, is entirely different. For him, rent is the economic form assumed by landed property. It is a consequence both of social relations governing access to land, labour and product, and of the material properties of the land itself however these may have been created. Moreover, the rent relation can be displaced from those on or immediately around the land to agents 'networked' to it – from moneylenders funding seeding or subsistence, for example, to multinationals tying in producers by subcontracting. The social and natural are inextricably connected for Marx but he remains open to be interpreted as guilty of dualism.[10]

ANT is liable to prove a passing fad in food studies but it has usefully raised the issue of nature and its relationship to society. Rather than address this directly, consider why food should have been so relevant for, and in the forefront of, the study of consumption more generally. Apart from the reasons already given, the most notable distinguishing feature of food studies is the extent to which they have been organised around the idea of food systems, chains or foodways.[11] Such approaches have survived the vagaries of shifting methods, topics and emphases. In short, it has been readily if not universally accepted that to understand any one aspect of food, it is necessary to follow its provision from land to lip.

Why has this been so? Elsewhere it has been argued that food is uniquely 'organic' (Fine 1994a, b, 1998c, Fine et al. 1996). By this is meant that the material properties of food itself are of considerable importance and concern because food is ingested by the consumer. But other products are also ingested, such as medicines. A further feature of food, though, is that it is grown and thereby dependent upon (non-human) living organisms from the outset of supply. Consequently, the food system necessarily negotiates the organic in the passage to ultimate consumption. Lest this be considered too dualistic or biologically deterministic, such an observation is entirely compatible with the ANT approach, merely emphasising the heavy presence of the natural in, to use the vernacular, actor–network translation of agriculture into food. Despite the critique of the notion of organic from an ANT perspective in Goodman (1999, 2001) and Lockie and Kitto (2000), the food system approach otherwise appears to escape unscathed and is even strengthened. Buttel (1996: 35), for example, albeit in an industry versus agriculture setting, sees emphasis on the organic as[12]

> a useful extension of the 'particularities argument', since it is able not only to incorporate, but also transcend, the biologism of earlier perspectives, by giving ample stress to the cultural and social constructions of foods as representing limits to full-blown industrialization of the food system.

Why the organic nature of food should encourage analysis to follow food systems has in part been revealed by Fischler's (1980, 1988, 1989) idea of the omnivore's paradox. His argument is that, with development and urbanisation, consumers are displaced from contact with, and knowledge of, the sources and hence content of food.[13] The paradox is that because, as omnivores, we can eat anything, we have to be wary of everything. As a result, there is a pervasive, if dulled, incentive to trace back food to its origins. Fischler's paradox, however, needs to be so heavily qualified that it scarcely survives close examination as a hypothesis about food.

First the paradox focuses exclusively on anxiety about food, particularly its organic properties and its corresponding safety for consumption. The idea that we are being poisoned or contaminated by foods of unknown origin and content is a genuine fear but is far removed from our general and daily experiences. Motivations around food have never been confined to physiological survival; we eat and do not feed. Even putting aside stigma and taboos, the tastes and distastes attached to food have long since buried its organic content beyond dominant influence. And just as the physiological has given way to the psychological, so the psychological has conceded to the cultural. Nor is it simply a matter of the intellectual omnivore's capacity for hunting and gathering a few more paradoxes around psychological and cultural factors. For the meaning of food to its consumers is inextricably bound together by its complex of material and cultural properties. These cannot, respectively, be correspondingly reduced to distance and content, and anxiety, even presuming these could be precipitated for scrutiny from one another and other ingredients. As Fitzsimmons and Goodman (1998: 214) put it within an ANT framework, in referring to BSE:

> A food scare of this magnitude opens up the 'black box' of the modern agro-food system to wider scrutiny, revealing the scope of enlistment of human and non-human actants in prosaic decisions of everyday life.

More generally, for Probyn (2000: 14):

> I want to use eating and its associations in order to think about how this most ordinary of activities can be used to help us reflect on how we are connected to others and to large and small social issues.

Indeed, this leads her to question food in terms of 'articulating what we are, what we eat and what eats us' (p. 32). And, as Shaw (1999: para 13.2) concludes:

> It appears that public understanding of issues such as microbiological safety, BSE and GM food may carry with them many wider questions relating to the nature of society, the environment, the food chain, science and technology, industry, politics, and the complex relationships between these.

In this respect, recent consumer activism around food is highly instructive. For it is scarcely confined to concerns and agitation for personal health and safety. Food activism has taken many other issues on board, not least those involving the environment, animal rights, multinational corporations, international organisations, working conditions, and so on. Reaction against the food we eat, and its origins, reflects anxiety for others and other as much as for self. Vegetarianism is a classic illustration, incorporating internal disputes over how far animal products need to be eschewed to claim authenticity. Thus, food activism offers a striking illustration of the arguments of Chapter 9. As soon as consumers address issues, they tend to be transformed into others with content that is both collective and, at least in part, removed from the act of consumption itself. At one level, in ranging critically over all of the issues associated with the fast-food chains, Schlosser (2001: 10) could not have been more wrong:

> Hundreds of millions of people buy fast food every day without giving it much thought, unaware of the subtle and not so subtle ramifications of their purchases. They rarely consider where this food came from, how it was made, what it is doing to the community around them. They just grab their tray off the counter, find a table, take a seat, unwrap the paper, and dig in. The whole experience is transitory and soon forgotten. I've written this book out of a belief that people should know what lies behind the shiny, happy surface of every fast food transaction. They should know what really lurks behind those sesame-seed buns. As the old saying goes: You are what you eat.

His book found itself on the list of US non-fiction best-sellers! More constructively, as Isserman (2001: 1231) observes of Reisner's (2001) study in a special issue of the *American Behavioral Scientist*, devoted to 'Genetically Modified Food: Understanding the Societal Dilemma':

> Genetically modified food by its very nature simultaneously raises concern about human health, the environment, monopoly capital, and the food supply and therefore has led to unprecedented coalitions among social movement organizations.

218

Similar considerations apply where safe consumption is the initiating and remains the main issue. Recent scares around mad cow disease and GM food have challenged the nature of farming methods, the power of entrenched interests and so on (ESRC 1999). In this respect, a number of lessons can be gained from the past. As is evident from Burke's (1998) study of margarine, rumours about the content of food – margarine made out of human baby fat – may be fantastic, in part in order to mount a critique of capitalism. For him, sop and cultural system are intertwined (pp. 263–4):

> Thus, product rumours often lodge claims about precisely those matters which are most concealed from general knowledge under modern capitalism: the pathways by which innovation and newness enter the world of commodities, the origins of goods, the process of their manufacture, the intentions and outlook of their makers, the manner of their distribution. Rumours indirectly ask: where does this thing come from? How is it made? Why do they want me to buy it? What are 'they' anyway?

Thus, consumer activism is not always appropriately informed and focused on the most important matters. This is in part a consequence of how it is formed and informed as well as its mixed motives.[14] Food contamination, for example, receives much attention in the media because of its acute headline-grabbing consequences.[15] The dull and chronic results of poor diet tend to pass unremarked in premature illness and death. Further the food system's response to consumer activism reflects entrenched interests and processes. The history of the adulteration of food reveals a stance towards legislation that reflects those interests – as is evident in the remorseless campaign against margarine throughout the world on the part of dairy industries, thereby denying cheap spread to those on low incomes. Margarine has been legally and practically stigmatised as adulteration, needing to be coloured pink to distinguish it from butter, subject to heavy taxation, and so on, see Dupré (1999) most recently but see Fine and Leopold (1993: Chapter 12). 'Rumours' can be appropriated for commercial advantage as well as for anti-commercialism. Stances begin to change not only in response to consumers but also when new or newly emerging commercial interests prevail over the old. Not surprisingly, as in the political arena, yesterday's food terrorists become tomorrow's establishment.

The preceding discussion reveals a second deficiency in the omnivore's paradox. It inspires a particularly limited, and false, approach to the nature of food knowledge. At one level, it appears to suggest that the producer knows and the consumer does not, the more so the greater the distance between the two. This is simply false, certainly in some absolute sense, since the twentieth-century school child, who has never seen field or cow, knows more about nutrients and bacterial food poisoning than a subsistence farmer of bygone years. Nor, once again, is this a matter of adding in other sources of knowledge but in holding to a different understanding of knowledge itself. As argued in Chapter 6, it is subject to the five Cs (taken up below) and, in the context of consumption, is attached to a cultural system corresponding to an sop. In a sense, the omnivore's paradox is a highly simplified, unidimensional and unidirectional version of the circuit of culture which was rejected for its neglect of the systemic and for exaggeration of motion between more or less arbitrary nodal sources of cultural input.

Nonetheless, the power and the fallacy of the approach based, implicitly, on the omnivore's paradox are demonstrated by current campaigns around healthier eating. The diseases of affluence – most notably, excessive consumption of fat, sugar and salt – have led to a flood of informational campaigns designed to reduce their intake. They are motivated by what might be interpreted as an application of the omnivore's paradox. Consumers are perceived to be removed from appropriate knowledge of what they eat. They need to be properly informed and persuaded to respond accordingly. The result is a strategy of trickling-down knowledge from the experts, so-called current human nutritional thinking (CHNT), and regulation of other sources of (false) knowledge in labelling and other advertising of health claims.[16]

Set this model against the alternative based on the five Cs that is briefly and partially illustrated in what follows. First, food knowledge is contested at every stage, including the higher levels of science – as is evidenced by changing content of CHNT (ESRC 1999, Shaw 1999). At a mundane level, for example, eggs and dairy products are no longer perceived to be as healthy as previously, given preoccupation with excess cholesterol in the blood. Further, nutritional science is heavily embroiled in the commerce of food itself, with economic and political interests being served directly or indirectly by commercially funded research.

Second, food knowledge is constructed through the way it is represented. A product that is labelled as only containing 'natural' ingredients is liable both to carry the intended connotation of being healthy and to be packed with sugar. Similarly, advertising slogans along the lines '95 per cent fat free', 'only 5 per cent fat' or 'virtually fat free' do and do not mean the same as alternatives along the lines of 'at least 5 per cent fat'. This form will be used for what are perceived to be desirable ingredients of properties: '20 per cent pure fruit juice' for a product that is 80 per cent artificially flavoured and coloured sugar water. 'Made with 90 per cent meat' reveals nothing about permitted levels of water and gristle – quite apart from MRM (mechanically recovered meat).

Third, as is already apparent, food knowledge is construed and cannot simply be taken at face value by the consumer. For how we understand food is intimately bound up with how we understand 'healthy', 'natural' and, increasingly, 'organic', quite apart from beliefs about what is good or bad for you. Food beliefs are extraordinarily diverse and complex given the cultural content of food and, especially, how food is experienced. It is not simply a matter of taste and reflection but how we buy, prepare, eat, dispose of and socialise around food.

Fourth, food knowledge is thereby rendered chaotic. Its sources, offered meanings and received and reworked interpretations are rarely able to be ordered coherently and consistently since our experiences of food cut across one another and are attached to a wide variety of practices other than eating – not least dating, tourism, observance of family values or not, and the list could run on endlessly.

Finally, food knowledge is contradictory not only in the sense of inconsistency at the level of individual beliefs and actions but also systemically. Consider, for example, the failure of healthy eating campaigns. Like the ill-effects of smoking, none can surely now be unaware of the message. Yet it is not heeded and unhealthy levels of consumption of fat, sugar and salt persist.[17] Sufficient explanation might be thought to reside in the four previously elaborated features of food knowledge. But these need to be more fully rooted in the material realities of food systems. Consider, for example, the sugar system. This has been heavily organised around guaranteeing supply to serve commercial interests, both growers and refiners. The details need not detain us here, and they do differ over time and place (Fine *et al.* 1996: Chapters 5 and 6) . For the sake of argument, assume that sugar supply is predetermined. Then, waste aside, it must find its way into consumption (or exports). The net effect of healthy eating campaigns can only be to redistribute consumption across the population. What are the effects? First, consumption of sugar is liable to be disguised by its use as an ingredient in the manufacturing of food. All believe they are using less sugar, as they are in direct consumption in hot drinks, home-baking or the like. But more is being consumed indirectly in sweet goods as well as those that are not for which presence of sugar often passes unnoticed to the sweet and sweetened tooth.

Second, whilst not as cheap as air and water as the stuff of today's bread (in place of yesterday's chalk), sugar is a flexible ingredient in terms of its physical properties and palatability. Consequently, it is particularly attractive for the manufacture and sale of mass-produced, low-quality foods for mass and frequent consumption. Third, healthy eating advice is more open to be received, and acted upon, by those least in need of it, the more affluent by virtue of their higher incomes, education and readier access to sources of gratification other than cheap food. Fourth, then, the overall impact of healthy eating campaigns around sugar is liable to be to consolidate unhealthy eating patterns that are already heavily skewed against the poor. More generally, the point is to observe a close connection between the sugar system and the nature and distribution of food knowledge. With food, as with all, knowledge, there is a heavy bias towards conformity in belief to practice. If the latter is attached to sustained sugar supply, so will be consumption and the culture of sweetness, in part disguised in processed products.

Slightly different considerations apply in case of the dairy system and the unhealthy consumption of excessive quantities of cream (Fine *et al.* 1996: Chapter 12). In this case, British supermarkets have been praised for having made available a variety of healthy, more or less fat-free, milks and other products (as opposed to door-to-door milk delivery). Their capacity for doing so has been based upon the huge variety of products that can be stocked in support of one-stop weekly shopping. But something must happen to the cream that is skimmed. It finds its way into the equally large, if not larger, variety of fancy cheeses and desserts on display in the same supermarkets. Previous research on the UK Nation's Diet has shown that those in the forefront of purchasing healthy milks have been equally adept at placing high-cream products in their shopping trolleys. This might in part reflect a lite–heavy syndrome – the idea that a healthy warrants an unhealthy food as reward, with overall diet worsened.

These examples demonstrate that food supply and food (health) information policies need to be coordinated and consistent. This has rarely been the case in practice with the two ploughing separate furrows, with supply winning out. The classic exception of coordination and consistency, proving the rule, has been in Norway but only when dairy interests coincided with CHNT. When the latter changed away from dairy products, it was quickly subordinated. The deeper methodological point, though, is to relate food knowledge both through the five Cs and to corresponding food systems.

As a result, I have argued that the omnivore's paradox needs to be replaced by what I have termed the diet paradox, Fine (1993b, 1998c: Chapter 3). Somewhat misleadingly, the earlier discussion has made reference to healthy and unhealthy foods. With the exception of the unhealthy in the form of the poisonous or the contaminated, as the metaphorical school child knows, a healthy is a balanced diet in composition and amount to meet minimum daily nutritional requirements. No single food is healthy or unhealthy as such. As a result, in scholarly, professional and popular discourse, the idea prevails of a healthy diet as an organising principle. Who does or does not meet it, why, how and when? And, after the event, diets can be measured in principle in terms of intake and their deviation from the norm. So we all have a diet – good, bad or indifferent.

But do we? There is a parallel here with the idealised notion of the market – this is how it works perfectly but imperfections explain deviations from it. This cannot explain anything and borders on the tautological. Similarly, although we all have a diet, this in no way explains or helps to explain what we eat and drink. The consumption of food is rarely organised in practice around attaining a balanced, healthy diet, although it is one element in food knowledge and behaviour. Rather diet is fractured by a multiplicity of foods and their diverse practices and cultures so that the only thing they have in common is that they are filtered through the stomach. Thus, the diet paradox reveals that the closer we examine our 'diet', the more we find it does not exist.

This is to exaggerate lack of connectedness once the subject matter is socially and historically delimited. For diet has been increasingly tied to commodification, transforming not just the level and composition of what is eaten but the meaning of diet itself! It has taken on the guise of the opposite of itself, diet as not eating. The result over the course of the twentieth century has been the emergence of an epidemic of stunning proportions – at least amongst the affluent and within affluent countries. Eating disorders range from anorexia to obesity, affecting percentages of the population well into double figures. Those seeking medical advice or treatment are only the tip of the iceberg for the majority of the population relate to weight watching. Both cookery and diet books, videos and TV programmes, vie with one another to occupy top position for non-fiction.

Psychological studies reveal that eating disorders arise out of the twin compulsions to eat and to diet. Counihan (1999: 87) rightly observes: 'the economy depends on manipulating consumers to buy as much as possible, and one way is to project simultaneously the urge to eat and the need to diet'. We all have to resolve the associated tensions not because they are innate but because they are imposed. Anorexics, for example, do not lose appetite. On the contrary, they display the most extraordinary capacity to deny the most basic of natural urges, to the point of self-destruction. At the other extreme, the stigma and guilt associated with obesity arise out of the perceived failure to be able to exercise self-control and, hence, command over one's own appearance, with responses in the form of obsessive exercise and, ultimately, surgery.

In broad sweep, the literature on eating disorders exhibits the following characteristics. First, it is concerned with individual dysfunction and its incidence, whether for physiological or psychological reasons. Second, psychological approaches seek out neuroses that have been displaced onto food. Third, where social factors have been introduced, they have understandably focused on the shifting position of women, from generation to generation, as well as over the life-cycle. Emphasis has been placed upon multiple demands made upon women, especially those concerning body image, educational and other success, and familial obligations, to which eating disorders are perceived as a form of coping, distress or resistance. But, as the literature has increasingly and, hardly surprisingly, revealed, eating disorders are highly flexible in terms of who and what is involved. Food, after all, is closely bound to identity, anybody's.

What the literature tends to neglect, an essential element in explaining the historical nature and incidence of eating disorders, is the dull compulsion of economic factors. For the imposed compulsions to eat and to diet are heavily created and conditioned by the economics of food. Both eating and dieting are fed by huge industries, seeking to expand in whatever way possible. The truly remarkable if unfortunate achievement of the twentieth century is to have rendered these industries compatible with one another, the opposite sides of the same coin. Each feeds on, rather than negating, the other. This is sharply revealed by dieting foods, eating in order not to eat. Or, to subvert Brillat-Savarin, 'Tell me what you are and I will tell you what to eat'. The problem is that we have multiple food personalities created for us. In short, eating disorders are part and parcel of the food system and its cultural complements.

The commercial imperatives to force-feed and to force-diet are matched, at least potentially, by how we obtain our food. Families that eat together and, thereby, stay together may be looking a bit thin on the ground but, either way, they are liable to shop together in the same place. British supermarkets are the most concentrated in ownership and dominated by hyperstores. As a result, apart from holding tens of thousands of items, they compete with one another to win loyalty for the weekly shop that they make possible. One way of doing so is to offer cheaper, own-label, often identically manufactured, items. This cannot go too far in displacing branded goods, otherwise shoppers may be deterred by lack of availability of favoured brands. By the same token, for commercial viability, it is vital to brand manufacturers that they be stocked by supermarket chains. This gives rise to the paradox of own-label products competing in-store with branded rivals.

Two immediate results are striking for the functioning of the food system more generally. Not surprisingly, branded goods have sought to make themselves attractive to supermarkets/customers by highly fanciful advertising campaigns that have stretched the imaginations of both ad agencies and semiotic interpretation. Yet, at times, the fastest growing sector in advertising has been by the supermarket chains themselves, peddling the simple message along the lines 'come to us because we are cheapest'. In short, the cultural analysis of food advertising is liable to be seriously misinterpreted, selective and self-serving of postmodern themes unless grounded in the material practices of the advertisers themselves.

In this vein, second, in the 1990s, so-called store-wars were intensified in the UK and took the form of competition over purchases of land for out-of-town hypermarket development.[18] Temporarily collapsing property values threatened to bankrupt the supermarket chains, intensifying the competition for the weekly shop. Traditionally, Tesco has been the more down-market of the two leading companies, and Sainsbury's has been more up-market. Each sought the other's customers, broadening their appeal with advertising targeting the other's appeal – life-style and quality as opposed to cost, respectively.

These developments indicate how advertising and retailing (around food) can exhibit general trends, although why and how require investigation beyond the practices of the stores themselves. Over-generalisation is an ever-present danger, especially with self-selection of evidence. This is apparent from the use of fantasy, rather than mundane, ads in the interpretation of food and identity, in the exaggeration of the power of retailers over producers, and over the regulation of food itself (Marsden *et al.* 2000). Even though varieties of food may be gathered in one place for the purpose of retailing, their material and cultural lives, both before and afterwards, are liable to be distinctive, necessitating a finer grain in examining the food system or, more exactly, food systems.

The illusions shattered by the collapse of the simple globalisation of agriculture model have questioned the idea of deploying a food system approach more generally. Diversity, flexibility and perpetual change are perceived to rule in place of secure sops. Global, Fordist or nothing seem to be the alternatives on offer with the first two rejected. Such nihilism has been reinforced by the emphasis placed at the two extremes of the food chain. Consumer demand for organic produce and GM influence over agriculture are taken to be horizontal factors that increasingly cut across and undermine the presence of vertical food systems. But matters are not so simple, and there is nothing as such in these recent developments to justify rejection of the food system approach.

In the case of the demand for organic food, like the demand for quality, health and safety more generally, what it is is open to social reconstruction. Is it the content of the food or how it is produced and by whom? Or is it the wider anxieties that prevail over the emergence of 'Franken(stein)food' (Nerlich *et al.* 1999), although these are lesser and different than 'Frankenmedicine' (Gofton and Haimes 1999). Clearly, 'organic' food is subject to the five Cs. As such it is dependent upon how it is provided. As Buck *et al.* (1997) have argued in the context of north Californian vegetables, the sustainability of organic production depends upon limited economies of scale in mixed cropping and handling methods, and the vitality of social movements and niche demand for such products. On the other hand, organics are characterised by the entry of big business or commercial imperatives more generally (pp. 3–4):

> Explosive growth since the 1980s is both cause and effect of a prolifera-
> tion of new entrants who are attempting to capture the lucrative niche
> markets lurking behind organic products and the organic label.
> Consequently the field is experiencing rapid changes in production and
> marketing strategies, and a restructuring of economic imperatives. And
> while a plurality of economic and ideological actors continue to thrive
> within the organic sector, large business firms – or successful start-up
> firms which increasingly mirror agribusiness practices – are penetrating
> the most dynamic and profitable segments.

In particular, Buck *et al.* invoke the ideas of appropriationism and substitutionism to characterise recent developments in organic agriculture as well as pointing to the increasing role of large-scale capital in distribution and marketing (p. 16):[19]

> ... where the organic sector is beginning to look most like the conven-
> tional one. Although organic food provision is often represented as
> 'local production for local markets', the geographic reach of this sector
> is quite extensive, and follows cropping and distribution patterns similar
> to those of conventional. Peripatetic production and regional specializa-
> tion are becoming commonplace and the distribution of California
> organic produce is considerably far flung.

Further, imports are also serving Californian markets, with large-scale distribution and marketing squeezing smaller scale local producers.

In short, it is necessary to examine how organics are differentially sourced and how they articulate with the meaning of organic. Similarly, for GM crops, there are some common features. As King and Stabinsky (1998/9) reveal,[20] GM products are based on patenting for profit, thereby raising a host of issues and practices. Chemical companies have needed to acquire seed companies for developmental purposes. Their prices have been inflated, thereby constituting a form of displaced rent. Patenting needs to be protected against resowing, with outlawing of seed saving or research resources dedicated to 'terminator' projects that prevent seeds being propagated. Some research is public funded and open, other is private and closed. GM technology is distinguished according to whether it seeks to modify inputs (allowing for use of pesticides and weedkillers or obviating the need for them) or to improve quality of output (size, ripening, colour, flavour, etc.).

As Buttel (1999) observes, although GM crop areas are increasing rapidly, they remain limited and specialised in scope. Three-quarters of cropland is in the United States, with soybeans taking up over half of world GM production, corn a further 30 per cent, and most of the rest by cotton and canola (with practically none for wheat or rice). Why is this and what is distinctive about these crops as opposed to others? Murcott (1999) argues for a sociology of GM crops, of wider applicability across the social sciences, in which we follow the chain from eating through to the laboratory. Similarly, in seeking GM tomatoes, Harvey (1999) suggests that outcomes are liable to be different in the United States and the UK owing to the different organisation of retailing across the two countries. More generally, food systems are being constituted and reconstituted by the impact of GM foods. There is little or no evidence of their dissolution. Significantly, Grey (2000), in editing a special issue of *Human Organization* on 'Food and Power: Case Studies in Industrial Agriculture and Its Alternatives in the United States', begins by drawing a contrast between two food systems – the global vertically integrated and concentrated agribusinesses and direct marketing and natural foods. However, in concluding on the basis of the case studies in the collection, he is drawn to the conclusion that it is necessary to step back from such polarised perspectives and to recognise differentiation by setting and by product.

Gaze on the cluttered landscape of consumption

In his review of history and consumption studies, Glennie (1995) acknowledges that they can become or be interpreted as examples of their own object of study. For history is consumed as well as being produced and in ways and for reasons that potentially reflect the whole gamut of factors that have informed both academic and popular discourses. Having opened reflexive potential in the study of consumption, it is difficult to know where to stop, whether in a spirit of pastiche or a dose of heavy-handed humour. The title of this section is itself a hybrid, purloined from Goldman and Papson (1996) and Urry (1990) with tongue firmly positioned in cheek. Further exercise in turning the study of consumption back in upon itself is left to the reader as consumer at play.

But, as indicated in the introduction, the study of consumption is both chaotic and ordered, just as sport and leisure for pleasure are serious business. As a result, we are collectively caught in a good news/ bad news syndrome, of achievements matched by challenges. It is an achievement, not least through the circuits of culture, to have established a commitment to bring culture and the economy together, for everyday as for elite articles of consumption, to have avoided the colonial designs of mainstream economics, and to recognise that the economy is more than production as opposed to consumption. But the challenge is to go beyond such circuits of culture and to develop and employ a deeper political economy of capitalism.[21] The notion of consumer revolution has been discredited, the more so the more it is deployed. Yet, periodisation within the study of consumption remains extremely weak even, possibly especially, where it is not based on consumerism. Trickle theories and the like have been surpassed by a recognition of consumption as expressing relations, structures, tendencies and practices. But, not surprisingly, these have not been sufficiently well tied to understandings of capitalism and its periodisation.

I have outlined my own approach to these conundrums in terms of commitment to sops complemented by corresponding cultural systems. As is evident from the examples given, there is reason to be optimistic that this represents a feasible and attractive framework. In addition, the impact of a colonising mainstream economics may be counterproductive from its own perspective, inducing those with a genuine commitment to understand the social construction of (the meaning of) consumption to seek a more appropriate economic analysis. Yet, there are also reasons for pessimism. Social theory tends to dub mainstream economics and political economy with the same dismissive brush as sharing more in common in reductionism than they differ in shedding light on the creation of material culture. There is a danger, in the wake of postmodernism, of retreat into the interpretative side in the study of consumption at the expense of the material side. Not only will this impoverish the study of consumption, it will concede the economic territory to those who are most ill-suited to occupy it, namely mainstream economists. Further, whilst there is almost universal enthusiasm for interdisciplinary approaches to consumption, such enthusiasm is rarely matched by practice. To some extent, this is a consequence of interdisciplinary boundaries which are difficult to cross. As Nell (1996: 15) observes, 'there's no getting around the fact that economics is tough'. It might be added both that it is getting tougher and semiotics is hardly a piece of cake![22] Is it possible that any scholar can be sufficiently grounded in the combination of necessary disciplines, especially given their diversity of methods, techniques and traditions? Disciplinary and/or topic-based specialisations are inevitable, not least depending upon the issue at hand. But they need not exercise a stranglehold, a necessity made out of vice.

There is, however, a more serious aspect to this problem that I will illustrate from my own experience. For, the study of consumption depends less upon being interdisciplinary in the sense of occupying a command of more than one discipline.

Rather, it requires an abandonment of disciplinary loyalties, and a straddling of disciplines in place of multiple occupancy. Whilst recognisably grounded in political economy, my work on consumption has consistently attempted to incorporate the insights of other disciplines and pose questions about consumption as such, not simply apply a more rounded economics to consumption. Thus, in first proposing the sop approach in Fine and Leopold (1993), careful consideration was given to its relationship to other disciplines, approaches and issues including, for example, the study of adverts and the excesses of Baudrillard in his understanding of use value and its relation to the commodity. Significantly, references to my work tend to point to its particular approach as based on sops, but not to its implications for the culture of consumption. I am also often earmarked as an economist although, to the best of my knowledge, only social scientists who reject the hegemonic mainstream economics, and few heterodox economists, have ever shown any interest in my work.[23] This self-reference is not intended as an indulgent rebuff to the students of consumption but serves to illustrate what I take to be a continuing failure to confront economics with culture and vice versa. More generally, studies of consumption continue to be identified with the disciplines from which they or their authors hail. If the landscape of consumption studies is to exhibit order over chaos, we all need to play the game by taking one another a bit more seriously, rather than cluttering the terrain with marginal additions, vertical or horizontal, to our own established constructs.

NOTES

1 Introduction and overview

1 The selective bibliography of Furlough in de Grazia and Furlough (1996) runs to twenty pages, including sections on conceptualisations; historical perspectives; distribution, retailing and shopping as sites of consumption; marketing and design; spectatorship and reception; production of representations; domesticity, household and the family; sexuality; bodies, clothing and beauty as appearance; and politics and ideologies of consumption. On shopping alone, the brief history and selected literature of Hewer and Campbell in Falk and Campbell (1997), also of twenty pages, addresses typologising, instrumental and recreational, gendering, economics, geography, history, literature, marketing, psychology, and sociology. The unlimited scope for the study of consumption, however, arises out of its being attached to the formation of identity – for which anything goes.

2 Some do straddle consumer studies and the more scholarly study of consumption, notably Holbrook (1995), Belk (1995) and Firat and Dholakia (1998), for example.

3 That consumer studies remains in disarray, along the lines of throw in everything and select something, is evidenced for example by contributions to Ratneshwar *et al.* (2000).

4 Strangely, the boom in the study of consumption is seen as coinciding with the boom in consumption. But surely there is something of a lag between the two?

5 Ritzer also locates consumption in the conceptual space created between cathedrals of consumption, on the one hand, and Marx's Department II, on the other. See also Ritzer (1999b) for response to constructive criticism by incorporation of an ever-widening array of analytical elements.

6 See also Chaney (1998: 543) for whom, 'I hope to have established the substantial challenge of consumption for the practice of sociology'.

2 From economics imperialism to globalisation?

1 See Fine (1997a, 1998a, b, 1999a, 2000a, d–f, 2001a–f) and Fine and Milonakis (2001) and Milonakis and Fine (2001) – and Fine (1999b) in debate with Bowden and Offer (1994, 1996, 1999), and Fine (1999c) with Thompson (1997, 1999), and Fine and Lapavitsas (2000) with Zelizer (2000) – for the general argument as well as for specific case studies. See also Fine *et al.* (2001). For evidence from the mainstream itself, see Becker (1990) and Lazear (2000), both of whom refer to economic imperialism and Olson and Kähkönen (2000) who prefer the telling metaphor of economics as metropolis and other social science as the suburbs. See also Frey (1999) who attracts praise from Nobel Laureates Becker, Stigler and Buchanan.

2 What follows draws on Fine (2000f). This piece was returned by the editor of the *Quarterly Journal of Economics*, without being sent to referees, on the grounds that he did not wish to engage debate on the issue in the journal.

3 As Amariglio and Ruccio (1999: 23) put it:

> Academic economists tend to privilege the form of reasoning associated with economic science – the 'economic way of thinking' … the formal methods that serve to guarantee scientific rigor.

4 For a critique, to some extent within the context of economics imperialism, see Fine (1998a: Chapter 3) and Fine and Rose (2001).

5 Note that, over the past five years, the *Journal of Economic Literature* has published articles on economics and the arts, emotions, psychology (twice), religion, preference formation, political science, corruption, sociology (twice), the family and altruism.

6 This section was originally drafted in August 1998 following a selective but wide-ranging consultation of the literature on globalisation. As may be apparent, no attempt has been made to take account of the impossibly voluminous subsequent literature except in a casual way. But I suspect the conclusions drawn would only be strengthened.

7 As Therborn (2000a: 149) recognises:

> Basically it is a concern of the second half of the 1990s. … In the major dictionaries of English, French, Spanish and German of the 1980s or the first half of the 1990s the word is not listed. … The *Social Science Citation Index* records only a few occurrences of 'globalization' in the 1980s but shows its soaring popularity from 1992 onwards, which accelerated in the last years of the past century.

8 Social capital has also swept across the social sciences, with some contribution from economics, only lagging globalisation marginally in timing and weight. See Fine (2001a) for a comprehensive critical survey.

9 See also Bairoch (2000) and Khondker (1994). Wallerstein (2000: 249) is the most extreme in the nothing-new stance:

> Globalization is a misleading concept, since what is described as globalization has been happening for 500 years.

10 See Lee (1997) for insistence on the continuing importance of the developmental state for South Korea despite the impact of globalisation and liberalisation, and Hamilton *et al.* (2000) for the importance of nationally organised private capital in a comparative study of South Korea and Taiwan.

11 Note that the state versus globalisation revisits a debate begun, or highlighted, by Murray (1971) over the significance of multinational corporations in this respect. See Fine and Harris (1979) for a critique along the lines that such is a false opposition, not least because the state tends to promote internationalisation of capital.

12 See MacLean (2000) who raises the issue of doxa (taken for granted or unexamined) across positions in debate around globalisation as opposed to doxy (differences between orthodoxy and heterodoxy). He stresses the doxa of international relations and empiricist methodology.

13 See also the collection in *Review of International Political Economy* on globalisation and food edited by Ward and Almas (1997) (and also vol. 4, no 3, Autumn, 1997, for relevant discussion of many of the issues presented here), but especially Held and McGrew (2000a) for overview of debate between globalisation sceptics and enthusiasts.

14 See also Beck (2000) for a few more factors in the style of Appadurai. For Amin and Thrift (1994a) the dialectic between global and local needs to be unpacked through

seven aspects of globalisation – finance, knowledge, technology, oligopolies, diplomacy and loss of state power, communications, and culture and migration. See also Robinson (1996).

15 See also Dunning and Hamdani (1997) and Dunning (2000).

16 See Therborn (2000b) and, for example, in the context of global cultural political economy, Stevenson (2000) who examines five themes: McDonaldisation, cultural imperialism, postmodernisation, democratisation and nationalism.

17 See Griffin and Khan (1992), Thomas and Wilkin (1997), Vandenbroucke (1998), Wilding (1997) and Rhodes (1996, 1997). The issue of the necessity for class compromise (or some form of Third Way) in light of globalisation has been heavily debated. See Webster and Adler (1999), Lambert (2000) and Fine (2000c), for example. Discussion of the relationship between globalisation and class has been more muted than mooted, but see Sklair (2000) and Robinson and Harris (2000), for example.

18 See also Albrow et al. (1997) who make a similar point, adding how the globalisation literature seeks to free traditional concepts from territorial reference.

19 See Berger (1996) and Boyer (1996) for discussion of recent developments within mainstream economics in the context of globalisation.

20 See Stiglitz (1998) and Fine et al. (2001) for critical assessments.

21 As in Amin and Thrift (1994a), Berger and Dore (1996), Boyer (1996) and Archibugi and Michie (1997).

22 See Evans (1997), for example.

23 See Lewis et al. (1996).

24 See Weiss (1998).

25 The metaphor can also prevail in the absence of reference to the economic or finance, as for Meyer (2000: 246):

> Globalization of instrumental culture is a product of a stateless world that is filled out with 'social actors' who are legitimated in rationalistic and universalistic terms.

26 See Fine (1997b) and Aybar and Lapavitsas (2001).

27 For a critical exposition in the context of a case study, South Africa, see Fine (1997b).

28 If, as in game-theoretic strategies, agents choose to behave probabilistically, then imperfect information is endogenous as in the definition of equilibrium as a probability distribution of the behaviour of otherwise identical firms. For a critique of the treatment of information in this way, and uncertainty as risk, see Dixon (1986) and Slater and Spencer (2000).

29 In a limited way, this is recognised by Douglass North in rejecting the new economic history based on neo-classical economics, for its failure to deal properly with formal and informal 'institutions'. For a critique, see Fine and Milonakis (2001) and Milonakis and Fine (2001).

30 Thus, for example, long-term finance by Japanese banks has been provided through guaranteed rollover of short-term credits so that differences in the time structure of loans can be a poor index of commitment between finance and industry.

31 For a fuller exposition of what follows, see Fine (1989) and, for the distinctiveness of Marx's theory of capital in exchange, the debate between Panico (1988) and Fine (1985/6, 1988). For discussion of the relevance of Marx's theory of capital for globalisation, see articles for example collected in *Environment and Planning D – Society and Space*, vol. 18, no. 1, 2000.

32 It is estimated, for example, that at least 20 per cent of employment in both New York and London is devoted to financial services, 443,000 and 617,000 workers, respectively. For the UK, the contribution of financial services to GDP has risen from 13 to 25 per cent between 1970 and 1999. For overview of globalisation of finance, see Singh (1999).

33 Corresponding to models of imperfect competition with excessive product innovation and differentiation. Note also that models of exhaustible resources conclude that monopolies overproduce in the short run relative to competitive outcomes (in order to earn more at earlier and higher levels of present value).

34 For Marxist political economy, one implication is that finance and industry are not subject to the same process of equalisation of rate of return. Rather, surplus value is divided between the rate of interest and profit of enterprise, with the former not governed by underlying 'fundamentals'.

35 For an excellent taste of the flavour of current mainstream understandings and proposals around international finance, see special section in *Journal of Economic Perspectives*, vol. 13, no. 4, 1999.

36 For dated views of economists and economics as wedded to *laissez-faire*, see discussion of Bourdieu in Fine (2001a: Chapter 4). See also Esping-Andersen (2000d) discussed in Chapter 10.

3 The world of commodities

1 At the time of writing, an email has been winging around the world recounting the tale of the unsuccessful attempt to obtain personal trainers from Nike with the words 'sweated labour' embossed upon them.

2 See Lippincott (1995) for discussion of the common confusion between commodity and commodity form, in the context of eighteenth-century portraiture and the different markets served.

3 It has become a cliché of embedded markets to refer to the diamond traders of New York or elsewhere, for whom a community of trust is essential for the way that they go about their business (Slater and Tonkiss 2001: 101, most recently). What is always overlooked is the wider context of the international diamond cartel that makes this both possible and necessary.

4 This is not quite correct but close enough for the purposes here. Commodity exchange can become so regularised that money falls away from transactions (other than in ultimately settling accounts). Also the emergence of money should not be seen as the cause of the emergence of commodities. Rather, it is the other way about. What is important for commodities is that the social relations of production lead to production for the market.

5 Note, however, as an early example of economics imperialism, that Akerlof (1982) interprets labour contracts in terms of the gift, where loyal and dedicated workers are rewarded with higher pay and more secure employment, in one enterprise compared with another where individualism prevails.

6 See Caplow (1982, 1984) for the gift, cited in Lapavitsas (2000). More generally, see Eco (1976), for example, for the notion of exchange as a system of signs and communication.

7 See also the comment on Mauss by Godelier (1999: 15), 'he thought he had found this condition in the belief that *things given have a soul that compels them to return to their original owner who gave them away*'. Lapavitsas (2000) provides further discussion and references.

8 See also Clammer (1997: 19):

> Gift-giving then appears as a commercialized form of modern intimacy, or rather as the form of intimacy without its substance, of creating bonds without a moral substance.

9 See Fine (1982).

10 See Carrier (1995a) for an excellent discussion of gifts under capitalism in the tradition of Mauss.

11 The opposite practice is to be found to some extent in the principle of pricing at marginally just below a round figure.

12 Thus, Gregory (1997: 42–6) heavily criticises Appadurai (1986a) for elevating commodity fetishism to a methodological principle, for failing to recognise that gifts prosper through contact with the world of commodities, and for universalising the commodity form.

13 See also p.155:

> The case of self-provisioning, of DIY furniture, has been mentioned previously and is an excellent example of how furniture firms transfer 'productive' labour to the 'consumer' and extract something similar to surplus value from him/her without even entering into a labour/capital relationship.

14 At a deeper theoretical level, this is argued in Fine (1979, 1980) in debate with Catephores (1980). It concerns the so-called historical transformation problem for which the traditional interpretation, adopted by the latter, is that commodities exchange at their value for pre-capitalist simple commodity production before exchanging at prices that diverge from values under capitalism. The alternative interpretation is that the nature of value itself is transformed, as opposed to whether it does or does not equal price. See also Milonakis (1995).

15 In later work, Gregory (1997) rejects the simple dichotomy between gift and commodity by adding a third category, 'good', something that is not exchanged by any mechanism. Possibly this reflects the influence of the arguments of Weiner (1992) and Godelier (1999) that it is unexchangeable 'sacred' objects that distinguish societies from one another. Gregory also denies the continuum between gift and commodity but only in favour of multidimensional outcomes as gifts, commodities and goods are deployed as universal ingredients in constructing societies and their values. Note that, of his ingredients, only the commodity is socially and historically specific. Gregory also fails to distinguish between commodity production and capitalist commodity production (the only capital he really considers is merchant capital which he incorrectly depicts, for Marx, as buying cheap and selling dear). For Marx, merchant capital buys below and sells at value. Further, his understanding of power is primarily as an ahistorical distributional category, paradoxically reflecting the influence of Sraffa for whom the distinction between commodities, goods and gifts is notable for its absence. And, in addressing monetary exchange, he displays a limited understanding of money within capitalism (primarily addressed only as means of payment and store of value) and as capital itself. These heavy criticisms are, however, only possible because Gregory does seek to address the issues that others avoid.

16 See also Gregory (1997: 6):

> The university educated Trobriander of today has not given up the values of *kula* exchange but has acquired those of the international businessman. *Kula* is now done at the weekends in Port Moresby with the aid of a Mercedes.

17 See essays collected in Lunt and Furnham (1996), for example.

18 See also Stone *et al.* (2000: 8–9) who adopted a 'more expansive definition of commodities' for which 'the presence of money is not necessarily an indication that commodified relationships exist'. Indeed:

> A commodity is any good that can be exchanged for other goods. Commodities existed in precapitalist economies, are culturally defined and molded, and are embedded in political and social systems which they both reflect and help to shape.

4 Use value and consumption

1 See also Williamson (1986: 229), who points to the neglect in forging an analytical unity between production and circulation. This coincides with the priority of production. For Preteceille and Terrail:

> A proper insistence on the determining character of the social relations of production has overshadowed not only the necessary analysis of the specific modes of consumption, but also an analysis of the relation between the two spheres, which has been reduced to a single, mechanistic determination.

> (Preteceille and Terrail 1985: 4)

2 Thus Duesenberry's (1967) relative income hypothesis found only a temporary and uneasy home within the theory of the consumption function, presumably because of its use of interdependent and path-dependent preferences. Its attraction was its ability to explain empirically the divergence between short-run and long-run saving propensities.

3 Sahlins (1976), erroneously, suggests that there is an affinity between neo-classical and Marxist economics in their mutual neglect of the social meaning of objects as opposed to their physical properties. In the context of a cultural account of production, this has immediate application to the sphere of consumption.

4 It may be slightly inappropriate to include post-Fordism within an approach that autonomises consumption in that it is heavily technologically determinist, with the availability of production through flexible specialisation proving decisive in economic and social organisation. However, it does tend to take as axiomatic, and unexplored historically and analytically, the simplistic proposition that there has been satiation in the consumption of mass-produced commodities.

5 See also Galbraith (1969: 46, 1973: 134–8), Packard (1960) and Marris (1968: Chapter 4). These ideas have their intellectual origins in Veblen's *The Theory of the Leisure Class* (Veblen 1924), although there the forces at work are confined to a specific 'class' rather than generalised to the population as a whole.

6 *La Physiologie du gout*, Paris, 1825, as quoted in Burnett (1968: 98).

7 See also Johnston (1977: 19), Burgoyne and Clarke (1983) and Goody (1982: 115) quoting Prakash (1961). The expression is particularly compelling in German: '*man ist was er isst*'. Of course, the dictum is intended metaphorically. Yet, in Mintz's outstanding study of the relationship between sugar and power, the phrase is modified into: 'We are *made* more and more into what we eat' (Mintz 1985: 211). And for Barthel (1989: 431), noting the ideological association between sweetness and women: 'Self-identified "chocoholics" are overwhelmingly female. For them chocolate provides the primary identity: *quite literally*, they are what they eat; they have a relationship with food.'

8 For a full treatment of these issues, see also Keen (1991).

9 See Fine (1985/6) for a discussion of Marx's theory of money and interest-bearing capital, and Itoh and Lapavitsas (1998) for a fuller treatment.

10 For an elementary elaboration of these ideas, see Fine (1989).

11 For a discussion of fixed capital in Marx, see Weeks (1981).

12 See Soper (1981) for further discussion.

13 See Preteceille and Terrail (1985: 6), for whom the representation of consumption as a specific autonomous practice gained precision with the historical development of capitalism.

14 As Marx (1969a: 298) observes by way of a different sort of production, drinking champagne is not productive consumption even if it produces a hangover.

15 A similar point can be made by referring to the distinction between wholesale and retail trade. Each is concerned with the buying and selling of use values but they are surrounded by different cultures due, in part, to their different economic locations.

16 See Tomlinson and Warde (1993) and Fine *et al.* (1996: Chapter 11) for the relationship between food and class.

17 See Baudrillard (1981: 89). Reference to Baudrillard is generally to early if not earliest work where the connection of his analysis both with Marx and with the economy is at its strongest. Consequently, the points made here are even more pertinent to his later contributions.

18 See also Carrier and Heyman (1997) and Corrigan (1997: 32).

19 D. Clarke (1996: 296) cites Massumi (1992: 179) to the effect that, 'Baudrillardians never make it past the shopping mall'. According to Woodward *et al.* (2000), it is arguable that they do not even make it that far. For their study finds that mall rats perceive themselves as totally free from the postmodern condition. It is a matter of choosing whether shoppers or social theorists are the more disoriented. On commodity fetishism and consumption in Marx, see Shumway (2000).

20 Symptomatic of this is the discussion of exchange in terms of a self-confessedly, formalistic, unarticulated division into the four logics of use value, exchange value, symbolic exchange and sign value.

21 For Ewen:

> The relationship between style and social power is not a creation of the twentieth century consumer culture in particular. This alliance has a long history. Before the rise of a mass market in style, style was already a viable embodiment of power relations.
>
> (Ewen 1990: 47)

22 And when unwanted opportunities do initially arise for income to overcome social distinctions through consumption, then sumptuary laws are enacted.

23 The treatment of emulation and discrimination as motive forces independent of production leans on the conservative side in so far as the behaviour of the rich is inevitably seen as the prime mover. See Braudel (1974) and especially Sombart (1967) for the idea that luxury consumption is an engine of history. See also Fine and Leopold (1993: Chapters 10 and 11).

24 Hence, Baudrillard's infamous comment that the Gulf War does not exist because it is a product of the media – and his refusal to travel and see for himself; see Fine (2001a: 54).

25 See Taussig (1980) for commodity fetishism in the context of non-capitalist commodity production, for which the devil functions to bridge the gap between production and alienation of the product.

26 See also Miller (1987: 157).

27 See Lovell (1995) and Wayne (1995). Agnew (1993: 300) observes:

> What began after 1968 as a legitimate effort to correct the labour metaphysic of classical and Marxist political economy and to restore the symbolic dimension of consumption has given way to a blanket dismissal of such categories as subsistence, use-value and labour.

28 For further discussion, see Fine and Leopold (1993: Chapters 18 and 19) and, especially in the context of foods, Fine *et al.* (1996: Chapter 11). For de Grazia (1996: 152), there is 'no uniform pattern across classes for Mr. Breadwinner and Mrs. Consumer'. For contrasting outcomes in terms of the transparency of class in consumption, see Wight (1993) for the working class in the context of unemployment and, for Johnson (1988: 42):

> It is always possible to identify complex status hierarchies in any society, but it is not always the case that these run counter to more fundamental class divisions. In late-Victorian and Edwardian Britain, however, the immediacy of the status

divisions of all levels of working-class society, and the precarious nature of most families' income and social respectability, acted as a barrier to the development of a more cohesive working class outlook. This was not false consciousness, it was real life.

29 Interestingly, recent translation of Baudrillard's (1998) earlier work reveals that he had yet to have broken with a heavy, if simplistic, dose of economic determinism as monopoly capitalism is seen as homogenising people and products, thereby creating a cult of differentiation (pp. 89–90). Moreover, the view from this perspective that only the idea, and not the fulfilment, of consumption has been created becomes very different within a postmodernist framework in which the economic determinism has fallen away, and only subjective notions of consumption remain.

30 As Burke recognises, goods also have other material properties, such as those attached to their role in production and reproduction.

31 Unfortunately, they incorrectly continue, 'But for Marx, this additional complexity applied only to commodities in a capitalist society.' This is asserted despite Marx's analysis of commodity fetishism preceding any discussion of capital in Volume I of *Capital*, in his initial dissection of the anatomy of the commodity in general.

32 As a result, Burke's claim that 'Marx felt that fetishism was particular to capitalism' is incomprehensible unless this be confined to wage labour and commodity fetishism. Burke (1998) seems more favourably inclined to Marx and, to anticipate, in studying commodity rumours adopts an approach consistent with that developed in Chapter 6 (and 9) (pp. 263–4):

> The pathways by which innovation and newness enter the world of commodities, the origins of goods, the process of their manufacture, the intentions and outlook of their makers, the manner of their distribution. Rumors indirectly ask: where does this thing come from? How is it made? Why do they want me to buy it? Who are 'they', anyway?

33 See Clarke's (1999b) discussion, drawing upon Hounshell (1984), of the aesthetic trade-off between productivity and product or, in the more mundane terms of the automobile industry, how and how often to change models for marketing purposes. Sex and advertising sell cars, but there is much more to it than that.

5 Consumption through systems of provision

1 See Fine *et al.* (1996) for the idea of a single meat system in the UK but a difference between the sugar system and that attached to artificial sweeteners.

2 Goodman (1999), for example, appears to dismiss the system of provision method for failing to overcome the dualism between nature and society but not the system of provision approach itself.

3 This is posited for consumption alone and not as a general proposition for all social theory. See Fine (1998a) for example on labour market analysis and the need to deploy and integrate both horizontal and vertical analysis.

4 As will be clear, the following discussion draws upon the references and themes taken up by Church (1999) whose concern is to identify sources of competitive success for which serving the demand for consumption is but an immediate part at the point of sale.

5 See Clarke (1997) for a discussion in the context of bringing studies of the managerial and consumer revolutions together, and also S. Clarke (1996) for market research and its interaction with General Motors' strategy towards distribution networks.

6 Lemire (1992, 1997) provides an exemplary historical and empirical account of the distinction between mass production and mass consumption, the latter not requiring the former. Note also the importance of the military (and slavery and the state) in

promoting mass consumption. For a critique of 'flec-spec' see Fine (1995a), and for an account of its intellectual origins and content, see Fine (1998a: Chapter 4).

7 See also Scranton (1991, 1999).

8 See also Cohen (1990).

9 On the other hand, witness the praise for Sutton from the mainstream. For Cable (1994a: 6), 'the exquisite blend of theory and empirics in Sutton (1991) may prove a model for future work', and Waterson (1994: 133) 'endorses the approach of authors such as Sutton (1991), who have shifted away from the proliferation of theoretical nuances towards a search for empirical regularities'. Note that in his most recent work, Sutton (1998) has addressed economies of scope in a limited way, and interprets it as 'the central theme: the problem of market definition', the latter representing the creation of boundaries between sectors. This might be interpreted as an implicit and partial recognition of the importance of systems of provision!

10 For more detail in the context of the associated (re)structuring of labour markets, see Fine (1998a: Chapter 7).

11 In Marx's striking image, commodities are in love with money – but the course of true love never did run smooth. See also Carruthers and Babb (2000: 4):

> Given the near-complete penetration of market relations into our modern economic lives, it is not surprising that we tend to use the market metaphor for other areas of social life, such as dating and marriage.

12 For the relation between advertising and women as sex objects, see Williamson (1978) and also Fine and Leopold (1993: Chapter 14); for the media and commodification, see Dunn (1986); for the state, there is some discussion in Miller (1987); and for the family, this is a favoured ground for marketing and the sociology of socialisation.

13 They cite Lash and Urry (1994: 4) for whom, 'the aestheticization of material objects takes place in the production, circulation or the consumption of such goods'.

14 In Marx's terms, labour is only formally subordinated to capital in the production process which has yet to seize the methods of production that it inherits and transform them to the specifically capitalist method of production or real subordination, see Appendix to Marx (1976).

15 This might be termed Accam's Razor after the nineteenth-century chemist concerned with exposing and obliterating adulteration of foods (by which genuine ingredients were confined to a minimum), and by analogy with Occam's Razor which seeks to eliminate any step in an argument that is not strictly required! See Fine and Leopold (1993: Chapter 12).

16 More generally, for the selling of authenticity in the form of a constructed British heritage, see Samuel (1989).

17 For biscuits, see Corley (1976), and for canned products, see Johnston (1976).

18 In foods, sugar is even combined with fat, a source of heart and circulation disease, in a ratio of roughly one to one by weight since this raises the 'go-away' factor, the illusion in taste that food has left the mouth (and teeth!). See Cantor and Cantor (1977).

6 Systems of provision and cultural systems

1 See the more general debate in *Critical Studies in Mass Communication*, vol. 12, no. 1, 1995, pp. 62–100.

2 But see Kammen (2000) for the need to be cautious about the timing, pacing and rhythm of commercialisation of culture.

3 Just as we should be aware of failed technologies and products, see Lebergott (1993: 18) who reports that 70 per cent of market-tested products fail for major corporations; for grocery stores, estimates that only 5,000 of 30,000 products survived

between 1960 and 1980, and of 84,933 between 1980 and 1990, 86 per cent failed. See also Forty (1986).

4 Latouche (1993: 24) observes of westernisation that it is made up of 'economy and culture as two primeval dimensions of human experience, conforming to two antagonistic logics'.

5 Muggleton (2000) is an exception, pinpointing two supposed methodological weaknesses in CCCS (Centre for Contemporary Cultural Studies, University of Birmingham) work: a totalising framework, and a prior commitment to analytical principles in terms of which the empirical is interpreted. He is concerned that there is a 'failure to take seriously enough the subjective viewpoints of the youth subculturalists themselves' (p. 3), rather than imposing increasingly esoteric and exoteric theory upon them through reading of their 'texts', in place of their own representations. In contrast,

> categories and definitions of sociologists must be derived from, rather than imposed upon, the sensibilities of the people under study. To claim, from the outside as it were, that people's indigenous meanings are contradictory is to ignore how such apparent contradictions can make perfect, logical sense to those involved given their own definitions of the situation.
>
> (p. 59)

Consequently, distinctive individuality and subcultural affiliation 'can therefore be understood, somewhat paradoxically, as collective expressions and celebrations of individualism' (p. 79). Whatever the validity of these criticisms, they are not intrinsic to the circuit of culture approach as it is sufficiently malleable to accommodate them.

6 Thus, Andrews and Talbot (2000a: 2) cite Johnson (1986), partly wrongly, for the source of understanding consumption as 'but one point on ... the cultural circuit, consisting of representation, identity, consumption, production and regulation'.

7 See, for example, the diagram offered by Goldman and Papson (1998: 8) in constructing their study of Nike's 'swoosh'.

8 The expression is due to Baron and Hannan (1994).

9 See also Alfino (1998: 182) for whom:

> The 'scandal' of Baudrillard's theory is that we have to begin by saying that a trip to McDonald's is not about eating. McDonald's is not selling hamburgers which first satisfy our hunger and happen also to have various social connotations. Rather, as a form of consumption, eating at McDonald's is about consuming (and reproducing) the message of McDonald's.

On a different tack, returning to the theme of deficient economics, Livingston (1994) mechanically deploys Marx's reproduction schema to periodise capital, and consumption, according to whether Department I (means of production) predominates over Department II (means of consumption) or vice versa. This is arbitrary but, interestingly, can be interpreted as a crude form of McDonaldisation for the contemporary phase where the imperative to consume predominates.

10 See also Miller and Rose (1997) for how the consumer as subject is constructed for advertising agencies.

11 See also Winship (2000: 38) for whom the chain store's 'uniformity and conservatism were the means to a more democratic participation in the culture of the nation' as against the 'cultured middle classes'.

12 See also Cockburn (1992) for the idea of a circuit of technology especially in order to examine gendering. See also Cowan (1997: 218):

> The history of ideas about technology is, like the history of all ideas, both very complex and very subtle. Objects, technologies, even technological systems ... carry, as a result of the complexity and subtlety, many levels of cultural meaning

... those meanings can sometimes be more potent to people than the social and economic functions those objects and technologies and technological systems were designed to perform.

13 He continues, however:

> Yet engaging as these individual narratives are, it is also intriguing to observe the ways in which they subsequently converged ... [on] the prevalent association of the great corporation with small-town Main Street ... a contrived sentimentalism ... to address the disproportions in size and power that the giant corporation still signified.

14 More generally, see Bermingham (1995: 14):

> The modernist distrust of mass culture which has to a large extent both written the history of consumption and blinded us to its history rests on a tendency to think in essentialist terms about culture, class and identity. Accordingly, culture is high and pure, classes are homogeneous and stable, and identity is unified and transparent. All of these assumptions need to be questioned if we are to write a history of consumption since the seventeenth century. Instead of seeing culture in simple productivist terms as the creation of unique objects by individuals not alienated from their labor, we need to look at uses of culture, at the social context of cultural change and innovation, and at the solutions cultural forms propose to the social contradictions that have generated them.

15 See Porter (1993) for consumption conceived as (unhealthy) disorder.
16 The notion of circuits of knowledge is appropriate to the study of creolisation of consumption, which tends to be understood in terms of a meeting of, rather than a dialogue between, cultures. See Lien (1997) for the Norwegian pizza and Howes (1996a: 5) who contrasts creolisation with coca-colonisation both for flow to, rather than from, the west and the 'creativity of the consumer' rather than the 'intentionality of the producer'. It is 'neither homogenization nor fragmentation (nor any dialectical synthesis of the two), but the multiplicity of possible local-global articulations' (p. 6). See also Colloredo-Mansfeld (1999: 32) who argues that 'cash infusions and indigenous cultures mix in unpredictable ways', not least reinforcing, undermining and shifting the contours of power and differentiation as well as cultural meanings (not simply reducible to dependence versus enhancement).
17 Circulatory or similar models of the culture of consumption can lead but not be reduced to notions of consumption as communication, as in Cosgel (1997), for example. For a critique, see Campbell (1997).
18 See, for example, McGovern (1998: 40–1):

> Whereas admen and consumer advocates were fiercely opposed on the questions of the consumer's best interest or the important characteristics of buyers, these two professions shared remarkably similar views about consumers. They placed themselves squarely in a cultural elite, whose tastes paralleled and reinforced their own social position. They embraced the language of authenticity to discredit mass consumption and elevate their own tastes. By investing their own preferences with the authority of the 'real' in a culture long suspicious of artifice, they made those tastes the yardstick of reality.

See also Auslander (1996a), and Walton (1992) for the desire of workmen to maintain both their skills and product quality.
19 Ritzer (1999a: 194), however, observes of Schor (1991) that she

> offers nine principles designed to deal with the problem of overspending. Virtually all of them focus on things consumers should do such as controlling

desire, imposing voluntary restraints on themselves, sharing more with others, becoming more educated consumers, and avoiding shopping for therapeutic reasons.

20 See also Sulkunen (1997) and Lunt and Livingstone (1992: 167) who observe that, 'time and again, the contradictions of previous times [are seen as] being hard but secure, limited but moral, oppressive but authentic'. Increasingly, though, science (and truth), morality (and values), and art (and beauty) have been brought together in acts of consumption (p. 168).

21 As discussed in Chapter 9, this is in part explained by the impact of tracing back the sources of consumption to other practices around labour, the environment, quality, etc. See Cooper (1998), for example, and Johns and Vural (2000) for a contemporary account.

22 See McGovern (1998) for the notion of consumer democracy as a means of denying (class) stratification in consumption. See Mullins (1999) for lack of democracy in consumption in the context of race.

23 See also Folbre and Nelson (2000) and Fine (1992) and Fine (1995d) in debate with Kotz (1994, 1995). For Frost (1993: 1289):

> Domestic technologies saw little diffusion for other reasons as well. The argument that seemed compelling for rationalization and automation in industry was economic: machines would replace workers and thus save employers considerable wage expenses. Once women were cajoled or forced back into the home, what point was there, in an economic sense, to put them out of 'work'. Even for well-heeled, middle-class families, expenditures on costly home appliances were hard to justify.

Note, however, that the counterpart to commodification of domestic consumption, the emergence of the welfare state, tends to be studiously ignored in the sticky comparative advantage accounts of the division of labour between household and commercial private sector. Esping-Andersen's highly influential theory of welfare regimes emphasises decommodification. But, even for him in his most recent work (Esping-Andersen 1999), the new household economics exerts its crude charms. For a critique, see Chapter 10.

24 See Clunas (1999) for the shifting and expansive scope of what constitutes consumption across historical studies, his focusing on the marked passage from Brewer and Porter (1993) to Bermingham and Brewer (1995), and in such a short time.

25 For Scranton (1999: 60), in the context of urban manufacturing:

> If the simplifying assumption that the significance of Midwestern cities lay in their service to the emergence of mass production is refused, a more nuanced account of territorial industrialization will be feasible.

But see Roy (1997) for the argument that the dominance of large-scale corporations far exceeded their weight and representativity.

26 But, for the very close relations between Disney and McDonald's in practice, see Schlosser (2001).

27 See debate in *Review of International Political Economy*, vol. 1, no. 3, 1994.

28 But note the more favourable response to the food systems approach in Watts and Goodman (1997) compared to debate with Fine (1994a, b) in Goodman and Redclift (1994) and Watts (1994). See Chapter 11 for further discussion.

29 Fine (1995b, 1998c: Chapter 3). Note that Becker (1996) has argued that eating disorders are the consequence of rational intertemporal choice (for an appropriately specified utility function).

NOTES

30 In response, both to Pennell and to the literature more generally, we can make the countercharge of neglect of public consumption, raised in the closing chapter of Fine and Leopold (1993), and taken up here in Chapters 10 and 11.

31 Most notably for Lash and Urry (1994) of whom, presumably, Glennie and Thrift (1996: 221) observe the view that because 'the increased speed of circulation of objects and images empties out both subjects and objects of meaning ... a chaotic process of *cultural fragmentation* has been occurring'. Hence, far from anticipating despair, they offer a warm embrace for 'reflexive modernization' as opening a world of possibilities.

32 This is to have anticipated the reservations of Edwards (2000: 42) over the system of provision approach:

> Although it is clearly true that the consumption, or indeed production, of packets of crisps is not easily equated with the demand for, or supply of, Armani suits, there remains some connection, or at least clustering, in the patterns of development and practice across quite different goods and their respective systems of provision.

In seeking to pinpoint consumer society (itself a 'horizontal' category, see Chapter 8), he stacks three horizontal factors – that consumption is multifaceted, expansive in ethos and practice, and divisive and oppressive – around social stratification.

33 See Palumbo-Liu (1997).

34 For a particularly sympathetic account, see McLennan (1998).

35 Similarly, what is being reworked and what are its origins when Miller *et al.* (1998: 185) argue that 'through shopping ... consumers are involved in a creative *reworking* of gender, ethnicity, class and space' (emphasis added)?

36 Thus, Fine (1998a) argues that it can be appropriate to analyse certain labour markets from a 'horizontal' perspective.

37 Nonetheless, the approach raises delicate and difficult issues such as whether theme parks, shopping malls, tourism and the like constitute systems of provision of their own or are the interaction of many different ones.

38 See also Horowitz and Mohun (1998) which, in the context of consumption, gender and technology, finds much commendable in the 'consumption junction' framework of Cowan (1982) that has considerable affinities to the systems of provision approach. Note that in her later work, Cowan (1997) posits the importance of technological systems and organises her account around particular sectors. For Lubar (1998: 32),

> creation of a consumer society is an ongoing process ... a negotiation of value and meaning between manufacturer and worker. Each person who participates in the design, manufacture, sale or use of an object brings meaning to it, each helps to construct it.

39 See also James (2000) for a parallel acknowledgement of the impact of globalisation from this perspective. Rosenbaum (1999: 317) goes further than James in seeking to incorporate 'the cultural significance of commodities', but his contribution remains marked by its taking economics as its starting point, for which culture is initially left out. Thus, 'if commodities have important non-material characteristics, then taking goods at face value would run the risk of overlooking substantial, if not decisive, reasons why individuals value and choose goods in the first place' (p. 326). But commodities always have non-material characteristics, and their face value is a major part of their culture!

40 The latest contribution ranges, for example, over networks, social capital and competitiveness of nations. For work within the global chain approach, see Gwynne (1999) and, in a more critical vein, Raikes *et al.* (2000) and Raikes and Gibbon (2000). See

241

also Haugerud *et al.* (2000) for some case studies that loosely use the global commodity chain approach, primarily to motivate ethnographic considerations.

41 Hartwick (2000) seeks to add this element to the global commodity chain approach in order to establish a radical political geography.

42 This is also characteristic of his treatment of globalisation (Appadurai 1996) whereby it is constructed out of five different landscapes – those of ethnos, media, techno, finance and ideo. See Chapter 2 for a critique.

43 In 1986, Mattel claimed Barbie's wardrobe had made it the world's largest producer of women's wear (p. 87), and the most popular toy in history (p. 88). Barbie demonstrates the two rules of toy making: nothing is for ever – except for Barbie. But she needs freshening up (p. 88). On toys, see Cross (1997) and Kline (1998) who observe the switch from toys as preparation for work to toys as entertainment with strong links to TV, Disney, etc., and multimillion-dollar business.

44 Apart from labour, the material content of Barbie is highly dependent upon the pliability, and yet solidity, of plastic, on which see Meikle (1995). He establishes that plastic is the ideal raw material for capitalist production and consumption as a result of these properties. But it can only reflect, not create, social characteristics – just like money – with the two interestingly meeting up nicely with one another in our flexible friend, the credit card. For plastic in the construction of domesticity, see Clarke (1999). For an attempt to draw out the meaning of clothes from their physical form alone, see Barnes and Eicher (1992a).

45 Purdy (1998: 74) cites Ambrose Bierce, *The Devil's Dictionary*, 'Fashion – a despot whom the wise ridicule and obey'.

46 For Auslander (1996b: 101):

> To adequately explain the gendering of consumer practices in the nineteenth century one must ultimately locate that process within the dynamics of making nation and state and of capitalist expansion in the post-revolutionary era ... and the political and social ... of everyday life, including the acquisition, use and disposal of goods.

See also Walton (1992) on French furnishing.

47 See also Coffin (1996).

7 Economics and consumption

1 These claims to science (falsifiability) and rigour (mathematical modelling) are used by mainstream economics to dismiss any deviation from its methods and assumptions. There are, however, doubts over whether it does itself practise what it preaches (Blaug 1980, McCloskey 1986, Lawson 1997 and Boland 1997), and whether it could do so. See Hausman and McPherson (1996: 56–7) and Slater and Tonkiss (2001: 61), citing Boland to the effect that:

> Models of rational choice – especially as these have been extended to increasing domains of economic and social action – do not themselves subscribe to a methodology of falsification. If all action is assumed to be maximizing, then the assumption of maximization is itself non-falsifiable. The hypothesis falls into the trap of *si omnia nullia* – as a theory of everything, it ends up accounting for very little. It becomes difficult to think of an example of social action that *could not* be read as maximizing.

2 Almost equally rare is account taken of postmodernism in radical political economy, but see Cornwall (1997). An exception might be thought to be theories of post-

Fordism but these tend to appeal to an exogenously imposed desire of otherwise satiated consumers for niche products.

3 See Fine (1982) for an appropriate discussion in this context of the relationship between neo-classical economics and classical political economy but especially de Vroey (1975) on the differences between the two schools of thought.

4 This was most forcibly brought to the notice of anthropologists by Douglas and Isherwood (1980). Note, somewhat optimistically, in the new introduction to the *World of Goods*, they judge (Douglas and Isherwood 1996: xxvi):

> Methodological individualism is now so much under attack that the only thing wanting for its defeat is a range of alternative assumptions to take its place, and several are in the air.

5 For a critique of which, see Godelier (1973), Sen (1977), Hollis and Nell (1975) and Hargreaves-Heap (1992).

6 More generally, income is not simply taken as given but can be earned through the disutility of engaging in work. So, in standard treatments of work and leisure by economists, the two are seen as mutually exclusive, adding up to the twenty-four hours of the day. Each is reduced to an effect on the level of utility, negative and positive, respectively. See Spencer (1998) for a critique and also Roberts *et al.* (1988) for a discussion of producers who perceive their work as consumption. Saving is also extremely simply treated – as a guarantee of future consumption (commanding rate of interest as reward). For a critique of this, see Green (1990).

7 An exception that lays down the rule is Becker's new household economics in which households produce for own consumption as if a commercial firm (as understood by the mainstream).

8 See Deaton and Muellbauer (1980) and Blundell (1988).

9 Interestingly, there has recently been a renewed interest amongst economists in Scitovsky's empirical anomaly between cross-section and time-series reports of well-being, as in the collection edited by Dixon (1997). At core, an attempt to resolve the conundrum by economists proceeds by appeal to rising aspirations over time. Higher income makes you happier in the short run but is nullified in the long run by raising your standards. In effect, you need at least two variables to do the work for you – one to explain cross-section, the other to explain time series. Income and aspirations do it, respectively. This constitutes an extraordinary reductionism in two senses. First, even accepting its own way of proceeding, there is a vast literature on the variety of variables that influence well-being. Why confine attention to aspirations? The second reductionism is to set aside social relations (apart from relative comparisons) and simply to grind aspirations onto income as a determinant of well-being. But people feel happier or not according to the sort of society in which they live. Once again, this has a very large number of attributes, none of which is reducible to individual subjectivity. If pushed to be reductionist, regularity of sex, health and sleep might figure highly, none of which is inevitably closely or directly associated with income in the long run!

10 It is not intended here to enter into debate over the distinction between rational, irrational and non-rational – only to observe that use of the terms tends to act illegitimately and by tautology to support the arguments in which they are employed.

11 Consequently, the demand system for animals can be estimated empirically by using rewards/punishments (foods/electric shocks) as a proxy for prices, see Kagel (1981). Animals are more rational than humans in revealed preferences!

12 Economics is highly dependent upon the division between the exogenous (factors taken as given) and the endogenous (those determined within the model).

13 See Green (1979) for a critical assessment.

14 See Stigler (1954: 95) and Brown and Deaton (1972: 1155), the latter reporting that 'nor has recent research discovered more enduring or more complex "universal laws" relating to income elasticities than those put forward by Engel and Schwabe more than a century ago'. Schwabe's law suggests that the income elasticity of housing is usually less than one, i.e. expenditure rises less than income.

15 This remains true of the Lancaster (1966) model of characteristics even though in principle it breaks down items of consumption into their constituent properties. It simply moves the issue one stage back to the unexamined characteristics of goods rather than the goods themselves.

16 Similarly, Rosenbaum (1999: 319) argues that mainstream economics (and, it must be said, much heterodox) 'regards commodities as being usefully describable in terms of physical properties', with a corresponding focus on choice as opposed to consumption itself, thereby effectively excluding cultural considerations. Note, however, in his critique of Sen's capability approach from this perspective, he essentially seeks to add culture etc. as another, socially derived, set of characteristics of goods (Fine 2001b).

17 Note also the impoverished notion of subsistence that is tied to some absolute standard of physical survival, as opposed to relative standards and capabilities as pioneered by Amartya Sen for example.

18 See Fine (1982). Note that in its formal general equilibrium models, the distinction between supply and demand is explicitly obliterated in so far as excess demand functions, or the algebraic differences between supply and demand, suffice for analytical purposes.

19 For a survey of relevant developments in industrial economics, see Schmalansee (1988), although, more recently, attention has been dedicated to informational problems and game theory. In addition, technology is no longer taken as given in wake of endogenous growth theory. See Fine (2000a) for a critical assessment.

20 See Deaton and Muellbauer (1980), Blundell (1988) and Deaton (1997).

21 On these issues, see Keen (1987), Pudney (1989) and Meghir and Robin (1992), for example.

22 See Deaton's entry in the *New Palgrave Dictionary of Economics* (p. 592).

23 Of course, it might be argued that the *New Palgrave* is unrepresentative of the discipline, as is argued by Blaug (1988) who accuses the work of ideological bias. But, whilst he lists twenty-four omitted topics, none of these essentially involves consumption. So the relative unimportance of consumption to economics is common to widely different conceptions of the field.

24 Interestingly, Dickson and Sawyer (1984) suggest that analysis of consumer behaviour might be taken up by analogy with the economics of oligopoly by exploring why consumers enter and exit the market.

25 The acceptability of human capital theory has been subject to a very wide debate, although more in education than in economics. For a critique of the new household economics, see Fine (1992), and for a critique of 'consumer capital' theory, Fine (1995c). For more contributions in the Becker vein, see especially Febrero and Schwartz (1995) and Tommasi and Ierulli (eds) (1995).

26 See also Becker (1992) and Becker *et al.* (1994). Although Becker and Murphy refer to 'his preferences', my own interest in eating disorders was prompted by a citation search on gender and consumption in which such conditions, and tobacco and alcohol consumption, were by far the most referenced topics, with women disproportionately represented.

27 See also Becker (1992: 327) where it is argued in addition that:

> The assumption of independence [of influence of one person's preferences on another] is not 'nonsense', for it usefully simplifies many problems that are not crucially affected by dependencies over time.

This article is also notable for accepting in its closing words what almost seems like a recantation (p. 341):

> With a still bolder vision and a lot of luck, the link between the past and present choices may also explain why and how parents influence the formation of children's preferences, how people get committed to future decisions, and the formation and support of institutions and culture.

Surely, however, this is heavily ironic in that each of these social determinants, including parenting, is in the article constructed on the basis of methodological individualism.

28 See also Becker (1992: 328) where explanations for habitual behaviour are understood within a common analytical framework: 'well-known examples include smoking, using heroin, eating ice cream or Kellogg's Corn Flakes, jogging, attending church, telling lies, and often intimacy with a lover'.

29 Not surprisingly, Becker is dismissively harsh on psychology, for its reliance upon multiple personalities (p. 12) and cognitive imperfections (p. 22). See also Gray (1987: 35) who advises that optimisation on the basis of fixed objects:

> Should not be taken as reason against fashioning better theories of belief formation which deploy the Becker scheme. In fact, the application of the economic approach to questions of cognitive psychology would seem to be one of its most promising research prospects.

This does not seem to have been borne out in practice.

30 This means that Becker (1996: 16–18) rejects Sen's notion of a distinction between ethical and personal preferences on the grounds that the one is reducible to the other. For more discussion, see Fine (2001a: Chapter 3), Etzioni (1988), Hausman and McPherson (1996), Redmond (2000) and, in the wider context, especially Walsh (2000). See also Wolfe (1989) for a critical account of Becker's economics imperialism particularly from an ethical perspective.

31 See also Swedberg (1991a) for an account of the separation of economics from sociology with emphasis upon 'methodenstreiten', concerning the dispute between historical and theoretical methods for economics.

32 See also Bowden and Offer (1999), in debate with Fine (1999b), and Bowden (1990), Bowden and Turner (1993) and Offer (1998).

33 Yet, closing their reply (p. 567):

> We remain committed, unrepentantly, to the familiar category of household appliances, and to the study of consumer behaviour through the attributes of people and the attributes of goods, in an historical environment of changing technologies, prices, norms, and yes (why not), 'systems of provision'.

34 See Becker (1965, 1991). See also Becker (1993, 1996).

35 Bowden and Offer (1999: 563) remark upon this interpretation of them as a 'translation' but they do not otherwise question it.

36 For some discussion of the shifting meaning of the telephone, not least in relation to gender, see Fine *et al.* (1992b).

37 Bowden and Offer (1999: 563–4) reasonably observe that there is some discipline associated with the household, presumably as time is a constraint or condition of all activity. But this is not really the point – that the imperative of profitability does not govern the household. This perhaps explains why they should see the domestic labour debate as irrelevant to the issue of time, as it contains 'only a discussion of a debate on value' (p. 563). But this debate is precisely concerned with which labour *time*

counts as value, with the presence of capitalist control as decisive for some contributors but not for others.

38 Apparently not, see later footnote on the lack of arousal attached to clean floors.

39 More generally, Bowden and Offer take an uncritical stance towards diffusion, a more or less valid descriptive device but with no explanatory content of its own. See Fine *et al.* (1992a, 1993) in the context of videos and microwaves, and Fine (1990: Chapter 7) in the different context of technology diffusion in the British coal industry.

40 But see Fine *et al.* (1996: Chapter 7), and earlier in this chapter, for the argument, in the context of food, that the calculation of such elasticities is highly questionable both theoretically and empirically.

41 Ultimately, B&O seem to rest the distinction between time saving and time using on whether the products address unpleasant tasks or arousal, presumably pleasant; '"arousal" is just what differentiates between the two types of goods: entertainment provides arousal, clean floors do not' (p. 564). But time can be saved in providing entertainment/arousal, by video in lieu of cinema trip etc. In answering the furniture/housing issue, they also adopt an extraordinarily reductionist approach to explanation of suburbanisation in terms of (individual) trade-offs between space, rural amenities, cleaning and travel times, etc.

42 Bowden and Offer (1999: 565) unhappily seek to resolve this issue by insisting:

> We did not label goods as gendered according to the gender of those who might consume them, but according to whether the benefit was direct or indirect.

The ambiguity around such a distinction of proximate benefit is surely far from helpful.

43 As recognised by Bowden and Offer (1996: 247).

44 Bowden and Offer (1999: 565) seem to question whether they use the notion of patriarchy. Thus:

> We observe that women's labour is worth less in the market place than men's. We do not attempt to encompass the reasons, nor all the implications, for market and household production.

Compare, however, with the view (Bowden and Offer 1994: 740) that 'status goods … impinge … on the satisfaction of males, and to the extent that males have greater power within households, these goods acquire priority for purchase'.

45 Bowden and Offer (1994: 740, 1996: 245, 261).

46 Somewhat lamely, B&O claim that this is in part explained by the greater numbers of females!

47 Thus, for Bowden and Offer (1999: 565):

> To say that advertising might cause the product mix to be biased towards expensive goods is odd … credit allowed consumers to acquire appliances which they could not have purchased, other things being equal.

48 As recognised by Bowden and Offer (1994: 742–3, 1996: 254).

49 See Atkinson (1995a) for such an argument, and also Fine and Leopold (1990, 1993: Chapter 11) for the view that such elite consumption obstructed rather than promoted a putative consumer revolution in the eighteenth century.

50 See Fine and Harris (1985) on the oligopolistic character of the British car market, sharply revealed by recent price comparisons with identical European models, and leading to newly established Internet traders importing directly from abroad.

51 See also Offer (1998).

52 As recognised by Bowden and Offer (1994: 743), even if with some inconsistency (p. 739). See also Bowden and Offer (1996: 261) and Seiter (1993) but especially Fine *et al.* (1992a, 1993).

53 See also pp. 727, 738 and 744, where equalities of marginal utilities are attached to the idea of equilibrium outcomes, a peculiarity in view of the wish to explain extensive economic and social change. Bowden and Offer (1999: 565) also claim:

> Fine smuggles in an assumption of insatiable demand (which we do not make). In fact (like most economists and psychologists), we assume that stimulation delivers diminishing returns, which is why sets are eventually turned off.

This is, with one proviso lest the diminishing returns become zero or negative (rarely assumed by most economists and psychologists), mutually contradictory. For diminishing but positive returns are sufficient condition for non-satiety!

54 Bowden and Offer (1999: 565–6) seek to resolve this issue either by reverting to the notion of 'reproducible machinery' or by listing the items concerned. This does not address the analytical issues involved, especially in light of the paragraph following here.

55 Thus, for economics imperialist Lazear (1999), language and culture simply become efficient mechanisms for forming collectives.

56 It involved departing critically from the standard technique for estimating the order of acquisition of durables and developing an alternative. See Fine (1983) and Fine and Simister (1995), the latter also providing a review of the literature more generally.

57 See especially Simister (1998).

58 Different effects for age and gender (and single parents, usually female) are also found for videos, microwaves and telephones.

59 Thoms *et al.* (1998a: 5) report that almost half of new cars in the UK are now bought by women. Even so, Rice and Saunders (1998: 284) conclude:

> If the car industry is to gear itself up for the future market dominated by women buying new cars, it needs to urgently address its marketing strategies and in particular start presenting advertisements that recognise the changed economic and social positions of women in the late twentieth century.

60 See also Fagnani (1990) and Pickup (1984, 1989).

61 See also Leopold (1989: 1) who finds that 'wage poverty among women is linked to lack of mobility in housing'.

62 Principal component, factor analysis and analysis of variance are excellent techniques for uncovering (ir)regularities across data and, hence, social norms. They are neglected by economists and econometricians who are obsessively attached to regression analysis because of its putative explanatory power.

8 What is consumer society?

1 Consumerism in the United States has come to mean (the movement) to represent the interests of consumers.

2 See Fine and Leopold (1990, 1993: Chapters 7 and 10) for further commentary on McKendrick *et al.*

3 See also Clunas (1999) for a critique of indiscriminate use of consumer revolution and, yet, its heavy Eurocentrism.

4 Crafts (1996, 1999a, b) has subsequently embraced the new growth theory. For critical commentary, see Fine (2000a, 2001c).

5 For an account and its implications, see Fine (1982). See also Perrotta (1997) for an outstanding account of how political economy prior to Adam Smith understood expanding consumption as a potential source of economic development.

6 It must be emphasised that the demand-led and the consumer-led explanations for growth are not the same since the latter focuses entirely upon final consumption to the neglect of other sources of demand. In doing so, consumption is presumed to drag investment demand and, even more neglected, intermediate inputs, behind it. This raises problems in the context of innovation since, as in energy conservation and efficiency, for example, this will lead to lower demand for inputs and a contraction of the market!

7 See Gilboy (1932), Mokyr (1977, 1984), Ben-Shachar (1984), McCloskey (1981) and Musson (1972), for example. It has been seen as the source of a 'monocausal' explanation of growth. See Gaski (1982), Inkster (1983) and Bruland (1985) for a critique.

8 See previous chapter and also James (1993, 2000) in the broader context of how western consumption habits amongst Third World elites hold back economic development. Note also that the consumer revolution approach to economic development is the positive counterpart to underconsumptionism, not least the idea that only factors such as militarisation prevent permanent stagnation.

9 See also Weatherill (1986b: 40).

10 See Flinn (1984), Nef (1932), Smith (1961), Dietz (1986) and Pollard (1983) for some discussion of the complexities in the marketing and distribution of coal.

11 Agnew (1993) makes the same point from a different perspective in emphasising McKendrick's reliance upon the *producer* Wedgwood.

12 An interesting convert in this respect is Mokyr (1998), with his effectively relying upon the impact of consumerism through (a weak form of technological) path dependence – the way in which ahistorical economics now allows for history. For a critique, see Fine (2000d).

13 See Marx's (1973: 100) discussion of production, distribution and consumption in the *Grundrisse*.

14 See Narotzky (1997) for use of the notion of social reproduction as multidimensional and as an instrument for avoiding simple dualisms – micro and macro, material and cultural, economy and society, and so on. See also Carrier and Heyman (1997) for emphasis on reproduction in the context of the study of consumption.

15 For specific critical discussion of imitation and emulation, see Campbell (1993). For men as consumers, against the interpretative grain, in the industrial/consumer revolution, see Finn (2000). See also Kowaleski-Wallace (1996) for the emergence only with the 'consumer revolution' of the idea of women as voracious (mouth and womb) at the expense of men. Interestingly, she deploys the examples of tea and sugar to explore (colonialism and slavery) contradictions in the ideology of the refined, civilised, sexuality of feminine consumption practices.

16 For a critique of this comparative advantage approach to the household, which has its radical counterpart in the domestic labour debate, see Fine (1992) and Fine (1995d) in debate with Kotz (1994, 1995). See also Folbre and Nelson (2000).

17 Witness the tautological in his arguments (p. 168):

> The increase in 'leisure' over the past one hundred years has to be interpreted as a consequence of … high income elasticity of demand for earnings intensive commodities.

If history had been different, it would be 'explained' by different values for the elasticities. Further, for him, such conclusions have to be investigated over longer periods to ascertain the exact balance of income and substitution effects throughout history. Unfortunately, history has a habit of undermining the assumptions under which elasticities can be meaningfully defined let alone measured.

18 See Featherstone (1983: 4) who, in referring to McKendrick *et al.*, suggests that: 'Although the term "consumer society" is normally applied to post-war western societies, we should remember that many of the central features of the consumer way of life are by no means new'.

19 For the transition to mass production, see Hounshell (1984). Piore and Sabel (1984) questionably argue that there was no necessity for fragmented production to have given way to mass production if institutional arrangements had evolved to support flexible, small-scale production.

20 See Leach (1984), Williams (1984) and Miller (1981). Cheney (1983: 28) points to the salience of women in the culture of consumerism and hence to the role of department stores (for whom women act both as employees and as customers).

21 See also Hirschman (1982), Riesman (1964) and the British Council of Churches (1978: 24/5), for whom:

> In summary, our study has indicated that along with the undoubted benefits of the consumer goods society there are major problems. There is the danger that men and women may be valued not for who they are but for what they possess. Some producers stimulate conspicuous consumption by advertising that emphasises status and social esteem and they encourage the desire for goods by playing on people's greed, envy or insecurity. There is a threat to minority tastes from the spread of mass-production. There is a danger that the really poor in our society may be overlooked amidst the general affluence and finally there is a weak sense of interdependence at a world level. A primary Christian duty is neglected. 'If anyone has the world's goods and sees his brother in need, yet closes his heart against him, how does God's love abide in him?'

See also discussion in Chapter 8.

22 Even physical subsistence is socially determined, as demonstrated by the preference for starvation over food relief with unfamiliar staples, not only in undeveloped communities but also, for example, in the case of US PoWs in the Korean War.

23 This notion of relative deprivation was most recently initiated by Sen (1983), ultimately leading through capabilities to the idea of development as freedom (Sen 1999). For commentary, see Cameron and Gasper (2000) and Fine (2001b) for example.

24 See also Gardner and Sheppard (1989: 46–7) for whom domestic consumption, as the female agenda, is now in the ascendancy following a retail revolution, although this has also witnessed a breakdown of the previous cultural divisions between male production and female consumption, now taken as inseparable. Fox and Lears (1983), however, see consumer culture as having been founded on the culture of a dominant white male elite for turn-of-the-century United States. See also, however, Gordon and McArthur (1985).

25 For a critical assessment of trickle-down effects, see Fine and Leopold (1993: Chapter 11).

26 For critical assessments of post-Fordism, see Sayer (1989), Pollert (1991) and Fine (1995a, 1998a: Chapter 4).

27 For an early, more favourable but questioning assessment of postmodernism, see Harvey (1989). See also Callinicos (1989).

9 Whatever happened to public consumption?

1 For presentation and critique, see Fine and Leopold (1993: Chapter 17), but especially Gurney (1999: 64) for failure of form of housing tenure to hold fixed relationships to other practices, especially representations of status or identity – 'our existing "common-sense" knowledge about home owners and local authority tenants … is at best partial and at worst prejudicial'.

2 The notion of collective consumption was popularised by Manuel Castells in the context of urban studies. As will be seen, it is not surprising that it should only enjoy a short life.

3 And as Baudrillard (1998: 32) argues in his early work: 'Consumer goods thus present themselves as *a harnessing of power*, not as products embodying work'. For an excellent

illustration, see Burke's (1996) account of the selling of cosmetics to black Zimbabweans.

4 See Wyrwa (1998) for the idea that questioning consumption tends to involve a critical element – although the notion of consumer sovereignty is an exception. However, Livingston (1998) is wrong to suggest such critiques of consumer society inevitably involve a nostalgia for the artisan, traditional female roles and a failure to embrace a world opening up to the pleasures of, and potential for, subjectivity.

5 See Uusitalo (1998) for the idea that ecological preferences represent a form of collective consumption. See also contributions to *Capital and Class*, no.72, Autumn, 2000.

6 See Johns and Vural (2000) for a recent illustration.

7 This is unwittingly acknowledged by Chaney (1998: 535) without drawing out the implications offered here: 'the increasing importance of consumer issues has fundamentally blurred distinctions between public and private spheres'.

8 Note, even if in the most crass way, the Blair government's response in 2000 to protests against the price of fuel is systemic – lower taxes on fuel means higher interest rates and lower pensions.

9 In the context of food, this has yielded what Fischler (1980, 1988, 1989) terms the omnivore's paradox – capacity to eat anything but fear of poisoning. For a critique, see Fine (1993b, 1998c: Chapter 2) and Chapter 11. But food poisoning and safety, for example, are increasingly a matter of public concern and not just private care and knowledge.

10 See McNally (1993: 112) in quoting E. P. Thompson: 'One of the great achievements of Owenism was that it taught many working-class radicals "to see capitalism, not as a collection of discrete events, but as a *system*".'

11 For a close review of the literature on labour chits, see Saad-Filho (1993).

12 Note, this is not the same as the working class as workers collectively consuming all that they produce. As Marx indicates in the *Critique of the Gotha Programme*, it is necessary to make allowance for those who are incapable of work, for the social expenses of production, and for investment for future production.

13 Marx is equally scathing over the analytical content underlying such schemes, not least in his critique of Proudhon. See Oishi (2001) for a recent commentary on the relationship between Marx and Proudhon.

14 See Bowring (1998) for a contemporary assessment.

15 As will be apparent, what follows depends heavily on Furlough (1991), but see also Gurney (1996) and Furlough and Strikwerda (1999).

16 See also Cooper (1998).

17 For an account of the National Consumer League to the present day, focusing on the New Deal era, see Storrs (2000). She finds it at the fore in struggling for minimum wages and improvement in working conditions, but also needing to finesse between progress for women (and children) and for the working class as a whole. Ultimately, 'in the 1990s the NCL was a lead organization on President Clinton's antisweatshop task force' (p. 2).

18 It would also be appropriate to relate public consumption to (corporate) welfare capitalism (see Cohen (1990) for an illustration), to pension funds (and their potentially 'ethical' application; see Blackburn (1999) for a recent contribution) and to profit-related pay (PRP) and employee shareownership plans (ESOPs) (see Fine (2000b) for a critical assessment).

19 See also Finnegan (1999) for the relationship between the suffragette movement and consumerism in the United States. More critically on consumerism and citizenship, see also Cronin (2000: 174) who closes:

> 'Consumer citizenship' may be an emergent rhetoric of defining belonging, but it is one based on *new forms* of exclusion and subordination which actively redefine categories of 'race', gender and national/European belonging.

20 Equally, this all induces a counter-reaction in which it is denied that simple measures are appropriate for individual or social welfare or whatever.

21 See Zelizer's (1987) outstanding account of the shifting evaluation of children from little workers to priceless offspring over the past century.

22 See Carter (1998) for a mercifully rare account of the welfare state from a postmodernist framework.

23 Cited in Radin (1996: 75–6).

24 See Gilliatt *et al.* (2000) for an excellent discussion of public services and the use of consumer 'empowerment' to retain rather than to devolve or reallocate responsibility and control.

10 Welfarism in light of globalisation

1 But see MERG (1993) in which I contributed the section on social and economic infrastructure. Here, despite many common features inherited from the South African apartheid system across various welfare programmes, is shown how outcomes, challenges and prospects have been very different – from health to education, and from housing to electrification. This prognosis has been fully borne out by subsequent developments.

2 This example is taken from Besley and Coate (1995) and is discussed more fully in Fine (1998a: Chapter 4) including a workfare scheme which brings further refinement to social stratification.

3 Not an entirely appropriate term for mainstream economics for, underlying all of its analysis, is the notion that all work is undesirable to the individual, a 'bad' as opposed to a good, thereby inducing disutility. For a critique, see Spencer (1998).

4 But see also Taylor-Gooby (2000a) on 'risk and welfare' and 'trust' as well, Taylor-Gooby (2000b). Quadagno (1999) places the intellectual context of the shifting understanding of the welfare state in more worldly terms, reflecting the realities of the increasing influence of finance and the market:

> Social insurance beneficiaries have become unfunded liabilities; the grand distributional issues of the day have become budget dilemmas; the objective of social welfare expenditures has become to increase savings and investments.

This view is stunningly confirmed, for example, by Tanzi's (2000) working paper for the IMF, where globalisation is seen as undermining the capacity of the nation-state to raise tax revenue, thereby justifying the greater participation of the private sector in sourcing welfare provision.

5 This would follow Mancur Olson's theory of collective action which ultimately suggests high gains and low costs for small groups and, potentially, vice versa for large groups.

6 He has also served as Chair of the Committee for awarding the Nobel Prize in Economics but was forced into resignation as 'the indirect result of a worldwide protest about the continuous bias toward neoliberal economics in awarding the Nobel Prize' (Navarro 1999: 674). See also Navarro's comments on Lindbeck's 'faulty data and sloppy work' and its adoption by Giddens in promoting the Third Way. Frank Field (1996: 19) is Lindbeck's political counterpart in the UK in the way in which he understands behavioural responses to the social security system:

> Self-interest, not altruism, is mankind's main driving force.

7 Andersen *et al.* (1995) provide a sequence of papers constructing the welfare state as a response to market imperfections. More generally, the *Journal of Public Economics* is full of such models.

8 This is a perverse counterexample to Mason's (1998: 160) observation that

the emphasis on mathematical economics and econometrics has, at the least, marginalised research into the causes and effects of consumption for status and display.

9 For the limited understanding of history as path dependence or multiple equilibria, see Fine (2000d).

10 See also Suzumura (1999: 127) for whom:

> The task of the *welfare economics of the welfare state* ... is to deliberately design the main system – the competitive mechanism – and three sub-systems – the competition policy sub-system, the coordination policy sub-system, and the social security sub-system – of the welfare state so that the whole system will be incentive-compatible and work effectively. The task of the *ethics of the welfare state* is to clarify the philosophical foundations of the welfare state policies on the informational basis of individual advantages.

11 Leading to criticism of traditional methods for assessing economic performance (e.g. Stewart 1996). For assessment of Sen's approach, see special issue of *Journal of International Development* (Cameron and Gasper 2000). Note that others, such as Tony Atkinson, are also prepared to fight Lindbeck and the like on their own analytical terrain. See Atkinson (1995b, 1997) and Lindbeck (1997). See also Atkinson (1999a) for an excellent critique of the 'transatlantic consensus' on the inevitability of rising inequality but one entirely based on the social as derived from micro-foundations. Note that Atkinson (1999b: 187) closes as follows: 'Calls by economists for rolling back the welfare state are themselves part of the political process; we have not just endogenous politicians but also endogenous economists, whose behavior has to be explained'. But he offers no explanation himself for this example of the new phase of economics imperialism.

12 Blundell *et al.* (1994a: 41) also express the need to take account of rights, entitlements and obligations but ultimately, as leading theoretical and empirical practitioners, their goal is 'how to measure social welfare, inequality and poverty from individual welfare measures'.

13 I have explored this tension in some detail in an assessment of the literature induced by Sen's entitlement approach to famine (Fine 1997d). See also Fine (2001b).

14 Even so, Laybourn (1995: 10) suggests that there have been eight approaches to the study of the British welfare state – Whig, pragmatic, bureaucratic, ideological, conspiratorial, capitalistic, democratic and the latter's generalisation as pluralism.

15 It led Klein (1993) to dub their approach 'O'Goffe's Tale'.

16 Note how the use of the term social capital introduced by O'Connor has been entirely overlooked in the social capital literature that has shot to prominence over the last decade (Fine 2001a).

17 Block (1990) also points to the crudeness of the legitimation versus accumulation framework as do Friedland and Sanders (1990) in questioning simple substitutability between private and social 'wages'. Esping-Andersen (1994: 714) perceives O'Goffe as functionalist and economic reductionist for perceiving the welfare state as resolving the contradictions of capitalism. For more general critique of Gough's political economy and debate with him, see Fine and Harris (1976, 1979) and Gough (1975).

18 Offe (1995) has also succumbed to the globalisation limits to the welfare state analytical syndrome.

19 This is in effect a special case of a more general argument that social and political democracy itself is undermined by globalisation, as in Wilber (1998) for example.

20 That this is empirically false is established by Swank (1998).

21 See Alber and Standing (2000) for a critical exposition of the inevitability of social dumping, and its association with the 'recommodification' of labour. See also Bonoli *et al.* (2000).

22 Interestingly, Glyn (1998), a longstanding and leading proponent of the (international) profit-squeeze hypothesis, considers that the crisis of the welfare state continues to derive from intra-national conflicts and the global at most serves in an ideological contagion role.

23 See, for example, Geyer (1998), Clayton and Pontusson (1998), Myles and Pierson (1997), Fazeli (1996), Pierson (1996, 1998b) and Pierson (1994) for various interpretations of the crisis of the welfare state as obituary, restructuring or resilience, etc. See also Navarro (2000) and van Kersbergen (2000) for the idea that the welfare state remains resilient, and Kuhnle (2000) for comparative West European experience.

24 See also Ferrera and Rhodes (2000: 9) in their introduction to an edited collection:

> In sum, the process of welfare state 'recasting' involves a number of dimensions of change in response to a set of pressures which are largely domestically generated. Globalisation is compatible with several different institutional and normative projects, including those projects that aim at reconciling the imperatives of economic growth with the quest for more cohesion, solidarity and 'real' freedom.

25 For a critical assessment of this voluminous literature, see Fine (2000a).

26 Post-Fordism might be thought to provide an alternative avenue along which to pursue the political economy of the welfare state. Its increasingly exposed theoretical and empirical weaknesses have, however, predominantly left it high and dry in the face of such an applied topic. The boldest attempt has been made by Jessop (1994) in positing the shift from a Keynesian welfare to a Schumpeterian workfare system. More generally, see Burrows and Loader (1994) and the collection in *Environment and Planning A*, vol. 27, no. 10, 1995. Essentially, this work does little more than engage in conceptual translations and over-generalisations, with a theory that 'was developed at a more abstract (but still intermediate) level and needs to be concretized *and complexified* for the analysis of any specific historical object' (Jessop 1995: 1623). Pinch (1994: 222) is more blunt if still unduly positive:

> Post-Fordist concepts are beginning to look like an ornate sandcastle that is rapidly being engulfed by a tide of criticism. Yet a few battered turrets – such as the flexible-firm model – still remain. If used carefully, such concepts can provide insights into the complex character of recent changes in the welfare state.

See also Harris and McDonald (2000) who provide a comparative case study of personal social service provision in the UK and Australia. They point to the insensitivity of the post-Fordist approach to the differences in programmes and institutions, and the mimetics involved in imposing an industrial metaphor. Their own attempt to rescue the approach – by reference to spread of managerialism, development of quasi-markets, and shifts from users to customers, from unitary to mixed models of delivery, and in relations between central and local state – is, however, marked by a departure from anything specifically post-Fordist in content.

27 See also Gornick and Jacobs (1998: 692):

> Largely due to Esping-Andersen's (1990) influence, it is now commonplace for scholars of the welfare state to focus on welfare state regime types (i.e. groups of countries with similar characteristics).

28 See, for the interim, Esping-Andersen (1996a, b).

29 Before comparing and classifying welfare states, account should be taken of the conceptual and empirical difficulties laid out in Spicker (1995: Chapter 13).

30 See also Kloosterman (1994) who argues that the Netherlands is not German-like, as suggested by Esping-Andersen, in its labour market response to 'post-industrialism' (since it has not depended on growth in service sector employment). See also Goodin *et al.* (1999) for the Netherlands as an anomalous social democratic regime. Ultimately, this leads Goodin (2001) to pose the Netherlands as a post-productivist regime, one for which the non-utopian claim is made (p. 16):

> On the 'work' side of the ledger, the problem is presented more as one of rationing jobs than of filling them. On the 'welfare' side of the ledger, the problem is presented as one of decoupling income from paid labour, securing a decent level of income for those who (by choice or necessity) fail to secure one for themselves in the ordinary labour market.

31 And differences in benefits are perceived as 'screening out the rich rather than, more narrowly, "screening in" only the abject poor' (Esping-Andersen 1999: 75).

32 See Peng (2000) for a critique of Esping-Andersen on Japan. Jones (1993) includes contributions which demonstrate how Esping-Andersen needs to be refined to accommodate European welfare states let alone those of Asia.

33 For an overview of Mediterranean welfare states, see Rhodes (1997b) and also Katrougalos (1996) and Ferrera (1996). See also Cousins (1997) who, in the context of Ireland, suggests that Esping-Andersen neglects relevance of core and periphery in the functioning of the world system, as well as religion and farming!

34 Ultimately, Esping-Andersen (1999: 11) is drawn to the conclusion that 'a sound understanding of postindustrial society must be anchored in the household economy'.

35 Esping-Andersen's (1999: 86–7) upbeat and explicit response to three more sophisticated studies, as providing 'some support for the three clusters' is misplaced. Shalev (1996a) finds five of eighteen countries do not fit into the three clusters, Kangas (1994) finds some support but it is highly limited by time, countries and programmes, and Ragin (1994) rejects his hypothesis. More generally, Janoski and Hicks (1994a, b) see rational choice as one of four models for future work on the political economy of the welfare state, the others depending on more sophisticated structural statistical work, tagged to more qualitative hypotheses. But see van Kersbergen (1995) for the argument that improved data and statistical techniques will not suffice to settle disputes over interpretation of the number and incidence of welfare regimes.

36 Hence, Gough (2000c: 19) advises: 'One thing we can be certain of: globalisation will not call forth uniform policy responses in the [East Asian] region, let alone across the developing world'. In a personal communication, however, Gough concedes: 'I think the most powerful critique of WRs [welfare regimes] is the one you mention – that it varies so much according to social programme'.

37 This leads Taylor-Gooby (1996) to launch a critique of Esping-Andersen for not taking sufficient account of inertia, institutions, politics and dynamics in general.

38 As O'Connor (1996: 107) puts it:

> This complexity can only be captured by an analysis that recognizes the welfare state as a mechanism of stratification that can simultaneously deal with structuring by class and gender, and in some countries race.

See Claramunt and Arroyo (2000) for a review of PRT, and a qualified attempt to apply it to post-Franco Spain. Note, though, that Navarro and Shi (2001) perceive the need for a fourth ex-fascist welfare regime in considering the politics of social inequalities and health.

39 Here, there is an interesting parallel with bringing the (developmental) state back in

literature for which increasingly refined concepts around autonomy and embedded-ness are introduced to accommodate the mounting variety in state types – just as new welfare regimes or hybrids are required. See Fine and Rustomjee (1997: Chapter 3) and Fine (2001c).

40 As O'Connor (1996) more modestly puts it, there is a need to move beyond women as an issue to gender as a dimension of analysis. For consideration of gender and the welfare state, a rapidly growing literature, see also, for example, O'Connor *et al.* (1999), Haney (1998) and Cousins (1999).

41 See also Esping-Andersen (2000a).

42 See also Esping-Andersen (2000d: 69) with its acknowledged debt for his most recent work to that of Gershuny (1978, 1988). The latter is essentially a sticky comparative advantage version of the new household economics, with social factors impeding the economic.

43 Note the affinities with the newly emerging approach of the World Bank, as revealed in Holzmann and Jørgensen (2000), for example.

44 Esping-Andersen (1999: 37) indicates the 'discussion is indebted to the work of Barr (1993)', now in a third edition (Barr 1998), an entirely orthodox economics text. Thus, Esping-Andersen (2000a: 7) adopts the vernacular:

> Most welfare states, therefore, have moved from a positive-sum to a negative-sum-trade-off; they not only are increasingly unsustainable but are arguably hindering an optimal welfare-efficiency combination.

45 See also Esping-Andersen (2000b: 2) for evidence of shift in approach with the idea that 'welfare policy ... can base itself on two distinct "philosophies". The most widespread is to define the issue in terms of *social risks*. The alternative is to focus on resource command or, to follow Amartya Sen, *capabilities*', to which he adds basic needs, opting for a longitudinal monitoring of outcomes.

46 His irony is in response to postmodernism, but see debate with Hay (1998) who is less concerned with the new sociology as much as the new economic ideology of no alternative.

47 See Daly and Lewis (2000), for example, for an attempt to unpick the complex and shifting understandings attached to social care in the context of the welfare state. They are appropriately concerned with the extent to which the welfare regime literature has focused on cash benefits. On a different tack, see Ervasti (2001) who shows that (Finnish) middle-class support for the welfare state does not collapse in the face of post-industrialism as suggested by the saturation as opposed to the irreversibility hypothesis.

48 Thus, for Goodin and Mitchell (2000a: xiii) in introducing their edited collection on the welfare state:

> Thinking in terms of 'regime types' ... serves to limit policy innovation by tying all aspects of socio-economic policy together in a tight package. ... The rigidities of regime logic prevent mixing and matching, even among the very familiar components of the policy package that constitutes the modern welfare state.

See also Spicker (2000: 1–2) who suggests of both Titmuss and Esping-Anderson that 'these models have important deficiencies, and the kinds of generalization they make are difficult to relate to welfare states in practice'. His alternative, however, builds up a general theory of the welfare state from a wide-ranging notion of collectively expressed individualism. See also Spicker (1996).

49 He attempts to bring together three clusters of welfare state research – political economy, gender and developmentalism. For a theoretical and empirical critique of

the retrenchment hypothesis from the perspective of the logic of industrialism, the contradictions of capitalism, and the hypothesis of nation-state building, see Scarbrough (2000).

11 Whither consumption studies?

1 Reference is made to earlier work providing detailed studies and references for those who wish to follow them up.
2 See also Petridou (2001) with Greek dairy industry as case study.
3 But see also Hoff *et al.* (1993) for influential application of the new information-theoretic economics to rural development issues.
4 For a retrospective account, see Bernstein and Byres (2001), for example. See also Buttel (2001) for discussion of many of the issues to follow.
5 See Fine *et al.* (1996: Chapter 3) for commentary.
6 For a telling recent illustration, see the special issue on 'changing agro-food and fiber systems in Asia' edited by Thompson and Cowan (2000). In commenting on the far from accidental merits of the studies of Chari (2000) and Ramamurthy (2000), they fail to recognise that globalisation is not so much grounded as operating as an analytical constraint (that can be overlooked at a more general level) (pp. 405–6):

> These two papers bring together the interconnections between industrial and agricultural sectors, between the urban and the rural, between the local and the global, and between production and consumption that are less detailed in the other papers. Further they provide examples of the types of spatially specific, historical, and commodity-chain analyses needed to better ground globalization processes empirically.

7 Note that Gereffi (2001) continues to posit the two ideal types of producer- and seller-driven global commodity chains, cars and clothes, respectively.
8 See also Goodman (1997), Burch *et al.* (1996) (and special issue of *Rural Sociology*, vol. 64, no. 2, 1999) for a number of arguments and case studies, Murdoch and Miele (1999) for quality and organic in products for eggs and meat, Roche *et al.* (1999) global apple industries, and Renard (1999) for fair coffee.
9 See Fine (2001f) for critical account of ANT in the context of both food and economics imperialism.
10 Note, in parallel, that Marx's theory of the (capitalist) labour process is also about the material and social production of surplus value.
11 Note, in passing, that the Presidential Address to the US Agricultural History Society (Coclanis 1998) addresses 'Food Chains'.
12 See Busch and Juska (1997) for the bringing together of ANT, the global and Canadian rapeseed.
13 See Miller (1995a) for the more general argument of displacement or distancing of the consumer from the producer.
14 Thus, Juanillo (2001) argues that there are inherent difficulties for public participation in food science issues because of their technical difficulty and the dangers of hijacking by the, possibly wilfully, ignorant.
15 On food scares and the media, see MacIntyre *et al.* (1998).
16 One model is of government proscribing health claims, the other is to allow them to be harnessed to commerce with healthy information and foods driving out the bad. See Ippolito (1999) for a more general discussion, and Fine (1998c: Chapter 4) for a critique on this and other such issues.
17 Hence the ESRC's UK Nation's Diet Programme (Murcott 1998). Bring in social scientists when the scientists fail. Even so, corresponding research on nutrition still remains dominated by how to make healthy products more palatable.

18 As Schlosser (2001: 4) reveals, McDonald's makes more 'profit' out of its property portfolio than out of selling food. Note that another vital issue for supermarkets and fast-food chains is how they relate to labour markets.

19 See also Delind (2000: 198) who, in referring to the 'O-word', argues:

> This paper questions whether national standards designed to increase national and international commerce and thus 'grow the [organic] industry' can produce anything other than a slightly 'greener' version of the existing agrofood system.

20 See also Buttel (1999) and Rifkin (1998).

21 In this light, it is worrisome, in the context of retailing, that Lowe and Wrigley (1996) and Blomley (1996) should consider the bringing together of culture and economy to be more important than how it is done – in response to critique by Fine and Leopold (1993: Chapter 20) denying that retailing defines a meaningful category of capital. See D. Clarke (1996) for spirited support of the latter's position.

22 For simple exposition of the technical formalities of the semantic and syntactic in the context of advertising, see Messaris (1997: vii–xxi), and for a diagrammatic representation of the logic of sign value, see Goldman and Papson (1996: 22).

23 As the reviewer for Fine *et al.* (1996) kindly put it in the *Economic Journal*, Cameron (1998: 1590), 'this is an interesting book, but is hardly going to be required reading for many economists'.

REFERENCES

Adshead, S. (1997) *Material Culture in Europe and China, 1400–1800: The Rise of Consumerism*, London: Macmillan.

Agnes, P. (2000) 'The "End of Geography" in Financial Services? Local Embeddedness and Territorialization in the Interest Rate Swaps Industry', *Economic Geography*, vol. 76, no. 4, pp. 347–66.

Agnew, J. (1993) 'Coming up for Air: Consumer Culture in Historical Perspective', in J. Brewer and R. Porter (eds) *Consumption and the World of Goods*, London: Routledge.

Akerlof, G. (1970) 'The Market for "Lemons": Quality Uncertainty and the Market Mechanism', *Quarterly Journal of Economics*, vol. 84, no. 3, pp. 488–500.

Akerlof, G. (1982) 'Labor Contracts as Partial Gift Exchange', *Quarterly Journal of Economics*, vol. 97, no. 4, pp. 543–69, reprinted in G. Akerlof (1984) *An Economic Theorist's Book of Tales*, Cambridge: Cambridge University Press.

Akerlof, G. (1984) *An Economic Theorist's Book of Tales*, Cambridge: Cambridge University Press.

Akerlof, G. (1990) 'George A. Akerlof', in R. Swedberg (ed.) *Economics and Sociology, Redefining Their Boundaries: Conversations with Economists and Sociologists*, Princeton, NJ: Princeton University Press..

Alber, J. and G. Standing (2000) 'Social Dumping, Catch-Up, or Convergence? Europe in a Comparative Global Context', *Journal of European Social Policy*, vol. 10, no. 2, pp. 99–119.

Albrow, M. *et al.* (1997) 'The Impact of Globalization on Sociological Concepts: Community, Culture and Milieu', in J. Eade (ed.) *Living the Global City: Globalization as Local Process*, London: Routledge.

Alfino, M. (1998) 'Postmodern Hamburgers: Taking a Postmodern Attitude toward McDonald's', in M. Alfino *et al.* (eds) *McDonaldization Revisited: Critical Essays on Consumer Culture*, Westport, CT: Praeger.

Alfino, M. *et al.* (eds) (1998) *McDonaldization Revisited: Critical Essays on Consumer Culture*, Westport, CT: Praeger.

Alt, J. (1976) 'Beyond Class: The Decline of Industrial Labor and Leisure', *Telos*, no. 28, Summer, pp. 55–80.

Amariglio, J. and D. Ruccio (1999) 'The Transgressive Knowledge of "Ersatz" Economics', in R. Garnett (ed.) *What Do Economists Know?: New Economics of Knowledge*, London: Routledge.

Amin, A. and N. Thrift (1994a) 'Living in the Global', in A. Amin and N. Thrift (eds) *Globalization, Institutions, and Regional Development in Europe*, Oxford: Oxford University Press.

Amin, A. and N. Thrift (1994b) 'Holding Down the Global', in A. Amin and N. Thrift (eds) *Globalization, Institutions, and Regional Development in Europe*, Oxford: Oxford University Press.

Amin, A. and N. Thrift (eds) (1994c) *Globalization, Institutions, and Regional Development in Europe*, Oxford: Oxford University Press.

Andersen, T. *et al.* (eds) (1995) *The Future of the Welfare State*, Oxford: Blackwell.

Andrews, M. and M. Talbot (2000a) 'Introduction: Women in Consumer Culture', in M. Andrews and M. Talbot (eds) *All the World and Her Husband: Women in Twentieth-Century Consumer Culture*, London: Cassell.

Andrews, M. and M. Talbot (eds) (2000b) *All the World and Her Husband: Women in Twentieth-Century Consumer Culture*, London: Cassell.

Antle, J. (1999) 'The New Economics of Agriculture', *American Journal of Agricultural Economics*, vol. 81, no. 5, pp. 993–1010.

Appadurai, A. (1986a) 'Introduction: Commodities and the Politics of Value', in A. Appadurai (ed.) *The Social Life of Things: Commodities in Cultural Perspective*, Cambridge: Cambridge University Press.

Appadurai, A. (ed.) (1986b) *The Social Life of Things: Commodities in Cultural Perspective*, Cambridge: Cambridge University Press.

Appadurai, A. (1996) *Modernity at Large: Cultural Dimensions of Globalization*, Minneapolis: University of Minnesota Press.

Appadurai, A. (1997) 'Consumption, Duration, and History', in D. Palumbo-Liu and H. Gumbrecht (eds) *Streams of Cultural Capital*, Stanford, CA: Stanford University Press.

Appadurai, A. (2000) 'Grassroots Globalization and the Research Imagination', *Public Culture*, vol. 12, no. 1, pp. 1–19.

Arce, A. and E. Fisher (1999) 'The Accountability of Commodities in a Global Market Place: The Cases of Bolivian Coca and Tanzanian Honey', in R. Fardon *et al.* (eds) *Modernity on a Shoestring: Dimensions of Globalization, Consumption and Development in Africa and Beyond*, Leiden: EIDOS.

Archibugi, D. and J. Michie (eds) (1997) *Technology, Globalisation and Economic Performance*, Cambridge: Cambridge University Press.

Ashkenazi, M. and J. Clammer (2000a) 'Introduction: The Japanese and Their Goods', in M. Ashkenazi and J. Clammer (eds) *Consumption and Material Culture in Contemporary Japan*, London: Kegan Paul International.

Ashkenazi, M. and J. Clammer (eds) (2000b) *Consumption and Material Culture in Contemporary Japan*, London: Kegan Paul International.

Aston, T. and C. Philpin (eds) (1985) *The Brenner Debate: Agrarian Class Structure and Economic Development in Pre-Industrial Europe*, Cambridge: Cambridge University Press.

Atkinson, A. (1995a) 'Capabilities, Exclusion, and the Supply of Goods', in K. Basu *et al.* (eds) *Choice, Welfare, and Development: A Festschrift in Honour of Amartya K. Sen*, Oxford: Clarendon Press.

Atkinson, A. (1995b) 'Is the Welfare State Necessarily an Obstacle to Economic Growth?', *European Economic Review*, vol. 39, pp. 723–70.

Atkinson, A. (1997) 'The Economics of the Welfare State: An Incomplete Debate', in EC (1997) *The Welfare State in Europe: Challenges and Reforms, European Economy*, no. 4, Luxembourg: Official Publications of the European Communities.

Atkinson, A. (1999a) 'Is Rising Inequality Inevitable? A Critique of the Transatlantic Consensus', Third WIDER Annual Lecture, Helsinki.

Atkinson, A. (1999b) *The Economic Consequences of Rolling Back the Welfare State*, Cambridge, MA: MIT Press.

Auslander, L. (1996a) *Taste and Power: Furnishing Modern France*, Berkeley, CA: University of California Press.

Auslander, L. (1996b) 'The Gendering of Consumer Practices in Nineteenth-Century France', in V. de Grazia and E. Furlough (eds) *The Sex of Things: Gender and Consumption in Historical Perspective*, London: University of California Press.

Aybar S. and C. Lapavitsas (2001) 'Financial System Design and the Post-Washington Consensus', in B. Fine *et al.* (eds) *Neither Washington Nor Post-Washington Consensus: Challenging Development Policy in the Twenty-First Century*, London: Routledge.

Bairoch, P. (2000) 'The Constituent Economic Principles of Globalization in Historical Perspective: Myths and Realities', *International Sociology*, vol. 15, no. 2, pp. 197–214.

Bairoch, P. and R. Kozul-Wright (1996) 'Globalization Myths: Some Historical Reflections on Integration, Industrialization and Growth in the World Economy', UNCTAD Discussion Paper, no. 113.

Baldarassi, M. *et al.* (eds) (1996) *Equity, Efficiency and Growth: The Future of the Welfare State*, London: Macmillan.

Ball, M. (1983) *Housing Policy and Economic Power: The Political Economy of Owner Occupation*, London: Methuen.

Banks, R. (1985) *Continental Drift*, New York: Harper and Row.

Barnes, R. and J. Eicher (1992a) 'Introduction', in R. Barnes and J. Eicher (eds) *Dress and Gender: Making and Meaning in Cultural Context*, Oxford: Berg.

Barnes, R. and J. Eicher (eds) (1992b) *Dress and Gender: Making and Meaning in Cultural Context*, Oxford: Berg.

Baron, J. and M. Hannan (1994) 'The Impact of Economics on Contemporary Sociology', *Journal of Economic Literature*, vol. XXXII, no. 3, pp. 1111–46.

Barr, N. (1998) *The Economics of the Welfare State*, third edition, Oxford: Oxford University Press.

Bartelson, J. (2000) 'Three Concepts of Globalization', *International Sociology*, vol. 15, no. 2, pp. 180–96.

Barthel, D. (1989) 'Modernism and Marketing: The Chocolate Box Revisited', *Theory, Culture and Society*, vol. 6, August, pp. 429–38.

Barthes, R. (1985) *The Fashion System*, London: Jonathan Cape.

Basu, K. *et al.* (eds) (1995) *Choice, Welfare, and Development: A Festschrift in Honour of Amartya K. Sen*, Oxford: Clarendon Press.

Baudrillard, J. (1981) *For a Critique of the Political Economy of the Sign*, St Louis, MO: Telos Press.

Baudrillard, J. (1988) *Selected Writings*, London: Polity Press.

Baudrillard, J. (1998) *The Consumer Society: Myths and Structures*, London: Sage (original of 1970).

Baylis, J. and S. Smith (1997a) 'Introduction', in J. Baylis and S. Smith (eds) *The Globalization of World Politics: An Introduction to International Relations*, Oxford: Oxford University Press.

Baylis, J. and S. Smith (eds) (1997b) *The Globalization of World Politics: An Introduction to International Relations*, Oxford: Oxford University Press.

Beck, U. (2000) *What is Globalization?*, Cambridge: Polity Press.

Becker, G. (1965) 'A Theory of the Allocation of Time', *Economic Journal*, vol. 75, no. 299, pp. 493–517.

Becker, G. (1990) 'Gary S. Becker', in R. Swedberg (ed.) *Economics and Sociology, Redefining Their Boundaries: Conversations with Economists and Sociologists*, Princeton, NJ: Princeton University Press.

Becker, G. (1991) *A Treatise on the Family*, Cambridge, MA: Harvard University Press.

Becker, G. (1992) 'Habits, Addictions, and Traditions', *Kyklos*, vol. 45, no. 3, pp. 327–46.

Becker, G. (1993) *Human Capital: A Theoretical and Empirical Analysis, with Special Reference to Education*, third edition, London: University of Chicago Press.

Becker, G. (1996) *Accounting for Tastes*, Cambridge, MA: Harvard University Press.

Becker, G. and K. Murphy (1988) 'A Theory of Rational Addiction', *Journal of Political Economy*, vol. 96, no. 4, pp. 675–700.

Becker, G. *et al.* (1994) 'An Empirical Analysis of Cigarette Addiction', *American Economic Review*, vol. 84, no. 3, pp. 396–418.

Belk, R. (1995) *Collecting in a Consumer Society*, London: Routledge.

Beng-Huat, C. (2000a) 'Consuming Asians: Ideas and Issues', in C. Beng-Huat (ed.) *Consumption in Asia: Lifestyles and Identities*, London: Routledge.

Beng-Huat, C. (2000b) 'Singaporeans Ingesting McDonald's', in C. Beng-Huat (ed.) *Consumption in Asia: Lifestyles and Identities*, London: Routledge.

Beng-Huat, C. (ed.) (2000c) *Consumption in Asia: Lifestyles and Identities*, London: Routledge.

Ben-Shachar, A. (1984) 'Demand versus Supply in the Industrial Revolution: A Comment', *Journal of Economic History*, vol. 44, no. 3, September, pp. 801–5.

Benson, J. (1994) *The Rise of Consumer Society in Britain, 1880–1980*, London: Longman.

Berg, M. (1998) 'Product Innovation in Core Consumer Industries in Eighteenth-Century Britain', in M. Berg and K. Bruland (eds) *Technological Revolutions in Europe: Historical Perspectives*, Cheltenham: Edward Elgar.

Berg, M. and K. Bruland (eds) (1998) *Technological Revolutions in Europe: Historical Perspectives*, Cheltenham: Edward Elgar.

Berg, M. and H. Clifford (eds) (1999) *Consumers and Luxury: Consumer Culture in Europe, 1650–1850*, Manchester: Manchester University Press.

Berger, S. (1996) 'Introduction', in S. Berger and R. Dore (eds) *National Diversity and Global Capitalism*, Ithaca, NY: Cornell University Press.

Berger, S. and R. Dore (eds) (1996) *National Diversity and Global Capitalism*, Ithaca, NY: Cornell University Press.

Bermingham, A. (1995) 'Introduction: The Consumption of Culture: Image, Object, Text', in A. Bermingham and J. Brewer (eds) *The Consumption of Culture, 1600–1800: Image, Object, Text*, London: Routledge.

Bermingham, A. and J. Brewer (eds) (1995) *The Consumption of Culture, 1600–1800: Image, Object, Text*, London: Routledge.

Bernstein, H. and T. Byres (2001) 'From Peasant Studies to Agrarian Change', *Journal of Agrarian Change*, vol. 1, no. 1, pp. 1–56.

Besley, T. and S. Coate (1995) 'The Design of Income Maintenance Programmes', *Review of Economic Studies*, vol. 62, no. 2, pp. 187–221.

Bianchi, M. (ed.) (1998) *The Active Consumer: Novelty and Surprise in Consumer Choice*, London: Routledge.

Bishop, R. and L. Robinson (1998) *Night Market: Sexual Cultures and the Thai Economic Miracle*, London: Routledge.

Blackburn, R. (1999) 'The New Collectivism: Pension Reform, Grey Capitalism and Complex Socialism', *New Left Review*, no. 233, pp. 3–65.

Blaug, M. (1980) *The Methodology of Economics: Or How Economists Explain*, Cambridge: Cambridge University Press.

Blaug, M. (1988) *Economics Through the Looking Glass: The Distorted Perspective of the New Palgrave Dictionary of Economics*, Occasional Paper, no. 78, London: Institute of Economic Affairs.

Block, F. (1990) 'Political Choice and the Multiple "Logics" of Capital', in S. Zukin and P. DiMaggio (eds) *Structures of Capital: The Social Organization of the Economy*, Cambridge: Cambridge University Press.

Blomley, N. (1996) 'I'd Like to Dress Her All Over: Masculinity, Power and Retail Space', in N. Wrigley and M. Lowe (eds) *Retailing, Consumption and Capital: Towards the New Retail Geography*, London: Longman.

Blundell, R. (1988) 'Consumer Behaviour: Theory and Empirical Evidence – A Survey', *Economic Journal*, vol. 98, March, pp. 16–65.

Blundell, R. *et al.* (1994a) 'An Introduction to Applied Welfare Analysis', in R. Blundell *et al.* (eds) *The Measurement of Household Welfare*, Cambridge: Cambridge University Press.

Blundell, R. *et al.* (eds) (1994b) *The Measurement of Household Welfare*, Cambridge: Cambridge University Press.

Boland, L. (1997) *Critical Economic Methodology: A Personal Odyssey*, London: Routledge.

Bonoli, G. *et al.* (2000) *European Welfare Futures: Towards a Theory of Retrenchment*, London: Polity Press.

Boorstin, D. (1973) *The Americans: The Democratic Experience*, New York: Random House.

Bourdieu, P. (1977) *Outline of a Theory of Practice*, Cambridge: Cambridge University Press.

Bowden, S. (1990) 'Credit Facilities and the Growth of Consumer Demand for Electric Appliances in England in the 1930s', *Business History*, vol. 32, no. 1, pp. 52–75.

Bowden, S. and A. Offer (1994) 'Household Appliances and the Use of Time: The United States and Britain since the 1920s', *Economic History Review*, vol. XLVII, no. 4, pp. 725–48.

Bowden, S. and A. Offer (1996) 'The Technological Revolution that Never Was: Gender, Class, and the Diffusion of Household Appliances in Interwar England', in V. de Grazia and E. Furlough (eds) *The Sex of Things: Gender and Consumption in Historical Perspective*, London: University of California Press.

Bowden, S. and A. Offer (1999) 'Household Appliances and "Systems of Provision": A Reply', *Economic History Review*, vol. LII, no. 3, pp. 563–7.

Bowden, S. and P. Turner (1993) 'The Demand for Consumer Durables in the United Kingdom in the Interwar Period', *Journal of Economic History*, vol. 53, no. 2, pp. 244–58.

Bowring, F. (1998) 'LETS: An Eco-Socialist Alternative?', *New Left Review*, no. 232, pp. 91–111.

Boyer, R. (1996) 'The Convergence Hypothesis Revisited: Globalization but Still the Century of Nations', in S. Berger and R. Dore (eds) *National Diversity and Global Capitalism*, Ithaca, NY: Cornell University Press.

Boyer, R. and D. Drache (eds) (1996) *States Against Markets: The Limits of Globalization*, London: Routledge.

Braudel, H. (1974) *Capitalism and Material Life 1400–1800*, New York: Harper and Row.

Braun, B. and N. Castree (eds) (1998) *Remaking Reality: Nature at the Millennium*, London: Routledge.

Breen, T. (1986) 'An Empire of Goods: The Anglicization of Colonial America, 1690–1776', *Journal of British Studies*, vol. 25, October, pp. 467–99.

Breen, T. (1988) ' "Baubles of Britain": The American and Consumer Revolutions of the Eighteenth Century', *Past and Present*, no. 119, May, pp. 73–104.

Brewer, J. (1995) ' "The Most Polite Age and the Most Vicious": Attitudes towards Culture as a Commodity', in A. Bermingham and J. Brewer (eds) *The Consumption of Culture, 1600–1800: Image, Object, Text*, London: Routledge.

Brewer, J. and R. Porter (eds) (1993) *Consumption and the World of Goods*, London: Routledge.

British Council of Churches (1978) *The Consumer Goods Society*, London.

Brown, A. and A. Deaton (1972) 'Surveys in Applied Economics: Models of Consumer Behaviour', *Economic Journal*, vol. 82, December, pp. 1145–1236.

Bruland, K. (1985) 'Say's Law and the Single-Factor Explanation of British Industrialization: A Comment', *Journal of European Economic History*, vol. 14, no. 1, pp. 187–91.

Bruland, K. and P. O'Brien (eds) (1998) *From Family Firms to Corporate Capitalism: Essays in Business and Industrial History in Honour of Peter Mathias*, Oxford: Clarendon Press.

Brumann, C. (2000) 'Materialistic Culture: The Uses of Money in Tokyo Gift Exchanges', in M. Ashkenazi and J. Clammer (eds) *Consumption and Material Culture in Contemporary Japan*, London: Kegan Paul International.

Bryman, A. (1999) 'The Disneyization of Society', *Sociological Review*, vol. 47, no. 1, pp. 25–47.

Buck, D. *et al.* (1997) 'From Farm to Table: The Organic Vegetable Commodity Chain of Northern California', *Sociologia Ruralis*, vol. 37, no. 1, pp. 3–20.

Burch, D. *et al.* (eds) (1996) *Globalization and Agri-Food Restructuring: Perspectives from the Australasia Region*, Aldershot: Avebury.

Burgoyne, J. and D. Clarke (1983) 'You Are What You Eat: Food and Family Reconstitution', in A. Murcott (ed.) *The Sociology of Food and Eating*, Aldershot: Gower.

Burke, T. (1996) *Lifebuoy Men, Lux Women: Commodification, Consumption, and Cleanliness in Modern Zimbabwe*, London: Leicester University Press.

Burke, T. (1998) 'Cannibal Margarine and Reactionary Snapple: A Comparative Examination of Rumours about Commodities', *International Journal of Cultural Studies*, vol. 1, no. 2, pp. 253–70.

Burman, B. (1999a) 'Introduction', in B. Burman (ed.) *The Culture of Sewing: Gender, Consumption and Home Dressmaking*, Oxford: Berg.

Burman, B. (ed.) (1999b) *The Culture of Sewing: Gender, Consumption and Home Dressmaking*, Oxford: Berg.

Burnett, J. (1968) *Plenty and Want: A Social History of Diet in England from 1815 to the Present Day*, Harmondsworth: Pelican (third edition, 1989, London: Routledge).

Burrows, R. and B. Loader (eds) (1994) *Towards a Post-Fordist Welfare State?*, London: Routledge.

Burrows, R. and C. Marsh (eds) (1992) *Consumption and Class: Divisions and Change*, London: Macmillan.

Busch, L. and A. Juska (1997) 'Beyond Political Economy: Actor Networks and the Globalization of Agriculture', *Review of International Political Economy*, vol. 4, no. 4, pp. 688–708.

Buttel, F. (1996) 'Theoretical Issues in Global Agri-Food Restructuring', in D. Burch *et al.* (eds) *Globalization and Agri-Food Restructuring: Perspectives from the Australasia Region*, Aldershot: Avebury.

Buttel, F. (1999) 'Agricultural Biotechnology: Its Recent Evolution and Implications for Agrofood Political Economy', *Sociological Research Online*, vol. 4, no. 3, <http://www.socresonline.org.uk/socresonline/4/3/buttel.html> (accessed 6 October 2001).

Buttel, F. (2001) 'Some Reflections on Late Twentieth Century Agrarian Political Economy', *Sociologia Ruralis*, vol. 41, no. 2, pp. 165–81.

Cable, J. (1994a) 'Introduction and Overview: Recent Developments in Industrial Economics', in J. Cable (ed.) *Current Issues in Industrial Economics*, London: Macmillan.

Cable, J. (ed.) (1994b) *Current Issues in Industrial Economics*, London: Macmillan.

Cain, L. and P. Uselding (eds) (1973) *Business Enterprise and Economic Change: Essays in Honour of Harold F. Williamson*, Kent, OH: Kent State University Press.

Calder, L. (1999) *Financing the American Dream: A Cultural History of Consumer Credit*, Princeton, NJ: Princeton University Press.

Callinicos, A. (1989) *Against Postmodernism: A Marxist Critique*, Cambridge: Polity Press.

Callon, M. (1998a) 'Introduction: The Embeddedness of Economic Markets in Economics', in M. Callon (ed.) *The Laws of the Market*, Oxford: Blackwell.

Callon, M. (1998b) 'An Essay on Framing and Overflowing: Economic Externalities Revisited by Sociology', in M. Callon (ed.) *The Laws of the Market*, Oxford: Blackwell.

Callon, M. (ed.) (1998c) *The Laws of the Market*, Oxford: Blackwell.

Cameron, G. (1998) Book Review of Fine *et al.* (1996), *Economic Journal*, vol. 108, no. 450, pp. 1589–90.

Cameron, J. and D. Gasper (eds) (2000) 'Amartya Sen on Inequality, Human Well-Being, and Development as Freedom', *Journal of International Development*, vol. 12, no. 7.

Campbell, C. (1993) 'Understanding Traditional and Modern Patterns of Consumption in Eighteenth-Century England: A Character-Action Approach', in J. Brewer and R. Porter (eds) *Consumption and the World of Goods*, London: Routledge.

Campbell, C. (1997) 'When the Meaning is Not a Message: A Critique of the Consumption as Communication Thesis', in M. Nava *et al.* (eds) *Buy This Book: Studies in Advertising and Consumption*, London: Routledge.

Cannadine, D. (1983) 'The Context, Performance and Meaning of Ritual: The British Monarchy and the "Invention of Tradition"', in E. Hobsbawm and T. Ranger (eds) *The Invention of Tradition*, Cambridge: Cambridge University Press.

Cannadine, D. (1984) 'The Present and the Past in the English Industrial Revolution 1880–1980', *Past and Present*, no. 103, pp. 131–72.

Cannon, G. (1987) *The Politics of Food*, London: Hutchinson.

Cantor, S. and B. Cantor (1977) 'Socioeconomic Factors in Fat and Sugar Consumption', in M. Kare and O. Maller (eds) *The Chemical Senses and Nutrition*, New York: Academic Press.

Caplow, T. (1982) 'Christmas Gifts and Kin Networks', *American Sociological Review*, vol. 47, no. 3, pp. 383–92.

Caplow, T. (1984) 'Rule Enforcement without Visible Means: Christmas Gift Giving in Middletown', *American Journal of Sociology*, vol. 89, no. 4, pp. 1306–23.

Carrier, J. (1992) 'Occidentalism: The World Turned Upside-Down', *American Ethnologist*, vol. 19, no. 2, pp. 195–212.

Carrier, J. (1995a) 'Maussian Occidentalism: Gift and Commodity Systems', in J. Carrier (ed.) *Occidentalism: Images of the West*, Oxford: Oxford University Press.

Carrier, J. (ed.) (1995b) *Occidentalism: Images of the West*, Oxford: Oxford University Press.

Carrier, J. (1997a) 'Introduction', in J. Carrier (ed.) *Meanings of the Market: The Free Market in Western Culture*, Oxford: Berg.

Carrier, J. (1997b) 'Mr Smith, Meet Mr Hawken', in J. Carrier (ed.) *Meanings of the Market: The Free Market in Western Culture*, Oxford: Berg.

Carrier, J. (ed.) (1997c) *Meanings of the Market: The Free Market in Western Culture*, Oxford: Berg.

Carrier, J. and J. Heyman (1997) 'Consumption and Political Economy', *Journal of the Royal Anthropological Institute*, vol. 3, no. 2, pp. 355–73.

Carrier, J. and D. Miller (eds) (1998) *Virtualism: The New Political Economy*, London: Berg.

Carruthers, B. and S. Babb (2000) *Economy/Society: Markets, Meanings, and Social Structure*, Thousand Oaks, CA: Pine Forge Press.

Carter, E. (1997) *How German Is She? Postwar West German Reconstruction and the Consuming Woman*, Ann Arbor: University of Michigan Press.

Carter, J. (ed.) (1998) *Postmodernity and the Fragmentation of Welfare*, London: Routledge.

Castles, F. and D. Mitchell (1992) 'Identifying Welfare State Regimes: The Links between Politics, Instruments and Outcomes', *Governance*, vol. 5, no. 1, pp. 1–26.

Catephores, G. (1980) 'The Historical Transformation Problem – A Reply', *Economy and Society*, vol. 9, no. 3, pp. 332–6.

Cerny, P. (1994) 'The Dynamics of Financial Globalization: Technology, Market Structure, and Policy Response', *Policy Sciences*, vol. 27, no. 4, pp. 319–42.

Chan, S. *et al.* (eds) (1998) *Beyond the Developmental State: East Asia's Political Economies Reconsidered*, London: Macmillan.

Chaney, D. (1998) 'The New Materialism? The Challenge of Consumption', *Work, Employment and Society*, vol. 12, no. 3, pp. 533–44.

Chari, S. (2000) 'The Agrarian Origins of the Knitwear Industrial Cluster in Tiruppur, India', *World Development*, vol. 28, no. 3, pp. 579–99.

Cheal, D. (1988) *The Gift Economy*, London: Routledge.

Cheney, D. (1983) 'The Department Store as a Cultural Form', *Theory, Culture and Society*, vol. 1, no. 3, pp. 10–21.

Church, R. (1999) 'New Perspectives on the History of Products, Firms, Marketing, and Consumers in Britain and the United States since the Mid-Nineteenth Century', *Economic History Review*, vol. LII, no. 3, pp. 405–35.

Clammer, J. (1997) *Contemporary Urban Japan: A Sociology of Consumption*, Oxford: Blackwell.

Claramunt, C. and S. Arroyo (2000) 'The Role of the "Resources of the Power Hypothesis" in Explaining the Spanish Welfare State between 1975–1995', *European Journal of Political Research*, vol. 38, no. 2, pp. 261–84.

Clarke, A. (1999) *Tupperware: The Promise of Plastic in 1950s America*, Washington, DC: Smithsonian Institution Press.

Clarke, D. (1996) 'The Limits to Retail Capital', in N. Wrigley and M. Lowe (eds) *Retailing, Consumption and Capital: Towards the New Retail Geography*, London: Longman.

Clarke, S. (1996) 'Consumers, Information, and Marketing Efficiency at GM, 1921–1940', *Business and Economic History*, vol. 25, no. 1, pp. 186–95.

Clarke, S. (1997) 'Consumer Negotiations', *Business and Economic History*, vol. 26, no. 1, pp. 101–22.

Clarke, S. (1999a) 'Consumers and the Study of the Firm: The Experience of General Motors during the Great Depression', Paper presented to Business History Conference, University of Glasgow, 3 July.

Clarke, S. (1999b) 'Managing Design: The Art and Colour Section at General Motors, 1927–1941', *Journal of Design History*, vol. 12, no. 1, pp.65–79.

Clayton, R. and J. Pontusson (1998) 'The New Politics of the Welfare State Revisited: Welfare Reforms, Public-Sector Restructuring and Inegalitarian Trends in Advanced Capitalist Societies', EUI Working Paper, Robert Schumann Centre, RSC no. 98/26.

Clunas, C. (1999) 'Modernity Global and Local: Consumption and the Rise of the West', *American Historical Review*, vol. 104, no. 5, pp. 1497–1512.

Cockburn, C. (1992) 'The Circuit of Technology: Gender, Identity and Power', in R. Silverstone and E. Hirsch (eds) *Consuming Technologies: Media and Information in Domestic Spaces*, London: Routledge.

Coclanis, P. (1998) 'Food Chains: The Burdens of the (Re)past', *Agricultural History*, vol. 72, no. 4, pp. 661–74.

Coffin, J. (1994) 'Credit, Consumption, and Images of Women's Desires: Selling the Sewing Machine in Nineteenth-Century France', *French Historical Studies*, vol. 18, no. 3, Spring, pp. 749–83.

Coffin, J. (1996) 'Consumption, Production, and Gender: The Sewing Machine in Nineteenth Century France', in L. Frader and S. Rose (eds) *Gender and Class in Modern Europe*, Ithaca, NY: Cornell University Press.

Cohen, B. (1998) 'Money in a Globalized World: From Monopoly to Oligopoly', *Oxford Development Studies*, vol. 26, no 1, pp. 111–25.

Cohen, L. (1990) *Making a New Deal: Industrial Workers in Chicago, 1919–1939*, Cambridge: Cambridge University Press.

Cole, A. (ed.) (1932) *Facts and Figures in Economic History: Articles by Former Students of Edwin Francis Gay*, Cambridge, MA: Harvard University Press.

Cole, W. (1981) 'Factors in Demand', in R. Floud and D. McCloskey (eds) *The Economic History of Britain since 1700, vol. 1, 1700–1860*, Cambridge: Cambridge University Press.

Coleman, W. (1996) *Financial Services, Globalization and Domestic Policy Change*, London: Macmillan.

Colloredo-Mansfield, R. (1999) *The Native Leisure Class: Consumption and Cultural Creativity in the Andes*, Chicago: Chicago University Press.

Cook, I. *et al.* (1998) 'Category Management and Circuits of Knowledge in the UK Food Business', Mimeo, University of Wales, Lampeter.

Cooper, G. (1998) 'Love, War, and Chocolate: Gender and the American Candy Industry, 1890–1930', in R. Horowitz and A. Mohun (eds) *His and Hers: Gender, Consumption, and Technology*, Charlottesville: University Press of Virginia.

Corley, B. (1987) 'Consumer Marketing in Britain, 1914–60', *Business History*, vol. 29, no. 4, pp. 65–83.

Corley, T. (1976) 'Nutrition, Technology and the Growth of the British Biscuit Industry, 1820–1900', in D. Oddy and D. Miller (eds) *The Making of the Modern British Diet*, London: Croom Helm.

Cornwall, R. (1997) 'Deconstructing Silence: The Queer Political Economy of the Social Allocation of Desire', *Review of Radical Political Economics*, vol. 29, no. 1, pp. 1–130.

Corrigan, P. (1997) *The Sociology of Consumption: An Introduction*, London: Sage.

Cosgel, M. (1997) 'Consumption Institutions', *Review of Social Economy*, vol. LV, no. 2, pp. 153–71.

Counihan, C. (1999) *The Anthropology of Food and Body*, London: Routledge.

Cousins, C. (1999) *Society, Work, and Welfare in Europe*, New York: St Martin's Press.

Cousins, M. (1997) 'Ireland's Place in the Worlds of Welfare Capitalism', *Journal of European Social Policy*, vol. 7, no. 3, pp. 223–36.

Cowan, R. (1982) 'The "Industrial Revolution" in the Home: Household Technology and Social Change in the Twentieth Century', in T. Schlereth (ed.) *Material Studies in*

America, Nashville, TN: The American Association for State and Local History. Reproduced from *Technology and Culture*, vol. 17, no. 1, 1976, pp. 1–23.

Cowan, R. (1997) *A Social History of American Technology*, Oxford: Oxford University Press.

Crafts, N. (1981) 'The Eighteenth Century: A Survey', in R. Floud and D. McCloskey (eds) *The Economic History of Britain since 1700, vol. 1, 1700–1860*, Cambridge: Cambridge University Press.

Crafts, N. (1996) 'Post-Neoclassical Endogenous Growth Theory: What Are Its Policy Implications?', *Oxford Review of Economic Policy*, vol. 12, no. 2, pp. 30–47.

Crafts, N. (1999a) 'East Asian Growth Before and After the Crisis', *IMF Staff Papers*, vol. 46, no. 2, pp. 139–66.

Crafts, N. (1999b) 'Implications of Financial Crisis for East Asian Trend Growth', *Oxford Review of Economic Policy*, vol. 15, no. 3, pp. 110–31.

Cramer, C. (1999) 'Can Africa Industrialize by Processing Primary Commodities? The Case of Mozambique Cashew Nuts', *World Development*, vol. 27, no. 7, pp. 1247–66.

Crane, D. (1999) 'Diffusion Models and Fashion: A Reassessment', *Annals of the American Academy of Political and Social Science*, vol. 566, pp. 13–24.

Crang, P. (1997) 'Introduction: Cultural Turns and the (Re)Constitution of Economic Geography', in R. Lee and J. Wills (eds) *Geographies of Economies*, London: Arnold.

Crewe, L. (2000) 'Geographies of Retailing and Consumption', *Progress in Human Geography*, vol. 24, no. 2, pp. 275–90.

Cronin, A. (2000) 'Advertising Difference: Women, Western Europe and "Consumer-Citizenship" ', in M. Andrews and M. Talbot (eds) *All the World and Her Husband: Women in Twentieth-Century Consumer Culture*, London: Cassell.

Cross, G. (1997) *Kids' Stuff: Toys and the Changing World of American Childhood*, Cambridge, MA: Harvard University Press.

Crossick, G. and S. Jaumain (1999a) 'The World of the Department Store: Distribution, Culture and Social Change', in G. Crossick and S. Jaumain (eds) *Cathedrals of Consumption: The European Department Store, 1850–1939*, Aldershot: Ashgate.

Crossick, G. and S. Jaumain (eds) (1999b) *Cathedrals of Consumption: The European Department Store, 1850–1939*, Aldershot: Ashgate.

Daly, M. and J. Lewis (2000) 'The Concept of Social Care and the Analysis of Contemporary Welfare States', *British Journal of Sociology*, vol. 51, no. 2, pp. 281–98.

Damer, S. (2000) ' "The Clyde Rent War!": The Clydebank Rent Strike of the 1920s', in M. Lavalette and G. Mooney (eds) *Class Struggle and Social Welfare*, London: Routledge.

Davis, D. (ed.) (2000) *The Consumer Revolution in Urban China*, Berkeley, CA: University of California Press.

Davis, J. (1992) *Exchange*, Buckingham: Open University Press.

Davis, P. (2000) 'Rethinking the Welfare Regime Approach: The Case of Bangladesh', Global Social Policy Programme, Institute for International Policy Analysis, University of Bath, Mimeo.

de Grazia, V. (1996) 'Introduction', in V. de Grazia and E. Furlough (eds) *The Sex of Things: Gender and Consumption in Historical Perspective*, London: University of California Press.

de Grazia, V. and E. Furlough (eds) (1996) *The Sex of Things: Gender and Consumption in Historical Perspective*, London: University of California Press.

De Vries, J. (1993) 'Between Purchasing Power and the World of Goods: Understanding the Household Economy in Early Modern Europe', in J. Brewer and R. Porter (eds) *Consumption and the World of Goods*, London: Routledge.

de Vroey, M. (1975) 'The Transition from Classical to Neoclassical Economics: A Scientific Revolution', *Journal of Economic Issues*, vol. IX, no. 3, pp. 415–39.

Deaton, A. (1997) *The Analysis of Household Surveys: A Microeconometric Approach to Development Policy*, Baltimore, MD: Johns Hopkins University Press.

Deaton, A. and J. Muellbauer (1980) *Economics and Consumer Behaviour*, Cambridge: Cambridge University Press.

Delind, L. (2000) 'Transforming Organic Agriculture into Industrial Organic Products: Reconsidering National Organic Standards', *Human Organization*, vol. 59, no. 2, pp. 198–208.

Dickson, P. and A. Sawyer (1984) 'Entry/Exit Demand Analysis', *Advances in Consumer Research*, vol. XI, pp. 617–22.

Dietz, B. (1986) 'The North-East Coal Trade, 1550–1750: Measures, Markets and the Metropolis', *Northern History*, vol. 22, pp. 280–94.

Dilnot, A. (1995) 'The Assessment: The Future of the Welfare State', *Oxford Review of Economic Policy*, vol. 11, no. 3, pp. 1–10.

Dixon, H. (1997) 'Controversy: Economics and Happiness', *Economic Journal*, vol. 107, no. 3, pp. 1812–14.

Dixon, R. (1986) 'Uncertainty, Unobstructedness, and Power', *Journal of Post-Keynesian Economics*, vol. 8, no. 4, pp. 585–90.

Dodd, N. (1994) *The Sociology of Money: Economics, Reason and Contemporary Society*, Cambridge: Polity Press.

Douglas, M. and B. Isherwood (1980) *The World of Goods*, London: Penguin.

Douglas, M. and B. Isherwood (1996) *The World of Goods: Towards an Anthropology of Consumption*, second edition with new introduction, London: Routledge.

du Gay, P. (1997a) 'Introduction', in P. du Gay (ed.) *Production of Culture, Cultures of Production*, London: Sage.

du Gay, P. (ed.) (1997b) *Production of Culture, Cultures of Production*, London: Sage.

du Gay, P. *et al.* (1996) *Doing Cultural Studies: The Story of the Sony Walkman*, London: Sage.

Duesenberry, J. (1967) *Income, Saving and the Theory of Consumer Behaviour*, Cambridge, MA: Harvard University Press.

Dunn, R. (1986) 'Television, Consumption and the Commodity Form', *Theory, Culture and Society*, vol. 3, no. 1, pp. 49–64.

Dunning, J. (1993) *The Globalization of Business*, London: Routledge.

Dunning, J. (2000) 'The New Geography of Foreign Direct Investment', in N. Woods (ed.) *The Political Economy of Globalization*, London: Macmillan.

Dunning, J. and K. Hamdani (eds) (1997) *The New Globalism and Developing Countries*, Tokyo: United Nations University Press.

Dupré, R. (1999) ' "If It's Yellow, It Must Be Butter": Margarine Regulation in North America since 1886', *Journal of Economic History*, vol. 59, no. 2, pp. 353–71.

Eade, J. (1997a) 'Introduction', in J. Eade (ed.) *Living the Global City: Globalization as Local Process*, London: Routledge.

Eade, J. (ed.) (1997b) *Living the Global City: Globalization as Local Process*, London: Routledge.

Eatwell, J. *et al.* (eds) (1987) *The New Palgrave: A Dictionary of Economics*, London : Macmillan.

EC (1997) *The Welfare State in Europe: Challenges and Reforms*, European Economy, no. 4, Luxembourg: Official Publications of the European Communities.

Eco, U. (1976) *A Theory of Semiotics*, Bloomington: Indiana University Press.

Edwards, T. (2000) *Contradictions of Consumption: Concepts, Practices and Politics in Consumer Society*, Buckingham: Open University Press.

Elson, D. (ed.) (1979) *Value: The Representation of Labour in Capitalism*, London: CSE Books.

Eriksen, E. and J. Loftager (eds) (1995) *The Rationality of the Welfare State*, Oslo: Scandinavian University Press.

Ervasti, H. (2001) 'Class, Individualism and the Finnish Welfare State', *Journal of European Social Policy*, vol. 11, no. 1, pp. 9–23.

Esping-Andersen, G. (1990) *The Three Worlds of Welfare Capitalism*, Princeton, NJ: Princeton University Press.

Esping-Andersen, G. (1994) 'Welfare States and the Economy', in N. Smelser and R. Swedberg (eds) *The Handbook of Economic Sociology*, Princeton, NJ: Princeton University Press.

Esping-Andersen, G. (1996a) 'After the Golden Age? Welfare State Dilemmas in a Global Economy', in G. Esping-Andersen (ed.) *Welfare State in Transition: National Adaptations in Global Economies*, London: Sage.

Esping-Andersen, G. (1996b) 'Positive-Sum Solutions in a World of Trade-Offs', in G. Esping-Andersen (ed.) *Welfare State in Transition: National Adaptations in Global Economies*, London: Sage.

Esping-Andersen, G. (ed.) (1996c) *Welfare State in Transition: National Adaptations in Global Economies*, London: Sage.

Esping-Andersen, G. (1997) 'Hybrid or Unique? The Japanese Welfare State between Europe and America', *Journal of European Social Policy*, vol. 7, no. 3, pp. 179–90.

Esping-Andersen, G. (1999) *Social Foundations of Postindustrial Economies*, Oxford: Oxford University Press.

Esping-Andersen, G. (2000a) 'The Sustainability of Welfare States into the Twenty-First Century', *International Journal of Health Services*, vol. 30, no. 1, pp. 1–12.

Esping-Andersen, G. (2000b) 'Social Indicators and Welfare Monitoring', UNRISD Social Policy and Development Programme, Paper no. 2.

Esping-Andersen, G. (2000c) 'Multi-Dimensional Decommodification: A Reply to Graham Room', *Policy and Politics*, vol. 28, no. 3, pp. 353–9.

Esping-Andersen, G. (2000d) 'Two Societies, One Sociology, and No Theory', *British Journal of Sociology*, vol. 51, no. 1, pp. 59–77.

ESRC (1999) 'The Politics of GM Food: Risk, Science and Public Trust', ESRC Global Environmental Change Programme, Special Briefing No. 5, University of Sussex.

Etzioni, A. (1988) *The Moral Dimension: Towards a New Economics*, New York: Free Press.

Etzioni, A. and P. Lawrence (eds) (1991) *Socio-Economics: Toward a New Synthesis*, Armonk, NY: M.E. Sharpe.

Evans, P. (1997) 'The Eclipse of the State? Reflections on Stateness in an Era of Globalization', *World Politics*, vol. 50, no. 1, pp. 62–87.

Evans, P. *et al.* (eds) (1985) *Bringing the State Back In*, Cambridge: Cambridge University Press.

Ewen, S. (1976) *Captains of Consciousness: Advertising and the Social Roots of the Consumer Culture*, New York: McGraw-Hill.

Ewen, S. (1990) 'Marketing Dreams: The Political Elements of Style', in A. Tomlinson (ed.) *Consumption, Identity and Style*, London: Routledge.

Fagnani, J. (1990) 'City Size and Mothers' Labour Force Participation', *Tijdschrift voor Economische en Sociale Geografie*, vol. 81, no. 3, pp. 182–8.

Falk, P. and C. Campbell (eds) (1997) *The Shopping Experience*, London: Sage.

Fardon, R. (1999) 'Consumption and Identification: The Question of Public Goods', in R. Fardon *et al.* (eds) *Modernity on a Shoestring: Dimensions of Globalization, Consumption and Development in Africa and Beyond*, Leiden: EIDOS.

Fardon, R. *et al.* (eds) (1999) *Modernity on a Shoestring: Dimensions of Globalization, Consumption and Development in Africa and Beyond*, Leiden: EIDOS.

Fazeli, R. (1996) *The Economic Impact of the Welfare State and Social Wage: The British Experience*, Aldershot: Avebury.

Featherstone, M. (1983) 'Consumer Culture: An Introduction', *Theory, Culture and Society*, vol. 3, no. 1, pp. 4–9.

Febrero, R. and P. Schwartz (eds) (1995) *The Essence of Becker*, Stanford, CA: Hoover Institution Press.

Ferrera, M. (1996) 'The "Southern Model" of Welfare in Social Europe', *Journal of European Social Policy*, vol. 6, no. 1, pp. 17–37.

Ferrera, M. and M. Rhodes (2000) 'Recasting European Welfare States: An Introduction', *West European Politics*, vol. 23, no. 1, pp. 1–10.

Field, F. (1996) *Stakeholder Welfare*, London : IEA Health and Welfare Unit.

Fine, B. (1979) 'On Marx's Theory of Agricultural Rent', *Economy and Society*, vol. 8, no. 3, pp. 241–78.

Fine, B. (1980) 'On the Historical Transformation Problem', *Economy and Society*, vol. 9, no. 3, pp. 337–9.

Fine, B. (1982) *Theories of the Capitalist Economy*, London: Edward Arnold.

Fine, B. (1983) 'The Order of Acquisition of Consumer Durables: A Social Choice Theoretic Approach', *Journal of Economic Behaviour and Organization*, vol. 4, no. 2, pp 239–48.

Fine, B. (1985/6) 'Banking Capital and the Theory of Interest', *Science and Society*, vol. XLIX, no. 4, pp. 387–413.

Fine, B. (ed.) (1986) *The Value Dimension: Marx versus Ricardo and Sraffa*, London: Routledge & Kegan Paul.

Fine, B. (1988) 'From Capital in Production to Capital in Exchange', *Science and Society*, vol. 52, no. 3, pp. 326–37.

Fine, B. (1989) *Marx's 'Capital'*, third edition, London: Macmillan.

Fine, B. (1990) *The Coal Question: Political Economy and Industrial Change from the Nineteenth Century to the Present Day*, London: Routledge.

Fine, B. (1992) *Women's Employment and the Capitalist Family*, London: Routledge.

Fine, B. (1993a) 'Modernity, Urbanism, and Modern Consumption – A Comment', *Environment and Planning D, Society and Space*, vol. 11, no. 5, pp. 599–601.

Fine, B. (1993b) 'Resolving the Diet Paradox', *Social Science Information*, vol. 32, no. 4, December, pp. 669–87.

Fine, B. (1994a) 'Towards a Political Economy of Food', *Review of International Political Economy*, vol. 1, no. 3, pp. 519–45.

Fine, B. (1994b) 'Towards a Political Economy of Food: A Response to My Critics', *Review of International Political Economy*, vol. 1, no. 3, pp. 579–86.

Fine, B. (1995a) 'Flexible Production and Flexible Theory: The Case of South Africa', *Geoforum*, vol. 26, no. 2, pp. 107–19.

Fine, B. (1995b) 'Towards a Political Economy of Anorexia?', *Appetite*, vol. 24, no. 3, pp. 231–42.

Fine, B. (1995c) 'From Political Economy to Consumption', in D. Miller (ed.) *Worlds Apart: Modernism through the Prism of the Local*, London: Routledge.

Fine, B. (1995d) 'Reconsidering "Household Labor, Wage Labor, and the Transformation of the Family"', *Review of Radical Economics*, vol. 27, no. 2, pp. 107–25.

Fine, B. (1997a) 'The New Revolution in Economics', *Capital and Class*, no. 61, Spring, pp. 143–8.

Fine, B. (1997b) 'Industrial Policy and South Africa: A Strategic View', NIEP Occasional Paper Series, no. 5, Johannesburg: National Institute for Economic Policy.

Fine, B. (1997c) 'Playing the Consumption Game', *Consumption, Markets, Culture*, vol. 1, no. 1, pp. 7–29.

Fine, B. (1997d) 'Entitlement Failure?', *Development and Change*, vol. 28, no. 4, pp. 617–47.

Fine, B. (1998a) *Labour Market Theory: A Constructive Reassessment*, London: Routledge.

Fine, B. (1998b) 'The Triumph of Economics: Or "Rationality" Can Be Dangerous to Your Reasoning', in J. Carrier and D. Miller (eds) *Virtualism: The New Political Economy*, London: Berg.

Fine, B. (1998c) *The Political Economy of Diet, Health and Food Policy*, London: Routledge.

Fine, B. (1999a) 'From Becker to Bourdieu: Economics Confronts the Social Sciences', *International Papers in Political Economy*, vol. 5, no. 3, pp. 1–43.

Fine, B. (1999b) ' "Household Appliances and the Use of Time: The United States and Britain since the 1920s" - A Comment', *Economic History Review*, vol. LII, no. 3, pp. 552–62.

Fine, B. (1999c) 'A Question of Economics: Is It Colonising the Social Sciences?', *Economy and Society*, vol. 28, no. 3, pp. 403–25.

Fine, B. (1999d) 'Competition and Market Structure', *Metroeconomica*, vol. 50, no. 2, pp. 1–25.

Fine, B. (2000a) 'Endogenous Growth Theory: A Critical Assessment', *Cambridge Journal of Economics*, vol. 24, no. 2, pp. 245–65, a shortened and amended version of identically titled SOAS Working Paper, no. 80, February 1998.

Fine, B. (2000b) 'ESOP's Fable: Golden Egg or Sour Grapes?', in J. Toporowski (ed.) *Political Economy and the New Capitalism: Essays in Honour of Sam Aaronovitch*, London: Routledge.

Fine, B. (2000c) 'Transition and the Political Economy of South Africa', *African Rural and Urban Studies*, forthcoming.

Fine, B. (2000d) 'New and Improved: Economics' Contribution to Business History', longer version of original SOAS Working Paper in Economics, no. 93.

Fine, B. (2000e) 'Economic Imperialism as Kuhnian Revolution', *International Papers in Political Economy*, forthcoming.

Fine, B. (2000f) ' "Economic Imperialism": A View from the Periphery', *Review of Radical Political Economics*, forthcoming.

Fine, B. (2001a) *Social Capital versus Social Theory: Political Economy and Social Science at the Turn of the Millennium*, London: Routledge.

Fine, B. (2001b) 'Amartya Sen: A Partial and Personal Appreciation', CDPR Discussion Paper, no.1601, SOAS.

Fine, B. (2001c) 'Beyond the Developmental State: Towards a Political Economy of Development', in H. Hirakawa, H. *et al.* (eds) *Beyond Market-Driven Development: A New Stream of Political Economy of Development*, Tokyo: Nihon Hyoron Sha (in Japanese), forthcoming.

Fine, B. (2001d) 'Economics Imperialism and Intellectual Progress: The Present as History of Economic Thought?', *History of Economics Review*, vol. 32, no. 1, pp. 10–36.

Fine, B. (2001e) 'Addressing the Critical and the Real in Critical Realism', in P. Lewis (ed.) *Transforming Economics: Perspectives on the Critical Realist Project*, London: Routledge, forthcoming.

Fine, B. (2001f) 'From Laws of the Market to Political Economy of Capitalism', Paper arising out of workshop on 'The Technological Economy', Goldsmith College, University of London, December.

Fine, B. and L. Harris (1976) 'State Expenditure in Advanced Capitalism: A Critique', *New Left Review*, no. 98, pp. 97–112.

Fine, B. and L. Harris (1979) *Rereading 'Capital'*, London: Macmillan.

Fine, B. and L. Harris (1985) *The Peculiarities of the British Economy*, London: Lawrence and Wishart.

Fine, B. and C. Lapavitsas (2000) 'Markets and Money in Social Theory: What Role for Economics?', *Economic and Society*, vol. 29, no. 3, pp. 357–82.

Fine, B. and E. Leopold (1990) 'Consumerism and the Industrial Revolution', *Social History*, vol. 15, no. 2, May, pp. 151–79.

Fine, B. and E. Leopold (1993) *The World of Consumption*, London: Routledge.

Fine, B. and D. Milonakis (2001) 'From Principle of Pricing to Pricing of Principle: Rationality and Irrationality in the Economic History of Douglass North', Mimeo.

Fine, B. and A. Murfin (1984) *Macroeconomics and Monopoly Capitalism*, Brighton: Wheatsheaf.

Fine, B. and P. Rose (2001) 'Education and the Post-Washington Consensus', in B. Fine *et al.* (eds) *Neither Washington Nor Post-Washington Consensus: Challenging Development Policy in the Twenty-First Century*, London: Routledge.

Fine, B. and Z. Rustomjee (1997) *South Africa's Political Economy: From Minerals-Energy Complex to Industrialisation*, Johannesburg: Wits University Press.

Fine, B. and J. Simister (1995) 'Consumption Durables: Exploring the Order of Acquisition', *Applied Economics*, vol. 27, no. 11, pp. 1049–57.

Fine, B. *et al.* (1992a) 'Consumption Norms, Diffusion and the Video/Microwave Syndrome', SOAS Working Papers in Economics, no. 19, May.

Fine, B. *et al.* (1992b) 'Access to Phones and Democracy in Personal Communication: Myth or Reality?', SOAS Working Papers in Economics, no. 20, May.

Fine, B. *et al.* (1992c) 'Who Owns and Who Wants to Own a Car? An Empirical Analysis', SOAS Working Papers in Economics, no. 21, May.

Fine, B. *et al.* (1992d) 'Consumption Norms: A Definition and an Empirical Investigation of How They Have Changed, 1975–1990', SOAS Working Papers in Economics, no. 22, May.

Fine, B. *et al.* (1992e) 'Consumption Norms for Durables: Evidence from the General Household Survey', SOAS Working Papers in Economics, no. 23, May.

Fine, B. *et al.* (1993) 'Consumption Norms, Trickle-Down and the Video/Microwave Syndrome', *International Review of Applied Economics*, vol. 7, no. 2, pp. 123–43.

Fine, B. *et al.* (1996) *Consumption in the Age of Affluence: The World of Food*, London: Routledge.

Fine, B. *et al.* (eds) (2001) *Neither Washington Nor Post-Washington Consensus: Challenging Development Policy in the Twenty-First Century*, London: Routledge.

Finn, M. (2000) 'Men's Things: Masculine Possession in the Consumer Revolution', *Social History*, vol. 25, no. 2, pp. 133–55.

Finnegan, M. (1999) *Selling Suffrage: Consumer Culture and Votes for Women*, New York: Columbia University Press.

Firat, A. and N. Dholakia (1998) *Consuming People: From Political Economy to Theaters of Consumption*, London: Routledge.

Fischler, C. (1980) 'Food Habits, Social Change and the Nature/Culture Dilemma', *Social Science Information*, vol. 19, no. 6, pp. 937–53.

Fischler, C. (1988) 'Food, Self and Identity', *Social Science Information*, vol. 27, no. 2, pp. 275–92.

Fischler, C. (1989) 'Cuisines and Food Selection', in D. Thomson (ed.) *Food Acceptability*, London: Elsevier.

Fitzsimmons, M. and D. Goodman (1998) 'Incorporating Nature: Environmental Narratives and the Reproduction of Food', in B. Braun and N. Castree (eds) *Remaking Reality: Nature at the Millennium*, London: Routledge.

Flinn, M. with the assistance of D. Stoker (1984) *The History of the British Coal Industry, vol. 2, 1700–1830: The Industrial Revolution*, Oxford: Clarendon Press.

Floud, R. and D. McCloskey (eds) (1981) *The Economic History of Britain since 1700, vol. 1, 1700–1860*, Cambridge: Cambridge University Press.

Folbre, N. and J. Nelson (2000) 'For Love or Money?', *Journal of Economic Perspectives*, vol. 14, no. 4, pp. 123–40.

Forty, A. (1986) *Objects of Desire: Design and Society from Wedgwood to IBM*, London: Thames and Hudson.

Foster, H. (ed.) (1985) *Postmodern Culture*, London: Pluto.

Fox, R. and T. Lears (eds) (1983) *The Culture of Consumption: Critical Essays in American History, 1880–1980*, New York: Pantheon.

Frader, L. and S. Rose (eds) (1996) *Gender and Class in Modern Europe*, Ithaca, NY: Cornell University Press.

Fraser, W. (1981) *The Coming of the Mass Market, 1850–1914*, London: Macmillan.

Freeman, R. (1995) 'The Large Welfare State as a System', *American Economic Review*, vol. 85, no. 2, pp. 16–21.

Frey, B. (1999) *Economics as a Science of Human Behaviour: Towards a New Social Science Paradigm*, extended second edition of that of 1992, Boston: Kluwer Academic.

Friedland, R. and J. Sanders (1990) 'Private and Social Wage Expansion in the Advanced Market Economies', in S. Zukin and P. DiMaggio (eds) *Structures of Capital: The Social Organization of the Economy*, Cambridge: Cambridge University Press.

Friedland, W. (1997) 'Commentary on Part III: "Creating Space for Food" and "Agro-Industrial Just-in-Time" ', in D. Goodman and M. Watts (eds) *Globalising Food: Agrarian Questions and Global Restructuring*, London: Routledge.

Friedman, M. (1957) *A Theory of the Consumption Function*, Princeton, NJ: Princeton University Press.

Friedmann, H. (1993) 'The Political Economy of Food: A Global Crisis', *New Left Review*, no. 197, pp. 29–57.

Friedmann, H. (1994) 'Premature Rigour: Can Ben Fine Have His Contingency and Eat It, Too?', *Review of International Political Economy*, vol. 1, no. 3, Autumn, pp. 553–61.

Friedmann, H. and McMichael, P. (1989) 'Agriculture and the State System: The Rise and Fall of National Agricultures, 1870 to the Present', *Sociologia Ruralis*, vol. 19, no. 2, pp. 93–117.

Frost, R. (1993) 'Machine Liberation: Inventing Housewives and Home Appliances in Interwar France', *French Historical Studies*, vol. 18, no. 1, pp. 109–30.

Fulcher, J. (2000) 'Globalisation, the Nation-State and Global Society', *Sociological Review*, vol. 48, no. 4, pp. 522–43.

Furlough, E. (1991) *Consumer Cooperation in France: The Politics of Consumption, 1834–1930*, Ithaca, NY: Cornell University Press.

Furlough, E. and C. Strikwerda (eds) (1999) *Consumers against Capitalism? Consumer Cooperation in Europe, North America, and Japan, 1840–1990*, Oxford: Rowman and Littlefield.

Gabriel, Y. and T. Lang (1995) *The Unmanageable Consumer: Contemporary Consumption and Its Fragmentation*, London: Sage.

Galbraith, J. (1962) *The Affluent Society*, Harmondsworth: Penguin.

Galbraith, J. (1969) *The New Industrial Estate*, Boston: Houghton Mifflin.

Galbraith, J. (1973) *Economics and the Public Purpose*, New York: Basic Books.

Gardner, C. and J. Sheppard (1989) *Consuming Passion: The Rise of Retail Culture*, London: Unwin Hyman.

Garnett, R. (ed.) (1999) *What Do Economists Know? New Economics of Knowledge*, London: Routledge.

Garnham, N. (1995) 'Reply to Grossberg and Carey', *Critical Studies in Mass Communication*, vol. 12, no. 1, pp. 95–100.

Garrett, G. (1998) 'Shrinking States? Globalization and National Autonomy in the OECD', *Oxford Development Studies*, vol. 26, no. 1, pp. 71–98.

Garvey, E. (1996) *The Adman in the Parlor: Magazines and the Gendering of Consumer Culture, 1880s to 1910s*, New York: Oxford University Press.

Gaski, J. (1982) 'The Causes of the Industrial Revolution: A Brief, "Single Factor" Argument', *Journal of European Economic History*, vol. 11, no. 1, pp. 227–33.

Gereffi, G. (1998) 'More than Market, More than the State: Global Commodity Chains and Industrial Upgrading in East Asia', in S. Chan *et al.* (eds) *Beyond the Developmental State: East Asia's Political Economies Reconsidered*, London: Macmillan.

Gereffi, G. (1999) 'International Trade and Industrial Up-Grading in the Apparel Commodity Chain', *Journal of International Economics*, vol. 48, no. 1, pp. 37–70.

Gereffi, G. (2001) 'Shifting Governance Structures in Global Commodity Chains, with Special Reference to the Internet', *American Behavioral Scientist*, vol. 44, no. 10, pp. 1616–37.

Gereffi, G. and M. Korzeniewicz (eds) (1994) *Commodity Chains and Global Capitalism*, Westport, CT: Greenwood Press.

Germain, R. (ed.) (2000) *Globalization and Its Critics: Perspectives from Political Economy*, London: Macmillan.

Gershuny, J. (1978) *After Industrial Society: The Emerging Self-Servicing Economy*, London: Macmillan.

Gershuny, J. (1988) *The Social Economics of Postindustrial Societies*, A Report to the Joseph Rowntree Trust, University of Bath.

Gertler, M. (1997) 'Globality and Locality: The Future of "Geography" and the Nation-State', in P. Rimmer (ed.) *Pacific Rim Development: Integration and Globalisation in the Asia-Pacific Economy*, St Leonards: Allen and Unwin.

Geyer, R. (1998) 'Globalisation and the (Non-)Defence of the Welfare State', *West European Politics*, vol. 21, no. 3, pp. 77–102.

Gibbon, P. (2001) 'Upgrading Primary Production: A Global Commodity Chain Approach', *World Development*, vol. 29, no. 2, pp. 345–63.

Gilboy, E. (1932) 'Demand as a Factor in the Industrial Revolution', reproduced in R. Hartwell (ed.) *The Causes of the Industrial Revolution*, London: Methuen.

Gilliatt, S. *et al.* (2000) 'Public Services and the Consumer: Empowerment or Control?', *Social Policy and Administration*, vol. 34, no. 3, pp. 333–49.

Ginsburg, N. (1979) *Class, Capital and Social Policy*, London: Macmillan.

Glennie, P. (1995) 'Consumption within Historical Studies', in D. Miller (ed.) *Worlds Apart: Modernism through the Prism of the Local*, London: Routledge.

Glennie, P. and N. Thrift (1992) 'Modernity, Urbanism, and Modern Consumption', *Environment and Planning D: Society and Space*, vol. 10, no. 4, pp. 423–43.

Glennie, P. and N. Thrift (1993) 'Modern Consumption: Theorising Commodities and Consumers', *Environment and Planning D: Society and Space*, vol. 11, no. 5, pp. 603–6.

Glennie, P. and N. Thrift (1996) 'Consumption, Shopping and Gender', in N. Wrigley and M. Lowe (eds) *Retailing, Consumption and Capital: Towards the New Retail Geography*, London: Longman.

Glickman, L. (1999a) 'Bibliographic Essay', in L. Glickman (ed.) *Consumer Society in American History: A Reader*, Ithaca, NY: Cornell University Press.

Glickman, L. (ed.) (1999b) *Consumer Society in American History: A Reader*, Ithaca, NY: Cornell University Press.

Glyn, A. (1998) 'The Assessment: Economic Policy and Social Democracy', *Oxford Review of Economic Policy*, vol. 14, no. 1, pp. 1–18.

Godbout, J. with A. Caillé (1998) *The World of the Gift*, Montreal: McGill–Queen's University Press.

Godelier, M. (1973) *Rationality and Irrationality in Economics*, New York: Monthly Review Press.

Godelier, M. (1999) *The Enigma of the Gift*, Chicago: Chicago University Press (original of 1996).

Gofton, L. and E. Haimes (1999) 'Necessary Evils? Opening up Closings in Sociology and Biotechnology', *Sociological Research Online*, vol. 4, no. 3, <http://www.socresonline.org.uk/socresonline/4/3/gofton.html> (accessed 6 October 2001).

Goldman, R. and S. Papson (1996) *Sign Wars: The Cluttered Landscape of Advertising*, New York: Guilford Press.

Goldman, R. and S. Papson (1998) *Nike Culture: The Sign of the Swoosh*, London: Sage.

Gollan, P. (1995a) 'Introduction', in P. Gollan (ed.) *Globalization and Its Impact on the World of Work*, University of Sydney: ACIRRT Working Paper, no. 38.

Gollan, P. (ed.) (1995b) *Globalization and Its Impact on the World of Work*, University of Sydney: ACIRRT Working Paper, no. 38.

Goodin, R. (2001) 'Work and Welfare: Towards a Post-Productivist Welfare Regime', *British Journal of Political Science*, vol. 31, no. 1, pp. 13–39.

Goodin, R. and D. Mitchell (2000a) 'Foundations of the Welfare State: An Overview', in R. Goodin and D. Mitchell (eds) *The Foundations of the Welfare State*, three volumes, Cheltenham: Edward Elgar.

Goodin, R. and D. Mitchell (eds) (2000b) *The Foundations of the Welfare State*, three vols, Cheltenham: Edward Elgar.

Goodin, R. *et al.* (1999) *The Real Worlds of Welfare Capitalism*, Cambridge: Cambridge University Press.

Goodman, D. (1997) 'World-Scale Processes and Agro-Food Systems: Critique and Research Needs', *Review of International Political Economy*, vol. 4, no. 4, pp. 663–87.

Goodman, D. (1999) 'Agro-Food Studies in the "Age of Ecology": Nature, Corporeality, Bio-Politics', *Sociologia Ruralis*, vol. 39, no. 1, pp. 17–38.

Goodman, D. (2001) 'Ontology Matters: The Relational Materiality of Nature and Agri-Food Studies', *Sociologia Ruralis*, vol. 41, no. 2, pp. 182–200.

Goodman, D. and M. Redclift (1994) 'Constructing a Political Economy of Food', *Review of International Political Economy*, vol. 1, no. 3, Autumn, pp. 547–52.

Goodman, D. and M. Watts (1994) 'Reconfiguring the Rural or Fording the Divide?: Capitalist Restructuring and the Global Agro-Food System', *Journal of Peasant Studies*, vol. 22, no. 1, October, pp. 1–49.

Goodman, D. and M. Watts (eds) (1997) *Globalising Food: Agrarian Questions and Global Restructuring*, London: Routledge.

Goodman, D. *et al.* (1987) *From Farming to Biotechnology: A Theory of Agro-Industrial Development*, Oxford: Blackwell.

Goodman, R. *et al.* (eds) (1998) *The East Asian Welfare Model: Welfare Orientalism and the State*, London: Routledge.

Goody, J. (1982) *Cooking, Cuisine and Class: A Study in Comparative Sociology*, Cambridge: Cambridge University Press.

Gordon, J. and J. McArthur (1985) 'American Women and Domestic Consumption, 1800–1920: Four Interpretive Themes', *Journal of American Culture*, vol. 18, no. 3, Fall, pp. 35–46.

Gornick, J. and J. Jacobs (1998) 'Gender, the Welfare State, and Public Employment: A Comparative Study of Seven Industrialized Countries', *American Sociological Review*, vol. 63, no. 5, pp. 688–710.

Gottdiener, M. (1997) *The Theming of America: Dreams, Visions and Commercial Spaces*, Boulder, CO: Westview Press.

Gough, I. (1975) 'State Expenditure in Advanced Capitalism', *New Left Review*, no. 92, pp. 53–92.

Gough, I. (1979) *The Political Economy of the Welfare State*, London: Macmillan.

Gough, I. (1999) 'The Needs of Capital and the Needs of People: Can the Welfare State Reconcile the Two?', Inaugural Lecture, University of Bath.

Gough, I. (2000a) 'Welfare Regimes: On Adapting the Framework to Developing Countries', Global Social Policy Programme, Institute for International Policy Analysis, University of Bath, Mimeo.

Gough, I. (2000b) 'Welfare Comparisons in East Asia and Europe: Comparisons and Lessons', Annual World Bank Conference on Development Economics, Paris.

Gough, I. (2000c) 'Globalisation and Regional Welfare Regimes: The East Asian Case', Global Social Policy Programme, Institute for International Policy Analysis, University of Bath, Mimeo.

Granovetter, M. (1985) 'Economic Action and Social Structure: The Problem of Embeddedness', *American Journal of Sociology*, vol. 91, no. 3, pp. 481–510, reproduced in R. Swedberg (ed.) *Economic Sociology*, Cheltenham: Edward Elgar.

Gray J. (1987) 'The Economic Approach to Human Behavior: Its Prospects and Limitations', in G. Radnitzky and P. Bernholz (eds) *Economic Imperialism: The Economic Method Applied Outside the Field of Economics*, New York: Paragon House.

Green, F. (1979) 'The Consumption Function: A Study of a Failure in Positive Economics', in F. Green and P. Nore (eds) *Economics: An Anti-Text*, London: Macmillan.

Green, F. (1990) 'Institutional and Other Unconventional Theories of Saving', Discussion Paper, University of Leicester.

Green, F. and P. Nore (eds) (1977) *Economics: An Anti-Text*, London: Macmillan.

Green, F. and P. Nore (eds) (1979) *Issues in Political Economy: A Critical Approach*, London: Macmillan.

Gregory, C. (1982) *Gifts and Commodities*, London: Academic Press.

Gregory, C. (1987) 'Gifts', in J. Eatwell *et al.* (eds) *The New Palgrave: A Dictionary of Economics*, London : Macmillan.

Gregory, C. (1997) *Savage Money: The Anthropology and Politics of Commodity Exchange*, Amsterdam: Harwood Academic.

Grey, M. (2000) 'The Industrial Food Stream and Its Alternatives in the United States: An Introduction', *Human Organization*, vol. 59, no. 2, pp. 143–50.

Grieco, M. *et al.* (eds) (1989) *Gender, Transport and Employment: The Impact of Travel Constraints*, Aldershot: Gower.

Griffin, K. and A. Khan (1992) *Globalization and the Developing World: An Essay on the International Dimensions of Development in the Post-Cold War Era*, Geneva: UNRISD.

Gronow, J. (1997) *The Sociology of Taste*, London: Routledge.

Grossberg, L. (1995) 'Cultural Studies Vs. Political Economy: Is Anyone Else Bored with This Debate?', *Critical Studies in Mass Communication*, vol. 12, no. 1, pp. 72–81.

Gurney, C. (1999) ' "We've Got Friends Who Live in Council Houses": Power and Resistance in Home Ownership', in J. Hearn and S. Roseneil (eds) *Consuming Cultures: Power and Resistance*, London: Macmillan.

Gurney, P. (1996) *Cooperative Culture and the Politics of Consumption in England, 1870–1930*, Manchester: Manchester University Press.

Gwynne, R. (1999) 'Globalization, Commodity Chains and Fruit Exporting Regions in Chile', *Tijdschrift voor Economische en Sociale Geografie*, vol. 90, no. 2, pp. 211–25.

Hamilton, G. *et al.* (2000) 'Neither States nor Markets: The Role of Economic Organization in Asian Development', *International Sociology*, vol. 15, no. 2, pp. 288–305.

Hamilton, K. and L. Jenkins (1989) 'Why Women and Travel?', in M. Grieco *et al.* (eds) *Gender, Transport and Employment: The Impact of Travel Constraints*, Aldershot: Gower.

Haney, L. (1998) 'Engendering the Welfare State: A Review Article', *Comparative Studies in Society and History*, vol. 40, no. 4, pp. 748–67.

Hansen, K. (2000) *Salaula: The World of Secondhand Clothing and Zambia*, Chicago: Chicago University Press.

Hantrais, L. and S. Mangen (eds) (1996) *Cross-National Research Methods in the Social Sciences*, London: Pinter.

Hardyment, C. (1988) *From Mangle to Microwave: The Mechanisation of Household Work*, London: Polity Press.

Hargreaves-Heap, S. (1992) *The Theory of Choice: A Critical Guide*, Oxford: Blackwell.

Harrington, C. and D. Bielby (2001a) 'Constructing the Popular: Cultural Production and Consumption', in C. Harrington and D. Bielby (eds) *Popular Culture: Production and Consumption*, Oxford: Blackwell.

Harrington, C. and D. Bielby (eds) (2001b) *Popular Culture: Production and Consumption*, Oxford: Blackwell.

Harris, J. and C. McDonald (2000) 'Post-Fordism, the Welfare State and the Personal Social Services: A Comparison of Australia and Britain', *British Journal of Social Work*, vol. 30, no. 1, pp. 51–70.

Hartwell, R. (ed.) (1967) *The Causes of the Industrial Revolution*, London: Methuen.

Hartwick, E. (2000) 'Towards a Geographical Politics of Consumption', *Environment and Planning A*, vol. 32, no. 7, pp. 1177–92.

Harvey, D. (1989) *The Condition of Post-Modernity: An Enquiry into the Origins of Cultural Change*, Oxford: Blackwell.

Harvey, M. (1999) 'Cultivation and Comprehension: How Genetic Modification Irreversibly Alters the Human Engagement with Nature', *Sociological Research Online*, vol. 4, no. 3, <http://www.socresonline.org.uk/socresonline/4/3/harvey.html> (accessed 6 October 2001).

Haug, W. (1986) *Critique of Commodity Aesthetics: Appearance, Sexuality and Advertising in Capitalist Society*, London: Polity Press.

Haugerud, A. *et al.* (eds) (2000) *Commodities and Globalization: Anthropological Perspectives*, Lanham, MD: Rowman and Littlefield.

Hausman, D. and M. McPherson (1996) *Economics and Moral Philosophy*, Cambridge: Cambridge University Press.

Hausmann, W. (1984a) 'Cheap Coals or Limitation of the Vend? The London Coal Trade, 1770–1845', *Journal of Economic History*, vol. XLIV, no. 2, June, pp. 321–8.

Hausmann, W. (1984b) 'Market Power in the London Coal Trade: The Limitations of the Vend, 1770–1845', *Explorations in Economic History*, vol. 21, pp. 383–405.

Hay, C. (1998) 'Globalisation, Welfare Retrenchment, and the "Logic of No Alternative": Why Second-Best Won't Do', *Journal of Social Policy*, vol. 26, no. 4, pp. 525–32.

Hayden, D. (1982) *The Grand Domestic Revolution: A History of Feminist Designs for American Homes, Neighborhoods, and Cities*, Cambridge: Cambridge University Press.

Headey, B. *et al.* (1997) 'Welfare over Time: Three Worlds of Welfare Capitalism in Panel Perspective', *Journal of Public Policy*, vol. 17, no. 3, pp. 329–59.

Hearn, J. and S. Roseneil (eds) (1999) *Consuming Cultures: Power and Resistance*, London: Macmillan.

Held, D. and A. McGrew (2000a) 'The Great Globalization Debate', in D. Held and A. McGrew (eds) *The Global Transformations Reader*, Cambridge: Polity Press.

Held, D. and A. McGrew (eds) (2000b) *The Global Transformations Reader*, Cambridge: Polity Press.

Helleiner, E. (1997a) 'The World of Money: The Political Economy of International Capital Mobility', *Policy Sciences*, vol. 27, no. 4, pp. 295–8.

Helleiner, E. (1997b) 'Freeing Money: Why Have States Been More Willing to Liberalize Capital Controls than Trade Barriers?', *Policy Sciences*, vol. 27, no. 4, pp. 299–318.

Hilton, M. (1998) 'Retailing History as Economic and Cultural History: Strategies of Survival by Special Tobacconists in the Mass Market', *Business History*, vol. 40, no. 3, pp. 115–37.

Hirakawa, H. *et al.* (eds) (2001) *Beyond Market-Driven Development: A New Stream of Political Economy of Development*, Tokyo: Nihon Hyoron Sha (in Japanese), forthcoming.

Hirschman, A. (1982) *Private Interest and Public Action*, Oxford: Martin Robertson.

Hirst, P. and G. Thompson (1996) *Globalization in Question*, Cambridge: Polity Press (second edition, 1999).

Hobsbawm, E. and Ranger, T. (eds) (1983) *The Invention of Tradition*, Cambridge: Cambridge University Press.

Hoff, K. *et al.* (eds) (1993) *The Economics of Rural Organisation: Theory, Practice, and Policy*, New York: Oxford University Press.

Holbrook, M. (1995) *Consumer Research: Introspective Essays on the Study of Consumption*, London: Sage.

Hollis, M. and E. Nell (1975) *Rational Economic Man: A Philosophical Critique of Neoclassical Economics*, Cambridge: Cambridge University Press.

Holmwood, J. (1997) 'Citizenship and Inequality in Postmodern Social Theory', in P. Sulkunen *et al.* (eds) *Constructing the New Consumer Society*, New York: St Martin's Press.

Holzmann, R. and S. Jørgensen (2000) 'Social Risk Management: A New Conceptual

Framework for Social Protection, and Beyond', World Bank, Social Protection Discussion Paper, no. 0006.

Horowitz, D. (1985) *The Morality of Spending: Attitudes to the Consumer Society in America, 1875–1940*, London: Johns Hopkins University Press.

Horowitz, R. and A. Mohun (eds) (1998) *His and Hers: Gender, Consumption, and Technology*, Charlottesville: University Press of Virginia.

Hounshell, D. (1984) *From the American System to Mass Production, 1800–1932: The Development of Manufacturing Technology in the United States*, Baltimore, MD: Johns Hopkins University Press.

Howes, D. (1996a) 'Introduction: Commodities and Cultural Borders', in D. Howes (ed.) *Cross-Cultural Consumption: Global Markets, Local Realities*, London: Routledge.

Howes, D. (ed.) (1996b) *Cross-Cultural Consumption: Global Markets, Local Realities*, London: Routledge.

Hudson, K. (1983) *The Archaeology of the Consumer Society: The Second Industrial Revolution in Britain*, London: Heinemann.

Humphery, K. (1998) *Shelf Life: Supermarkets and the Changing Cultures of Consumption*, Cambridge: Cambridge University Press.

Humphrey, C. and S. Hugh-Jones (1992a) 'Barter, Exchange and Value', in C. Humphrey and S. Hugh-Jones (eds) *Barter, Exchange and Value: An Anthropological Approach*, Cambridge: Cambridge University Press.

Humphrey, C. and S. Hugh-Jones (eds) (1992b) *Barter, Exchange and Value: An Anthropological Approach*, Cambridge: Cambridge University Press.

Inkster, I. (1983) 'Technology as the Cause of the Industrial Revolution, Some Comments', *Journal of European Economic History*, vol. 12, no. 3, pp. 651–8.

Ippolito, P. (1999) 'How Government Policies Shape the Food and Nutritional Information Environment', *Food Policy*, vol. 24, no. 2–3, pp. 295–310.

Isserman, A. (2001) 'Genetically Modified Food: Understanding the Societal Dilemma', *American Behavioral Scientist*, vol. 44, no. 8, pp. 1225–32.

Itoh, M. and C. Lapavitsas (1998) *Political Economy of Money and Finance*, London: Macmillan.

James, J. (1993) *Consumption and Development*, New York: St Martin's Press.

James, J. (2000) *Consumption, Globalization and Development*, New York: St Martin's Press.

Jameson, F. (1985) 'Postmodernism and Consumer Society', in H. Foster (ed.) *Postmodern Culture*, London: Pluto.

Janoski, T. and A. Hicks (1994a) 'Methodological Innovations in Comparative Political Economy: An Introduction', in T. Janoski and A. Hicks (eds) *The Comparative Political Economy of the Welfare State*, Cambridge: Cambridge University Press.

Janoski, T. and A. Hicks (1994b) 'Conclusion: *Quo Vadis* Political Economy: Theory and Methodology in the Comparative Analysis of the Welfare State', in T. Janoski and A. Hicks (eds) *The Comparative Political Economy of the Welfare State*, Cambridge: Cambridge University Press.

Janoski, T. and A. Hicks (eds) (1994c) *The Comparative Political Economy of the Welfare State*, Cambridge: Cambridge University Press.

Jefferys, J. (1954) *Retail Trading in Britain, 1850–1950*, Cambridge: Cambridge University Press.

Jessop, B. (1994) 'The Transition to Post-Fordism and the Schumpeterian Workfare State', in R. Burrows and B. Loader (eds) *Towards a Post-Fordist Welfare State?*, London: Routledge.

Jessop, B. (1995) 'Towards a Schumpeterian Workfare Regime in Britain? Reflections on Regulation, Governance, and Welfare State', *Environment and Planning A*, vol. 27, no. 10, pp. 16–21.

Jirousek, C. (2000) 'The Transition to Mass Fashion System Dress in the Later Ottoman Empire', in D. Quataert (ed.) *Consumption Studies and the History of the Ottoman Empire, 1550–1922*, Albany, NY: State University of New York Press.

Johns, R. and L. Vural (2000) 'Class, Geography, and the Consumerist Turn: UNITE and the Stop Sweatshops Campaign', *Environment and Planning A*, vol. 32, no. 7, pp. 1193–1214.

Johnson, P. (1988) 'Conspicuous Consumption amongst Working Class Consumers in Victorian England', *Transactions of the Historical Society*, vol. 38, pp. 27–42.

Johnson, R. (1986) 'The Story so far: And Further Transformations?', in D. Punter (ed.) *Introduction to Contemporary Cultural Studies*, London: Longman.

Johnston, J. (1976) 'The Development of the Food-Canning Industry in Britain during the Inter-War Period', in D. Oddy and D. Miller (eds) *The Making of the Modern British Diet*, London: Croom Helm.

Johnston, J. (1977) *A Hundred Years of Eating: Food, Drink and the Daily Diet in Britain since the Late Nineteenth Century*, Dublin: Gill and Macmillan.

Jones, B. (1995) *Globalisation and Interdependence in the International Political Economy: Rhetoric and Reality*, London: Pinter.

Jones, C. (ed.) (1993) *New Perspectives on the Welfare State in Europe*, London: Routledge.

Jones, E. (1973) 'The Fashion Manipulators: Consumer Tastes and British Industries; 1660–1800', in L. Cain and P. Uselding (eds) *Business Enterprise and Economic Change: Essays in Honour of Harold F. Williamson*, Kent, OH: Kent State University Press.

Juanillo, N. (2001) 'The Risks and Benefits of Agricultural Biotechnology: Can Scientific and Public Talk Meet?', *American Behavioral Scientist*, vol. 44, no. 8, pp. 1246–66.

Kagel, J. (1981) 'Demand Curves of Animal Consumers', *Quarterly Journal of Economics*, vol. XCVI, no. 1, February, pp. 1–15.

Kammen, M. (2000) *American Culture, American Tastes: Social Change and the Twentieth Century*, New York: Alfred A. Knopf.

Kangas, O. (1994) 'The Politics of Social Security: On Regressions, Qualitative Comparisons, and Cluster Analysis', in T. Janoski and A. Hicks (eds) *The Comparative Political Economy of the Welfare State*, Cambridge: Cambridge University Press.

Kare, M. and O. Maller (eds) (1977) *The Chemical Senses and Nutrition*, New York: Academic Press.

Katona, G. (1964) *The Mass Consumption Society*, New York: McGraw-Hill.

Katrougalos, G. (1996) 'The South European Welfare Model: The Greek Welfare State in Search of a Model', *Journal of European Social Policy*, vol. 6, no. 1, pp. 39–60.

Keat, R. *et al.* (eds) (1994) *The Authority of the Consumer*, London: Routledge.

Keen, M. (1987) 'Zero Expenditures and the Estimation of Engel Curves', *Journal of Applied Econometrics*, vol. 41, pp. 277–86.

Keen, S. (1991) 'Paul Sweezy and the Misinterpretation of Marx', *School of Economics Discussion Paper*, no. 91/1, January, University of New South Wales.

Kemeny, J. (1995) 'Theories of Power in *The Three Worlds of Welfare Capitalism*', *Journal of European Social Policy*, vol. 5, no. 2, pp. 87–96.

Khondker, H. (1994) 'Globalisation Theory: A Critical Appraisal', Department of Sociology Working Paper no. 123, National University of Singapore.

Kidd, A. and D. Nicholls (1999a) 'Introduction: History, Culture and the Middle Classes', A. Kidd and D. Nicholls (eds) *Gender, Civic Culture and Consumerism: Middle Class Identity in Britain, 1800–1940*, Manchester: Manchester University Press.

Kidd, A. and D. Nicholls (eds) (1999b) *Gender, Civic Culture and Consumerism: Middle Class Identity in Britain, 1800–1940*, Manchester: Manchester University Press.

King, J. and D. Stabinsky (1998/9) 'Biotechnology under Globalisation: The Corporate Expropriation of Plant, Animal and Microbial Species', *Race and Class*, vol. 40, no. 2/3, pp. 73–89.

Klein, R. (1993) 'O'Goffe's Tale, or What Can We Learn for the Success of the Capitalist Welfare States?', in C. Jones (ed.) *New Perspectives on the Welfare State in Europe*, London: Routledge.

Kline, S. (1998) 'Toys, Socialization, and the Commodification of Play', in S. Strasser *et al.* (eds) *Getting and Spending: European and American Consumer Societies in the Twentieth Century*, Cambridge: Cambridge University Press.

Kloosterman, R. (1994) 'Three Worlds of Welfare Capitalism? The Welfare State and the Post-Industrial Trajectory in the Netherlands after 1980', *West European Politics*, vol. 17, no. 4, pp. 166–89.

Kopytoff, I. (1986) 'The Cultural Biography of Things: Commoditization as Process', in A. Appadurai (ed.) *The Social Life of Things: Commodities in Cultural Perspective*, Cambridge: Cambridge University Press.

Korpi, W. and J. Palme (1998) 'The Paradox of Redistribution and Strategies of Equality: Welfare State Institutions, Inequality, and Poverty in the Western Countries', *American Sociological Review*, vol. 63, no. 5, pp. 661–87.

Kotz, D. (1994) 'Household Labor, Wage Labor, and the Transformation of the Family', *Review of Radical Political Economics*, vol. 26, no. 2, June, pp. 24–56.

Kotz, D. (1995) 'Analyzing the Transformation of the Family', *Review of Radical Economics*, vol. 27, no. 2, pp. 116–23.

Kowaleski-Wallace, E. (1996) *Consuming Subjects: Women, Shopping, and Business in the Eighteenth Century*, New York: Columbia University Press.

Kryk, H. (1923) *A Theory of Consumption*, Cambridge: Riverside Press, reprinted in 1976, New York: Arnos Press.

Kuhnle, S. (ed.) (2000) *Survival of the European Welfare State*, London: Routledge.

Kwon, H. (1997) 'Beyond European Welfare Regimes: Comparative Perspectives on East Asian Welfare Systems', *Journal of Social Policy*, vol. 26, no. 4, pp. 467–84.

Kwon, S. (2000) 'East Asian Social Policy in Global Context: The Korean Case', UNRISD Conference on Social Policy and Social Development, Stockholm, September.

Lambert, R. (2000) 'Globalization and the Erosion of Class Compromise in Contemporary Australia', *Politics and Society*, vol. 28, no. 1, pp. 93–118.

Lancaster, K. (1966) 'A New Approach to Consumer Theory', *Journal of Political Economy*, vol. 74, pp. 132–57.

Langlois, R. and M. Cosgel (1998) 'The Organization of Consumption', in M. Bianchi (ed.) *The Active Consumer: Novelty and Surprise in Consumer Choice*, London: Routledge.

Lapavitsas, C. (2000) 'Commodity versus Gift as Metaphor for Market versus Non-Market', SOAS, Mimeo.

Lasch, C. (1979) *The Culture of Narcissism: American Life in an Age of Diminishing Expectations*, New York: Norton.

Lash, S. and J. Urry (1994) *Economies of Signs and Space*, London: Sage.

Latouche, S. (1993) *In the Wake of Affluent Society: An Exploration of Post-Development*, London: Zed Books.

Lavalette, M. and G. Mooney (eds) (2000) *Class Struggle and Social Welfare*, London: Routledge.

Lawson, T. (1997) *Economics and Reality*, London: Routledge.

Laybourn, K. (1995) *The Evolution of British Social Policy and the Welfare State*, Keele: Keele University Press.

Lazear, E. (1999) 'Culture and Language', *Journal of Political Economy*, vol. 107, Supplement, pp. S95–S126.

Lazear, E. (2000) 'Economic Imperialism', *Quarterly Journal of Economics*, vol. 115, no. 1, pp. 99–146.

Leach, W. (1984) 'Transformations in a Culture of Consumption: Women and Department Stores, 1890–1925', *Journal of American History*, vol. 71, no. 2, September, pp. 319–42.

Leach, W. (1993) *Land of Desire: Merchants, Power, and the Rise of a New American Culture*, New York: Pantheon Books.

Lears, J. (1998) 'Reconsidering Abundance: A Plea for Ambiguity', in S. Strasser *et al.* (eds) *Getting and Spending: European and American Consumer Societies in the Twentieth Century*, Cambridge: Cambridge University Press.

Lebergott, S. (1993) *Pursuing Happiness: American Consumers in the Twentieth Century*, Princeton, NJ: Princeton University Press.

Lee, M. (1993) *Consumer Culture Reborn: The Cultural Politics of Consumption*, London: Routledge.

Lee, R. and J. Wills (eds) (1997) *Geographies of Economies*, London: Arnold.

Lee, Y. (1997) 'The Limits of Economic Globalization in East Asian Developmental States', *Pacific Review*, vol. 10, no. 3, pp. 366–90.

Lefebvre, H. (1971) *Everyday Life in the Modern World*, London: Allen Lane.

Leiss, W. *et al.* (1986) *Social Commodities in Advertising: Person, Products, and Images of Well-Being*, London: Methuen.

Lemire, B. (1984) 'Developing Consumerism and the Ready-Made Clothing Trade in Britain, 1750–1800', *Textile History*, vol. 15, no. 1, Spring, pp. 21–44.

Lemire, B. (1992) *Fashion's Favourite: The Cotton Trade and the Consumer in Britain, 1660–1800*, Oxford: Oxford University Press.

Lemire, B. (1997) *Dress, Culture and Commerce: The English Clothing Trade before the Factory, 1660–1800*, New York: St Martin's Press.

Leopold, E. (1989) 'Women's Employment in the London Boroughs of Hackney and Bromley: A Report of the Findings of the Survey of Londoners' Living Standards', London: Association of London Authorities.

Leslie, D. (1998) 'Consumer Subjectivity, Space, and Advertising Research', *Environment and Planning A*, vol. 31, no. 8, pp. 1443–57.

Leslie, D. and S. Reimer (1999) 'Spatializing Commodity Chains', *Progress in Human Geography*, vol. 23, no. 3, pp. 401–20.

Levi-Faur, D. (1997) 'Friedrich List and Political Economy of the Nation-State', *Review of International Political Economy*, vol. 4, no. 1, pp. 154–78.

Lewis, M. *et al.* (1996) *The Growth of Nations: Culture, Competitiveness, and the Problem of Globalization*, Bristol: Bristol Academic Press.

Lewis, P. (ed.) (2001) *Transforming Economics: Perspectives on the Critical Realist Project*, London: Routledge.

Lien, M. (1997) *Marketing and Modernity*, Oxford: Berg.

Lindbeck, A. (1995) 'Hazardous Welfare-State Dynamics', *American Economic Review*, vol. 85, no. 2, pp. 9–15.

Lindbeck, A. (1997) 'Welfare State Dynamics', in EC (1997) *The Welfare State in Europe: Challenges and Reforms*, European Economy, no. 4, Luxembourg: Official Publications of the European Communities.

Lindbeck, A. (2000) 'The Sveriges Riksbank (Bank of Sweden) Prize in Economic Sciences in Memory of Alfred Nobel, 1969–1998', <http://www.nobel.se/economics/articles/lindbeck/index.html> (accessed 6 October 2001).

Lindbeck, A. *et al.* (1999) 'Social Norms and Economic Incentives in the Welfare State', *Quarterly Journal of Economics*, vol. CXIV, no. 1, pp. 1–35.

Lippincott, L. (1995) 'Expanding on Portraiture: The Market, the Public, and the Hierarchy of Genres in Eighteenth-Century Britain', in A. Bermingham and J. Brewer (eds) *The Consumption of Culture, 1600–1800: Image, Object, Text*, London: Routledge.

Livingston, J. (1994) *Pragmatism and the Political Economy of Cultural Revolution, 1850–1940*, Chapel Hill: University of North Carolina Press.

Livingston, J. (1998) 'Modern Subjectivity and Consumer Culture', in S. Strasser *et al.* (eds) *Getting and Spending: European and American Consumer Societies in the Twentieth Century*, Cambridge: Cambridge University Press.

Lockie, S. and S. Kitto (2000) 'Beyond the Farm Gate: Production-Consumption Networks and Agri-Food Research', *Sociologia Ruralis*, vol. 40, no. 1, pp. 3–19.

Lovell, T. (1995) 'Subjective Power? Consumption, the Reading Public, and Domestic Women in Early Eighteenth-Century England', in A. Bermingham and J. Brewer (eds) *The Consumption of Culture, 1600–1800: Image, Object, Text*, London: Routledge.

Lowe, M. and N. Wrigley (1996) 'Towards the New Retail Geography', in N. Wrigley and M. Lowe (eds) *Retailing, Consumption and Capital: Towards the New Retail Geography*, London: Longman.

Lubar, S. (1998) 'Men/Women/Production/Consumption', in R. Horowitz and A. Mohun (eds) *His and Hers: Gender, Consumption, and Technology*, Charlottesville: University Press of Virginia.

Lunt, P. and A. Furnham (eds) (1996) *Economic Socialization: The Economic Beliefs and Behaviours of Young People*, Cheltenham: Edward Elgar.

Lunt, P. and S. Livingstone (1992) *Mass Consumption and Personal Identity: Everyday Economic Experience*, Buckingham: Open University Press.

Lury, C. (1996) *Consumer Culture*, Cambridge: Polity Press.

Lütz, S. (1998) 'The Revival of the Nation-State? Stock Exchange Regulation in an Era of Globalized Financial Markets', *Journal of European Public Policy*, vol. 5, no. 1, pp. 153–68.

McCloskey, D. (1981) 'The Industrial Revolution 1780–1860: A Survey', in R. Floud and D. McCloskey (eds) *The Economic History of Britain since 1700, vol. 1, 1700–1860*, Cambridge: Cambridge University Press.

McCloskey, D. (1986) *The Rhetoric of Economics*. Brighton: Wheatsheaf.

McCracken, G. (1987) 'The History of Consumption: A Literature Review and Consumer Guide', *Journal of Consumer Policy*, vol. 10, pp. 139–66.

McGovern, C. (1998) 'Consumption and Citizenship in the United States: 1900–1940', in S. Strasser *et al.* (eds) *Getting and Spending: European and American Consumer Societies in the Twentieth Century*, Cambridge: Cambridge University Press.

MacIntyre, S. *et al.* (1998) 'Food Choice, Food Scares, and Health: The Role of the Media', in A. Murcott (ed.) (1998) *The Nation's Diet: The Social Science of Food Choice*, London: Longman.

Mackay, H. (1997a) 'Introduction', in H. MacKay (ed.) *Consumption and Everyday Life*, London: Routledge.

Mackay, H. (ed.) (1997b) *Consumption and Everyday Life*, London: Routledge.

McKendrick, N. (1982) 'Commercialization and the Economy', in N. McKendrick *et al. The Birth of a Consumer Society: The Commercialization of Eighteenth Century England*, London: Europa.

McKendrick, N. *et al.* (1982) *The Birth of a Consumer Society: The Commercialization of Eighteenth Century England*, London: Europa.

McKenzie, G. and M. Khalidi (1996) 'The Globalization of Banking and Financial Markets: The Challenge for European Regulators', *Journal of European Public Policy*, vol. 3, no. 4, pp. 629–46.

MacLean, J. (2000) 'Philosophical Roots of Globalization and Philosophical Routes to Globalization', in R. Germain (ed.) *Globalization and Its Critics: Perspectives from Political Economy*, London: Macmillan.

McLennan, G. (1998) '*Fin de Sociologie?* The Dilemmas of Multidimensional Social Theory', *New Left Review*, no. 230, pp. 58–90.

McMichael, P. (ed.) (1994) *The Global Restructuring of Agro-Food Systems*, Ithaca, NY: Cornell University Press.

McNally, D. (1993) *Against the Market: Political Economy, Market Socialism and the Marxist Critique*, London: Verso.

Mahatoo, W. (1985) *The Dynamics of Consumer Behavior*, Toronto: Wiley.

Malhotra, N. (1988) 'Some Observations on the State of the Art in Marketing Research', *Journal of the Academy of Marketing Science*, vol. 16, no. 1, Spring, pp. 4–24.

Marchand, R. (1998a) *Creating the Corporate Soul: The Rise of Public Relations and Corporate Imagery in American Big Business*, Berkeley, CA: University of California Press.

Marchand, R. (1998b) 'Customer Research as Public Relations: General Motors in the 1930s', in S. Strasser *et al.* (eds) *Getting and Spending: European and American Consumer Societies in the Twentieth Century*, Cambridge: Cambridge University Press.

Marcuse, H. (1964) *One-Dimensional Man: Studies in the Ideology of Advanced Industrial Society*, Boston: Beacon Press.

Marris, R. (1968) *The Economic Theory of 'Managerial Capitalism'*, New York: Basic Books.

Marsden, T. *et al.* (2000) *Consuming Interests: The Social Provision of Foods*, London: UCL Press.

Marx, K. (1969a) *Theories of Surplus Value*, Part I, London: Lawrence and Wishart.

Marx, K. (1969b) *Theories of Surplus Value*, Part II, London: Lawrence and Wishart.

Marx, K. (1973) *Grundrisse*, Harmondsworth: Penguin.

Marx, K. (1976) *Capital*, Volume I, Harmondsworth: Penguin (original of 1867).

Mason, R. (1981) *Conspicuous Consumption: A Study of Exceptional Consumer Behaviour*, Farnborough: Gower.

Mason, R. (1984) 'Conspicuous Consumption: A Literature Review', *European Journal of Marketing*, vol. 18, no. 3, pp. 26–39.

Mason, R. (1998) *The Economics of Conspicuous Consumption: Theory and Thought since 1700*, Cheltenham: Edward Elgar.

Massumi, B. (1992) *A User's Guide to Capitalism and Schizophrenia: Deviations from Deleuze and Guattari*, London: Swerve.

Mauss, M. (1925) *The Gift*, London: Routledge & Kegan Paul, 1974.

Meghir, C. and J. Robin (1992) 'Frequency of Purchase and the Estimation of Demand Systems', *Journal of Econometrics*, vol. 53, no. 1, pp. 53–85.

Meikle, J. (1995) *American Plastic: A Cultural History*, New Brunswick, NJ: Rutgers University Press.

Mennell, S. (1985) *All Manners of Food*, Oxford: Blackwell.

Mennell, S. *et al.* (1992) *The Sociology of Food: Eating, Diet and Culture*, London: Sage, reproduction of the special issue of *Current Sociology*, vol. 40, no. 2.

MERG (Macroeconomic Research Group) (1993) *Making Democracy Work: A Framework for Macroeconomic Policy in South Africa*, Cape Town: CDS.

Messaris, P. (1997) *Visual Persuasion: The Role of Images in Advertising*, London: Sage.

Meyer, J. (2000) 'Globalization: Sources and Effects on National States and Societies', *International Sociology*, vol. 15, no. 2, pp. 233–48.

Miklitsch, R. (1998) *From Hegel to Madonna: Towards a General Economy of 'Commodity Fetishism'*, Albany, NY: State University of New York Press.

Miles, S. (1998) *Consumerism – As a Way of Life*, London: Sage.

Miller, B. (1981) *The Bon Marché: Bourgeois Culture and the Department Store, 1869–1920*, Princeton, NJ: Princeton University Press.

Miller, D. (1987) *Material Culture and Mass Consumption*, Oxford: Blackwell.

Miller, D. (1995a) 'Introduction: Anthropology, Modernity and Consumption', in D. Miller (ed.) *Acknowledging Consumption*, London: Routledge.

Miller, D. (1995b) 'Consumption in the Vanguard of History', in D. Miller (ed.) *Acknowledging Consumption*, London: Routledge.

Miller, D. (ed.) (1995c) *Worlds Apart: Modernism through the Prism of the Local*, London: Routledge.

Miller, D. (ed.) (1995d) *Acknowledging Consumption*, London: Routledge.

Miller, D. (1997) 'Consumption and Its Consequences', in H. Mackay (ed.) *Consumption and Everyday Life*, London: Routledge.

Miller, D. (2001a) 'Alienable Gifts and Inalienable Commodities', in F. Myers and B. Kirshenblatt-Gimblett (eds) *The Unsettled Empire of Things: Regimes of Value and Material Culture*, Sante Fe, NM: School of American Research.

Miller, D. (ed.) (2001b) *Car Cultures*, Oxford: Berg.

Miller, D. (ed.) (2002) *Consumption: Critical Concepts in the Social Sciences*, London: Routledge.

Miller, D. *et al.* (1998) *Shopping, Place and Identity*, London: Routledge.

Miller, P. and N. Rose (1997) 'Mobilizing the Consumer: Assembling the Object of Consumption', *Theory, Culture and Society*, vol. 14, no. 1, pp. 1–36.

Milonakis, D. (1995) 'Commodity Production and Price Formation before Capitalism: A Value-Theoretic Approach', *Journal of Peasant Studies*, vol. 22, no. 2, pp. 327–55.

Milonakis, D. and B. Fine (2001) 'From New to Newest: The Economic History of Douglass North', Mimeo.

Mintz, S. (1985) *Sweetness and Power*, New York: Viking.

Mishra, R. (1998) 'Beyond the Nation State: Social Policy in an Age of Globalization', *Social Policy and Administration*, vol. 32, no. 5, pp. 481–500.

Mishra, R. (1999) *Globalization and the Welfare State*, Cheltenham: Edward Elgar.

Mishra, R. and M. Asher (2000) *Welfare Capitalism in Southeast Asia: Social Security, Health and Education Policies*, London: Macmillan.

Moeran, B. (1996) *A Japanese Advertising Agency: An Anthropology of Media and Markets*, Richmond: Curzon.

Mohun, S. (1977) 'Consumer Sovereignty', in F. Green and P. Nore (eds) *Economics: An Anti-Text*, London: Macmillan.

Mokyr, J. (1977) 'Demand vs Supply in the Industrial Revolution', *Journal of Economic History*, vol. 37, pp. 981–1008.

Mokyr, J. (1984) 'Demand versus Supply in the Industrial Revolution: A Reply', *Journal of Economic History*, vol. 44, pp. 806–9.

Mokyr, J. (1998) 'The Political Economy of Technological Change: Resistance and Innovation in Economic History', in M. Berg and K. Bruland (eds) *Technological Revolutions in Europe: Historical Perspectives*, Cheltenham: Edward Elgar.

Moorhouse, H. (1988) 'American Automobiles and Workers' Dreams', *Sociological Review*, vol. 31, pp. 403–26.

Morley, D. (1998) 'So-Called Cultural Studies: Dead Ends and Reinvented Wheels', *Cultural Studies*, vol. 12, no. 4, pp. 476–97.

Mort, F. (1996) *Cultures of Consumption: Masculinities and Social Space in Late Twentieth-Century Britain*, London: Routledge.

Mort, F. (1997) 'Paths to Mass Consumption: Britain and the USA since 1945', in M. Nava *et al.* (eds) *Buy This Book: Studies in Advertising and Consumption*, London: Routledge.

Möser, K. (1998) 'World War I and the Creation of Desire for Automobiles in Germany', in S. Strasser *et al.* (eds) *Getting and Spending: European and American Consumer Societies in the Twentieth Century*, Cambridge: Cambridge University Press.

Muggleton, D. (2000) *Inside Subculture: The Postmodern Meaning of Style*, Oxford: Berg.

Mukerji, C. (1983) *From Graven Images: Patterns of Modern Materialism*, New York: Columbia University Press.

Mullins, P. (1999) *Race and Affluence: An Archaeology of African America and Consumer Culture*, New York: Kluwer Academic.

Murcott, A. (ed.) (1983) *The Sociology of Food and Eating*, Aldershot: Gower.

Murcott, A. (ed.) (1998) *The Nation's Diet: The Social Science of Food Choice*, London: Longman.

Murcott, A. (1999) ' "Not Science but PR": GM Food and the Makings of a Considered Sociology', *Sociological Research Online*, vol. 4, no. 3, <http://www.socresonline.org.uk/socresonline/4/3/murcott.html> (accessed 6 October 2001).

Murdoch, J. (1997) 'Inhuman/Nonhuman/Human: Actor-Network Theory and the Prospects for a Non-Dualistic and Symmetrical Perspective on Nature and Society', *Environment and Planning D: Society and Space*, vol. 15, no. 6, pp. 731–56.

Murdoch, J. (1998) 'The Spaces of Actor-Network Theory', *Geoforum*, vol. 29, no. 4, pp. 357–74.

Murdoch, J. and M. Miele (1999) ' "Back to Nature": Changing "Worlds of Production" in the Food Sector', *Sociologia Ruralis*, vol. 39, no. 4, pp. 465–82.

Murray, R. (1971) 'The Internationalisation of Capital and the Nation State', *New Left Review*, no. 67, pp. 46–60.

Musson, A. (ed.) (1972) *Science, Technology, and Economic Growth in the Eighteenth Century*, London: Methuen.

Myers, F. and B. Kirshenblatt-Gimblett (eds) (2001) *The Unsettled Empire of Things: Regimes of Value and Material Culture*, Sante Fe, NM: School of American Research.

Myles, J. and P. Pierson (1997) 'Friedman's Revenge: The Reform of "Liberal" Welfare States in Canada and the United States', EUI Working Paper, Robert Schumann Centre, RSC no. 97/30.

Narotzky, S. (1997) *New Directions in Economic Anthropology*, London: Pluto Press.

Nava, M. *et al.* (eds) (1997) *Buy This Book: Studies in Advertising and Consumption*, London: Routledge.

Navarro, V. (1999) 'Is There a Third Way? A Response to Giddens's *The Third Way*', *International Journal of Health Services*, vol. 29, no. 4, pp. 667–77.

Navarro, V. (2000) 'Are pro-Welfare State and Full Employment Policies Possible in the Era of Globalization?', *International Journal of Health Services*, vol. 30, no. 2, pp. 231–51.

Navarro, V. and L. Shi (2001) 'The Political Context of Social Inequalities and Health', *Social Science and Medicine*, vol. 52, no. 3, pp. 481–91.

Nef, J. (1932) *The Rise of the British Coal Industry*, vols I & II, London: Routledge.

Negus, K. (1997) 'The Production of Culture', in P. du Gay (ed.) *Production of Culture, Cultures of Production*, London: Sage.

Nell, E. (1996) *Making Sense of a Changing Economy: Technology, Markets and Morals*, London: Routledge.

Nerlich, B. *et al.* (1999) 'The Influence of Popular Cultural Imagery on Public Attitudes towards Cloning', *Sociological Research Online*, vol. 4, no. 3, <http://www.socresonline.org.uk/socresonline/4/3/nerlich.html> (accessed 6 October 2001).

Nixon, S. (1997) 'Circulating Culture', in P. du Gay (ed.) *Production of Culture, Cultures of Production*, London: Sage.

Noble, D. (1985) 'Command Performance: A Perspective on Military Enterprise and Technological Change', in M. Smith (ed.) *Military Enterprise and Technological Change: Perspectives on the American Experience*, Cambridge, MA: MIT Press.

Nussbaum, M. and A. Sen (eds) (1993) *The Quality of Life*, Oxford: Clarendon Press.

O'Connell, S. (1998) *The Car and British Society: Class, Gender and Motoring, 1896–1939*, Manchester: Manchester University Press.

O'Connor, J. (1973) *The Fiscal Crisis of the State*, New York: St Martin's Press.

O'Connor, J. (1996) 'From Women in the Welfare State to Gendering Welfare State Regimes', *Current Sociology*, vol. 44, no. 2, pp. 1–130.

O'Connor, J. and G. Olsen (1998a) 'Introduction, Understanding the Welfare State: Power Resources Theory and Its Critics', in J. O'Connor and G. Olsen (eds) *Power Resources Theory and the Welfare State: A Critical Appraisal. Essays Collected in Honor of Walter Korpi*, Toronto: University of Toronto Press.

O'Connor, J. and G. Olsen (eds) (1998b) *Power Resources Theory and the Welfare State: A Critical Appraisal. Essays Collected in Honor of Walter Korpi*, Toronto: University of Toronto Press.

O'Connor, J. *et al.* (1999) *States, Markets, Families: Gender, Liberalism and Social Policy in Australia, Canada, Great Britain and the United States*, Cambridge: Cambridge University Press.

Oddy, D. and D. Miller (eds) (1976) *The Making of the Modern British Diet*, London: Croom Helm.

Offe, C. (1984) *The Contradictions of the Welfare State*, London: Hutchinson.

Offe, C. (1995) 'Full Employment: Asking the Wrong Question?', in E. Eriksen and J. Loftager (eds) *The Rationality of the Welfare State*, Oslo: Scandinavian University Press.

Offer, A. (ed.) (1996) *In Pursuit of the Quality of Life*, Oxford: Oxford University Press.

Offer, A. (1997) 'Between the Gift and the Market: The Economy of Regard', *Economic History Review*, vol. l, no. 3, pp. 450–76.

Offer, A. (1998) 'The American Automobile Frenzy of the 1950s', in K. Bruland and P. O'Brien (eds) *From Family Firms to Corporate Capitalism: Essays in Business and Industrial History in Honour of Peter Mathias*, Oxford: Clarendon Press.

Oishi, T. (2001) *The Unknown Marx: Reconstructing a Unified Perspective*, London: Pluto Press.

Olson, M. and S. Kähkönen (2000a) 'Introduction: The Broader View', in M. Olson and S. Kähkönen (eds) *A Not-So-Dismal Science: A Broader View of Economies and Societies*, Oxford: Oxford University Press.

Olson, M. and S. Kähkönen (eds) (2000b) *A Not-So-Dismal Science: A Broader View of Economies and Societies*, Oxford: Oxford University Press.

Otnes, P. (ed.) (1988) *The Sociology of Consumption: An Anthology*, Oslo: Solum Forlag and New Jersey: Humanities Press International.

Packard, V. (1957) *The Hidden Persuaders*, London: Longmans, Green.

Packard, V. (1960) *The Status Seekers: An Exploration of Class Behaviour in America*, London: Longmans.

Palumbo-Liu, D. (1997) 'Introduction: Unhabituated Habituses', in D. Palumbo-Liu and H. Gumbrecht (eds) *Streams of Cultural Capital*, Stanford, CA: Stanford University Press.

Palumbo-Liu, D. and H. Gumbrecht (eds) (1997) *Streams of Cultural Capital*, Stanford, CA: Stanford University Press.

Panico, C. (1988) 'Marx on the Banking Sector and the Interest Rate: Some Initial Notes for a Discussion', *Science and Society*, vol. 52, no. 3, pp. 310–25.

Paulson, R. (1995) 'Emulative Consumption and Literacy: The Harlot, Moll Flanders, and Mrs Slipsop', in A. Bermingham and J. Brewer (eds) *The Consumption of Culture, 1600–1800: Image, Object, Text*, London: Routledge.

Pendergast, T. (2000) *Creating the Modern Man: American Magazines and Consumer Culture, 1900–1950*, Columbia, MO: University of Missouri Press.

Peng, I. (2000) 'A Fresh Look at the Japanese Welfare State', *Social Policy and Administration*, vol. 34, no. 1, pp. 87–114.

Pennell, S. (1999) 'Consumption and Consumerism in Early Modern England', *Historical Journal*, vol. 42, no. 2, pp. 549–64.

Perelman, M. (2000) *The Invention of Capitalism: Classical Political Economy and the Secret History of Primitive Accumulation*, Durham, NC: Duke University Press.

Perrotta, C. (1997) 'The Preclassical Theory of Development: Increased Consumption Raises Productivity', *History of Political Economy*, vol. 29, no. 2, pp. 295–326.

Petras, J. and H. Veltmeyer (2000) 'Globalisation and Imperialism', *Cambridge Review of International Affairs*, vol. XIV, no. 1, pp. 32–48.

Petridou, E. (2001) 'Milk Ties: A Commodity Chain Approach to Greek Culture', Doctoral thesis, University College London.

Pfaller, A. *et al.* (1991a) 'The Issue', in A. Pfaller *et al.* (eds) *Can the Welfare State Compete? A Comparative Study of Five Advanced Capitalist Countries*, London: Macmillan.

Pfaller, A. *et al.* (eds) (1991b) *Can the Welfare State Compete? A Comparative Study of Five Advanced Capitalist Countries*, London: Macmillan.

Phelps, E. (1996a) 'On the Damaging Side Effects of the Welfare System: How, Why and What to Do', in M. Baldarassi *et al.* (eds) *Equity, Efficiency and Growth: The Future of the Welfare State*, London: Macmillan.

Phelps, E. (1996b) 'Conclusions', in M. Baldarassi *et al.* (eds) *Equity, Efficiency and Growth: The Future of the Welfare State*, London: Macmillan.

Pickup, L. (1984) 'Women's Gender-Role and Its Influence on Travel Behaviour', *Built Environment*, vol. 10, pp. 61–8.

Pickup, L. (1989) 'Hard to Get Around: A Study of Women's Travel Mobility', in M. Grieco *et al.* (eds) *Gender, Transport and Employment: The Impact of Travel Constraints*, Aldershot: Gower.

Pierson, C. (1996) 'The New Politics of the Welfare State', *World Politics*, vol. 48, no. 2, pp. 143–79.

Pierson, C. (1998a) 'Contemporary Challenges to Welfare State Development', *Political Studies*, vol. XLVI, no. 3, pp. 777–94.

Pierson, C. (1998b) *Beyond the Welfare State: The New Political Economy of Welfare*, Cambridge: Polity Press.

Pierson, P. (1994) *Dismantling the Welfare State? Reagan, Thatcher, and the Politics of Retrenchment*, Cambridge: Cambridge University Press.

Pierson, P. (2000) 'Three Worlds of Welfare State Research', *Comparative Political Studies*, vol. 33, no. 6/7, pp. 791–821.

Pinch, S. (1994) 'Labour Market Flexibility and the Changing Welfare State: Is There a Post-Fordist Model', in R. Burrows and B. Loader (eds) *Towards a Post-Fordist Welfare State?*, London: Routledge.

Piore, M. and C. Sabel (1984) *The Second Industrial Divide: Possibilities for Prosperity*, New York: Basic Books.

Pollard, S. (1983) 'Capitalism and Rationality: A Study of Measurements in British Coal Mining, ca. 1750–1850', *Explorations in Economic History*, vol. 20, pp. 110–29.

Pollert, A. (ed.) (1991) *Farewell to Flexibility*, Oxford: Blackwell.

Porter, R. (1993) 'Consumption: Disease of the Consumer Society? ', in J. Brewer and R. Porter (eds) *Consumption and the World of Goods*, London: Routledge.

Porter, T. (1996) 'Capital Mobility and Currency Markets: Can They Be Tamed?', *International Journal*, vol. LI, no. 4, pp. 669–89.

Powell, M. and M. Hewitt (1998) 'The End of the Welfare State?', *Social Policy and Administration*, vol. 32, no. 1, pp. 1–13.

Prakash, O. (1961) *Food and Drinks in Ancient India*, Delhi: Munshi Ram Manohar Lal.

Preteceille, E. and J.-P. Terrail (1985) *Capitalism, Consumption and Needs*, Oxford: Blackwell.

Probyn, E. (2000) *Carnal Appetites: FoodSexIdentities*, London: Routledge.

Pudney, S. (1989) *Modelling Individual Choice: The Econometrics of Corners, Kinks and Holes*, Oxford: Blackwell.

Punter, D. (ed.) (1986) *Introduction to Contemporary Cultural Studies*, London: Longman.

Purdy, D. (1998) *The Tyranny of Elegance: Consumer Cosmopolitanism in the Era of Goethe*, Baltimore, MD: Johns Hopkins University Press.

Quadagno, J. (1999) 'Creating a Capital Investment Welfare State: The New American Exceptionalism', *American Sociological Review*, vol. 64, no. 1, pp. 1–10.

Quataert, D. (ed.) (2000) *Consumption Studies and the History of the Ottoman Empire, 1550–1922*, Albany, NY: State University of New York Press.

Radin, M. (1996) *Contested Commodities*, Cambridge, MA: Harvard University Press.

Radnitzky, G. and P. Bernholz (eds) (1987) *Economic Imperialism: The Economic Method Applied Outside the Field of Economics*, New York: Paragon House.

Ragin, C. (1994) 'A Qualitative Comparative Analysis of Pension Systems', in T. Janoski and A. Hicks (eds) *The Comparative Political Economy of the Welfare State*, Cambridge: Cambridge University Press.

Raikes, P. and P. Gibbon (2000) ' "Globalisation" and African Export Crop Agriculture', *Journal of Peasant Studies*, vol. 27, no. 2, pp. 50–93.

Raikes, P. *et al.* (2000) 'Global Commodity Chain Analysis and the French *Filière* Approach', *Economy and Society*, vol. 29, no. 3, pp. 390–417.

Ramamurthy, P. (2000) 'The Cotton Commodity Chain, Women, Work and Agency in India and Japan: The Case for Feminist Agro-Food Systems Research', *World Development*, vol. 28, no. 3, pp. 551–78.

Ratneshwar, S. *et al.* (eds) (2000) *The Why of Consumption: Contemporary Perspectives on Consumer Motives, Goals, and Desires*, London: Routledge.

Reagin, N. (1998) 'Comparing Apples and Oranges: Housewives and the Politics of Consumption in Interwar Germany', in S. Strasser *et al.* (eds) *Getting and Spending: European and American Consumer Societies in the Twentieth Century*, Cambridge: Cambridge University Press.

Redmond, W. (2000) 'Consumer Rationality and Consumer Sovereignty', *Review of Social Economy*, vol. LVIII, no. 2, pp. 177–96.

Reisner, A. (2001) 'Social Movement Organizations' Reactions to Genetic Engineering in Agriculture', *American Behavioral Scientist*, vol. 44, no. 8, pp. 1389–1404.

Renard, M. (1999) 'The Interstices of Globalization: The Example of Fair Coffee', *Sociologia Ruralis*, vol. 39, no. 4, pp.484–500.

Rhodes, M. (1996) 'Globalization and West European Welfare States: A Critical Review of Recent Debates', *Journal of European Social Policy*, vol. 6, no. 4, pp. 305–27.

Rhodes, M. (1997a) 'Globalisation, Labour Markets and Welfare States: A Future of "Competitive Corporatism"', EUI Working Paper, Robert Schumann Centre, RSC no. 97/36.

Rhodes, M. (ed.) (1997b) *Southern European Welfare States: Between Crisis and Reform*, London: Frank Cass.

Rice, J. and C. Saunders (1998) ' "Mini Loves Dressing Up": Selling Cars to Women', in D. Thoms *et al.* (eds) *The Motor Car and Popular Culture in the Twentieth Century*, Aldershot: Ashgate.

Riesman, D. (1964) *Abundance for What: And Other Essays*, London: Chatto and Windus.

Rifkin, J. (1998) *The Biotech Century: Harnessing the Gene and Remaking the World*, New York: Tarcher/Putnam.

Rimmer, P. (ed.) (1997) *Pacific Rim Development: Integration and Globalisation in the Asia-Pacific Economy*, St Leonards: Allen and Unwin.

Ritzer, G. (1993) *The McDonaldization of Society: An Investigation into the Changing Character of Contemporary Social Life*, Thousand Oaks, CA: Pine Forge Press.

Ritzer, G. (1998) *The McDonaldization Thesis: Exploration and Extensions*, London: Sage.

Ritzer, G. (1999a) *Enchanting a Disenchanted World: Revolutionizing the Means of Consumption*, Thousand Oaks, CA: Pine Forge Press.

Ritzer, G. (1999b) 'Assessing the Resistance', in B. Smart (ed.) *Resisting McDonaldization*, London: Sage.

Roberts, S. *et al.* (1988) 'The Fortunate Few: Production as Consumption', *Advances in Consumer Research*, vol. XV, pp. 430–5.

Robinson, W. (1996) 'Globalisation: Nine Theses on Our Epoch', *Race and Class*, vol. 38, no. 2, pp. 13–32.

Robinson, W. and J. Harris (2000) 'Towards a Global Ruling Class? Globalization and the Transnational Capitalist Class', *Science and Society*, vol. 64, no. 1, pp. 11–54.

Roche, D. (2000) *A History of Everyday Things: The Birth of Consumption in France, 1600–1800*, Cambridge: Cambridge University Press (originally published in French, 1997).

Roche, M. *et al.* (1999) 'Making Fruitful Comparisons: Southern Hemisphere Producers and the Global Apple Industry', *Tidjschrift voor Economische en Sociale Geografie*, vol. 90, no. 4, pp. 410–26.

Rodrik, D. (1997) *Has Globalization Gone Too Far?*, Washington, DC: International Economics.

Rogers, M. (1998) *Barbie Culture*, London: Sage.

Room, G. (2000) 'Commodification and Decommodification: A Developmental Critique', *Policy and Politics*, vol. 28, no. 3, pp. 331–51.

Rosdolsky, R. (1977) *The Making of Marx's 'Capital'*, London: Pluto.

Roseberry, W. (1996) 'The Rise of Yuppie Coffees and the Reimagination of Class in the United States', *American Anthropologist*, vol. 98, no. 4, pp. 762–75.

Rosenbaum, E. (1999) 'Against Naive Materialism: Culture, Consumption and the Causes of Inequality', *Cambridge Journal of Economics*, vol. 23, no. 3, pp. 317–36.

Rostow, W. (1967) *The Stages of Economic Growth: A Non-Communist Manifesto*, Cambridge: Cambridge University Press.

Roy, W. (1997) *Socializing Capital: The Rise of the Large Industrial Corporation in America*, Princeton, NJ: Princeton University Press.

Saad-Filho, A. (1993) 'Money, Labour and "Labour-Money": A Review of Marx's Critique of John Gray's Monetary Analysis', *History of Political Economy*, vol. 25, no. 1, pp. 65–84.

Saad-Filho, A. (1997) 'Concrete and Abstract Labour in Marx's Theory of Value', *Review of Political Economy*, vol. 9, no. 4, pp. 457–77.

Sack, R. (1992) *Place, Modernity, and the Consumer's World: A Relational Framework for Geographical Analysis*, Baltimore, MD: Johns Hopkins University Press.

Sahlins, M. (1972) *Stone Age Economics*, London: Tavistock.

Sahlins, M. (1976) *Culture and Political Reason*, Chicago: Chicago University Press.

Sainsbury, D. (1999a) 'Gender, Policy Regimes, and Politics', in D. Sainsbury (ed.) *Gender and Welfare State Regimes*, Oxford: Oxford University Press.

Sainsbury, D. (ed.) (1999b) *Gender and Welfare State Regimes*, Oxford: Oxford University Press.

Salaman, G. (1997) 'Culturing Production', in P. du Gay (ed.) *Production of Culture, Cultures of Production*, London: Sage.

Samuel, R. (1989) *Patriotism: The Making and Unmaking of British National Identity, vol. 1, History and Politics*, London: Routledge.

Sassen, S. (1995) *Losing Control? Sovereignty in an Age of Globalization*, New York: Columbia University Press.

Saunders, P. (1984) 'Beyond Housing Classes: The Sociological Significance of Private Property Rights in Means of Consumption', *International Journal of Urban and Regional Research*, vol. 8, pp. 202–25.

Saunders, P. (1988) 'The Sociology of Consumption: A New Research Agenda', in P. Otnes (ed.) *The Sociology of Consumption: An Anthology*, Oslo: Solum Forlag and New Jersey: Humanities Press International.

Sayer, A. (1989) 'Postfordism in Question', *International Journal of Urban and Regional Research*, vol. 13, no. 4, pp. 666–95.

Sayer, A. (1997) 'The Dialectic of Culture and Economy', in R. Lee and J. Wills (eds) *Geographies of Economies*, London: Arnold.

Scarbrough, E. (2000) 'West European Welfare States: The Old Politics of Retrenchment', *European Journal of Political Research*, vol. 38, no. 2, pp. 225–59.

Scharpf, F. (2000) 'The Viability of Advanced Welfare States in the International Economy: Vulnerabilities and Options', *Journal of European Public Policy*, vol. 7, no. 2, pp. 190–228.

Schlereth, T. (ed.) (1982) *Material Studies in America*, Nashville, TN: American Association for State and Local History.

Schlosser, E. (2001) *Fast Food Nation: The Dark Side of the All-American Meal*, Boston: Houghton Mifflin.

Schmalansee, R. (1988) 'Industrial Economics: An Overview', *Economic Journal*, vol. 98, September, pp. 643–81.

Schor, J. (1991) *The Overworked American: The Unexpected Decline of Leisure*, New York: Basic Books.

Schrift, A. (1997a) 'Introduction: Why Gift?', in A. Schrift (ed.) *The Logic of the Gift: Toward an Ethic of Generosity*, London: Routledge.

Schrift, A. (ed.) (1997b) *The Logic of the Gift: Toward an Ethic of Generosity*, London: Routledge.

Scitovsky, T. (1976) *The Joyless Economy: An Inquiry into Human Satisfaction and Dissatisfaction*, New York: Oxford University Press.

Scranton, P. (1991) 'Diversity in Diversity: Flexible Production and American Industrialisation', *Business History Review*, vol. 65, no. 1, pp. 27–90.

Scranton, P. (1994) 'Manufacturing Diversity: Production Systems, Markets, and an American Consumer Society', *Technology and Culture*, vol. 35, no. 3, pp. 476–505.

Scranton, P. (1998) *Endless Novelty: Speciality Production and American Industrialisation, 1865–1925*, Princeton, NJ: Princeton University Press.

Scranton, P. (1999) 'Multiple Industrializations: Urban Manufacturing Development in the American Midwest, 1880–1925', *Journal of Design History*, vol. 12, no. 1, pp. 45–63.

Seiter, E. (1993) *Sold Separately: Children and Parents in Consumer Culture*, New Brunswick, NJ: Rutgers University Press.

Sen, A. (1977) 'Rational Fools: A Critique of the Behavioral Foundations of Economic Theory', *Philosophy and Public Affairs*, vol. 6, no. 4, pp. 317–44, reprinted in A. Sen (1982) *Choice, Welfare and Measurement*, Blackwell: Oxford.

Sen, A. (1982) *Choice, Welfare and Measurement*, Blackwell: Oxford.

Sen, A. (1983) 'Poor, Relatively Speaking', *Oxford Economic Papers*, no. 35, pp. 153–69.

Sen, A. (1993) 'Capability and Well-Being', in M. Nussbaum and A. Sen (eds) *The Quality of Life*, Oxford: Clarendon Press, pp. 30–53.

Sen, A. (1999) *Development as Freedom*, Oxford: Oxford University Press.

Shalev, M. (1996a) 'Introduction', in M. Shalev (ed.) *The Privatization of Social Policy? Occupational Welfare and the Welfare State in America, Scandinavia and Japan*, London: Macmillan.

Shalev, M. (ed.) (1996b) *The Privatization of Social Policy? Occupational Welfare and the Welfare State in America, Scandinavia and Japan*, London: Macmillan.

Shammas, C. (1990) *The Pre-Industrial Consumer in England and America*, Oxford: Clarendon Press.

Shaw, A. (1999) ' "What Are 'They' Doing to Our Food?": Public Concerns about Food in the UK', *Sociological Research Online*, vol. 4, no. 3, <http://www.socresonline.org.uk/socresonline/4/3/shaw.html> (accessed 6 October 2001).

Shin, D. (2000) 'Financial Crisis and Social Security: The Paradox of South Korea', *International Security Review*, vol. 53, no. 3, pp. 83–107.

Shumway, D. (2000) 'Fetishizing Fetishism: Commodities, Goods, and the Meaning of Consumer Culture', *Rethinking Marxism*, vol. 12, no. 1, pp. 1–15.

Silverstone, R. and E. Hirsch (eds) (1992) *Consuming Technologies: Media and Information in Domestic Spaces*, London: Routledge.

Simister, J. (1998) 'Women's Employment and the Ownership of Household Durable Goods in Britain and India', PhD thesis, University of London.

Simmel, G. (1900) *The Philosophy of Money*, London: Routledge & Kegan Paul (edition published in 1978).

Singh, K. (1999) *Globalisation of Finance: A Citizen's Guide*, London: Zed Books.

Sklair, L. (2000) 'The Transnational Capitalist Class and the Discourse of Globalisation', *Cambridge Review of International Affairs*, vol. XIV, no. 1, pp. 67–85.

Sklar, K. (1998) 'The Consumers' White Label Campaign of the National Consumers' League, 1898–1918', in S. Strasser *et al.* (eds) *Getting and Spending: European and American Consumer Societies in the Twentieth Century*, Cambridge: Cambridge University Press.

Slater, D. and F. Tonkiss (2001) *Market Society: Markets and Modern Social Theory*, Cambridge: Polity Press.

Slater, G. and D. Spencer (2000) 'The Uncertain Foundations of Transaction Costs Economics', *Journal of Economic Issues*, vol. XXXIV, no. 1, pp. 61–87.

Smart, B. (ed.) (1999) *Resisting McDonaldization*, London: Sage.

Smelser, N. and R. Swedberg (eds) (1994) *The Handbook of Economic Sociology*, Princeton, NJ: Princeton University Press.

Smith, M. (ed.) (1985) *Military Enterprise and Technological Change: Perspectives on the American Experience*, Cambridge, MA: MIT Press.

Smith, R. (1961) *Sea-Coal for London*, London: Longmans.

Snower, D. (1996) 'What is the Domain of the Welfare State?', in M. Baldarassi *et al.* (eds) *Equity, Efficiency and Growth: The Future of the Welfare State*, London: Macmillan.

Sombart, W. (1967) *Luxury and Capitalism*, Ann Arbor: University of Michigan Press.

Soper, K. (1981) *On Human Needs*, Brighton: Harvester.

Spencer, D. (1998) 'Economic Analysis and the Theory of Production: A Critical Appraisal', PhD thesis, University of Leeds.

Spicker, P. (1995) *Social Policy: Themes and Approaches*, London: Prentice Hall.

Spicker, P. (1996) 'Normative Comparisons of Social Security Systems', in L. Hantrais and S. Mangen (eds) *Cross-National Research Methods in the Social Sciences*, London: Pinter.

Spicker, P. (2000) *The Welfare State: A General Theory*, London: Sage.

Stevenson, N. (2000) 'Globalization and Cultural Political Economy', in R. Germain (ed.) *Globalization and Its Critics: Perspectives from Political Economy*, London: Macmillan.

Stewart, F. (1996) 'Basic Needs, Capabilities, and Human Development', in A. Offer (ed.) *In Pursuit of the Quality of Life*, Oxford: Oxford University Press.

Stigler, G. (1954) 'The Early History of Empirical Studies of Consumer Behavior', *Journal of Political Economy*, vol. LXII, no. 2, April, pp. 95–113.

Stiglitz, J. (1994) *Whither Socialism?*, Cambridge, MA: MIT Press.

Stiglitz, J. (1998) 'More Instruments and Broader Goals: Moving Toward the Post Washington Consensus', Second WIDER Annual Lecture, Helsinki.

Stone, M. *et al.* (2000) 'Commodities and Globalization: Anthropological Perspectives', in A. Haugerud *et al.* (eds) *Commodities and Globalization: Anthropological Perspectives*, Lanham, MD: Rowman and Littlefield.

Storey, J. (1999) *Cultural Consumption and Everyday Life*, London: Arnold.

Storrs, L. (2000) *Civilizing Capitalism: The National Consumers' League, Women's Activism, and Labor Standards in the New Deal Era*, Chapel Hill: University of North Carolina Press.

Strasser, S. *et al.* (eds) (1998) *Getting and Spending: European and American Consumer Societies in the Twentieth Century*, Cambridge: Cambridge University Press.

293

Strathern, M. (1988) *The Gender of the Gift: Problems with Women and Problems with Society in Melanesia*, Berkeley, CA: University of California Press.

Strathern, M. (1992) 'Qualified Value: The Perspective of Gift Exchange', in C. Humphrey and S. Hugh-Jones (eds) *Barter, Exchange and Value: An Anthropological Approach*, Cambridge: Cambridge University Press.

Strathern, M. (1997) 'Partners and Consumers: Making Relations Visible', in A. Schrift (ed.) *The Logic of the Gift: Toward an Ethic of Generosity*, London: Routledge.

Stuard, S. (1985) 'Medieval Workshop: Toward a Theory of Consumption and Economic Change', *Journal of Economic History*, vol. 45, no. 2, June, pp. 447–51.

Sulkunen, P. (1997) 'Introduction: The New Consumer Society – Rethinking the Social Bond', in P. Sulkunen *et al.* (eds) *Constructing the New Consumer Society*, New York: St Martin's Press.

Sulkunen, P. *et al.* (eds) (1997) *Constructing the New Consumer Society*, New York: St Martin's Press.

Sutcliffe, B. and A. Glyn (2000) 'Still Underwhelmed: Indicators of Globalization and Their Misinterpretation', *Review of Radical Political Economy*, vol. 31, no. 1, pp. 111–32.

Sutton, J. (1991) *Sunk Costs and Market Structure: Price Competition, Advertising, and the Evolution of Concentration*, Cambridge, MA: MIT Press.

Sutton, J. (1998) *Technology and Market Structure: Theory and History*, Cambridge, MA: MIT Press.

Suzumura, K. (1999) 'Welfare Economics and the Welfare State', *Review of Population and Social Policy*, vol. 8, no. 1, pp. 119–38.

Swank, D. (1998) 'Funding the Welfare State: Globalization and the Taxation of Business in Advanced Market Economies', *Political Studies*, vol. XLVI, no. 4, pp. 671–92.

Swedberg, R. (1990a) 'Introduction', in R. Swedberg (ed.) *Economics and Sociology, Redefining Their Boundaries: Conversations with Economists and Sociologists*, Princeton, NJ: Princeton University Press.

Swedberg, R. (ed.) (1990b) *Economics and Sociology, Redefining Their Boundaries: Conversations with Economists and Sociologists*, Princeton, NJ: Princeton University Press.

Swedberg, R. (1991) ' "The Battle of Methods": Toward a Paradigm Shift?', in A. Etzioni and P. Lawrence (eds) *Socio-Economics: Toward a New Synthesis*, Armonk, NY: M.E. Sharpe.

Swedberg, R. (ed.) (1996) *Economic Sociology*, Cheltenham: Edward Elgar.

Tang, K. (2000) *Social Welfare Development in East Asia*, Basingstoke: Palgrave.

Tanzi, V. (2000) 'Globalization and the Future of Social Protection', IMF Working Paper, no. 00/12.

Taussig, M. (1980) *The Devil and Commodity Fetishism in South America*, Chapel Hill: University of North Carolina Press.

Taylor-Gooby, P. (1996) 'Eurosclerosis in European Welfare States: Regime Theory and the Dynamics of Change', *Policy and Politics*, vol. 24, no. 2, pp. 143–79.

Taylor-Gooby, P. (1997) 'In Defence of Second-Best Theory: State, Class and Capital in Social Policy', *Journal of Social Policy*, vol. 27, no. 2, pp. 171–92.

Taylor-Gooby, P. (1998a) 'Choice and the Policy Agenda', in P. Taylor-Gooby (ed.) *Choice and Public Policy: The Limits to Welfare Markets*, London: Macmillan.

Taylor-Gooby, P. (1998b) 'Choice and the New Paradigm in Policy', in P. Taylor-Gooby (ed.) *Choice and Public Policy: The Limits to Welfare Markets*, London: Macmillan.

Taylor-Gooby, P. (ed.) (1998c) *Choice and Public Policy: The Limits to Welfare Markets*, London: Macmillan.

Taylor-Gooby, P. (2000a) 'Risk and Welfare', in P. Taylor-Gooby (ed.) *Risk, Trust and Welfare*, London: Macmillan.

Taylor-Gooby, P. (ed.) (2000b) *Risk, Trust and Welfare*, London: Macmillan.

Tedlow, R. (1990) *New and Improved: The Story of Mass Marketing in America*, Oxford Heinemann.

Therborn, G. (2000a) 'Introduction: From the Universal to the Global', *International Sociology*, vol. 15, no. 2, pp. 149–50.

Therborn, G. (2000b) 'Globalizations: Dimensions, Historical Waves, Regional Effects, Normative Governance', *International Sociology*, vol. 15, no. 2, pp. 151–79.

Thirsk, J. (1978) *Economic Policy and Projects: The Development of a Consumer Society in Early Modern England*, Oxford: Clarendon Press.

Thomas, C. and P. Wilkin (eds) (1997) *Globalization and the South*, London: Macmillan.

Thomas, H. (ed.) (1995) *Globalization and the Third World Trade Unions: The Challenge of Rapid Economic Change*, London: Zed Press.

Thompson, G. (1997) 'Where Goes Economics and the Economies?', *Economy and Society*, vol. 26, no. 4, pp. 599–610.

Thompson, G. (1999) 'How Far Should We Be Afraid of Conventional Economics? A Response to Ben Fine', *Economy and Society*, vol. 28, no. 3, pp. 426–33.

Thompson, S. and J. Cowan (2000) 'Globalizing Agro-Food Systems in Asia: Introduction', *World Development*, vol. 28, no. 3, pp. 401–8.

Thoms, D. *et al.* (1998a) 'Introduction', in D. Thoms *et al.* (eds) *The Motor Car and Popular Culture in the Twentieth Century*, Aldershot: Ashgate.

Thoms, D. *et al.* (eds) (1998b) *The Motor Car and Popular Culture in the Twentieth Century*, Aldershot: Ashgate.

Thomson, D. (ed.) (1989) *Food Acceptability*, London: Elsevier.

Titmuss, R. (1969) *The Gift Relationship: From Human Blood to Social Policy*, London: Routledge.

Tomlinson, A. (ed.) (1990) *Consumption, Identity and Style*, London: Routledge.

Tomlinson, M. and A. Warde (1993) 'Social Class and Change in Eating Habits', *British Food Journal*, vol. 95, no. 1, pp. 3–10.

Tommasi, M. and K. Ierulli (eds) (1995) *The New Economics of Human Behaviour*, Cambridge: Cambridge University Press.

Toporowski, J. (ed.) (2000) *Political Economy and the New Capitalism: Essays in Honour of Sam Aaronovitch*, London: Routledge.

Torfing, J. (1998) *Politics, Regulation and the Modern Welfare State*, London: Macmillan.

Trifiletti, R. (1999) 'Southern European Welfare Regimes and the Worsening Position of Women', *Journal of European Social Policy*, vol. 9, no. 1, pp. 49–64.

Urry, J. (1990) *The Tourist Gaze: Leisure and Travel in Contemporary Societies*, London: Sage.

Uusitalo, L. (1998) 'Consumption in Postmodernity: Social Structuration and the Construction of the Self', in M. Bianchi (ed.) *The Active Consumer: Novelty and Surprise in Consumer Choice*, London: Routledge.

Uzzi, B. (1999) 'Embeddedness in the Making of Financial Capital: How Social Relations and Networks Benefit Firms Seeking Financing', *American Sociological Review*, vol. 64, no. 4, pp. 481–505.

Valentine, G. (1999) 'Eating In: Home, Consumption and Identity', *Sociological Review*, vol. 47, no. 3, pp. 491–524.

Valeri, V. (1994) 'Buying Women and Selling Them: Gift and Commodity Exchange in Huaulu Alliance', *Man*, vol. 29, no. 1, pp. 1–26.

van Kersbergen, K. (1995) *Social Capitalism: A Study of Christian Democracy and the Welfare State*, London: Routledge.

van Kersbergen, K. (2000) 'The Declining Resistance of Welfare States to Change?', in S. Kuhnle (ed.) *Survival of the European Welfare State*, London: Routledge.

Vandenbroucke, F. (1998) *Globalisation: Inequality and Social Democracy*, London: IPPR.

Veblen, T. (1924) *The Theory of the Leisure Class: An Economic Study of Institutions*, London: Allen and Unwin.

Velthuis, O. (1999) 'The Changing Relationship between Economic Sociology and Institutional Economics: From Talcott Parsons to Mark Granovetter', *American Journal of Economics and Sociology*, vol. 58, no. 4, pp. 629–49.

Voth, H. (1998) 'Work and the Sirens of Consumption in Eighteenth-Century London', in M. Bianchi (ed.) *The Active Consumer: Novelty and Surprise in Consumer Choice*, London: Routledge.

Wade, R. (1996) 'Globalization and Its Limits: Reports of the Death of the National Economy Are Greatly Exaggerated', in S. Berger and R. Dore (eds) *National Diversity and Global Capitalism*, Ithaca, NY: Cornell University Press.

Waller, W. (1988) 'The Concept of Habit in Economic Analysis', *Journal of Economic Issues*, vol. XXII, no. 1, March, pp. 113–26.

Wallerstein, I. (2000) 'Globalization or the Age of Transition? A Long-Term View of the Trajectory of the World System', *International Sociology*, vol. 15, no. 2, pp. 249–65.

Walsh, V. (2000) 'Smith after Sen', *Review of Political Economy*, vol. 12, no. 1, pp. 5–25.

Walton, W. (1986) ' "To Triumph Before Feminine Taste": Bourgeois Women's Consumption and Hand Methods of Production in Mid-Nineteenth-Century France', *Business History Review*, vol. 60, no. 4, pp. 541–63.

Walton, W. (1992) *France at the Crystal Palace: Bourgeois Taste and Artisan Manufacture in the Nineteenth Century*, Berkeley, CA: University of California Press.

Ward, N. and R. Almas (1997) 'Explaining Change in the International Agro-Food System', *Review of International Political Economy*, vol. 4, no. 4, pp. 611–29.

Warde, A. (1994) 'Consumers, Consumption and post-Fordism', in R. Burrows and B. Loader (eds) *Towards a Post-Fordist Welfare State?*, London: Routledge.

Warde, A. and L. Martens (2000) *Eating Out: Social Differentiation, Consumption and Pleasure*, Cambridge: Cambridge University Press.

Waterman, P. (1996) 'Beyond Globalism and Developmentalism: Other Voices in World Politics', *Development and Change*, vol. 27, no. 1, pp. 165–80.

Waterson, M. (1994) 'Models of Product Differentiation', in J. Cable (ed.) *Current Issues in Industrial Economics*, London: Macmillan.

Watson, S. *et al.* (1997) 'Conclusion: Global-Local Relations Revisited', in P. Rimmer (ed.) *Pacific Rim Development: Integration and Globalisation in the Asia-Pacific Economy*, St Leonards: Allen and Unwin.

Watts, M. (1994) 'What Difference Does Difference Make?', *Review of International Political Economy*, vol. 1, no. 3, Autumn, pp. 563–70.

Watts, M. and D. Goodman (1997) 'Agrarian Questions: Global Appetite, Local Metabolism: Nature, Culture, and Industry in *Fin-de-Siècle* Agrofood Systems', in D. Goodman and M. Watts (eds) *Globalising Food: Agrarian Questions and Global Restructuring*, London: Routledge.

Wayne, D. (1995) 'The "Exchange of Letters": Early Modern Contradictions and Postmodern Conundrums', in A. Bermingham and J. Brewer (eds) *The Consumption of Culture, 1600–1800: Image, Object, Text*, London: Routledge.

REFERENCES

Weatherill, L. (1986a) 'The Business of Middleman in the English Pottery Trade before 1780', *Business History*, vol. 28, no. 3, July, pp. 51–76.

Weatherill, L. (1986b) *The Growth of the Pottery Industry in England 1660–1815*, New York: Garland.

Weatherill, L. (1988) *Consumer Behaviour and Material Culture in Britain 1660–1760*, London: Routledge.

Webster, E. and G. Adler (1999) 'Toward a Class Compromise in South Africa's "Double Transition": Bargained Liberalization and the Consolidation of Democracy', *Politics and Society*, vol. 27, no. 3, pp. 347–85.

Weeks, J. (1981) *Capital and Exploitation*, London: Edward Arnold.

Weiner, A. (1992) *Inalienable Possessions*, Berkeley, CA: University of California Press.

Weiss, L.(1998) *The Myth of the Powerless State: Governing the Economy in a Global Era*, Cambridge: Polity Press.

Westall, O. (1994) 'Marketing Strategy and the Competitive Structure of British General Insurance, 1720–1980', *Business History*, vol. 36, no. 2, pp. 20–46.

Westley, W. and M. Westley (1971) *The Emerging Worker: Equality and Conflict in the Mass Consumption Society*, Montreal: McGill–Queen's University Press.

Whipp, R. and M. Grieco (1989) 'Time, Task and Travel: Budgeting for Interdependencies', in M. Grieco *et al.* (eds) *Gender, Transport and Employment: The Impact of Travel Constraints*, Aldershot: Gower.

White, G. (1998) 'Social Security Reforms in China: Towards an East Asian Model', in R. Goodman *et al.* (eds) *The East Asian Welfare Model: Welfare Orientalism and the State*, London: Routledge.

White, G. and R. Goodman (1998) 'Welfare Orientalism and the Search for an East Asian Welfare Model', in R. Goodman *et al.* (eds) *The East Asian Welfare Model: Welfare Orientalism and the State*, London: Routledge.

Whitfield, D. (2001) *Public Services or Corporate Welfare*, London: Pluto Press.

Wight, D. (1993) *Workers not Wasters – Masculine Respectability, Consumption and Unemployment in Central Scotland: A Community Study*, Edinburgh: Edinburgh University Press.

Wilber, C. (1998) 'Globalization and Democracy', *Journal of Economic Issues*, vol. XXXII, no. 2, pp. 465–71.

Wilding, P. (1997) 'Globalization, Regionalism and Social Policy', *Social Policy and Administration*, vol. 31, no. 4, pp. 410–28.

Williams, R. (1984) 'Review of McKendrick *et al.* (1982)', *Technology and Culture*, vol. 15, pp. 337–9.

Williamson, J. (1978) *Decoding Advertisements: Ideology and Meaning in Advertising*, London: Marion Boyars.

Williamson, J. (1986) *Consuming Passions: The Dynamics of Popular Culture*, London: Marion Boyars.

Winship, J. (2000) 'New Disciplines for Women and the Rise of the Chain Store in the 1930s', in M. Andrews and M. Talbot (eds) *All the World and Her Husband: Women in Twentieth-Century Consumer Culture*, London: Cassell.

Wolfe, A. (1989) *Whose Keeper? Social Sciences and Moral Obligation*, Berkeley, CA: University of California Press.

Woods, N. (ed.) (2000) *The Political Economy of Globalization*, London: Macmillan.

Woodward, I. *et al.* (2000) 'Consumerism, Disorientation and Postmodern Space: A Modest Test of an Immodest Theory', *British Journal of Sociology*, vol. 51, no. 2, pp. 339–54.

297

Wrigley, N. and M. Lowe (eds) (1996) *Retailing, Consumption and Capital: Towards the New Retail Geography*, London: Longman.

Wyrwa, U. (1998) 'Consumption and Consumer Society: A Contribution to the History of Ideas', in S. Strasser *et al.* (eds) *Getting and Spending: European and American Consumer Societies in the Twentieth Century*, Cambridge: Cambridge University Press.

Yang, Y. (2000) 'The Rise of the Welfare State amid Economic Crisis, 1997–99: Implications for the Globalisation Debate', *Development Policy Review*, vol. 18, no. 3, pp. 235–56.

Zafirovski, M. (2000) 'The Rational Choice Generalization of Neoclassical Economics Reconsidered: Any Theoretical Legitimation for Economic Imperialism', *Sociological Theory*, vol. 18, no. 3, pp. 448–71.

Zelizer, V. (1987) *Pricing the Priceless Child: The Changing Social Value of Children*, New York: Basic Books.

Zelizer, V. (1988) 'Beyond the Polemics on the Market: Establishing a Theoretical and Empirical Agenda', *Sociological Forum*, vol. 3, no. 4, pp. 614–34, reproduced in R. Swedberg (ed.) (1996) *Economic Sociology*, Cheltenham: Edward Elgar.

Zelizer, V. (1994) *The Social Meaning of Money*, New York: Basic Books.

Zelizer, V. (1996) 'Payments and Social Ties', *Sociological Forum*, vol. 11, no. 3, pp. 481–95.

Zelizer, V. (1998) 'The Proliferation of Social Currencies', in M. Callon (ed.) *The Laws of the Market*, Oxford: Blackwell.

Zelizer, V. (2000) 'Fine-Tuning the Zelizer View', *Economy and Society*, vol. 29, no. 3, pp. 383–9.

Zukin, S. and P. DiMaggio (eds) (1990) *Structures of Capital: The Social Organization of the Economy*, Cambridge: Cambridge University Press.

NAME INDEX

SUBJECT INDEX